Shaping the African Savannah

The southern African savannah landscape has been framed as an 'Arid Eden' in recent literature, as one of Africa's most sought after exotic tourism destinations by twenty-first century travellers, as a 'last frontier' by early twentieth-century travellers, and as an ancient ancestral land by Namibia's Herero communities. In this 150-year history of the region, Michael Bollig looks at how this 'Arid Eden' came into being, how this 'last frontier' was construed, and how local pastoralists relate to the landscape. Putting the intricate and changing relations between humans, arid savannah grasslands, and its co-evolving animal inhabitants at the centre of his analysis, this history tells the story of material relations, of power struggles between commercial hunters and wildlife, between wealthy cattle patrons and foraging clients, between established homesteads and recent migrants, conservationists and pastoralists. Finally, Bollig highlights how futures are being aspired to and planned for between the increasing challenges of climate change, global demands for cheap ores, and quests for biodiversity conservation.

MICHAEL BOLLIG is Professor of Social and Cultural Anthropology at the University of Cologne where his key interests lie in the environmental anthropology of sub-Saharan Africa. His current research projects focus on the social-ecological dynamics connected to large-scale conservation projects, the commodification of nature and the political ecology of pastoralism. He is the author of *Risk Management in a Hazardous Environment* (2006), co-author of *African Landscapes* (2009) with O. Bubenzer, *Pastoralism in Africa* (2013) with M. Schnegg and H. P. Wotzka, and *Resilience and Collapse in African Savannahs* (2017) with D. Anderson.

African Studies Series

The African Studies series, founded in 1968, is a prestigious series of monographs, general surveys, and textbooks on Africa covering history, political science, anthropology, economics, and ecological and environmental issues. The series seeks to publish work by senior scholars as well as the best new research.

Editorial Board:
David Anderson, *The University of Warwick*
Catherine Boone, *The London School of Economics and Political Science*
Carolyn Brown, *Rutgers University, New Jersey*
Christopher Clapham, *University of Cambridge*
Michael Gomez, *New York University*
Richard Roberts, *Stanford University, California*
David Robinson, *Michigan State University*
Leonardo A. Villalón, *University of Florida*

Other titles in the series are listed at the back of the book.

Shaping the African Savannah

From Capitalist Frontier to Arid Eden in Namibia

MICHAEL BOLLIG
University of Cologne

CAMBRIDGE
UNIVERSITY PRESS

University Printing House, Cambridge CB2 8BS, United Kingdom

One Liberty Plaza, 20th Floor, New York, NY 10006, USA

477 Williamstown Road, Port Melbourne, VIC 3207, Australia

314–321, 3rd Floor, Plot 3, Splendor Forum, Jasola District Centre, New Delhi – 110025, India

79 Anson Road, #06–04/06, Singapore 079906

Cambridge University Press is part of the University of Cambridge.

It furthers the University's mission by disseminating knowledge in the pursuit of education, learning, and research at the highest international levels of excellence.

www.cambridge.org
Information on this title: www.cambridge.org/9781108488488
DOI: 10.1017/9781108764025

© Michael Bollig 2020

This publication is in copyright. Subject to statutory exception and to the provisions of relevant collective licensing agreements, no reproduction of any part may take place without the written permission of Cambridge University Press.

First published 2020

A catalogue record for this publication is available from the British Library.

Library of Congress Cataloging-in-Publication Data
Names: Bollig, Michael, author.
Title: Shaping the African savannah : from capitalist frontier to arid Eden in Namibia / Michael Bollig, University of Cologne.
Description: Cambridge, United Kingdom ; New York, NY : Cambridge University Press, 2020. | Series: African studies | Includes bibliographical references and index.
Identifiers: LCCN 2019060071 (print) | LCCN 2019060072 (ebook) | ISBN 9781108488488 (hardback) | ISBN 9781108726399 (paperback) | ISBN 9781108764025 (ebook)
Subjects: LCSH: Savannas–Namibia–History. | Savanna ecology–Namibia–History. | Human ecology–Namibia–History.
Classification: LCC GB578.88.N3 B65 2020 (print) | LCC GB578.88.N3 (ebook) | DDC 577.27096881–dc23
LC record available at https://lccn.loc.gov/2019060071
LC ebook record available at https://lccn.loc.gov/2019060072

ISBN 978-1-108-48848-8 Hardback

Cambridge University Press has no responsibility for the persistence or accuracy of URLs for external or third-party internet websites referred to in this publication and does not guarantee that any content on such websites is, or will remain, accurate or appropriate.

Contents

List of Figures	page vii
List of Maps	viii
List of Tables	ix
Acknowledgements	x
Part 1 Introduction	1
1 Doing Research on a Changing Savannah Landscape	3
Part 2 The Evolution of Pre-Colonial Environmental Infrastructure	19
2 The Prehistory of North-Western Namibia and the Emergence of Pastoralism	21
3 Elephants and Humans in the Late Nineteenth and Early Twentieth Century	49
Part 3 Encapsulation and Pastoralisation, 1900s to 1940s	67
4 Scientists, Cartographers, Photographers, and the Establishment of Western Knowledge of the Kaokoveld	71
5 The Establishment of Colonial Administration and the Re-establishment of a Pastoral Livelihood	93
6 The Politics of Encapsulation: Game Protection, Instituting Borders, and Controlling Mobility	106

	Part 4 The State, Intervention, and Local Appropriations between the 1950s and 1980s	151
7	A Hydrological Revolution in an African Savannah	153
8	Conservation and Poaching in the 1970s and 1980s	196
	Part 5 Dynamics of Social-Ecological Relations between the 1990s and the Present	237
9	Pastoralism, Environmental Infrastructures, and State–Local Society Relations in the Late Twentieth and Early Twenty-First Century	241
10	The Establishment of 'New Commons' by Government Decree	279
11	Into the Future: Envisioning, Planning, and Negotiating Environmental Infrastructures	317
	Part 6 Theorising Time, Space, and Change in a Pastoral System	349
12	The Changing Environmental Infrastructure of the North-Western Namibian Savannah	351

Bibliography 366
Index 389

Figures

2.1	Heavily armed young Himba men belonging to a troop of irregular soldiers (*corpo de irregulares*). Photographed probably between 1900 and 1911	page 48
3.1	Group of Ovatjimba men with spears and ivory tusks, in Kaokoveld [original caption: Herero Ovashimba natives from Kaokoveld]	60
4.1a	Taxidermist N. Arends posing with specimens of moles	88
4.1b	Carp Expedition, June 1951; collected moles	88
6.1	A pass created by the Truppenspieler movement	113
7.1	Registration sheet of a borehole	176
9.1	Young Himba children demonstrating for the coming elections for the NPF, a political party in Namibia, 17 April 1989	245
9.2	Himba woman milking; the milker takes milk from two teats while the calf is drinking from the other two teats at the same time	251
9.3	Dynamics of the regional cattle herd	255
9.4	Population increase 1963–2011	257
9.5a–b	Age pyramids for the populations of Epupa and Opuwo constituencies according to the 2011 National Census	258
9.5c	Age pyramid, data from a household survey from 2004–5	259
10.1	Dynamics of specific wildlife populations between 2000 and 2015	296

Maps

2.1 The immigration of herding communities to south-western Africa	page 25
2.2 Nineteenth-century settlement nuclei in north-western Namibia reconstructed on the basis of oral evidence	35
4.1 Manning's map of the Kaokoveld, part depicting the Omuhonga Basin cartographically	77
6.1 Etosha Park alias Game Park No. 2 in 1907	107
7.1 Map of boreholes established until 1999	177
8.1 Tinley's plan for two additional game parks in north-western Namibia	207
8.2 Owen-Smith's plan for the Kaokoveld Game Reserve in north-western Namibia	210
8.3 Park boundaries and settlement areas according to the Eloff Plan	214
8.4 Distribution of wildlife and livestock according to the 1976 aerial census	220
9.1 Homesteads and gardens in the Omuhonga Valley	260
9.2 The dry-season grazing area of Oheuva showing dispersed cattle camps in the vicinity of the seasonal Oheuva River	262
9.3 Ombombo village	264
9.4a–c Expanding agriculture in the Omuhonga basin between 1975 and 2006	274
9.5 Gardens bordering Opuwo town in the south-west	275
10.1 Communal conservancies in north-western Namibia	282
10.2 Zonation map for Ehirovipuka conservancy	291
11.1 Consequences of global climatic change for agricultural production by 2080	321
11.2 Expansion of lions in north-western Namibia, 1995–2015	324
11.3 Mining concessions in north-western Namibia	331

Tables

4.1	Studying the Kaokoveld fauna	*page* 89
8.1	Wildlife counts between 1969 and 1976 based on aerial photography	221
10.1	Zonation of Ehirovipuka conservancy	293
10.2	Spatial extent of zones in five conservancies	294
10.3	Sources of income of conservancies	299
10.4	Wildlife put on wildlife quotas of conservancies in Kunene Region and their use (conservancies located in Epupa and Opuwo constituencies) for 2013	303
10.5	Water-point contributions rules in the communities immediately surrounding Okangwati	310

Acknowledgements

I am grateful to the people of the Kaokoveld who have hosted me so many times over two and a half decades. First of all, of course, my thanks go to the Omuhonga-Omuramba community in the northernmost part of the Kaokoveld. There I spent two years of fieldwork in the 1990s, and during later years always came back to that region. The households of the late Kandjuhu Rutjindo and his son Mungerinyeu Rutjindo, and of Mutaambanda Kapika, hosted me many times, and I was privileged to be made to feel part of the household. The households' children, Mukatjikuvi in particular (now herself the mother of many children), taught me the local language. The late Katjira Muniombara introduced me to the intricate history of the region; Maongo Hembinda drew my attention to the close relation between history and politics; and Vahenuna Tjitaura explained to me the local attempts to come to terms with governmental institutions. Since the early 2000s I expanded my interviews to the central, western, and southern parts of the Kaokoveld. I never lived in those areas for long periods of time, but I visited some places frequently and I always felt welcome. Fortunately, the Otjiherero-speaking communities of the Kaokoveld do not strictly segregate men and women, and interviews with women were always possible: Mukaakaserari Rutjindo, Kazupotjo, Kozombandi, and Watundwa introduced me to female perspectives on pastoral labour, coping strategies during droughts, and kinship, health, and ancestral beliefs. It is not possible to thank all those people who contributed to this book in person, and I hope that those mentioned here by name may stand for the many people who answered my questions over more than two decades.

When I started fieldwork in 1994 I arrived with some rudimentary knowledge of Otjiherero. I was able to expand this knowledge during the coming years, and could conduct part of my research without a translator. However, during many interviews I had to rely on a translator. Since the late 1990s Uhangatenwa Kapi not only helped with

Acknowledgements

translations, he also became a true friend. Uhangatenwa took a great interest in my work, suggesting new kinds of questions and new approaches. He was able to visit me in Germany repeatedly, and during those visits entered data or translated longer interviews. This book has profited immensely from Uhangatenwa's inventiveness, intelligence, reliability, endurance, and talent for teamwork. Others assisted during fieldwork before Uhangatenwa joined me, when he was not available, or when larger teams, e.g. of enumerators, were necessary. Tjakazaapi Mbunguha, Magic Mburura, Yatemburaike Mutambo, and Mbandera Tjitaura were always reliable assistants.

This book has profited vastly from discussing its contents in part or as a whole with colleagues, fellow anthropologists, historians, and ecologists. Historians Patricia Hayes, Ciraj Rassool, Wolfgang Werner, Dag Henrichsen, Giogio Miescher, Lorena Rizzo, Jan Bart Gewald, and David Anderson urged me to discuss my local findings in the context of a wider colonial context and helped me to make good use of existing archives and to problematise archival evidence at the same time. Fellow anthropologists Rob Gordon, Steven van Wolputte, John Friedman, Laura Bleckmann, Silke Toensjost, Michael Schnegg, Julia Pauli, and Clemens Greiner helped me to gain other perspectives on the subject matter, with Steven van Wolputte and Laura Bleckmann adopting more symbolic and discursive approaches, John Friedman taking a political anthropology perspective, and Silke Toensjost working predominantly within the context of another regional focus in the southern Kaokoveld and focusing on female perspectives. Laura Bleckmann kindly allowed me to make use of her transcribed interviews on the history of the southern Kaokoveld. Rob Gordon continually supplied me with hard-to-find literature on the region. Both Rob Gordon and Patricia Hayes read early chapters of this book and contributed greatly to its final form with their commentaries. Together with Michael Schnegg I organised the LINGS project, which lasted for many years. With him as the driving force behind the project's methodological setup I had the chance to look at the wider ramifications of water management within the pastoral context and to compare contemporary water management with other fields of natural resource management. Michael also has been a knowledgeable and inspiring discussant in the background of this book. My colleagues Julia Pauli and Clemens Greiner, who worked (together with Michael Schnegg) south of the area I was focusing on, alerted me to processes of social differentiation and mobility, which took very different forms in the context in which they were working than in the Kaokoveld. Throughout the ten-year gestation of this book I profited a great deal from supervising and coordinating work with young scholars, besides Silke Toensjost and Laura Bleckmann; Thekla Kelbert, Theresa Linke, Elsemi Olwage, and Diego Menestrey-Schwieger contributed to this book with their thoughts and their critique. Diego has been especially helpful, as the community he worked with lies closest to mine. Many of his informants were related to men and women I worked with. In recent years Diego has also been helpful in organising some research in my absence, paying enumerators, taking questionnaires into the field, etc. Beyond anthropologists and historians, other scientists have contributed pertinently to this book. Archaeologist Ralf Vogelsang and palaeo-botanist Barbara Eichhorn alerted me to complex prehistoric settlement patterns and the difficulty of tracing the past human footprint in contemporary vegetation. Ecologist Anja Linstädter (née Schulte) sensitised me to the differential impact of livestock on perennial and annual grasses. Two anonymous reviewers gave very good advice on how to improve the overall structure of the book and pointed out a number of pertinent points I had not sufficiently thought about.

Of course, not only scientists contributed; the idea of the book emerged also in many discussions with practitioners and staff members of development projects. Garth Owen-Smith has been a source of inspiration, and I was fortunate to have the chance to tap into his vast knowledge on social-ecological relations in the region. Together with his partner Margie Jacobsohn Garth inspired me to think beyond the conventional social-science critique of community-based conservation. Beyond in-depth knowledge and enthusiasm for conservation, Garth's great respect for local pastoralists and his empathetic approach to local communities became an important inspiration. Collin Nott helped me to understand the vulnerability of the grazing system better and to alert me to the impact of different forms of grazing on perennial and annual grasses. Anna Davies shared important insights on the economic performance of conservancies. John Kasaona was always an inspiring discussant, linking local politics to pertinent development issues.

In Windhoek I and my family enjoyed the hospitality of the Gschwender family, and Frank Gschwender, a trained geographer, was an inspiring discussant on a number of topics that were salient for my research.

Acknowledgements

This book would not have been possible without the long-term funding by the German Research Council. A fieldwork stipend in the mid-1990s, which graciously allowed me to do fieldwork for two years (1994–6) in the region, laid the basis for my engagement with the environmental history and political ecology of the Kaokoveld. Subsequently two long-term projects – the collaborative research centre Arid Climate, Adaptation and Cultural Innovation in Africa, ACACIA (1996–2007), and the anthropological long-term project Local Institutions in a Global Setting, LINGS (2010–19) – rendered a framework in which to continue research. Research permits endorsed by responsible Namibian government agencies were important for conducting research, and made fieldwork in northern Namibia possible. I am also grateful to the staff of the Namibia National Archives; in particular the archives' former director, Werner Hillebrecht, has been very helpful in tracing sources.

Back in Cologne I always found a conducive working atmosphere, first in the collaborative research centre ACACIA, then in the Research Unit Resilience, Collapse and Reorganisation, in the LINGS project, and most recently in the new collaborative research centre Future Rural Africa. I was backed by administrative and technical staff at the University of Cologne. Monika Feinen drew all the maps for this book masterfully. Monika Böck, Werner Schuck, and during the past few years also Dominik Becker managed the finances of the diverse projects and helped with the complex accounting for expenditures. Student aide Nina Krömer worked on the bibliography and helped to organise the text's figures, tables, and maps. Independent text editor Pax Amphlett worked on the English throughout all chapters.

The book came into existence over ten to twelve years. My two children, Antonio and Vivian, as well as my former wife Heike spent months in northern Namibia and in Windhoek with me. While we greatly enjoyed being in Namibia, my children also bemoaned the temporary loss of contact with their friends, and Heike accepted setbacks in her professional career.

My partner, Kristin, accompanied me supportively during the difficult task of writing of the final chapters, and in the tedious work of transforming a first draft into a final manuscript.

I am greatly indebted to all those mentioned (and many more besides), and greatly appreciate their manifold contributions to this book.

Dedicated to my children Antonio and Vivian.

PART I
Introduction

1 | *Doing Research on a Changing Savannah Landscape*

This book is about changing social-ecological relations in a southern African savannah landscape framed as an 'Arid Eden' in recent literature (e.g. Owen-Smith 2010), as a 'last frontier' by early twentieth-century travellers (Green 1952), and as ancestral land by Namibia's Herero communities (Bollig 1997). How did change come about in this 'Arid Eden', and how did such a landscape become an Eden in the first place? How did a 'last frontier' become construed, and how did (and do) local pastoralists relate to this landscape? How does 'Arid Eden' develop today under the forces of globalisation and what do its future prospects look like in the face of climate change and quests for mineral resources? The intricate relations between humans, arid savannah grasslands, and co-evolving domesticated and non-domesticated fauna constitute the central focus of this book. What follows is a history of infrastructural change and local agency, violence and encapsulation, state power and local resistance, contested knowledge and globalisation. Humans have formed this arid landscape in many ways: through their ways of herding, by changing the hydrological system through extensive borehole-drilling, by eradicating wildlife in the twentieth century, and by creating conditions leading to a phenomenal resurgence of wildlife numbers in the early twenty-first century. The environment has not been a passive recipient of human action though: elephant herds have shaped riverine vegetation, and the grazing behaviour of non-domesticated herbivores has impacted the vegetation patterns of the wide pre-Namib plains. The story to be told is not only a history of an intense coupling of species but also a history of power struggles between wealthy cattle patrons and foraging clients, between established homesteads and recent migrants, between a repressive colonial regime and local herders, and between conservationists (national and international) and advocates of mining development. Beyond material relations and power, it is a history of imaginations of a fabled cattle country, a last wilderness, and a prizewinning conservation area – visions that are in outright conflict with narratives of the place as a terribly overgrazed landscape, a 'besieged desert' (Reardon 1986), and on account of its remoteness the 'Siberia of South West Africa'.[1]

After a short glance at the prehistory of the region and the manifold imaginaries of grand migration histories framing the Kaokoveld as corridor for early Bantu-speaking pastoralists moving from eastern Africa into the southern parts of the continent, the book takes up the story at a point when, in the eighteenth/early nineteenth century, north-western Namibia was still occupied by only a few thousand people. Hunting and gathering was the dominant livelihood strategy then and seemingly only a few households subsisted on larger herds of livestock. The area was then rapidly drawn into the emergent networks of mercantile globalisation and landscapes and their human and non-human inhabitants became 'entwined with specifically European and North American commodity markets' (Sullivan et al. 2016: 14). At the end of the nineteenth/beginning of the twentieth century elephants were butchered in the area in their hundreds and probably in their thousands. The dominant landscape architect was thereby removed from much of the terrain. The region then became part of colonial empires, first the German *Kaiserreich*, and then for many decades the South African empire (Henrichsen et al. 2015). The establishment of a colonial administration seeking to influence mobility patterns, political hierarchies, and exchange with external actors was the most salient feature of social-ecological development in the first half of the twentieth century. For most of the twentieth century pastoralism was on the increase. By the 1930s foraging had become a minority occupation; not only was hunting prohibited and sternly persecuted but so too did local motivations lead to the swift transition from hunting and gathering to cattle pastoralism (Rizzo 2012). Throughout the first half of the twentieth century north-western Namibia was kept separate from the remainder of the colony: the area was not a source of migrant labour (in stark contrast to neighbouring north-central Namibia; Hayes 1998; Kreike 2010; McKittrick 2002), nor was there a decisive move to make lands available to white settlers

---

[1] A colonial officer commented upon his placement in Opuwo (at that time Ohopoho) and likened it to the banishment of Russian administrators or dissidents to Siberia (NAN SWAA 2514 A552/3 30/09/1937).

(Bollig 1998a). The area became encapsulated, and access to and exit from the Kaokoveld was limited by anxiously controlled boundaries, notably the infamous Red Line, a mighty fence that since the 1950s has separated northern Namibia's African reserves (later homelands) from the settler colony (Miescher 2012).

The developmental visions of Apartheid administrators and planners for north-western Namibia changed drastically in the 1950s. Like other areas in northern Namibia (see e.g. Kreike 2013) the area's economy was now to be modernised. Livestock husbandry was to be intensified and the output of cattle to be increased. In order to set this development in motion an ambitious borehole-drilling programme was inaugurated leading to a veritable hydrological revolution in this water-scarce semi-arid landscape. The increased availability of water contributed to a massive increase of livestock holdings and a rapid expansion of livestock-related mobility. The changing material infrastructure entrapped the population in a specialised pastoral livelihood. After only a few decades the grave ecological consequences of intensification became visible: a rapid change from perennial to annual grasses and a loss of floristic and faunal biodiversity were hallmarks of this social-ecological transformation. Alternative approaches to resource management were discussed in administrative circles from the 1970s onward: putting further stretches of land under protection and concentrating the population in more restricted areas was one idea; making game management a source of a 'greener' livelihood another approach. Soon after Namibia gained independence the state delegated rights to game management, and also to water, forests, and pastures to local communities. Non-governmental organisations (NGOs) funded through international donors entered the scene. Communal resource management was reorganised according to global blueprints of successful common-pool resource management. Indeed, game numbers increased again in the 1990s and early 2000s. North-western Namibia became a haven for community-minded conservationists. Pastoral communities got involved in conservation and gained some income from tourism. Even limited commercial hunting was (re)introduced to the region for the sake of fostering local interest in conservation. Eventually a landscape that had witnessed colonial oppression, violence, and invasions (of people, microbes, and game), a landscape that had undergone tremendous ecological changes, became something that could be depicted as an 'Arid Eden'.

In the following sections I will outline the theoretical underpinnings of this volume. The book is informed by three theoretical strands. The first is the very recent neo-materialist approach, which emphasises the material constitution of social and political reproduction. The second strand is environmental history with its concern for the historical dynamics of relations between state, local community, and environment. The third is political ecology, which analyses the link between power imbalances and environmental processes and is concerned with the effects of global embeddedness on local social-ecological systems.

1.1 New Materialism

People travelling the arid plains and hills of north-western Namibia get a good idea of how the material givens of the savannah landscape impact human settlement and livelihoods. During the dry season the absence of grasses makes one wonder how any grazing animal could ever survive in such an environment. Locals frame accounts of their lifeworld with depictions of changing vegetation and fauna. During the rainy season the environment rapidly changes to an affording, overwhelmingly green landscape. However, this flush of biotic production also brings challenges: Malaria infections soar and cause deaths, roads are inundated and cannot be passed for many days. This first impression is misleading though: The landscape in which today's pastoralists live is itself the result of selective grazing by domesticated ruminants and infrastructure built up by humans. All too easily we slip into a discourse which juxtaposes humans to a natural environment and which emphasises the ingenuity of human adaptation to a challenging (natural) landscape and climate. The 'environment' is in parts the result of human action: domesticated herbivores produced the peculiar vegetation cover of the landscape. Humans actively manipulated the genetic basis of these herbivores, by selecting breeding bulls and castrating steers for example. Cattle were instrumental to concentrate the energy dispersed over the vast semi-arid savannah into 'relatively compact and portable bodies' (LeCain 2017: 36). Based on data on north-central Namibia, Kreike (2013: 139–56) suggests that the browsing capacity of the local Sanga cattle breed encouraged the expansion and structure of the dominant mopane savannah. Man-made infrastructures matter too for the emergence of this pastoral landscape: A vast network of boreholes drilled since the 1950s is the basis for today's nomadic livestock husbandry.

There are other material givens that are entangled with human livelihoods, social organisation, and culture. Local people would immediately name livestock as prominent almost human-like actors and would have little difficulty in ascertaining that cattle have their own will and their own intelligence. They are 'used to' certain pastures and 'remember' other pastures. During the dry season cattle herds are often left alone in riverine forests to look after themselves and, of course, they do well there because they 'know' how to do it. There are other animals that unfold their own agency. Elephants notably are such a species. In the early twenty-first century they roam the region in increasing numbers, also 'remembering' older paths and 'exploring' new terrains.

Recent debates on the Anthropocene have suggested that humans have completely colonised nature and have changed large parts of it according to their needs. The emphasis on human impact has glossed over the fact that to a great extent humans are a product of the material givens surrounding and in many ways constituting them. Chakrabarty (2009) has recently put forward the bold hypothesis that the advent of anthropogenically caused climate change necessitates the end of the conventional dichotomy between human culture and nature (for a discussion of Chakrabarty's ideas see Emmett and Lekan 2016). While Western philosophers and anthropologists would still feel uneasy with this end of the (scientific) world as we knew it, pastoralists in northwestern Namibia would find it much easier to acknowledge that natural history and human history are intertwined and barely separable. I remember interviewing a herder about his cattle. We stood at the edge of the cattle enclosure, and my informant said 'these cattle are very old', implying that they had very long 'family' histories. Retreating back into the long shadows of sunset we then sat down under a tree and he related the history of some of his cattle over a century. The genealogies of some cows he could trace back into the 1890s! Ambitiously he followed up on how ancestral cows were inherited, presented, and, notably, found their own ways, and how they had constituted places, moulded the environment, and created social relations. From a local perspective it was very much the cattle who involved themselves in the realm of humans. Other elements of the material world unfold other kinds of agency. Ancestral graveyards unfold their agency – they are powerful agents in a wider landscape. Ancestors guard and protect 'their land'; they contribute to good grazing conditions in ways that humans cannot fully grasp and their power is compressed in graveyards.

Ian Hodder has recently put forward the concepts of *entanglement* and *entrapment* in his analysis of interactions between humans and the non-human world. These I found helpful to capture the intricate relations between human culture and material dynamics. *Entanglement* he defines as the dialectic dependency between humans and things (Hodder 2014: 20). The term *entanglement* seeks to capture the ways in which humans and things *entrap* each other. Hodder's entanglement concept bears similarities with Bruno Latour's idea of actor-networks. Both concepts seek to overcome the dualisms between material world and culture and between agency and structure. Hodder, however, convincingly argues that 'to bring everything into the dispersed human/nonhuman network risks losing one of the main motors of change – the limited unfixed nature of things in themselves and their relationship with each other' (Hodder 2014: 24–5). Kreike (2013) conceptualises the process of entanglement with his concepts 'environmental infrastructure' and 'environing'. Echoing Hodder's main motivation to overcome the nature–culture dualism, Kreike uses the concept of environmental infrastructure in order to bridge the culture–nature dichotomy; he sees environmental infrastructure as being conditioned by 'both Nature's and Culture's creativity' (Kreike 2013: 1). It comprises the shaping and reshaping of the environment from 'mental abstraction to physical execution' and 'highlights the idea that human control, use and agency are neither absolute nor exclusive' (Kreike 2013: 22). In contrast to conventional infrastructure whose function is to support human agency, environmental infrastructure is shaped by and may serve both human and non-human actors. The creation and recreation of environmental infrastructure Kreike terms *environing* (Kreike 2013: 24). In processes of *environing* (Kreike 2013: 228–33) different actors (human and non-human) collaborate in the creation of an environmental infrastructure. Influenced by perspectives of Science and Technology Studies Blok et al. (2016: 9) regard infrastructures as both physical objects and knowledge objects that in 'both capacities ... need work of coordination and maintenance in order to function properly'. They are particularly interested in 'how environments get infrastructure ... attending to contested landscapes of knowledge, processes, and effects' (Blok et al. 2016: 3).[2]

1.2 The Environmental History Approach

Environmental history in southern Africa has focused on the interaction between colonial state, local resource users, and the environment (Beinart 2002; Beinart and Coates 1995; Carruthers 2005; Jacobs 2003; Kreike 2013). Prominently environmental perceptions and ideologies of colonial elites and administrations were described and ensuing colonial practice was critically portrayed. Environmental historians have shown that hegemonic European perceptions and the ideas of settler communities with regard to nature were often directly linked to issues of power and control. William Beinart (2000, 2007) and Jocelyn Alexander (2006) show to what extent environmental policies followed the calculus of imperial power politics. Environmental historians have shown how many uncertainties were rendered as certainties (e.g. overgrazing, soil erosion) in order to prove the destructiveness of local modes of production and legitimise heavy-handed state control (e.g. Botha 2005; Fairhead and Leach 1997; Kreike 2009).

A great deal of environmental historians' work concentrates on the views and actions of those in power, whereas the strategies of those subjected to administrative measures are often portrayed in a less detailed manner. This, of course, is an artefact of the availability of sources. Whereas oral accounts on, for example, African hunting in the 1920s and 1930s and local measures against contagious bovine pleuropneumonia are rare, there is an abundance of written statements by colonial administrators on these topics. Even in the 1950s and 1960s, decades for which both oral accounts and files are numerous, it is hard to reconstruct local perspectives and strategies. I have tried to do so: when dozens of boreholes were drilled in the 1950s and 1960s, local institutions of pasture management apparently changed rapidly.

---

[2] Blok et al.'s (2016) concept of *infrastructuring environments* is in many respects similar to Kreike's *environing*. There are some notable differences though: Kreike's environing embellishes a multi-species perspective in that it concedes that human and also non-human actors participate in the process. Blok et al. adopt a more anthropocentric perspective and highlight performative aspects. I will try to include both perspectives without advocating for yet another term.

Former rainy-season grazing areas became dry-season areas because then water could be provided permanently and new rules of cooperative grazing emerged. Information on how all this happened is not found in the archives, and astonishingly also not in oral traditions. The latter only reflect upon the results of this process, and portray institutional arrangements as a *fait accompli*. While oral traditions were almost mute on these deep infrastructural and environmental changes, they were vocal regarding chiefly conflicts and contestations between colonial administration and local traditional authorities. Furthermore, in many environmental history accounts material dynamics are not considered in great detail: nature remains an entity written upon by various kinds of invaders, and a passive object of exploitation, but is generally not attributed agency. In this book I attempt to acknowledge the material dynamics that unfold in a self-organised way and are only partially captured by humans.

1.3 The Political Ecology Approach

Power and the unequal distribution of costs and benefits accruing from the interaction of humans with their living and non-living surroundings as well as patterns of inclusion and exclusion are salient topics throughout this book. Political ecology which 'has sought... to understand the political dynamics surrounding material and discursive struggles over the environment' (Bryant 1998: 89; see also Blaikie 1985; Greenberg and Park 1994) is therefore the third theoretical vantage point relevant to this account. Political ecology has developed in different directions over the past fifty years. In the 1970s and 1980s a structuralist approach, looking at the interdependence between socio-economic inequality and geobiophysical dynamics dominated. Blaikie (1985) for example analysed soil degradation in connection with colonial land tenure policies, while others (e.g. Watts 1983) reported on the environmental consequences of local inequality. While both cultural ecology and systems theory looked for adaptation and homeostasis, political ecology focused on non-adaptive behaviour, degradation, and societal crisis (Walker 2005: 74). In recent decades a poststructuralist approach with a focus on the effects of discursive formations on environmental governance dominated. This shift showed how global discourses, for example on tropical forest loss (Fairhead and Leach 1997), desertification (Bassett and Crummey

2003), and climate change (Bollig 2018; De Wit 2017; Weiser et al. 2014) impacted local social-ecological systems and contributed to grave changes of environmental infrastructure in the past and in the present. This book will endeavour to combine both strands of political ecology: local inequalities have changed throughout the past two centuries, and such changes have always had pertinent effects on land use and social-ecological transformations connected to them. At the same time global flows of commodities, people, and ideas have influenced local social-ecological dynamics.

More so than environmental history, political ecology is geared towards a critique of present and past injustices (see e.g. Jacobs 2003). Kottak emphasises the emancipatory orientation of political ecology (Kottak 1999: 26) and environmental justice is an up-coming topic of political ecology with much potential for the analysis of local initiatives in globalised contexts (Kiaka 2018; Schnegg and Kiaka 2018). The Himba pastoralists of north-western Namibia nowadays frame themselves as indigenous people. They have just handed in a petition to the UN in which they complain about environmental injustices.

In all parts of this book I trace the manifold entanglements – and in fact the mutual constitution – of dynamic epistemic formations, political contestations, social change, and environmental infrastructural dynamics. Furthermore, I attempt to be sensitive to scale interactions impacting local ecological dynamics: even if north-western Namibia is (and has been) portrayed as isolated and remote, it has been connected to global flows of ideas, people, and commodities.

1.4 Doing Fieldwork in North-Western Namibia

I started fieldwork in north-western Namibia in the early 1990s. In 1993 I conducted a pre-tour to the region and in February 1994 started fieldwork and stayed in the region for twenty-five months until March 1996. Namibia had just become independent three years earlier. In order to reach Opuwo, the region's small administrative centre, one had to drive some 250 km on a gravel road. The town itself still showed the signs of civil war, with a barbed wire fence around part of the town. Opuwo had not much to offer beyond one working petrol station and a large shop which was devoid of any fresh produce but offered a limited choice of canned food, noodles, rice, sugar, and salt.

My primary fieldwork destination was about 150 km north of Opuwo, close to the Angolan border. In 1993 I had come with the idea of studying risk management in a pastoral society. I focused on ecological hazards (droughts, livestock diseases) as much as on economic and political hazards (market failure, denial of access to resources) and a range of strategies used by herders to adapt to these (Bollig 2006). After some months of fieldwork (and a number of language courses in Germany) I had gained some proficiency in Otjiherero and could do at least part of my fieldwork independently from field assistants. This significantly contributed to my gaining the trust of the local people even if for more complex issues I would come along with an assistant. I could travel on my own, find my way along hidden footpaths, and could address people appropriately.

When I left the field in early 1996 a large-scale interdisciplinary project in which I happened to be a co-applicant had started. Between 1996 and 2007 I visited north-western Namibia at least once a year and was able to do another twelve months of fieldwork. This time the thematic focus of my fieldwork differed. I was now engaged in a large interdisciplinary programme called Arid Climate, Adaptation and Cultural Innovation in Africa (ACACIA), and worked alongside botanists, archaeologists, linguists, and geographers; some of the anthropological work was directed towards interdisciplinary topics such as soil erosion and vegetation degradation (Bollig and Schulte 1999; Sander et al. 1998), settlement history (Bollig and Vogelsang 2002), and regional history (Bollig and Gewald 2000). The project also gave me the extraordinary chance to broaden my knowledge of the region in three important ways. First of all I expanded my work to other regions of Namibia's north-west and did work in the southern as much as in the western Kaokoveld. I had also the chance to work with a number of PhD and MA students who worked on different aspects of human–environment relations. Laura Bleckmann, for example, looked at the constitution of landscapes in praise songs (Bleckmann 2012), and Silke Tönsjost (2013) investigated wealth, consumption, and land use in the southern Kaokoveld. After the ACACIA programme came to an end in 2007 I gained some funding to conduct research on conservation and other community-based resource management issues (Bollig 2012). This refocusing of research was first of all brought about by pertinent changes in resource governance in the region. In harmony with globally shifting ideas about resource management the Namibian government was keen to hand over rights and obligations to local natural resources to local communities. Boreholes had been managed by the administration since the 1950s. Now the villagers had to care for these boreholes themselves and had to fix a price for water. In 2010 Michael Schnegg (University of Hamburg) and I secured a grant to study how local institutions for water management changed in reaction to this governmental programme. In connection with this project Thekla Kelbert (2016), Diego Menestrey-Schwieger (2017), Richard Kiaka (2018), and Elsemi Olwage (forthcoming) did further research in the region on institutional dynamics, land rights and mobility, and the translation of global concepts of water governance to the local level. In 2018 another survey of some 200 Himba households in the northern-most parts of the Kunene Region was conducted. Linking to earlier surveys in 1994 and 2004/5 the data of the 2018 survey sheds some light on continuities and discontinuities of social and economic change.

Throughout the past twenty years I did research in Namibia's National Archive. I first concentrated on early colonial times, particularly on the encapsulation of the Kaokoveld's social-ecological system[3] by the South African administration in the 1920s and 1930s (Bollig 1998b). Later on I worked on the comprehensive borehole-drilling programme of the administration from the 1950s to 1970s. More recently I did archival research on the beginnings of conservationist planning in the Kaokoveld in the 1970s.

---

[3] The basic idea of the concept of a social-ecological system is that societies and geobiophysical entities interact across spatio-temporal scales and mutually constitute each other. Anderies et al. (2004) define such a hybrid system as: 'an integrated system of geo-biophysical, social and cultural subsystems with reciprocal feedback and interdependence in which some of the interdependent relationships among humans are mediated through interactions with biophysical and non-human biological units'. I regard the concept 'social-ecological system' as the natural science/ecology correlate to the humanities concept 'environmental infrastructure'. Social-ecological systems are intricately coupled (Crumley 1994), which means that there exist strong mutual feedbacks between system elements and scales. In the context of this book, processes of enforced *decoupling* and *recoupling* are also important. The concept 'coupling' I regard as the natural sciences correlate to environing and environmental infrastructuring, though coupling focusses our attention more on material flows while environing and environmental infrastructuring give more attention to creativity and agency.

1.5 Chapter Outline

The book is organised into six parts consisting of twelve chapters. After the introductory Part 1, Part 2 outlines the pre-colonial history of north-western Namibia. Part 3 deals with the environmental history of the first part of the twentieth century, whereas Part 4 treats the history of environmental infrastructures between the 1950s and the 1980s. Part 5 focuses on the past three decades and analyses land use patterns between the late 1980s and the present. Part 5 also includes a chapter detailing recent attempts of future-making in and for the region. The final Part 6 theorises and generalises the findings.

In Part 1 (Chapter 1) the theoretical outlook of the study is depicted. Part 2 consists of two chapters. Chapter 2 describes the emergence of social-ecological relations as we find them today in the Kaokoveld. Archaeo-botanical and archaeological data shows that the vegetation patterns we see today came into being (only) about 8,000 years ago, replacing a vegetation that was typical for an earlier, drier climate. Pastoralists only entered the scene relatively recently, probably in the nineteenth century. Whereas some scientists have cited evidence for a much earlier immigration of pastoralists into the area, local sources (and also a number of written sources) speak of a gradual build-up of pastoralism *in situ* and a long co-existence of pastoralism and foraging. Archaeological records do not give a conclusive picture as to how early pastoralists and foragers shaped the local environmental infrastructure. While for example the planned burning of stretches of the savannah and the browsing of large herds of cattle in the vicinity of the few permanent water sources were of relevance, the ecological footprint of these activities is difficult to clearly associate with human action. This period, which can rightly be addressed as pre-colonial (i.e. with little influence from outside colonising forces) came to an end in the second half of the nineteenth century, when militarily superior groups from central Namibia raided the Kaokoveld and violently forced the local population to flee to south-western Angola and central Namibia.

Chapter 3 deals with the pertinent interlude of intensive elephant hunting between the 1880s and the 1910s. For roughly thirty years large numbers of elephants were killed for their ivory. It was mainly a group of Boers, the Dorsland Trekkers, settling close to Lubango in south-western Angola, who raided the Kaokoveld's elephant herds annually. The ivory was transported back to southern Angola and shipped from there abroad. Apart from the Boer hunters, locals and other hunters of European descent also operated in the Kaokoveld. Nobles and the kings of the westernmost Ovambo kingdoms Uukwaludhi and Ongandjera equipped locals with guns to hunt elephants on their behalf. The chapter argues that this onslaught on the most impactful herbivorous animal significantly influenced environmental infrastructures.

Chapters 4–6 of Part 3 deal with the first phase of colonial rule and roughly comprise developments from the 1890s to the 1940s. Chapter 4 deals with the build-up of knowledge on the region during the first few decades of colonial rule. Scientists, administrators, and agents of a mining company travelled the area, gathered information, produced maps, and took photographs. The chapter details how environmental knowledge was produced and what kind of knowledge was sought. Chapter 5 deals with the establishment of colonial administration and the development of pastoralism during the first three decades of colonial rule. At the end of German colonial rule the Kaokoveld saw a significant influx of population from southern Angola, where erstwhile refugees decided to return to their ancestral lands in reaction to more oppression by the Portuguese colonial forces. The South African administration rapidly gained influence in the early 1920s, nominated three chiefs, set boundaries and guarded them ambitiously. Chapter 6 describes how the Kaokoveld became an encapsulated part of the mandated territory and a true colonial frontier. Mobility of pastoralists was tightly controlled and a hunting ban strictly enforced. Compulsory livestock vaccination was instituted, despite strong local protests. Throughout these early decades of the twentieth century pastoralism grew in significance and foraging strategies lost importance.

Part 4 has two chapters. Chapters 7 and 8 deal with transformations of the environmental infrastructure under colonial rule during the second half of the twentieth century (1950s–1980s). Chapter 7 deals with the period between the late 1940s and the 1970s: the South African administration now sought to modernise its colony at all costs and to intensify livestock production. It envisaged that the Kaokoveld could produce significantly more livestock if water could be made available. By the mid-1950s a comprehensive borehole-drilling programme was instituted which was then rolled out in the 1960s and 1970s. This programme had tremendous effects: vast new stretches of land could now be used during the dry season (whereas previously they had only been used sporadically during the rainy season). Chapter 8 deals with the manifold contradictions of this period of pastoral intensification. The modernisation programme was strongly anti-conservationist. Predators were redefined as vermin and local herders were given poison, traps, and later guns to hunt them. In opposition to this programme of pastoral intensification a spate of plans was produced for how to best protect wildlife in the Kaokoveld in the 1970s. While none of the ambitious conservationist plans of the 1970s came about, they set the agenda for the last two decades of the twentieth century and the early twenty-first century: the Kaokoveld was to become a focal area for conservation efforts.

Part 5's three chapters deal with the present development of pastoralism, state-led efforts to introduce community-based natural resource management, and the future (as seen and planned for today). These three chapters cover three decades, the end of the 1980s until the present day. After a bloody war of liberation in the 1970s and 1980s Namibia finally became independent in 1990. In its policy towards the newly founded administrative unit Kunene Region, of which the Kaokoveld constituted the northern part, the new government sought to combine agricultural intensification and conservation. Chapter 9 deals with the current organisation of mobile livestock husbandry. The Kaokoveld's pastoral economy is still very much subsistence-oriented. The grazing is communal, and neither privatisation nor fencing of lands has taken place. Still only minor fractions of livestock are sold to obtain maize and other commodities. While integration into larger commodity markets is still restricted due to, for example, the infamous Red Line, a veterinary cordon fence that separates commercial rangelands from communal lands in northern Namibia, governmental programmes for community-based natural resource management bring the state much closer to locals than ever before. Chapter 10 then deals with two governmental programmes to reorganise natural resource tenure: The conservancy programme allows registered conservancies to make good use of game. They may either sell game allotted to them to trophy hunters or hunt a restricted number of animals themselves. They may also rent out land to tourism entrepreneurs for the construction of lodges and campsites. In return they have to flag out core conservation areas which they pledge not to use regularly. Conservancies also garner considerable outside support through NGOs. At the same time rural water supply was reorganised. While previously boreholes had been maintained by the government, now boreholes and all responsibilities and obligations connected with them were handed to newly formed water-point associations. These associations were to collect fees for the use of the water point and thereby earn the money necessary to run the borehole sustainably. Chapter 11 deals with the future – or, perhaps better, how the future is anticipated at present. Three possible futures are fleshed out. Conservation may indeed become the leading paradigm for rural development, with incomes from conservation and tourism replacing agricultural incomes to some extent. The second projected future scenario does not sit easily with the first: north-western Namibia may also have a significant industrial future. Recent geological surveys by Australian and Chinese companies have resulted in the formation of companies intending to exploit Namibia's riches. Then there is a third potential future trajectory: Local people, who progressively identify as indigenous, carve out more autonomy for themselves and organise land use semi-independently like the Canadian Cree or the Scandinavian Saami for example.

Part 6's Chapter 12 summarises the results of this study and attempts to link the dense empirical data to the different theoretical strands discussed earlier in this first chapter as well as to other literature on land use transformations in northern Namibia.

PART 2

The Evolution of Pre-Colonial Environmental Infrastructure

How did the environmental infrastructure of north-western Namibia develop in pre-colonial times and how did change come about in this social-ecological system? To start off with: we know fairly little about the region's prehistory. There has been a spate of excavations in rockshelters roughly between 1995 and 2005 (for a summary see Vogelsang and Eichhorn 2011). In an area as big as Switzerland these are, however, only first steps into an unknown territory. These excavations have documented the long persistence of a foraging lifestyle. While there are some few finds that seem to document the restricted use of goats and or sheep since about 2,000 years ago, there is no evidence that foragers turned to pastoralism. Unfortunately archaeological evidence does not stretch much into the eighteenth and nineteenth century. For these centuries oral traditions suggest the emergence of a pastoral tradition in north-western Namibia. Much in contrast to the sparse evidence from archaeological research and the analysis of oral traditions, the region features importantly in some grand tales of pastoral migration from eastern Africa to southern Africa. Some authors alleged that Bantu-speaking pastoralists entered the south-western part of Africa via the Kaokoveld some 300 years ago – as said, there is very little evidence for that from the region.

What about environmental infrastructure? We know that the mopane savannah is the dominant biome since about 8,000 years ago. Before that time it was considerably colder than today and only after a warmer period had set in could the mopane savannah establish itself. Humans have certainly been impacting this social-ecological system and built up an environmental infrastructure conducive to their livelihoods. It is certain that foragers used fires in order to rejuvenate vegetation; it is also probable that gatherers made use for example, of *Hyphaenae ventricosa*, the abundant palm in riverine valleys, and transported its nuts as food from valley to valley thereby adding to its expansion. There are more instances of alleged human impact on the vegetation cover. The problem is to find appropriate evidence for such assumptions. Oral evidence becomes denser for the period beginning in the mid-nineteenth century. Traditions suggest that by that time pastoral households settled many of the permanent springs and along the seasonal river courses. Still these households relied heavily on hunting and gathering and many people still lived a purely foraging life, but pastoralism had increasing impact by then. How these early pastoralists changed their environment and created a pastoral landscape has not been researched yet. The build-up of a pastoral lifestyle was violently interrupted in the 1860s–1890s when raiding commandos destroyed pastoral livelihoods in the region and forced people to either flee to southern Angola or to look for safer living conditions in the mountains of the Kaokoveld.

2 | *The Prehistory of North-Western Namibia and the Emergence of Pastoralism*

Humans have interacted with the environment in north-western Namibia for many thousands of years. In around 100 excavated sites, characteristic stone artefacts from the Early Holocene Later Stone Age (c. 12,000 to 8,000 BP) were found (Bollig and Vogelsang 2002: 146f.; Vogelsang and Eichhorn 2011; Vogelsang et al. 2002: 115). In contrast, artefacts related to the Middle Holocene Later Stone Age (8,000 to 4,000 BP) are very rare in the region. This corresponds to the near-absence of rock art in north-western Namibia. While rock art and Middle Holocene Later Stone Age remains are plentiful in the region adjoining north-western Namibia to the south (the southern parts of today's Kunene Region and the adjoining Erongo Region), the central and northern parts of the Kunene Region – the Kaokoveld – seem to have been avoided by humans during that time period.

Anthracological charcoal analysis indicates that the climate of the eastern parts of the Kunene Region around 12,000 BP was both drier and cooler than at present. The woody vegetation of that period was dominated by the genus Acacia. Taxa typical of today's mopane savannah, such as *Colophospermum mopane*, *Terminalia prunioides*, and *Combretum apiculatum*, were absent from the data. Marine pollen analysis (Shi et al. 1998, 2000) corroborates the assumption that temperatures were considerably lower during this time period. However, it is this dry period to which many Early Holocene Later Stone Age remains belong. The semi-arid savannah ecosystem as we know it today established itself between 9,000 and 8,000 BP (Blümel et al. 2000; Eichhorn and Vogelsang 2007) due to a significant increase in precipitation. Despite this climatic change towards more favourable conditions, human occupation in north-western Namibia remained ephemeral and at a low level for millennia.

Settlement in the area increased again around 2,500 BP. The research team of the Cologne-based ACACIA project located bones (which were tentatively classified as bones of ovicaprines) and pottery – both appearing independently in the record around 2,000 BP for the first time. Vogelsang et al. (2002: 121) report that settlement sites of hunter-gatherer communities absorbed these exotic materials and technologies with no transformation of the general subsistence pattern. Pastoral sites are notably absent from the record for the past 2,000 years, and there is a lot of evidence that the contact situation between foraging populations in north-western Namibia and livestock-keeping populations in the wider region did not result in a general change of forager livelihoods until the eighteenth or even nineteenth century (Vogelsang and Eichhorn 2011: 204–6).

Two types of foragers are to be differentiated on the basis of these accounts. I will first address the forager communities making use of the coastline, and then describe forager communities living further inland in the mountainous parts of the Kaokoveld in greater detail: van Warmelo (1951: 45) refers explicitly to a small 'Bushman' community living at the lower reaches of the Hoanib in the early 1950s.[1] While pastoralists in the nineteenth and twentieth century did not make use of the shoreline of north-western Namibia, Eichhorn and Vogelsang (2007) found evidence of an intensive use of the coast by forager communities in the pre-colonial past: large shell middens are a regular feature in the vicinity of the mouths of all larger rivers along the north-west Namibian coast. These middens are entirely composed of shells collected from the beach, along with a few stone artefacts, potsherds, ostrich eggshell beads, and bones. In these middens and settlement structures Vogelsang could locate hardly any artefacts of European origin. This stands in stark contrast to the evidence from coastal sites in more southerly regions of the Namib Desert (Kinahan 2000), where trade contacts between coastal foragers and European and North

---

[1] Apart from van Warmelo (1951), a letter by B. Carp to the Administrator of Southwest Africa, Windhoek, on his 'Kaokoexpedition' in the late 1940s (NAN SWAA Kaokoveld A522) mentions a forager population at the mouth of the Hoanib River. He records them as comprising '3 bushmen, 2 bushwomen, 3 Damas and 3 Dama-women', and continues: 'They were called Sandlopers as they lived in the sand and also part of the year on the beaches of the coast, where they ate dead fish etc. Inland their diet consisted of grass veldkos and anything they could catch. They lived in scherms, no proper huts and had a very primitive life.' Whether Carp confuses '*strandloper*' and '*sandloper*' or just plays on the terms is hard to say. Hartmann (1902/1903) had possibly met with the same community some four decades earlier while exploring the coast. Even around 1900 the community consisted of only a very few individuals.

American sailors have been recorded since the early nineteenth century. The lack of trade-goods is probably the consequence of the absence of any good harbouring place along that stretch of the coast. However, it may also provide evidence for the demise of a coastal forager culture before the advent of European colonialism, i.e. before the nineteenth century. Eichhorn and Vogelsang (2007) conclude that the archaeological evidence suggests a strong connection between the savannah hinterland and the coastal ecosystem. The beaches of what is today the Skeleton Coast Park were visited seasonally by foragers for the exploitation of marine food resources. Did these foragers – most of them probably of Khoisan descent – interact with Bantu-speaking communities further inland? While the archaeological record evidences the use of hinterland resources by coastal foragers, there is little oral evidence for the interaction between Bantu pastoralists and coastal foragers. In oral traditions collected from Himba and Herero informants in the 1990s and 2000s, Khoisan-speaking coastal foragers are not mentioned. This may suggest that by the time pastoralists had settled the highlands of the interior, the coastal forager population had shrunk in significance, and that coast–hinterland migrations did not feature prominently in the livelihoods of people dwelling in the Kaokoveld later on.

In contrast to the absence of Khoisan-speaking foragers in the oral record, there is evidence of two Bantu-speaking forager communities in oral traditions and written sources: On the one hand, various Tjimba communities, some of them in possession of some small stock and a few cattle, and others completely relying on foraging strategies; on the other hand, Thwa communities residing predominantly in the southernmost parts of south-western Angola, and operating occasionally in north-western Namibia.[2] Thwa communities hunted and gathered, but also displayed a number of craft specialisations (see Bollig 2004: 211f.): While the men were expert smiths, the women were masters of pottery. Oral traditions emphasise that whereas Tjimba, Himba, and Herero identities were flexible and permeable, with significant

---

[2] There is very little ethnographic research on the Thwa in general, and no research (that I know of) on their history. Estermann's (1981: 94, 153) ethnographic remarks remain the exception. Oral traditions of the Thwa gathered by the author indicate that Thwa foragers may have used resources in the northernmost part of the Kunene Region in pre-colonial times. However, their main area of activity was situated in south-western Angola.

shifts between these communities, the Thwa were an almost caste-like group. Whereas Tjimba communities turned fully to pastoralism during the course of the twentieth century, Thwa communities mainly relied on small herds of livestock and the production and exchange of metal adornments and pottery. In contrast to coastal foragers, the Tjimba and Thwa communities engaged extensively in exchanges with pastoral nomadic communities.

To what extent did foragers impact the social-ecological system and actively create environmental infrastructure? There is no evidence from oral history that could help to answer this question and unfortunately also archaeological evidence is sparse. On the basis of pollen evidence from hyrax middens Gil-Romera et al. (2007) find an increase in mopane trees and acacias from c. 1,300 cal yrs BP, while grasses decrease in the same time period. On the basis of their sources Gil-Romera et al. find it impossible to differentiate whether this trend towards a higher tree–grass ratio is attributable to inherent ecosystem dynamics, slightly drier climatic conditions and subsequent overgrazing, or simply to depositional effects and hyrax dietary habits (Gil-Romera et al. 2007: 12). On the basis of archaeological and archeo-botanical evidence Vogelsang and Eichhorn (2011: 148) tentatively connect an increase in bush vegetation along rivers to an increasing use of riverine valleys by humans. The lack of archaeological evidence certainly suggests that population numbers were very small and human impact on the environment transient and in most settings ephemeral. Nevertheless, foragers would have contributed to the emergence of an environmental infrastructure by the igniting of bush fires, the selective use of plants, and the targeted hunting of prey-species – the footprint they left, however, is hard to decipher.

2.1 The Emergence of Pastoralism

Despite the dearth of pertinent archaeological evidence for pastoralisation in the Kunene Region, there has been a lot of academic speculation on the topic. Strikingly, north-western Namibia has featured centrally in many early and some contemporary depictions of the spread of pastoralism to southern Africa. While the archaeological evidence is scanty, models of the spread of pastoralism have by and large relied on linguistic (e.g. Ehret 1998; Elphick 1977; Möhlig 2002) and ethnohistorical (e.g. Stow 1905; Vedder 1928, 1934) evidence. Recent archaeological publications, such as those of Henshilwood (1996) and Bousman (1998), still cite Stow (1905), who assumed that livestock-holding Khoekhoe migrated from the East African Lakes region in a westerly direction to the north-west of Namibia, and from there along the coast to the Cape region (hence the migration route passing through north-western Namibia). Stow suggests the Khoekhoe migrations were due to their replacement by Bantu-speaking agro-pastoralists, while in turn Khoekhoe herders on their way south replaced Bushmen foragers. Elphick (1977) offers another route: On the basis of linguistic evidence he assumes an expansion of livestock-keeping from northern Botswana to the Oranje, and from there a subsequent movement in both westerly and easterly directions. Cooke (1965) gives yet another route for early pastoralists; originating from the region south of Lake Malawi they venture through Zimbabwe and northern Botswana entering Namibia from the north-east (see Map 2.1). Stow (and others) see north-western Namibia as the cradle of livestock-keeping in southern Africa and in Elphick's model livestock husbandry expanded into north-western Namibia as a relatively late occurrence (Vogelsang 2002 offers a good summary of the discussion). A review of the literature shows three rather different models of pastoralisation in north-western Namibia.

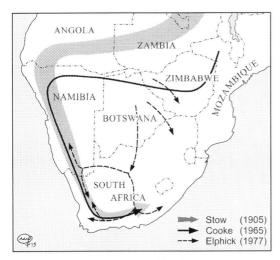

Map 2.1 The immigration of herding communities to south-western Africa.
Source: adapted from Vogelsang (2002)

While these scenarios attempt to capture the expansion of livestock husbandry to southern Africa, the models summarized in the subsequent sections deal with the expansion of Bantu-speaking herders (and not of livestock husbandry per se).

Model A: *Pastoral Migration into the Kunene Region*

Based on the comparative analysis of oral traditions collected at the beginning of the twentieth century, the missionary and lay ethnographer Vedder assumed that the Herero had entered north-western Namibia around 1700, or – as he claimed in a later publication – around 1550.[3] In Vedder's accounts the fabled origin of the Herero, a place called Mbandwa, referred to in traditional accounts as *ehi raruu* (the land of reed-grass), was to be found in the Kavango swamps, or alternatively near the East African Lakes. Vedder's account resounds with the diffusionist Hamitic theory (Rohrbacher 2002; Sanders 1996), which argued that herder communities (often framed as a specific race) originating in the Near East migrated to East Africa and then on to southern Africa, and brought with them not only livestock husbandry but also the capacity to establish states. This racist theory, which was first forwarded by German Africanists (Westermann, Meinhof), had a direct impact on Vedder's reading of Herero traditions, as the following quote shows:

The Hereros, with their coffee-coloured complexion, their tall, stately physique, their distinguished demeanour, their fine features, differ too much from the negro-type to warrant our including them in the negro-race without further investigation. The supposition has often been expressed that they might belong to the Hamite tribes of North Africa. If this be the case, this tribe must have emigrated thence in prehistoric times and have intermingled with Negro tribes in Central Africa and come to the south of Africa after long nomadic migrations. Presumably the ancestors of the Hereros lived for a considerable time in the regions of the Central African lakes. Not only do philological investigations point to this fact; so do vague recollections which

---

[3] For a critique of Vedder's approach see Lau (1981). Vedder visited the Kaokoveld only once, in 1914, for about two months (NAN, J XIIIb5, Vedder Reisebericht des Missionars Vedder an den Bezirksamtmann von Zastrow. Geographische und Ethnographische Forschungen im Kaokoveld 1900–1914). He stayed mainly at Kaoko Otavi and had contact with some pastoral-foragers there. Contact with the Himba settled along the Kunene River was, at best, spurious.

have been handed down in the form of legends among the Hereros as well. From the lake districts they seem to have migrated with their herds in a westerly direction through South Angola, until their arrival at the shores of the Atlantic Ocean compelled them to turn south. They crossed the Kunene and migrated into the Kaokoveld, but rich owners of large herds as they were, they did not stay there very long ... One would hardly be wrong in assuming that immigration into the Kaokoveld took place at about the year 1700 and that the first immigration into the present Hereroland commenced fifty years later. (Vedder 1928: 156–7)

Only a few years later, however, Vedder depicted a very different route of migration of Herero pastoralists into north-western Namibia. In his later version north-western Namibia is not the cradle of pastoralism but a periphery of pastoral expansion in south-western Africa:

In ancient times the Herero were not a people on their own. Their ancestors were not yet called Herero. The name of their people was Mbandu; others called them Mbundua. This people called Mbandu settled in a well-watered country in which reeds were plentiful. Because of this the country was called the land of reeds (ehi raruu). Some cattle owners did not like this land any longer. It is no longer known what prompted them to move. ... They went to the country of the Betchuanas and were well received by them. At this time the country of the Betchuanas was much bigger than it is today. Its western boundary extended to Oviombo (i.e. Okahandja) in contemporary Herero land. In this manner the emigrants reached pastures in southwest Africa, which later became their property, but which were still owned by the Betchuanas at that time. Herero cattle were grazing in Omuramba Omatako, even if places like Okahandja or even Otjiwarongo or Omaruru had not yet been reached. (Vedder 1934: 135, my translation)

Only after conflicts with Tswana communities did Herero pastoralists move westwards towards north-western Namibia:

In order to prevent the loss of cattle they migrated westwards, passing Grootfontein and Outjo. However, they did not dare to cross the boundary into Ovamboland because powerful chiefs were ruling there. Consequently they were forced to migrate to the Kaokoveld, which was unsettled at that time. The cattle were mainly herded in the flat country in the southern reaches of the Kaokoveld up to the Omaruru River. Otjitambi (now Schlettwein's farm) became the centre of occupation for these pastoralists. (Vedder 1934: 135, my translation)

The fact that Vedder depicted completely different routes of pastoralisation in north-western Namibia may be due to the shakiness of his evidence. Anthropologists working in north-western Namibia between the 1950s and 1970s, however, subscribed to Vedder's 1928 version of Herero migrations and assumed that north-western Namibia was the key transit zone through which Bantu-speaking pastoralists entered into south-western Africa. Van Warmelo (1951: 9) tried to make sense of the presence of Bantu-speaking herders and foragers in the region within a diffusionist framework. He asserted that there had been two distinct movements of Bantu-speaking people into the Kaokoveld, in which the first wave of pastoralists soon became impoverished and were forced to lead their lives as pastoral-foragers (the Tjimba), while the later migrants, the Herero, succeeded in keeping their cattle (for a critique of van Warmelo's writing see Bollig 1997; Gordon 2000).

Linguistic reconstructions have backed the idea of Herero migrations from the eastern part of the continent to the semi-arid lands in the continent's south-west. Based on an extensive analysis of phonological and lexical characteristics of Bantu languages, as well as in-depth research on loan-words, Möhlig (2000: 138) summarises a chronological order of pastoral migrations across the continent: As representatives of the oldest Bantu-speaking stratum, the 'proto-Herero lived at the southern end of this Stratum, in a region to the west of Lake Malawi'. According to Möhlig Herero pastoralists then migrated westwards across the Lunda corridor some time around the end of the sixteenth or beginning of the seventeenth century. In the eighteenth century the Herero migrated and/or fled across the Kunene into the Kaokoveld, away from Portuguese slave raids in south-western Angola.

In Model A, livestock and their herders are associated with an immigrant Bantu population, which settled the Kaokoveld as part of a major population movement. Both Vedder's earlier account and Möhlig's linguistic reconstruction show the Herero – and with them, a pastoral livelihood – moving into Namibia through the Kaokoveld around 1700.

Model B: Pastoralisation as Regional Specialisation

In contrast to the model of an expansion of pastoralism into north-western Namibia through the movements of a pastoralist community originating in eastern Africa, anthropologists and historians predominantly working with archival documents, oral histories, and languages from south-western Angola present an account that argues for a local emergence of pastoralism in south-western Angola and a gradual spread to Namibia. The German anthropologist Baumann (1975: 484) was perhaps the first to reject migration models and to argue that a group of specialised pastoralists developed gradually on the fringes of the south-western Angolan highlands. Due to their specialisation, and due to the pressure from Nyaneka polities, which became ever more centralised in the course of the seventeenth century due to slave trading in southern Angola, pastoralists descended from the Huila highlands and populated the semi-arid plains on both sides of the Kunene. Baumann argues that the Herero had already developed a highly specialised pastoral livelihood while settling in the south-western Angolan highlands (Baumann 1975: 487f.). Estermann, a missionary ethnographer working in south-western Angola and with extensive access to Portuguese documents, asserted that pastoralists were living in the hinterland of Benguela around 1600. These pastoralists became the targets of Portuguese raiding commandos and then migrated (or fled) from south-western Angola towards the more arid savannahs of the Kaokoveld (Estermann 1981: 5–18). In the 1760s those living in the highlands of south-western Angola had their first direct contact with the expanding mercantile capitalism, and at the same time were drawn into the Atlantic slave trade (Clarence-Smith, 1978: 165–6), bringing about a significant increase in violence and social disruption, but also a concentration of political power in those polities participating in the trade.

The mountainous and arid lands of the Kaokoveld may have offered more protection than the open and fertile plains south of Huila. Although Baumann's methods for the comparison of cultural traits are outdated, his assumption that Herero migrations and the development of a specialised livestock economy were linked to political centralisation and violent conflict in southern Angola has been supported by recent historical research. Miller assumed that major dry periods between 1620 and 1640, and again in the 1720s, sparked off political unrest all over southern Angola (Miller 1988: 21). Clarence-Smith and Miller describe the emergence of centralised political systems in the Huila highlands as being a consequence of slave raiding and the penetration of merchant capital in the eighteenth century (Clarence-Smith 1978, 1979; Miller 1988: 222), and Williams

(1991: 132ff.) relates early Herero migrations into north-western Namibia to the expansion of the Imbangala around 1600 in central Angola and as a by-product of the slave trade.

In a recent publication Jan Vansina (2004: 120) argues for two centres of pastoralisation in the south-western part of the continent. An earlier Khoe-related pastoralism, mainly focused on small-stock husbandry, established itself in central and southern Namibia, whereas independently of the Khoe a transition from agro-pastoralism to nomadic pastoralism occurred in the dry coastal plains of south-western Angola and in the adjacent parts of north-western Namibia among speakers of Bantu languages. Vansina assumes that this transition happened around 1300 (i.e. considerably earlier than all other writers). Vansina's dating is vague, however: He infers this date from 'the known climate change' and argues that 'agro-pastoralism in the inner Cunene basin of southern Angola had just been established by the time of the short wetter period, which began ca. 1200, so that agropastoralists established themselves well beyond the western borders of where rainfed farming is now possible' (Vansina 2004: 120). With the beginning of the Medieval Ice Age, conditions became drier and agro-pastoralists were trapped in a semi-arid savannah and had to become mobile and to abandon agriculture. While there is ample evidence of major climatic changes in Africa on a continental scale during the past 2,000 years (Verschuren et al. 2004 for East Africa;[4] Holmgren and Öberg 2006 for southern Africa), I am not aware of any palaeo-climatic data from the wider region (south-western Angola, north-western Namibia) which could corroborate Vansina's assumption of a large-scale aridisation in south-western Africa at that point in time. Recent climatic reconstructions of pollen captured in hyrax dung middens (Gil-Romera et al. 2007) do not corroborate Vansina's assumption of a large-scale climatic change in north-western Namibia around 1300.[5] Vansina argues

---

[4] On the basis of the analysis of diatoms and pollen from lake cores of various East African Lakes, Verschuren et al. (2004) assert such a change from an agro-pastoral to a pastoral nomadic livelihood in Kenya in connection with a major inter-decadal drought between 1760 and 1840 (see also Anderson 2016 and Bollig 2016).

[5] On the basis of extensive excavations in the region Vogelsang and Eichhorn (2011: 198) diagnose a settlement hiatus at the time Vansina suggests the immigration of pastoralists.

for pastoral specialisation enforced by climatic circumstances mainly on the basis of linguistic evidence, and reports that a number of south-western Bantu languages, referred to by him as Njila languages, are closely connected, and that the Herero pastoralists developed directly out of this predominantly agro-pastoral cluster of communities located within the wider Kunene basin. On the basis of the Herero lexicon, as well as on reconstructed lexical proto-forms, Vansina depicts an early pastoralist lifeworld, pertinent traits of social organisation (e.g. double descent), and emergent stratification (Vansina 2004: 123f.).

Model C: Mobility and Socio-Cultural Dynamics in a Pastoral-Forager Community

As the preceding paragraphs have shown, the question of when and how pastoralists started using the rangelands of north-western Namibia is still open to debate. We know that when the first European travellers met with inhabitants of north-western Namibia in the second half of the nineteenth century, at least some of them were livestock-owning. Oral traditions also assert that before the raids by Nama commandos during the latter part of the nineteenth century pastoralism was well established in north-western Namibia. Based on the missionary Irle's reconstructions, Henrichsen (2011: 119) argues that prominent Herero leaders like Kambazembi and Mureti migrated as rich pastoralists from the Kaokoveld to the Waterberg region (Kambazembi) or to the Omaruru region (Kamureti) in the early 1860s.[6] This suggests that a pastoral economy had been well established in north-western Namibia in the mid-nineteenth century. These historical inferences do not, however, necessarily suggest that all inhabitants of the Kaokoveld were living as pastoralists at that time. Extensive archaeological campaigns by Vogelsang et al. (2002) and others between 1995 and 2005 showed no evidence of a longstanding tradition of specialised pastoralists in north-western Namibia (see also Vogelsang and Eichhorn 2011).

---

[6] Van Warmelo (1951: 10) remarks that Hosea Kutako, Paramount Chief of the Herero in the mid-twentieth century, claimed that his ancestors had originated from Okangundumba in the central Kaokoveld.

What can we say then about the advent of pastoralism in north-western Namibia? Indeed, there is no evidence that a specialised pastoral economy emerged in the Kaokoveld at an early stage, as suggested by Vansina, and there is also no evidence that a pastoral community entered north-western Namibia at some stage during the past 200 or 300 years, as Vedder and van Warmelo have it. Oral traditions account for single pastoralist households moving into the area between six and nine generations ago. In the Kaokoveld they met with Bantu-speaking foragers who may have kept some livestock. Herders and foragers established patron–client relations in some places, while a predominant forager tradition continued to exist without much pastoral interference in others. Compared to pastoralist–forager interactions observed in other parts of southern Africa, patron–client relations in north-west Namibia did not result in more permanent forms of stratification, and contrary to forager–pastoralist interaction commented upon by Wilmsen (1989: 69) and Jacobs (2003: 32ff.), who both describe the interaction between highly stratified Tswana polities and Khoisan-speaking foragers, the pastoral households entering the Kaokoveld were not organised into chiefdoms. Pastoral *ovahona* (wealthy men) dominated local exchange networks and pastoral production, but they did not establish enduring political structures of dominance and territoriality. In stark contrast to the situation found in the Kalahari, where marriage taboos inhibited Khoisan-speaking foragers' entry into the dominant Tswana society, and where serf–patron-like constellations were present and manifest in the *mafisa* system of cattle loans (Jacobs 2003:40), in north-western Namibia marriage relations between Bantu-speaking foragers and Bantu-speaking pastoralists (both speaking Otjiherero or dialects of Otjiherero) did occur. Both oral traditions and early written reports emphasise the continued relevance of foraging strategies.

Is there any spatial pattern discernible in forager–pastoralist relations in north-western Namibia? Apparently yes: pastoral communities focused their settlements along the courses of the major ephemeral rivers of the northern and the central Kaokoveld (notably Omuhonga and Hoarusib). Here foragers were often attached to pastoral encampments, acting as shepherds, or settled in the vicinity of pastoral households relying on exchange with livestock owners.

In the drier western parts of the Kaokoveld and also in the Baynes and Otjihipa Mountains there were few pastoral households (if any) as water sources were highly unreliable. Here foragers subsisted independently of pastoralists.

2.2 Interactions between Pastoralists and Foragers in the Pre-Colonial Kaokoveld

This section aims at a reconstruction of pre-colonial pastoral-foraging in the Kaokoveld in the nineteenth century. The account is based on a number of oral traditions collected between 1994 and 2009. Oral traditions suggest that Otjiherero-speaking immigrants entered the region from lands north of the Kunene. Most traditions are fairly specific about the place of origin of their ancestors and depict Okarundu Kambeti, a hilly area north of Ruacana, as their ancestral land, from where their ancestors migrated some five to seven generations ago. The immigrants first settled in a small number of settlement-nuclei in north-western Namibia. In traditional narratives these places are often referred to as 'very old' places, and communities now living in other localities trace their histories back to these ancestral places. The histories of these places are not located in a mythical past; they are realistic accounts of migrations and genealogical relations. Informants usually remember well their ancestors' places of birth and, especially, their burial places. This information can be used to reconstruct mobility and expansion.

The places where people settled in the pre-colonial past were generally well endowed with natural wells and/or near river courses. Often they were situated in riparian environments where abundant palm stands (*Hyphaene ventricosa petersiana*)[7] along with a good number of other fruit-yielding trees and bushes supplied food. From these settlements foraging as well as pastoral strategies could be operated. In oral traditions, places like Ombuku and Ewe rondjima, in the Omuhonga Valley in the northern most part of the Kaokoveld, Ehomba in its north-eastern part, Ongongo, Ongango, and Owuatjivingo in its western parts, Kaoko Otavi, Okorosave, and Oukongo

---

[7] In another publication (Bollig 2006: 194) I reported on the abundance and high nutritional value of the nuts from these palms.

in its central part, and Ombombo in its southern parts are named (see Map 2.2).

From these central places others were colonised, either in an effort to reach for additional, or other, more reliable palm groves, or in a step towards reaching for new pastures in order to cater for expanding livestock herds in a 'ruminant grazer's paradise'.[8] Map 2.2 shows that early settlers mainly sought out places for settlement along the larger seasonal river courses.

Oral traditions from different parts of north-western Namibia describe a subsistence economy which is still largely based on foraging strategies. Livestock is mentioned in these traditions but in many accounts livestock husbandry is subordinate to foraging. Some informants stressed that only a few people owned cattle, and that even rich people did not own many cattle. These narratives also stress a high degree of mobility and that huge areas were used by single households. Franz Uarije from Oruvandjei, a man in his seventies interviewed in 2005, reports his family's early history as being shaped by considerations about where to find good hunting grounds and good opportunities for gathering food. He depicts his ancestors as using an enormous area – members of his family migrated from Okangundumba to Otjovasandu, then to Omakange and Oukongo, and eventually back to Okangundumba.

We came from Okangundumba, that is where we came from; when my mother was born in Otjitoko (near Otjiuu East), we came past and we settled at Otjovazandu and other places there. A man called Kamwe of Hawanga, who is praised in that place, Okangundumba, he is my grandfather. When they say the place is of Kamwe, Kamwe of Hawanga, it is my father who gave birth to my grandfather (i.e. my grandfather's mother originated from my father's matri-clan), who gave birth to my mother. My grandfather was born in Otjitutuma in this plain (between Omakange and Okahao), he was just born there, while he still had the umbilical cord he moved to Oukongo, that one of Ngeendepi, that means it (the place) is in the navel of Nderura in Oukongo.[9] He himself (the grandfather) died in Oruhungu-rwangwazera (east of Otwani).

---

[8] LeCain (2017) depicts the entry of Longhorns into the Montana Deer Lodge Valley in the USA as an intrusion of grazers into a grazing paradise: highly nutritious perennial grasses and only limited competition from other ruminants made it a perfect site for pastoral expansion. The Kaokoveld may have had similar qualities for the first pastoralists entering the area.

[9] The formula 'the navel of' addresses the place where somebody's umbilical cord has been buried shortly after birth.

The Prehistory of North-Western Namibia

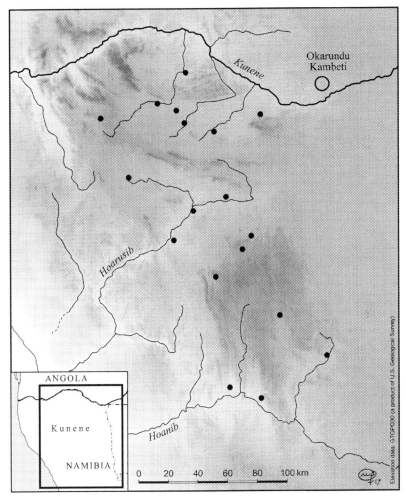

Map 2.2 Nineteenth-century settlement nuclei in north-western Namibia reconstructed on the basis of oral evidence.
Source: author's data

My grandfather Nderura is buried in Oruhungu; he is a grandfather of my biological father; he gave birth to my father, whose name is Ndere, who is buried in Okamanja (Kamanjab); that is how they migrated, but they were not chased. They had different homesteads, down to Outjo the land belonged to the people themselves, and there were not many communities who settled there. They lived well from their wild food, like game, like *ozombe* (fruits of

Berchemia discolour), like *omandjembere* (berries of *Grewia flava*), like *ozombapu* (probably berries of *Grewia bicolour*), wild animals like kudu, oryx and all this. They killed that game and they had their own way of protecting game.

When they killed, the people did not kill carelessly, so that they did not have to go too far away; they just killed a few animals. Then the people were hunting with arrows; the game was not aware; they were creeping, a person was creeping until he reached near the animal and then shot and lay down again. They used a poison which they used to dig out of the ground, it was called *ouzuwo*; it was put on the arrow, then a person shot with it, he was lying down, the game just went off, it went a bit because the person was not visible, it went a bit and then lay down. He just looked how it lay down and then it died; then he returned to the homestead to call people to transport the meat back home. There were no donkeys at that time. The meat was transported with the carrying sticks; the women carried the meat on their heads; they brought the meat to the homestead; they cut it – that was their food. When they got to know where the *ozombe* fruits were, they went there to spend the night where the *ozombe* were, they collected them and brought them to their houses. Sometimes the people built hunting huts at the spring where the game watered. When the game watered there then it was easy for the people to distinguish males from females. Only male animals were shot, and the females were left. They were also eating fruits and vegetables. There was a lot of food; some were *ovimaka* (*Coccinea sessilifolia*) and others were *ovitungwa* (not identified), there were a lot of different food plants that helped the people to survive; that is how they survived.

During those days there were not many cattle; only some men had cattle. One man had five cows, another one had ten cows. The grass was near and the cattle were not able to finish all the grass. In the dry season they stayed in the homesteads like in this place. Like in those places which have springs. Like Otjitunduuwa and Okozongwehe. In the dry season the cattle were kept near the water. In the rainy season they were brought to the pans (which then filled with rainwater). They did not do anything to the grass; a person who was called rich, he had perhaps ten head of cattle. In those days the cattle were properly herded because of hyenas and lions, which were all over here. During the night the people would not go out; sometimes the lions were even entering the homesteads to kill the cattle. Then the people were taking burning branches in order to protect the cattle. Again the cows were few ... five cattle per person, ten cattle per person. A rich person had perhaps some twenty cattle. (Frans Uarije, 2005)

Unlike Franz Uarije's ancestors Ndiri Ngombe's ancestors owned cattle. Like Uarije, Ngombe asserts that cattle were generally few.

Ndiri Ngombe's ancestors combined foraging strategies with cattle herding. According to the needs of their cattle they switched between rainy season pastures far away from their more permanent homesteads and grazing near to those homesteads. The places Ndiri Ngombe mentions in his account lie far apart from each other indicating a wide home range for grazing activities. Ndiri stresses that hunting was important for his ancestors and that they settled in a valley where antelopes were plentiful in order to hunt these.

When my father came here, he came to the plain of Tjavene of Mambepera to the homestead here your mother got married to.[10] When my father came here, he came to a place which was still looking like rainy season pasture even if it had not rained. When my father came, he came to the nice spring of Nahambo and Kambe the beloved one, the nice one that one can throw this Stipagrostis in, this arrow is stapling (perhaps indicating that arrows were many). When my father came here (Orotjitombo), he found a man of *Omukwahere* clan, he was my father's uncle Katweya,[11] the spy of the war of Mayova, this one of the shoes which do not wear out. There was no other homestead. He used to catch springbok to eat and he used the bark of the baobab trees for trapping the springbok.

He cut some trees called *omisepa*, which are good and strong; these trees he put into a hole which he had dug before. He tied this rope at the place where springbok used to graze. He was a man who caught springbok. When my father settled here at that time he (my father's uncle) was catching springbok. He was jumping like sparkling fire, this man; the spy of the war of Mayova with the shoes which did not wear out. He is my father's uncle Katweya, he is buried there at the end of this plain.

...

By that time we herded our cattle at Okazewana, we herded at Otjitunduuwa, they were grazing at Otjitunganane. The big cattle post was at Otuzemba; by that time my father's elder brother was still alive, and he was the one who was going with the cattle to the cattle posts at Otjitunduuwa, Otuzemba, Okazewana, Okangundumba, in the plain of small watercourses of the *ongange*-coloured cow of Tjao. In the place of the man of Omukwatjivi clan Mbambi of Henda who did not talk bad about other people. It is said that he was killed by a rhino while no rhino spoors were found in the place. At the small hill of Kouwe in the gently rising plain of

---

[10] Ndiri Ngombe here directly addressed my field assistant Uhangatenwa Kapi.
[11] Addressed as *hokuru*, father's mother's brother, i.e. the person father inherited from.

Utwa, that is Okangundumba. It is where our cattle were herded. Their cattle posts were there while gardening was taking place in Okapembambu. (Ndiri Ngombe, 2005)

Ndiri Ngombe's father resettled from Okapembambu, near Omuhiva, a place with plenty of water, to his father's maternal uncle's place at Orotjitombo; at the time his father went there his father's maternal uncle was living partially from hunting springbok with traps. Ndiri's father owned cattle, and Ndiri gives the names of cattle-post places used from their home base at Okapembambu: Otuzemba and Otjitunduua are far to the south-east near Otjondeka, about 100 km away from Okapembambu.

I did most of my ethnographic fieldwork in the northernmost part of the Kaokoveld, close to the Kunene River and in the vicinity of the Epupa Falls. In contrast to many other parts of the Kaokoveld, here a number of seasonal rivers, notably the Kunene River and the Omuhonga River, shape a mountainous landscape, well endowed with water. In subsequent chapters this community will often be referred to. What do we know about the early settlement of this area? Oral traditions claim that ancestors moved down the Kunene River from Okarundu Kambeti some six to nine generations ago. Along the river they herded their herds and made use of the dense palm forest along its banks. In contrast to the remainder of the Kaokoveld and the adjoining rocky and arid stretches of land in southern Angola, water availability was never an issue here. From the Kunene River ancestors first settled stretches of land along the tributary rivers of the Kunene, and in this context settlement in some places along the Omuhonga River is mentioned. Oral traditions collected by Alexander Kaputu talk about the birth and youth of Mureti, a person who is mentioned in written accounts by Dannert (1905: 15–17)[12] and the Swedish traveller de Vylder (Rudner and Rudner 1997: 187), as a wealthy herder living in the vicinity of Omaruru in the 1870s. If by that time Mureti was a senior man he was perhaps born in the first decades of the nineteenth century close

---

[12] Dannert (1905) places Mureti within the matrilineal and patrilineal kinship system and gives Ovahinaruzo as patrilineal clan (Dannert 1905: 15) and *Omukwendata wondjuwo okatiti* (sic) as matrilineal clan. Ovahinaruzo is a strange term for a patrilineal descent group: directly translated the term means 'those who do not belong to a patrilineal descent group'.

to the Kunene River in the Kaokoveld. These oral accounts mention that Mureti was herding his father's cattle, but they also refer to the hunting exploits of the young man.

Mureti was born in the river of Tjovatjorute which has no banks. It is said that his mother was nine months pregnant and he was born in the ninth month. And the month in which he was born was foretold by a baboon, the sun and the moon. His father was Kaupangua the son of Hengari: Hengari was the son of Ruzo. Ruzo was the son of Kaoko the son of Muhinaruzo. His mother was Nangava, the daughter of Ngotokera: and Ngotokera was the child of Tjikuva the eldest.... He grew up by the river Tjovatjorute, the river without banks, and he had no fear at all. But when he was about eight years old, there was a snake called *ongonga* living in a rock on the upper side of the village. As a Herero boy he was a good herdsman. Among the cattle there was a white oxen with long eyelashes. While all the cattle were grazing in the field the white oxen was bitten by the snake and died instantly. ... The following morning he went to the spot toward the east before the sun was up. The snake came out of the hole and went to lie on the rock as usual. When the snake had settled, he shot it with this arrow in the throat. Then it broke a branch of whitethorn tree trying to escape. He gave it another arrow which killed it. After he had killed the snake, he went to sleep at his cattle station but not at his father's home. (Narrated by A. Kaputu, March 1985, in Heywood et al. 1992: 62-4)

Some 20 kilometres down the Omuhonga River from Mureti's alleged place of birth in a place called Omiemire, the patrilineal clan of the present chief maintains an ancestral graveyard. The oldest grave identified belongs to an ancestor who had lived and died according to clan elders before Kwena raiders reached north-western Namibia, i.e. before the 1860s. This ancestor is also described as a herder. His homestead was situated close to the dense stands of *Hyphaene ventricosa petersiana* at the Omuhonga River at Ombuku according to traditions.

From this oral evidence we may deduce that by around 1800, herders were well established along the Kunene River and in the Omuhonga basin. These herders had their main settlements directly on the banks of the river, in close proximity to reliable water sources and in immediate proximity to large forests of *Faidherbia albida* and *Hyphaene petersiana*, two important food suppliers for small stock and humans. Although these ancestors are identified as herders, hunting and gathering were still of considerable importance to them.

2.3 Forager Resource Utilisation in the Pre-Colonial Setting

Oral traditions about the pre-1900 economy of the Kaokoveld are unanimous in emphasising the importance of foraging and the mutual interdependence of foraging and herding. These traditions are often explicit about hunting strategies, whereas pre-colonial herding is described with less detail. Hunting contributed significantly to subsistence; it was mainly conducted using poisoned arrows. Iron arrow points were bartered from the neighbouring Ovambo communities. Small gazelles and guinea fowl were hunted with slings. Hartmann (1941), a German geographer working for the Kaoko Land- und Minengesellschaft and exploring the Kaokoveld on behalf of the company around 1900 (see Chapter 4) describes roots, seeds, and berries as the staple food of most people in the region around 1900. Gatherers preyed especially on the nests of harvester ants, from which large amounts of grass seed could be excavated. The nuts of the *omarunga* palm (*Hyphaene ventricosa petersiana*) were also intensively used, according to his information (on the present-day use of these nuts see Bollig 2006: 192).

Next to a variety of hunting strategies a sizeable number of wild fruits and berries were mentioned by some informants in the mid 1990s (Bollig 2006: 195–6). Various species were named when referring to past food habits and especially to food sources available during droughts. *Cyperus fulgens* (*oseu*) is recounted as a major famine food. The seeds of various grasses and herbs, namely *Setaria verticillata*, *Eragrostis porosa*, and *Gisekia pharnaceoides* were mentioned as the basis for preparing porridge, especially by communities in the western parts of Kaokoveld (von Koenen and von Koenen 1964: 87). In the 1950s von Koenen filmed a community digging the seeds of *Setaria verticillata* from ants' nests (von Koenen and von Koenen 1964). In a personal communication Eberhard von Koenen reported in 2004 that the community he filmed in the western Kaokoveld in the early 1950s was still mainly subsisting on foraging and owned but a few goats. Foraging strategies were adapted to local traditions. Whereas seeds played a major role in the diet of communities living in the western more arid parts of the Kaokoveld, other communities – predominantly those living in mountainous areas – highlight the overall importance of *ozoseu* (*Cyperus fulgens*) for their diets. All informants stress the breadth of wild food that was available throughout the year and emphasise the abundance of game.

Before describing how this livelihood based on pastoralism and foraging came to an end due to massive violence and raiding in the second half of the nineteenth century, I will present a reconstruction of human–environment relations before the 1860s.

2.4 Population, Settlement, and Human–Environment Relations before the 1870s

How can human–environment interactions be characterised for the first part of the nineteenth century? Of course, any reconstruction of pre-colonial human–environment relations is beset with a number of methodological source-related problems. These are related to the paucity of written sources and the character of oral sources. All written accounts on the pre-colonial Kaokoveld refer to a time when herders had fled the region in the 1870s and 1880s due to attacks by Topnaar and Swartboois commandos. There is no written account referring to the time before the onslaught of raiders, i.e. to the time before the 1870s. However, oral traditions do refer to that time. In praise songs, settlements, graves, places of birth, and herders' names are mentioned.

It is difficult to come up with any estimate of population numbers. While Hartmann (1897, 1902/1903) described the Kaokoveld as almost uninhabited around 1900, Vedder, some fifteen years later, estimated the population to be somewhat less than 5,000 people.[13] Manning, in his report on his first tour to the Kaokoveld in 1917, likewise estimated population figures to be around 5,000. From oral traditions and written accounts we know that a number of families crossed the Kunene into north-western Namibia during the first two decades of the twentieth century. A number of these families had fled the Kaokoveld a few decades earlier when raiding commandos had destroyed their pastoral-foraging livelihood. These reports suggest that the population of north-western Namibia at the end of the nineteenth century was less than 5,000 people.

However, mid- and late nineteenth-century accounts on central and western Namibian Herero communities suggest much higher population numbers. Missionaries like Irle and Hahn travelled through much

---

[13] NAN, J XIIIb5, Reisebericht des Missionars Vedder an den Bezirksamtmann von Zastrow. Geographische und Ethnographische Forschungen im Kaokoveld 1900–1914, p. 28.

of Hereroland between the 1850s and the 1890s and they had come into direct contact with many communities. For our purposes, their estimates of Herero communities who had resettled from the Kaokoveld to central and western Namibia in the 1860s are interesting. Irle, for example, reported that Mureti, who had left the Kaokoveld in the 1860s, was regarded as the leader of about 6,000 people and owned huge herds in the 1870s. Kambazembi, who according to Hahn had left the Kaokoveld in 1863, led a community of some 12,000 people in the 1870s (Henrichsen 2011: 116). We are not able to ascertain whether all members of these two Herero communities had migrated from the Kaokoveld to central Namibia. Wealthy herders like Kambazembi and Mureti may have also gathered followers in their new places of residence. Nevertheless, it is likely that a substantial number of those followers had indeed migrated from the Kaokoveld with their leader, as it would be highly unlikely that both leaders gathered followers in such high numbers within a decade.

The figures given by Hahn and Irle suggest much higher population estimates for the pre-1860 Kaokoveld. Based on these figures I would rather suggest population figures between 10,000 and 15,000 for the pre-1860 period – population figures which the Kaokoveld only reached again in the 1960s. Unfortunately, though, any evidence from archaeological excavations that could sustain such a claim is still missing.

While in some households cattle may have numbered in the hundreds, in many households there were none. A first livestock census undertaken in 1927, which accounted for about 9,000 cattle, does not give any information about pre-1860 cattle holdings. The figures given by Hahn and Irle for Mureti's and Kambazembi's herds suggest much higher livestock numbers for the pre-1860 period. Drawing on the accounts of the two missionaries, Henrichsen (2011: 116, 119) gives a figure of 70,000 cattle for Kambazembi (in the early 1890s) and reports that Mureti's herds may have even been bigger than Kambazembi's. There is no way to prove or disprove that Kambazembi and Mureti brought such large herds of cattle from the Kaokoveld to central Namibia. If we assume for a moment that this was the case, we would depict a true pastoral Shangri-La with enormous numbers of cattle per capita. It would be immediately obvious why Swartbois and Topnaars focused their raids on the Kaokoveld. The lack of any archaeological evidence for such intense pastoral occupation, however, casts some doubts on such an assumption. Dense pastoral settlement along the reaches of the Kunene would be one possibility: here riverine prehistoric settlements would not easily be discernible due to frequent inundations. The regional pre-1860 herd may have been considerably smaller though and concentrated in a few places with reliable water. The accumulation of the enormous cattle herds observed in the 1860s and 1870s in central Namibia would by necessity then result from intense and successful raiding activities and less from a long-term build-up of herds.

There is, however, no doubt that those communities moving out of the Kaokoveld between the 1850s and 1870s were pastoralists. The pre-1860 regional herd of the Kaokoveld was concentrated for most of the year at perhaps thirty or so permanent water points. These cattle could easily be herded around a central water point and along the perennial Kunene River. They used an area with a radius of perhaps 10–12 km around that waterhole for some six to eight months of the year. During the rainy season these herds could make use of abundant forage in areas with seasonal water points. The effect of these herds on the environment would have been fairly small. Whereas in the vicinity of water sources a transition from perennial to annual grasses probably took place with the onset of intensive grazing, the short period of grazing on outlying pastures may even have contributed to the resilience of a productive perennial grass-cover. Beyond the vicinity of permanent waterholes, wild ungulates and elephants had a far greater impact on the structure of vegetation than cattle, goats, or sheep.

While there is little doubt that early pastoralists and foragers impacted the environment, there is little evidence on their specific contribution to environmental infrastructures. Kreike (2013) shows in great detail how pre-colonial farmers in north-central Namibia contributed to the build-up of fertile soils, the establishment of forest islands and the creation of a specific hydroscape by laying out a network of waterholes. Human impact on north-western Namibia's savannah is less obvious. On the basis of evidence presented here we may postulate that human impact may have been secondary to that of large herbivores, particularly elephants. Man-made fires and human settlement in a few places with permanent water sources will have left the most visible footprints. There is some likelihood that the extensive use of palm nuts contributed to the expansion of palm orchards:

Orchards constituted solely by *omarunga* palms (*Hyphaene ventricosa petersiana*) are found along all major river courses, perennial and seasonal and the extensive use of nuts will have contributed to their distribution and spread along all river courses in the Kaokoveld.

2.5 Violence and the Breakdown of the Foraging-cum-Pastoral Livelihood

While by the mid-nineteenth century the indigenous economies and societies of central Namibia had already been devastated by raiding and violence at the frontiers of the expanding Cape trading empire (Dedering 1997; Henrichsen 2000; Lau 1987), raiders probably started to launch attacks into north-western Namibia in the 1850s or 1860s. Anderson (1863: 271) reported that the Herero of the Kaokoveld had been devastated by Oorlam raiders in 1863 – as does another early traveller (Anon. 1878: 309), who described the Kaokoveld as deserted. While during the first phase of violence, i.e. in the 1850s, pastoralist households from central Namibia (Henrichsen speaks of 'entire clans') still fled to the Kaokoveld (Henrichsen 2011: 93), from the 1860s pastoralists began leaving the Kaokoveld, either turning towards central Namibia, where Oorlam power had been broken, or to south-western Angola. Only in the Kaokoveld did the raiding system centred upon the two Oorlam communities at Fransfontein and Sesfontein remain vibrant into the 1890s. Raided cattle were predominantly sold to traders connected to the expanding Cape trading network. Lau (1987: 88) gives an insight into the immense scale of the trade: cattle were traded for horses, guns, and cloth but also for domestic utensils, tools, and luxury goods. Henrichsen (2011: 171) reports on Swartboois living on the mission-station Ameib and in the southern Kaokoveld, as well as Damara of the Erongo-Brandberg region and San of the Etosha region, who engaged in heavily armed cattle raiding in the 1880s. Sesfontein emerged as the economic and political centre of a raiding economy in north-western Namibia (Rizzo 2012: 31–8). Men were engaged in commando groups which organised raids and hunting trips, and herded large livestock herds, which were partially the result from these raids. Dependent work relations within established patron–client bonds were frequent (Rizzo 2012: 33, 43). Raiders crossed the Kunene River several times into south-western Angola in the 1890s.

The communities of north-western Namibia were not armed with guns, nor had they any form of institutionalised military organisation. This period of raiding forms a prominent part in Himba oral history (Katjira Muniombara, Kozongombe Tjingee, and Tjikumbamba Tjambiru in Bollig, 1997). Battles, skirmishes, destruction, and escape are portrayed at length. Traditions do not allow for a detailed reconstruction of what happened: battles are not connected to specific years, nor even specific decades. Oral traditions emphasise high mortality rates and the brutality of attacks. As the raiders were mainly after cattle, the local livestock herd soon crumbled. Whereas Herero pastoral economy was rapidly expanding in central Namibia in the second half of the nineteenth century (Henrichsen 2000, 2011),[14] the north-western parts of Namibia underwent depopulation and depastoralisation during the last three decades of the nineteenth century. Processes which had been typical of the history of central Namibia in the 1840s and 1850s, such as a turn towards hunting and gathering[15] and dependence on Nama and Oorlam overlords, occurred in the Kaokoveld during the last thirty years of the nineteenth century. Only in the 1890s did the German colonial administration extend its control to Fransfontein and Sesfontein and put an end to raids by Swartboois and Topnaar commandos.

Himba oral traditions are full of detailed descriptions of these raids. The stories are clad in metaphors which make it hard for an outsider, and sometimes even for cultural insiders, to understand the course of action. During an interview in 1995 Katjira Muniombara recounted a traditional narrative which describes the destruction of pastoral communities in northern Kaokoveld:

---

[14] For central Namibia the rapid growth of cattle herds since the 1860s is well documented: Irle estimates that cattle numbers multiplied eightfold in the 1870s (Henrichsen 2011: 114). The Swedish trader Een estimates the number of cattle owned by Kamaherero to be c. 10,000 animals at the end of the 1860s (Henrichsen 2011: 114), while Kambazembi in the 1890s possessed some 70,000 cattle (Henrichsen 2011: 116).

[15] Henrichsen (2011: 96 based on the diary of missionary Rath), quotes traveller James Chapman, reporting on southern central Namibia: '[h]undreds, perhaps thousands, of Damaras (Herero bzw. Ovatjimba, Anm. Henrichsen) lived on roots and berries ...' and the traveller Green, who says that in northern Hereroland poor Herero lived 'chiefly upon nuts, beans and guinea fowls' (Henrichsen 2011: 96).

I will start with the gun of Kaukumuha; the man who killed us was called Kaukumuha – an Omukuena. Now they themselves say: '!aukumuha', the man who brought a raiding party into this land, first to Ombombo of Kazukotjiuma, where they destroyed the home of the Glowing Red Iron, Kakunotjivi, our senior mother's brother; they burnt (his home) to ashes. ... The troop of Kaukumuha came here, they came to Omuzengaturundu who ate a cow of yellow-black colour with thick jaws. There they found our two men, Uatuihi of Kavange, of Ndjara of Kaoko, who ate a female sheep; and Uambumba of Kaongo Tjimosenguaukamba, of the Mwatjikaku patriline, when the elephant of Rovingu was killed there. They found them there where they burnt it (the homestead) to ashes ...

The people were killed by the troop; the next day they fled in a hurry: 'So, Muje the war is near, the war is near. Let us separate, they will kill us, we will be destroyed.' After they said that, immediately afterwards Ndjoue was killed, and they separated there. The one of Mbumba, of the small kudu, passed through the mountain pass of Otjikotoona. He drove the cow of Ngao of Kasona, of the mother of Kuziruka, and they went down the valley; they crossed the river (Kunene) at Ohamurenge. ... The Ovakuena came down to Otjinduu, they raided the cow of Tjao which had a chest; they raided the Ouoruze area. Then it (the war?) crossed there straight towards the sun ... Those of Kaukumuha went and crossed the Kunene River. It was them who followed the home of Muje and burnt the people. ... The people of our fathers fled to Angola. (Katjira Muniombara in Bollig 1997)

In another oral account of Kwena raids, a protagonist desperately claims '*in this war there is nothing to fight; it is a fire which burns the people*'. This statement clearly suggests the inferiority of local people's weaponry: it was not worth fighting, the raid destroyed people like fire. The trauma and desperation of these events are well conserved in the metaphors and images of atrocities and plunder.

The foraging-cum-pastoral mode of production that had existed prior to this onslaught soon ceased to exist. Not only were livestock raided and driven to distant destinations, but locals seemingly also realised that 'cattle brought them their enemies'.[16] Informants described how people started consuming their cattle in a last effort to gain some benefits from their herds and in an attempt to render their

---

[16] In a recent volume on the relation between Turkana pastoral economy and raiding Terrence McCabe (2004) relates that the Turkana realise that it is mainly cattle that bring them into constant confrontations with their pastoral neighbours.

communities unattractive to raiders. The consequence of raiding and self-inflicted depastoralisation was a reversion to a livelihood completely based on foraging for those who remained in the Kaokoveld.[17] Others fled to southern Angola where they settled with other communities and came into close contact with the Portuguese colonial economy. Since the 1870s commercial hunters had been based in Mossamedes (today's Namibe), and operated mainly in the Kunene basin to procure ivory, ostrich feathers, and other tropical commodities for the world market (Bollig 1998a, 1998b). Oral accounts leave little doubt that Herero/Himba men eagerly looked for opportunities to earn money to invest in commodities such as guns, blankets, and clothes, and to restock their herds. Elephant hunting and ivory trading, which will be treated in some detail in the next chapter, became important elements of local livelihoods from the late 1880s. However, for the refugees, after 1890 the single most important employer was the Portuguese colonial army. Himba and Herero participated as mercenaries in so-called punitive expeditions, which were little more than governmentally endorsed raids on local communities.

The herds of the erstwhile refugees recovered in the 1890s but were then hit hard by a second catastrophe. The Rinderpest epidemic of 1887 is described in oral traditions as a major disaster. In Himba traditions the year is called *Otjita* – 'The Dying'. Oral traditions report that only one or two cattle survived per household and that people lived on small stock, bush resources, and, to a great extent, on income-generating activities other than pastoralism. Again, commercial soldiering was used as a means to limit losses. João de Almeida's publication (1936) reports on and provides photographs of Himba mercenaries – heavily armed young men and a *corpo de irregulares* – with their leader Vita Thom (Oorlog) (Almeida 1936: 151–2) (see Figure 2.1). Between 1898 and 1906 officially gazetted 'punitive raids' were frequent, and the mercenaries and especially their leaders profited directly from them. When after 1911 the Portuguese government decided to institute a civil administration and regular police, there was no longer any need for mercenaries (Stals and Otto-Reiner 1999: 34).

---

[17] See also interview with Ismael Mbunguha, Kaoko Otavi, conducted on 27 March 2007 by Laura Bleckmann.

Guerreiros muximbas (praça do corpo de irregulares). Gambos, 1910

Figure 2.1 Heavily armed young Himba men belonging to a troop of irregular soldiers (*corpo de irregulares*). Photographed probably between 1900 and 1911
Source: Almeida (1936: 151)

In the Kaokoveld the three decades from c. 1880 to 1910 are characterised by the massive impact of elephant hunting spurred by the global quest for ivory. The next chapter will detail this time of massive social-ecological change.

3 | *Elephants and Humans in the Late Nineteenth and Early Twentieth Century*

Elephants have been of tremendous importance for the social-ecological system of north-western Namibia. In the pre-colonial past they contributed significantly to the development of environmental infrastructure. In this chapter I will delineate to what extent elephants contributed to the environmental infrastructure of the Kaokoveld and portray the process and consequences of commercial elephant hunting on the society and environment of north-western Namibia around 1900.

3.1 Elephants as Landscape Architects

Laws (1970: 2) emphasises the impact of elephants, *Loxodonta africana*, on the environment, and states that 'after man himself, probably no other animal has had as great an effect on African habitats as the African bush elephant'. Their large body size, connected to their need for an immense input of biomass, their longevity, and the specific flocking and feeding behaviour of elephants together render them a primary factor in habitat change in many regions of Africa. Elephants are relatively unspecialised herbivores that need to consume about 6 per cent of their body weight daily (on a wet-weight basis; about 1.5 per cent dry weight). An average adult bull elephant (5,000 kg) requires 300 kg of food (75 kg dry weight) and an adult cow (2,800 kg) about 170 kg (42 kg dry weight) (all figures Laws 1970: 3). Under normal conditions elephants browse rather than graze. The heavy impact on bushland and woodland leads to a gradual change of these savannah habitats towards grassland communities (see also Håkansson 2004: 571). Leuthold (1996) observed in Tsavo National Park, Kenya, that the vegetation of this semi-arid savannah changed profoundly from the 1960s to the 1980s: the increase in elephant herd sizes in the 1960s led to a decrease in numbers of trees and bushes and an increasing number of bush fires due to intensive browsing. After elephant herds were seriously diminished by poachers in the 1970s and 1980s, trees and shrubs reappeared in large numbers and the grassland communities decreased. On the basis of historical data, Håkansson (2004: 572) depicts the land south of Lake Victoria in the mid-nineteenth century as rolling parkland with wide open grasslands and few trees. After massive commercial elephant hunting in the second part of the nineteenth century, travellers in the late 1880s and 1890s described the very same area as overgrown by bush and *miombo* woodland.

While elephants' impacts on wooded savannah landscapes of eastern and western Africa are well documented, it seems more difficult to assess the impact of elephant herds on the arid savannahs of southwestern Africa. In the last few years there has been some research into the effect elephants have on mopane savannahs, i.e. the vegetation type which is also typical of north-western Namibia. Smallie and O'Connor (2000) report on elephant–vegetation interaction in the Venetia Limpopo Nature Reserve, and describe C. *mopane* as a staple food item in the diet of elephants, with most individual trees being utilised lightly. Elephants preferred C. *mopane* trees of less than two metres in height. Trees which had been previously utilised by them – specifically trees whose terminal part of the main stem had been previously broken and/or which had been coppiced – were highly attractive. This led to a hedging effect: elephants at once shaped the structure of the vegetation and increased the availability of a preferred food item, i.e. they actively contributed to an environmental infrastructure that supported their feeding behaviour. The study recorded very little destruction of vegetation by elephants and concluded that 'on average Colophospermum mopane trees were lightly utilised, so that mortality of trees as a result of a single feeding event is likely to be uncommon', and that 'by continually hedging C. mopane, elephants maintain a supply of preferred coppice growth through time' (Smallie and O'Connor 2000: 358). Ben-Shahar (1996) observed elephant feeding behaviour in the mopane savannah of northern Botswana and found no evidence that elephants reduced the biomass of mopane woodlands there below a sustainable level. Only in the close vicinity of water sources were mopane woodlands susceptible to elephant browsing. Ben-Shahar also observed that elephants preferred to browse on mopane shrubs rather than on mopane trees. Intense coppicing made heavily used stretches of mopane savannah more prone to bush fires (Ben Shahar 1996: 513) creating space for grasses and other undergrowth. In a study on the impact of elephants on the woody vegetation in Etosha National Park,

Beer et al. (2006) document that elephants often change the structure and composition of the vegetation close to water sources. Especially during the dry season intense elephant browsing around waterholes leads to increased mortality of woody plants.

Du Toit et al. (2014: 35) analyse the contribution of elephants to landscape heterogeneity and biodiversity in Botswana's Chobe area. They describe how elephants select and actively maintain nutrient-rich patches by converting plants growing there into dung and urine (and also meat and bones). Through defecation, urination, and death and decomposition these nutrients become available for the uptake of grasses, forbs, and shrubs in the rainy season when soils are moist. This peculiar elephant-impacted environmental infrastructure is prioritised by other herbivores, because of good food availability. Skarpe et al. (2014) give rich evidence of the manifold ways elephants contribute to the environmental infrastructure of the Chobe Park with grave ecosystemic consequences for all other creatures living in this ecosystem.

3.2 Elephant–Environment Interaction in North-Western Namibia

Viljoen (1988: 238ff.) studied elephant–vegetation interaction in north-western Namibia in the 1970s and 1980s. When Viljoen did his study the elephant population of the Kaokoveld only comprised around 200–400 animals (Viljoen 1988: 67). Viljoen's observations on elephant–vegetation interaction are most detailed for the desert-dwelling elephants. He reports that elephants spend most of their time in the riparian forests feeding on the lush vegetation there. He monitored a total of 2,167 woody plants in 39 transects. Of the woody plants utilised (29 per cent of the total sample, i.e. 71 per cent of all examined plants were not used at all), 16 per cent were only slightly utilised; 10 per cent moderately utilised; 2 per cent were heavily utilised but were not dead, and only 1 per cent of all the plants sampled had been killed by elephants. The vast majority of dead woody plants had been killed by floods, drought, or fire (Viljoen 1988: 243ff.). Viljoen identified a clear order of preference for various woody plants: *Cordia gharaf*, *Pachypodium lealii*, and *Combretum wattii* were clearly the most preferred food plants of the desert-dwelling elephants. These woody plants, however, do not occur in dense stands and contribute little to the diet of elephants in terms of bulk. The most important food plants are *Colophospermum mopane*, *Tamarix usneoides*, and *Combretum imberbe*, which all occur in high density and have a high percentage of availability. Bark-stripping was only observed on three tree species, namely *Faidherbia albida*, *Acacia erioloba*, and *Colophospermum mopane*. While 68 per cent of the 213 *Faidherbia albida* trees in Viljoen's sample showed signs of debarking, only some 1.4 per cent of the 285 *Colophospermum mopane* trees checked showed signs of bark utilisation. While the utilisation of bark of *Faidherbia albida* trees was high, the number of trees killed through debarking was only 2.3 per cent. In a general estimation of elephant impact on the woody vegetation of the riparian zones of the western Kaokoveld, Viljoen judges that the rate of loss was insignificant. While elephants did not destroy a great deal of vegetation, they impacted upon the growth pattern of trees. By utilising thicket-forming plant species, elephants contributed significantly to the prevention of riverine thickets, thereby opening up paths through them, making it easy for other animals and also humans to gain access to water and the riparian vegetation.

Elephants influenced the vegetation structure in other ways: they showed a high feeding preference for *Faidherbia albida* pods, of which they ate large quantities between November and April. Viljoen collected seeds from freshly deposited elephant dung and from undigested pods, and the two samples were subjected to germination tests. He found that the germination success of seeds from elephant dung was significantly higher than that of seeds from undigested pods. Faidherbia seeds have a very hard testa, which needs weathering or some sort of damage before water can penetrate and trigger the germination process. Seeds from elephant dung had the testa softened by the elephant's digestive fluids, which then facilitated water penetration and subsequent germination. Viljoen argues that enhanced seed germination through elephant feeding was indeed a significant advantage for the population of *Faidherbia*. It is likely that the dense stands of *Faidherbia albida* trees along the Omuhonga/Ombuku or the Hoarusib drainage are attributable to the presence of large elephant herds.

It is hard to establish the number of elephants that roamed northwestern Namibia before the systematic raids by elephant hunters in the 1890s. The first reports by European travellers, natural scientists, and hunters visiting the area (e.g. Hartmann 1902/1903; Kuntz 1912a, 1912b; Stassen 2010; Steinhardt 1922; Vedder 1914; von Moltke

1943) stressed the great number of elephants in the area.[1] Beginning in about 1898, the Dorsland Trekkers launched annual elephant hunts into north-western Namibia from their settlements in south-western Angola. From a hunt in the early years of the 1900s, an erstwhile hunter reports the sighting of a major conglomeration of about 3,000 elephants in a valley near Okorosave, i.e. close to today's Opuwo (von Moltke 1943: 282).[2] If von Moltke's figures are taken at face value, it is possible to conceive of there being more than 10,000 elephants in the Kaokoveld. Based on comparative evidence, however, Viljoen (1988: 44) doubts that elephant numbers were as high as the figures given in von Moltke's report. He asserts that reports of high elephant numbers in the region may have been a protective device against public criticism of Boer elephant hunting: If elephant numbers were actually as high as alleged by von Moltke's informants, then the large numbers of elephants hunted in the last decade of the nineteenth and the first decade of the twentieth century did not matter so much. In fact, the Dorsland Trekkers were dependent on a good reputation at the Cape. They repeatedly received aid from the Cape (Stassen 2010: 320) or tried to solicit protection from South African politicians. Discourses on the protection of large game were popular at the Cape and many politicians were in favour of stricter laws against commercial hunting (Carruthers 1995: 29f.).[3] Viljoen (1988: 45) himself estimates that

---

[1] These reports pertain to the period between the 1880s and 1914. William Chapman, who resided with the Dorsland Trekker community in south-western Angola, visited the Kaokoveld several times for hunting tours, and on his way to the westernmost Ovambo kingdoms. Von Moltke's account in *Jagkonings* (*Kings of the Hunters*) (2003 [1943]) relies on interviews with hunters from the Dorsland Trekker community in the 1930s, and especially with descendants of F. Robbertse, who had been one of the most prolific elephant hunters of that community. Hartmann, Kuntz, Steinhardt, and Vedder visited the Kaokoveld after a period of intensive elephant hunting in the first decade of the twentieth century. Even von Moltke's account refers to a time (1898–1908) by which serious elephant hunting had already taken place.

[2] Von Moltke (1943: 282, my translation) reports his informants saying: 'It was more elephants than I could ever have dreamt about. Jakob and I counted the herds; it was eighteen, and they were not just big herds. It was incredibly big herds – we estimated from 150 till 200 in a herd, and if there was one elephant, there had to be 3000.'

[3] Recent evidence from southern Zambia's Sioma Ngwezi National Park, however, suggests that congregations of many hundreds of elephants are possible (Chase and Griffin 2008) and that very high elephant densities can be sustained over a long period of time (Skarpe et al. 2014).

prior to 1900 about 2,500–3,500 elephants roamed the Kaokoveld. He derives his estimate from the mean number of elephants shot per year according to von Moltke's report (von Moltke's account suggests that 2,000 animals were shot within a period of 28 years) and the assumption of a yearly calving increment of 2.7 per cent. There are, however, good reasons to assume that elephant numbers were somewhat higher than estimated by Viljoen. The elephant hunts of the Dorsland Trekkers in the Kaokoveld were at the end of a period of intense elephant hunting, not at the beginning of it. Oorlam commandos not only raided cattle from local communities but also hunted elephants in north-western Namibia in order to sell the ivory later on. Von Francois (1899: 107) reports that the Nama of Fransfontein undertook annual elephant hunts in the 1880s and 1890s. After elephant herds in central Namibia had been eradicated, the abundant herds in northern Namibia and the Ngamiland became attractive targets for elephant hunting.

Elephants had a profound impact on settlement patterns. Shortridge, who travelled north-western Namibia in the 1920s, observed that the local population's settlement patterns indicated an adjustment to high elephant numbers. He stated that huts were usually c. 200 yards away from waterholes in order to avoid direct contact with elephants using the wells. According to Shortridge, the wells were 'literally "shared" by the villagers (by day) and the elephants (by night) with a minimum of inconvenience' (Shortridge 1934: 366). In contrast to this image of easy cohabitation other authors stressed conflicting interests. Vedder, who travelled the Kaokoveld in 1914, emphasised the impact of elephants on settlement patterns. His group found many springs in the southern Kaokoveld had been trampled by elephants, making human consumption of water difficult. In the 1920s Deneys Reitz (1943: 105) observed how elephant herds chased cattle from a water pool in the southern Kaokoveld, and reported that gardening at Kaoko Otavi was severely hampered by a concentration of elephants in the vicinity. Informants reported that the Omuhonga valley, which around 2000 has several hundred gardens, in the past had only a very few, if any. Elephants roamed the valley and made any effort to plant millet, sorghum, or maize a risky exercise. One informant reported that in the past some households preferred to have their gardens in the inaccessible valleys of the Zebra Mountains, where no elephants were to be found. These narratives, however, stand in contrast to a report by the German traveller Kuntz, who travelled the Omuhonga valley in 1907 recording numerous gardens in the area (see Chapter 4). The Omuhonga valley was probably home to only a few elephants around 1900, since the Omuhonga River had been a primary target of the Dorsland Trekkers' hunting expeditions between 1896 and 1906.

3.3 The Demise of the Kaokoveld's Elephants: Commercial Hunting and the Ivory Trade in the Late Nineteenth and Early Twentieth Century

North-western Namibia's elephant herds were decimated during the last decades of the nineteenth century and the first two decades of the twentieth century. For the first time in north-western Namibia, humans had a massive and irreversible impact on the environment and changed environmental infrastructure profoundly and in a short time period. Commercial elephant hunting was coupled with an intense and violent reorganisation not only of human–environment relations but also of intercommunity relations. Weapons trading, slavery, raids, governmental 'punitive expeditions', and military rule led to changing patterns of social-ecological regulation. The major onslaught on elephants in the region occurred after herds in central Namibia were devastated in the mid-nineteenth century (Lau 1987: 91) and elephant herds in neighbouring Ovamboland were seriously diminished in the 1870s (Siiskonen 1990). Through elephant hunting and the ivory trade, the people of the Kaokoveld came into close contact with global exchange circuits for the first time. Over a period of perhaps four decades a local resource was heavily exploited and outsiders as well as locals traded ivory for cattle, guns, seed corn, iron beads, and probably money. A lot of commercial elephant hunting was conducted by outsiders (Boers, European hunters). If local people were engaged in the hunt themselves they often exchanged tusks according to customary prices (e.g. a tusk for a specific quantity of millet). Commercial hunting in north-western Namibia implicated a highly exploitative and sometimes violent regime of resource extraction: Whereas between the 1850s and the 1880s the Kaokoveld had been emptied of cattle in large-scale commercially oriented raids, the last two decades of the nineteenth century were characterised by the depletion of elephant herds.

Throughout the nineteenth century European demand for ivory grew as mass markets for items such as piano keys, billiard balls, and combs manufactured from African ivory emerged (Alpers 1992; Chaiklin 2010). Elephant hunting became a professional undertaking, and traditional hunting methods receded in favour of hunting with modern guns. While major hunting grounds were situated in East Africa – by 1891 Zanzibar provided about 75 per cent of the world's supply of ivory – other regions such as West Africa and southern Africa also attracted the attention of elephant hunters. Håkansson (2004: 571) shows how the price for ivory increased significantly throughout the nineteenth century, and especially during its last two decades. Regional trade systems in which the ivory trade was embedded changed greatly due to the upsurge of ivory trading.

Commercial elephant hunting in south-western Angola and north-western Namibia probably began in the 1860s. An important precondition for the rapid development of the trade was the dissolution of the Portuguese government's royal monopoly in the ivory trade in 1830, and the fact that the slave export trade from Angola was banned in 1836 (Miller 1988: 649). This made ivory a financially competitive substitute for slaves. Ovimbundu traded cattle for ivory with the Kwanyama and communities near the upper and middle courses of the Kunene River in the mid-nineteenth century. Petermann (1857) quotes from the diary of the Hungarian traveller, explorer, and hunter Ladislaus Magyar, who hunted elephants and lived for some years near the middle reaches of the Kunene River around 1850. Magyar observed a close relation between political power, access to elephant hunting grounds, and ivory trade. In Ovamboland commercial elephant hunting became important in the 1860s. There elephant hunting was embedded in the socio-political structure of the Ovambo kingdom. The trade in ivory remained a monopoly of the Ovambo kings. Siiskonen (1990: 84) reports that firearms entered the Oshivambo-speaking areas in substantial quantities from the 1850s onwards bringing about a change in hunting technology which spurred elephant hunting significantly. In the late 1870s and early 1880s elephant hunting climaxed (Siiskonen 1990: 121).

While lack of capital had hindered Mossamedes-based traders in the 1870s in expanding their activities further inland (Siiskonen 1990: 132), the settlement of Boers in the area in the early 1880s and the reorientation of many Walvis Bay-based traders to Mossamedes in the same time period greatly increased trading activities in the wider region. While in the 1890s ivory exports from Walvis Bay almost came to a standstill,

Mossamedes became the main outlet for both ivory and ostrich feathers in south-western Africa in the 1880s and 1890s (Siiskonen 1990: 148). In the 1880s the focal area of operations for hunters and traders was no longer Ovamboland but rather the northern side of the lower and middle Kunene. The ban on commercial hunting legislated by German authorities in 1892 made major hunting expeditions into German territory a risky undertaking. The 1890s, however, still saw major elephant hunts in the Kaokoveld, as German police only rarely patrolled the northernmost stretches of the region. Though local Tjimba communities traded ivory with Ovamboland, the major elephant hunts were conducted by Boer hunters from Humpata. Siiskonen (1990: 177) notes that after the Rinderpest outbreak of 1898, 'the ivory trade became irregular and marginal in significance'[4] in the German territory, but that ivory exports from Mossamedes continued for another two decades at least. The Rinderpest epidemic of 1898 may have spurred the hunting of elephants for another decade in south-western Angola and north-western Namibia: communities dependent on livestock husbandry vied for opportunities to procure commodities in order to exchange them for cattle. Oral traditions emphasise the eagerness of young men to obtain cattle and to restart a pastoral livelihood after massive herd losses in the Rinderpest epidemic of 1898. Large-scale commercial hunting in the Kaokoveld peaked around 1900.

Commercial Elephant Hunting in North-Western Namibia by Humpata's Dorsland Trekker Community

The Dorsland Trekker community had resided in the Kaokoveld for a short time between 1879 and 1881, and had then settled in Humpata at the south-western edge of the southern Angolan plateau (Stassen 2010: 327; von Moltke 1943: 96). There they established an economy based on agriculture, transportation business, and commercial hunting (Stassen 2010: 387). From their stronghold in south-western Angola they undertook major elephant hunts in the northern Kaokoveld in 1898 and continued to conduct major hunting expeditions into the

---

[4] Siiskonen (1990) supplies the following figures: The export of ivory from German south-west Africa was rapidly declining between 1898 and 1902: total amount by weight in 1898 was 1000 kg; in 1899, 35 kg; in 1900, 0 kg; in 1901, 0 kg; in 1902, 110 kg. Most of the exported ivory was procured from Ovamboland and the Okavango region in these years.

area every year until 1908 (von Moltke 1943: 222) thereby contributing significantly to social-ecological change. Von Moltke's informants stressed that these were highly profitable hunts (von Moltke 1943: 222).[5] The Dorsland Trekkers hunted in small groups of usually less than ten hunters. Elephant hunts were conducted on horseback, and herds were surrounded and chased in order to tire them (von Moltke 1943: 34). These hunts took place mainly along the Omuhonga and Ombuku rivers (von Moltke 1943: 260) and occasionally took Boer hunters to the upper reaches of the Hoarusib River, but apparently not further south. In the year 1900 a group of hunters conducted a 'record hunt' in the region. Altogether they spent five months in the Kaokoveld, starting their hunt with shooting hippos at Enyandi and then tracking further south via the Ondoto River to a place referred to as 'Otjiulunga' (Otjurunga, near Okahozu). According to von Moltke's informants the spring was settled by a bigger local community which served the hunters with further information on elephant herds near Okongo (Oukongo, in the vicinity of today's Opuwo) (von Moltke 1943: 276f.). Local scouts were usually made use of to track down elephant herds. At Oukongo thirteen bulls were shot. The hunt was continued at the upper reaches of the Hoarusib River. In two days another twenty bulls were shot there. In just a few days some fifty-two elephants were killed.[6] At the end of the hunt some 100 locally recruited black carriers transported elephant tusks across the Kunene River at Epupa (von Moltke 1943: 285; see also Rizzo 2012: 39–40). In 1901 some 182 elephants were shot, and in the following years the number killed was usually between 130 and 150 animals (von Moltke 1943: 289). In 1902 the hunt in north-western Namibia concentrated around the Ombuku River, called Riet Revier by the Boer hunters – again, a large number of elephants was shot there (von Moltke 1943: 297). Altogether some 160 elephants were killed during 1902. In 1903 – although the exact dating of the hunt is not clear – a Boer hunting expedition went down the Hoarusib River to Ekoto. Again a sizeable number of elephants was shot (von Moltke 1943: 303). The expedition then turned back towards the Kunene River, and on their way they shot

---

[5] Von Moltke (1943: 222, my translation) has one of his informants exclaim: 'The hunt in Kaokoveld was the biggest (hunt), and I can say that uncle Jannie made most of his money with ivory from Kaokoveld.'

[6] Von Moltke (1943: 284) reports that one of his informants sold ivory worth some £3,000 sterling after such a hunt.

a large number of elephants near Epembe and again near Omwangette, some 15 km further towards the river. From there the party descended down the Ombuku River to Otjikongo, where once again elephants were killed, and then to Otjijandjasemo (Bloemfontein). The severity of hunting apparently caused elephants to leave the basin.[7]

Next to elephants, rhinos and hippos were also hunted. Whips produced from rhino skin were sold at 2 Shilling for a large whip and 1 Shilling for a small whip. Von Moltke's informants reported that they made some £30 sterling profit from a single rhino skin. Within a decade some 150–200 rhinos had been killed in the region (von Moltke 1943: 297). In the same period about 313 hippos were shot along the Kunene River (von Moltke 1943: 308).

While the exact numbers of elephants shot are not clear[8] there is little doubt that probably between 1,000 and 2,000 animals were killed over a ten-year period (von Moltke 1943: 377). Elephant hunting was highly profitable. Von Moltke's informants state that they got about £30–£40 sterling per tusk (von Moltke 1943: 331). One thousand elephants shot would thus sell for some £60,000–£80,000, concentrated among a small group of hunters. Boer hunting concentrated on the Kunene River Valley and the river valleys of tributaries. Occasionally trips went as far as the Hoarusib but did not reach beyond that point. Elephant herds in the Kunene Valley were decimated while herds in the southern Kaokoveld and the eastern Sandveld (the western part of contemporary Etosha Park) were less affected. The distribution of elephants as captured in a map by Viljoen in the late 1970s seems to reflect this hunting scenario. Elephants then were still in some numbers only in the far western parts and the south-eastern parts of the Kaokoveld, those regions Boer hunters had not reached.

Commercial Hunting by Local African Hunters

Apart from the Dorsland Trekkers, men from the black communities settling with Boers at Humpata were engaged in elephant hunting,

---

[7] Von Moltke (1943: 307, my translation) reports that 'After we had shot so many elephants at Bloemfontein, we probably chased them away from the water.'

[8] Von Moltke's informant, Robbertse (von Moltke 1943: 150, 273) speaks of 50 to 182 elephants and later of 130 to 160 animals killed per year. He reports that only bulls were shot. The numbers he gives may include animals shot in the Western Ovamboland.

either as aides or on their own account. They were well armed as they had acted as mercenaries for the Portuguese army since the early 1890s. Written sources do not make any direct reference to these mercenary commando groups being involved in elephant hunting, but oral testimonies refer to elephant hunts conducted by members of these communities. Well-armed mercenaries probably took advantage of their guns and the easy access to ammunition and engaged in the lucrative elephant hunt during periods when no 'punitive expeditions' took place.

Beyond the Dorsland Trekkers and black commando groups, Tjimba communities resident in the Kaokoveld, and Thwa communities in south-western Angola were also preying on elephants (Figure 3.1). I will first turn to the Tjimba communities, who lived in small groups all over the Kaokoveld. In contrast to the other two groups of hunters mentioned, they did not directly sell tusks to traders acting within the Mossamedes trade network. Written and oral sources are unanimous that the Tjimba exchanged tusks with the king of Uukwaludhi, the westernmost Ovambo kingdom. Several Tjimba

Figure 3.1 Group of Ovatjimba men with spears and ivory tusks, in Kaokoveld [original caption: Herero Ovashimba natives from Kaokoveld].
Source: photographer Dickmann, NAN 14254

Elephants and Humans

communities apparently acknowledged the king of Uukwaludhi as their political leader and accepted his monopoly in ivory trading; i.e. they did not trade directly with the Portuguese but delivered the tusks to the royal court at Uukwaludhi, the neighbouring Ovambo kingdom. Rich Ovambo herd owners also made use of Tjimba communities as cattle posts, and loaned cattle to local Tjimba.[9] In contrast to commercial hunters, Tjimba hunters were not well equipped with guns. Vedder reports that they used old-fashioned muzzle-loaders, which they had received on a loan basis from their Ovambo overlords. The client status of the Tjimba becomes clear when looking at exchange rates: Vedder asserts that a great tusk was exchanged for two small sacks of seed-millet (whereas white hunters earned £30 sterling per tusk, as stated earlier).

The main exchange goods 'produced' by the Tjimba in the Kaokoveld for customers in western Ovamboland, however, were not tusks but ostrich egg shells. These were extremely valuable in the internal trade between Ovambo communities. Vedder reports that for a sack of ostrich egg shells, which had a value of some 100 marks in Ovamboland, they received a sack of seed-corn.[10] In addition to millet, the Tjimba tried to trade in iron arrowheads, blades for spears and axes, and iron beads and leg-rings. Oral traditions give a somewhat more favourable account of trade relations but do not question their asymmetric character: They also report that cattle were loaned by Ovambo leaders to Tjimba men, for example at Kaoko Otavi, and mention that occasionally such livestock loans were accompanied by the gift or loan of a gun. In an interview, a local elder, Eengombe Kapeke (Bollig 1997: 187), stressed that these asymmetric relations were embedded in kinship bonds. Reporting the story of the Ovambo leader Shikongo and

---

[9] Vedder reports on the situation in Kaoko Otavi in 1914: 'The chief of Otavi-Okorosave is the shepherd of an Omuambo, who loaned him 5 cattle without any rights to calves, because the property is very much endangered in Ovamboland. A Finish missionary gave him two additional cows.' NAN, J XIIIb5, Reisebericht des Missionars Vedder an den Bezirksamtmann von Zastrow. Geographische und Ethnographische Forschungen im Kaokoveld 1900–1914, my translation.

[10] Vedder also asserts that 'For a sack of ostrich egg shells, which is worth some hundred Marks in Ovamboland, they get an equal amount of seed-corn in their sack made from a hide.' NAN, J XIIIb5, Reisebericht des Missionars Vedder an den Bezirksamtmann von Zastrow. Geographische und Ethnographische Forschungen im Kaokoveld 1900–1914 (my translation).

his Tjimba client Tjongoha at Kaoko Otavi, Kapeke emphasised that both were of the Omukwendata matri-clan, and he also asserted that cattle were taken to and fro, ostensibly downplaying the patron–client character of the relationship. Himba living in the northernmost part of the Kaokoveld traded with the Portuguese directly, and apparently got more out of the ivory trade than the Tjimba of the central Kaokoveld: Vitunda Mutambo and Kandjuhu Rutjindo (in Bollig 1997: 247f.) asserted that blankets, alcohol, and also money were given by Portuguese traders in exchange for tusks.

The Thwa, a small ethnic community living mainly in south-western Angola close to the Kunene River, specialised in elephant hunting. Von Moltke's (1943: 353) informants asserted that the Thwa were highly successful elephant hunters.[11] Thwa informants whom I interviewed in the 1990s claimed that the term 'Thwa' was actually a misnomer and that the proper ethnonym would be 'Thwe', which they translated as 'the courageous ones', alluding to their exploits as elephant hunters. They asserted that in the past, when elephants were still plentiful, they had predominantly lived by hunting elephants and selling ivory. Oral traditions still convey an expert knowledge of elephant hunting. After the ivory boom was over, the Thwa found new income-generating activities in a growing local demand for iron products, pottery, and ritual services among their rich pastoral and agro-pastoral neighbours.

3.4 Violent Regulation of Human–Environment Relations

By 1910 the number of elephants had been considerably reduced. Although the Kaokoveld was still regarded as elephant-rich, the numbers of animals there had dwindled markedly. The remaining number of elephants was probably only about a third (and perhaps less) of the population roaming the Kaokoveld before 1870. This massive change within the social-ecological system was in itself violent, and was also connected to the use of violence by very different groups of actors. On the southern side of the Kunene, Swartboois and Topnaar raids into the Kaokoveld took place well into the 1890s,

[11] Von Moltke (1943: 353, my translation) reports on the Thwa community: 'The Thwa is a poor black tribe that lives in Angola on the other side of the Chella Mountains. They were slaves of their oppressors, the Makuari. But they were the most courageous and best elephant hunters that I ever came across among the black nations.'

and in south-western Angola the Portuguese government resorted to violence to stabilise its weak position.

Within this early colonial setting new forms of stratification and accumulation developed among the Himba and Herero. Warlords wielded significant power. They commanded armed groups of men which they hired out to the Portuguese army. Oral traditions and written sources (e.g. Stals and Otto-Reiner 1999: 35) leave little doubt that mercenary leaders enriched themselves enormously. The raiding of neighbouring communities at the command of the Portuguese military officials became a profitable business. The leaders of these mercenary bands formed commando-like groups with a strong leadership and a council of leading men. William Chapman's documentary on the Dorsland Trekkers gives a good (if somewhat biased) account of the extreme degree of violence used in the south-western part of Angola between the 1880s and the 1910s (Stassen 2010).

When the large-scale hunting of elephants came to an end in 1910, the number of elephants had massively declined. Estimates of elephant numbers in the 1920s and 1930s vary considerably. However, better-informed sources based on eyewitness observations (e.g. Green 1952; Shortridge 1934) mention numbers between 600 and 1,500. On the basis of comparative evidence from different sources, Viljoen (1988: 48) estimates the number of elephants remaining after the onslaught of commercial hunting in the Kaokoveld to be around 600–1,000 animals, implying a decline in numbers of 60–80 per cent. During the same period, hippos became nearly extinct in the lower reaches of the Kunene, a process which did not affect human–environment relations much but which may have caused pertinent changes in the river's ecology.[12] Also rhino numbers were significantly reduced. Hence, the entire megafauna of the Kaokoveld had completely changed its composition, size, and territory after this concerted and ruthless effort at extracting as much value as possible from the area.

What were the consequences for social-ecological relations? Håkansson (2004: 586) reports for the East African interior that 'the extinction or large-scale reduction in elephant herds may have caused significant changes in vegetation and in faunal composition. The disappearance of elephants may lead to the spread of woodland and

---

[12] Spinage (2012: 669) reports on pertinent changes in the vegetation after the removal of hippopotamus from Queen Elizabeth National Park in Uganda.

scrubs at the expense of grasses. This in turn brings tsetse flies and bovine sleeping sickness.' We do not have any data at hand which would suggest a similar trend in vegetation dynamics in north-western Namibia – the issue simply has not been researched yet. However, observations from East Africa on ecological dynamics after elephants have been removed from an ecosystem suggest that comparable processes may have been at work in the Kaokoveld: bush encroachment along the seasonal rivers may have increased, and the spread and rejuvenation of *Faidherbia albida* stands may have been hampered. Furthermore, the coppicing effect of heavy elephant browsing was significantly reduced or terminated, leading to a vegetation structure with more trees.

The effects of dramatically reduced elephant numbers on settlement patterns are more obvious. The riverine valleys could now be used more consistently for agricultural activities, without running the risk that elephant herds would destroy the harvest. Furthermore, settlement near waterholes became less risky, as humans were now in efficient control of permanent water sources. Stals and Otto-Reiner (1999: 41) give the following main wells for elephants in the Kaokoveld: Kaoko Otavi, Ombombo-Kaoko, Otjitundua, Epembe, Ombazu, Oruvandjei, Ombiha, Otjinyerese, Okamizi, and Okapembamba (next to the Kunene River itself); these wells became hubs of human settlement in the early twentieth century after the removal of significant elephant populations from the surrounding areas. Indirect effects of the ivory trade included a trend towards pastoral specialisation and an increase in hierarchical structures. An increase of stratification linked to commercial elephant hunting and ivory trading has been reported from other communities in Africa (e.g. Steinhart 2001: 339 on central Kenya). In north-western Namibia and south-western Angola too, commercial hunting was linked to an increase in stratification. Commercial hunting peaked during a period in which mercenary activities, violent engagements between local communities and colonial powers, and raiding between communities were of crucial importance. Mercenary leaders were also elephant hunters and raiders, and they thrived on the spoils of violent engagements with other communities or with game. Hence militarily prominent leaders also became wealthy livestock owners. However, between the 1880s and the 1910s the accumulation of political authority and wealth took place in south-western Angola rather than in the Kaokoveld. The close contact between the

Dorsland Trekker community at Humpata, near Lubango, and the Portuguese colonial administration brought distinct benefits for Herero and Himba communities residing in their vicinity. In contrast to this, the gains of Tjimba elephant hunters in north-western Namibia were marginal. The Tjimba communities that Hartmann, Kuntz, and Vedder met with between 1900 and 1914 owned only small cattle herds. Only in the second decade of the twentieth century did a rapid repastoralisation of the Kaokoveld occur. Since c. 1910 Himba and Herero who had accumulated large cattle herds in Angola crossed the Kunene and immigrated into the Kaokoveld.

With the repastoralisation of the Kaokoveld a second process set in. State control became more intense: German police patrols tried to inhibit elephant poaching in the Kaokoveld,[13] and in 1907 the German colonial administration incorporated the Kaokoveld into the newly founded Game Reserve No. 2. While German control of the area remained ephemeral despite attempts to administer the vast Kaokoveld, from 1917 onwards the South African administration stipulated the need for intense control. Encapsulation, increasing state control of human–environment relations, and the pastoralisation of the Kaokoveld will thus be the major topics of Chapter 4.

---

[13] Franke NAN A560 Accessions. Victor Franke reports in his diary on efforts in 1901 to curb hunting of 'Portuguese poachers'.

PART 3

Encapsulation and Pastoralisation, 1900s to 1940s

During the course of the first three decades of the twentieth century a number of major changes shaped the history of the Kunene Region. They led directly to the establishment of the colonial state in north-western Namibia and the inclusion of the local pastoral economy into wider administrative structures.[1] From the late 1910s the state and its administration became major actors in the regulation of human–environment relations in north-western Namibia. They claimed the right to oversee environmental infrastructure and to steer its development. Prohibitions (e.g. the ban on hunting), restrictions (e.g. control of mobility and trade), and the establishment of physical infrastructure (e.g. roads) heralded the rhizomatic expansion of the state. The area had been formally sold to a German merchant and his company in 1885 by a Swartboois leader residing in Fransfontein, had then fallen to the German state when this company collapsed in the early 1890s, and was resold by the German state to the Kaoko Land- und Minengesellschaft in 1894 – probably without the local population taking note of any of these changes. The Kaoko Land- und Minengesellschaft did not immediately start to develop its concession area. Only a limited number of cartographers, mining engineers, and police officers traversed the area between 1894 and 1915. Formally, however, the Kaokoveld had been included in a colony since 1884, when the German empire negotiated the Kunene border with the Portuguese state. Military control was expanded to cover the wider area from the late 1890s: in 1897 the power of Swartboois and Topnaar commandos was broken, when the German colonial military successfully intervened in a succession struggle in the Swartboois community in Fransfontein at the southern border of the Kaokoveld (Schnegg and

---

[1] The history of south-western Africa had been influenced by missionaries and traders of European descent since the 1830s (Lau 1987). However, the German state only took formal control of the area in 1884, and even then its presence on the ground in northern Namibia was very restricted (Emmett 1999; Gewald 1999).

Pauli 2008). Since then, 'Kwena'[2] raids into the Kaokoveld were discontinued. In 1901 the German military opened a small fort at Sesfontein, which was to control the vastness of the Kaokoveld. The elephant hunts by Dorsland Trekkers from south-western Angola were discontinued after 1906 due to expanded police control on both sides of the Kunene River. In 1907 the entire Kaokoveld was included in Game Park No. 2 – at that time the biggest conservation area in the world (Dieckmann 2007).

After the local population had been depleted during the last four decades of the nineteenth century, population numbers increased again through the arrival of migrants and returning refugees from south-western Angola, and refugees from the 1904 to 1907 war from central Namibia (Rizzo 2012: 103ff.). While the area had been destocked as a consequence of raids, outmigration, and Rinderpest for about three to four decades, a profound repastoralisation began to take place in the 1910s.

After a short war in 1915, German troops surrendered to South African forces, and in 1917 an initial military expedition was sent to the Kaokoveld to disarm the local population, followed by a second disarmament campaign in 1919.[3] South Africa ruled the colony with martial law until 1921, when a mandatory award by the League of Nations signalled the transmission to a civil administration (Wallace 2011: 205ff.). From the very beginning the South African administration of north-western Namibia shaped society, economy, and social-ecological relations much more than the German administration ever had. Borders were established and re-enforced, mobility was contained, and trade strictly controlled. Chiefs were named in 1921, and three reserves were gazetted in 1923.

This section is organized in three chapters: Chapter 4 discusses the emergence of scientific knowledge on the Kaokoveld. While scientists and mappers had gathered some information on the region, the accumulation of knowledge increased rapidly under South African rule. This knowledge laid the base for an understanding of the Kaokoveld by administrators, and established an epistemological framework for intervention. Chapter 5 describes the establishment of the colonial

---

[2] Nama are summarily addressed as *Kwena* in Otjiherero. The term glances over differences between various Nama communities (e.g. Swartboois and Topnaar).
[3] NAN SWAA 2516 A552/22. Report of Major Manning Tour to the Kaokoveld, Disarmament.

Encapsulation and Pastoralisation, 1900s to 1940s

administration in the Kaokoveld during a period of rapid demographic and economic change. The 1920s and 1930s were shaped by attempts to establish an efficient administration over a vast area. Until 1939 the region was administered from Ondangwa, and apart from the presence of a police station at Tjimuhaka, only occasional treks of administrators into this 'last frontier' area took place. Chapter 6 is constituted by an attempt to reconstruct social-ecological relations between the 1920s and the 1940s and describes the manifold ways the expanding colonial state impacted these relations. Despite the fact that the colonial administration repeatedly attempted, for example, to enforce boundaries, inhibit mobility, and criminalise hunting as poaching, the local population found space to manoeuvre and to (re-)establish a system of mobile livestock husbandry.

4 | *Scientists, Cartographers, Photographers, and the Establishment of Western Knowledge of the Kaokoveld*

Scientists, travellers, and cartographers collected information about the people and resources of north-western Namibia since the 1890s. This information provided the basis for the penetration of state institutions into a vast and largely unknown area. Visual presentations of people and landscape (maps and photographs) as well as scientific descriptions of north-western Namibia became key to the understanding of colonial hegemonic visions and the practice of colonial rule. Visual presentations are accompanied by travelogues, published papers, and inventories. Travellers like Hartmann, Toennissen, Kuntz, and Vedder left diary entries and published articles. South African administrators described their observations in lengthy reports to the government, and scientists like the zoologist Shortridge left voluminous books detailing the fauna of the region. It will be argued here that cartography and scientific inquiry were major strategies of colonial inscription during the early years of colonial rule. Far from being a simple and objective presentation of landscape, geographical features, and people, the cartography of the unknown fulfilled two goals: on the one hand the registration of resources allowed for better control and further commercial exploitation; on the other hand the inscription of colonial hegemony onto the local landscape took a more subtle but probably more enduring form. Mountains and valleys were labelled and took on the names of explorers of European descent; early travellers eagerly looked for the marks and spoors of their predecessors in the region, establishing an empirically based knowledge-grid, creating symbolically loaded places and colonial supremacy.

Visual material on the region from German times is scarce (Bollig and Heinemann 2004; Miescher and Rizzo 2000). The first series of articles, drawings, and photographs originate from the mining engineer Georg Hartmann who went on three expeditions to the Kaokoveld in the 1890s and early 1900s (1894, 1895/1896, and again in 1900/1901) on behalf of the Otavi Minen- und Eisenbahngesellschaft, to explore potential harbours along Namibia's northern coast, places worthwhile for guano exploitation, and possible railway lines (Abel 1954: 11). Captain Victor Franke, for some time stationed at Sesfontein on the southern fringe of the colonial Kaokoveld, traversed northwestern Namibia in 1901.[1] However, apart from the rather shallow descriptions of people and landscape in his diary, which says more about male supremacist and racialised attitudes than about his natural and social environment, he did not leave any published material, let alone photography. The Norwegian mineral explorer Toennissen travelled through the area from east to west in 1903 on behalf of the Kaoko Land- und Minengesellschaft but he left no published texts or photography either. However, his archived reports are filled with naturalistic and technical drawings of the landscape and its geomorphology.[2] Two geographers, Kuntz and Krause, travelled in northwestern Namibia while working for the same company between 1910 and 1912 (Abel 1954: 11f.). In addition to leaving extensive documentation of their travels in diaries and letters, Kuntz published fairly extensively, and also produced maps and photographs (Kuntz 1912a–c). The missionary-cum-anthropologist Heinrich Vedder travelled to the Kaokoveld in 1914. Although his texts and photography were only published from the 1920s onwards, he had already submitted to the German colonial government the first extensive report of his travels in 1914.[3] Vedder's account, along with Kuntz's and Hartmann's assumptions about race and identity, were influential on later dealings between the colonial state and local communities (Bollig and Heinemann 2004). Both German and South African administrators (notably Hahn) regarded the local population, and especially its 'big-men', with some degree of positive racial gaze. Early accounts by travellers and administrators often come from ardent commentators and not from distanced observers.[4] They began with the assumption

---

[1] NAN ADM 560 Diary Victor Franke.
[2] NAN ADM A326 Report of Toennissen on two expeditions to the Kaokoveld.
[3] NAN ZBU, J XIIIb5, Geographische Forschungen Kaokofeld 1900–1914. Bericht von H. Vedder an Bezirksamtmann von Zastrow, 28/10/1914.
[4] Stoler (2009) argues that affective states, in her case fear and uncertainty, constituted the common sense of Dutch colonial rule in Indonesia in the late nineteenth century. Stoler urges historians and anthropologist to look out for shifting notions of common sense on which colonial reports were based. In northwestern Namibia such affective states change during the course of eight decades of colonial rule: while a positive racial gaze dominates the first two decades of the

that the local society was strongly hierarchised and that authorities like chiefs were innate to the local political system. Gewald (2011) describes how Vita Thom was courted by the South African administration of the 1920s, and how, though an immigrant to the region, he was styled as the paramount chief of the Kaokoveld.

There are hardly any records of local voices reflecting changing human–environment relations for the first three decades of the twentieth century. There are echoes of such voices in oral traditions recorded today, and also in reports of white travellers who relied heavily on information from local actors. However, by and large it is not known how local herders narrativised the advent of colonial rule and repastoralisation. It is very difficult to reconstruct their motives and aspirations as first-hand sources are lacking. It is, however, feasible to reconstruct local adaptations to these dynamics. The changing settlement patterns and economic strategies are recorded in oral traditions as well as in archival files.

4.1 Maps and Photographic Representations of the Landscape

In the 1890s large companies and the military were particularly in need of more naturalistic descriptions of the land that they had leased from the German government, or that they were to control with a very limited number of staff. In north-western Namibia it was especially the Otavi-Minen und Eisenbahngesellschaft and the Kaoko Land- und Minengesellschaft which were interested in the exploration of the Kaokoveld. While the former was mainly interested in exploring a potential railway trajectory and a harbour on the northern Namibian coast in order to transport copper from the Otavi mines and then ship it overseas, the latter was more interested in the resources of the Kaokoveld itself. The expeditions were extensive and time-consuming: ox-wagons and ox-carts had to be taken along, as well as numerous trek-oxen and horses. Additionally, livestock for slaughter had to be herded along in order to provide meat for the journey, as local herders were frequently disinclined to sell any animals. To travel the distance from Otjitambi to Sanitatas, at the edge of the northern Namib Desert, for example, the Hartmann expedition took four weeks (Hartmann

colonial encounter, it gives way to authoritarian and extremely paternalistic attitudes in the 1930s and 1940s.

1902/1903: 403). Hartmann's expedition in 1895/96 was a joint venture with army officers who were seconded to the expedition, and Hartmann's second expedition in 1900/01 was also carried out in close cooperation with army officers. The diaries from the expeditions, and related published material, are explicit about distances and provide details about landscape features and water points.[5] Maps were drawn that showed crucial resources which were apt for exploitation (copper, iron), water sources, mountains, and sandy stretches. All this information was necessary in order to guarantee swift and safe movement in this remote part of the new colony. During his expeditions in 1894, 1895/96, and 1900/01 Hartmann collected extensive information, particularly on the Kaokoveld's western escarpment and the bordering Namib Desert. Like other travellers in the region, Hartmann interweaves clear-cut and detailed descriptions of physical properties of the landscape with emotional accounts of his observations. He describes the Kaokoveld as a dramatic landscape, claiming that the 'Kaokoveld [offers us] an arena for the wildest struggle with the forces of erosion and the land surface' (Hartmann 1902/1903: 122, my translation) and at the same time hints at the great potential of the area for livestock ranching (Hartmann 1902/1903: 126). The Groll map combines results from Hartmann's and Franke's expeditions.[6] The map marks the coastal desert and the semi-arid pro-Namib zone with shades of yellow, while further inland the use of green suggests abundant pastures. Elevations and escarpment features are rendered in a light brown colour. The ephemeral rivers draining towards the Atlantic Ocean as well as their basins are depicted in detail, as are the Marienfluss Valley and major dunes along the coast, reflecting the routes of Hartmann's three expeditions between 1894 and 1901. While details of observed topographical features along the travelling routes are rather dense, there are vast stretches of land which are not marked. However, these areas are not clearly marked as regions for which, apparently, no information was available at the time. They are

---

[5] See for example Vedder's report to von Zastrow, the *Bezirkshauptmann* at Outjo (NAN ZBU, J XIIIb5): The report includes a lengthy description of the places traversed, highlighting water availability and presence of people.
[6] The map is registered under the number Map XX, 81 ma, Max Groll in the Staatsbibliothek of Munich. Good accounts of Franke's, Toennissen's, and Kuntz's routes are found in their diaries and travelogues: Franke NAN A 560, Toennissen NAN A 326, Kuntz NAN A327.

shaded in the same green used to represent vegetation, suggesting a continuity of ranching land. (In fact, much of the land shaded in light green is rugged, mountainous desert-like country.) The landscape is only named in the spots that were actually visited. The only named rivers are the Kunene and the Marienfluss; strangely, no names are given for the ephemeral rivers, although they feature prominently in the travelling accounts, and their courses are sketched in detail on the Groll map. None of the mountains are named. 'Ovatjimba oder Wachimba' in the north, and 'Bergdamara' in mountainous stretches in the south, are given as the major populations. Occasionally there are remarks such as 'many elephants', or 'a lot of palms' scattered across the map.[7] Groll's map became the basis of the German war map of 1904 for these parts of the colony. For obvious reasons the war map included more detail about water sources, and for most places indicated whether there was a lot of water or only a little (Namibia National Archives 1997).

More detailed maps, based on earlier information and on the expeditions of Kuntz between 1907 and 1911 were produced about ten years later by Sprigade.[8] The Sprigade map shows much more detail than Groll's map of 1903, and covers most parts of north-western Namibia with detailed topographical information. The map is an attempt to satisfy two goals – to present visually the accumulated knowledge on the Kaokoveld and its inhabitants, and to highlight the resources available for exploitation. In a much more complex manner than in the Groll map, the topography of the entire Kaokoveld is represented. For the first time, mountains are named. Most Europeans who had explored the region had mountain ranges named after them (Toennissen Berge, Hartmann Berge, Joubert Berge, etc.). Other mountains were named after their topographical characteristics (Steilrandberge) or metaphorically after game (Zebraberge, Giraffenberge). It is mainly the mountains which received European names, while places and rivers were usually referred to using vernacular, indigenous names. The map provides details of where herds of large game like elephants, zebras, and giraffes had been seen, and locates exploitable minerals. As the

---

[7] Bollig and Heinemann (2004: 266–9) present the Groll map as well as the map by Sprigade in original colours in an analysis of historical photography of the Kaokoveld in German times.

[8] The map is registered under the number Map XX, 83 fa in the Staatsbibliothek Munich.

Kaokoveld was still considered for settler-farming purposes at that time, grazing qualities were also noted down. In comparison to the earlier map by Groll, more attention was given to portraying the human component; ethnic names were pinned down and chiefs' places were highlighted. One is surprised, though, that it was possible to present such a detailed image of the region at that time: after all, it was only the extensive expeditions of Kuntz which provided the informational basis for this map's increased detail compared with earlier maps – and yet, Kuntz did not reach the area north of today's Okangwati, towards the Kunene, nor did he venture into the Baynes Mountains. Nevertheless, his map bears topographical information about these areas, too. This suggests that the Sprigade map imaginatively added such information where data were missing to make the map look complete.

Map drawing continued into the South African period of colonial administration. Resident Commissioner Manning organised the South African administration in the north between 1915 and 1917. While residing in Ovamboland's Ondangwa he travelled the Kaokoveld several times, first to disarm locals there (1917, 1919) and then to fix the boundary with Portuguese West Africa (1920). Manning worked closely with his two deputies, Dickmann and Hahn, and an enormous number of photographs (mainly landscape photographs) were taken by both Hahn and Dickmann. Hayes (1998: 173) comments that 'under Manning's aegis, photography and cartography worked hand in hand in the construction of the international boundary and the production of geographic knowledge'. In 1923 at the latest, Manning added a more detailed map to the hitherto existing set of maps (see Map 4.1). Manning's map has a true working character: the map is a cyanotype – at that time, the simplest way to produce copies of complex, large-format maps. Cyanotypes utilise a chemical process in which photosensitive iron salts produce a deep blue colour where they are exposed to light. The map stored in the Namibia National Archives is a copy, and we may assume that several copies of the original map informed colonial officers working in or on the Kaokoveld from the 1920s to 1950s when other maps were produced based on aerial photography. Basic information about the landscape and natural resources could be disseminated quickly in this way. The map is very detailed, and contains numerous remarks which are extremely helpful when crossing the terrain. There are detailed notes on where water was

Western Knowledge of the Kaokoveld

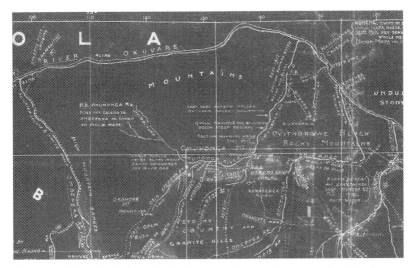

Map 4.1 Manning's map of the Kaokoveld, part depicting the Omuhonga Basin cartographically.
Source: NAN Map 00078, Storage: Rolled, ROLL-044, titled Travellers' map of Kaokoveld, Protectorate of South West Africa/by Major C. N. Manning, Resident Commissioner Ovamboland

to be found, and in what quantities. Many entries are qualified with a temporal specification: the map clearly differentiates Manning's observations from 1917 to 1919, and thereby adds information on the variability of water resources. Manning notes a great number of place names in Otjiherero, and also tries to map older wagon tracks to make navigation easier. He also notes down the whereabouts of leading political figures such as Vita Thom and Muhona Katiti. The mapping of chiefly homesteads is the basis for developing a system of indirect rule in the region. Local 'big-men' are mapped into a grid of colonial power, and so made accessible and controllable.

Carl (Cocky) Hahn, the long-term Native Commissioner of the Ovamboland and the Kaokoveld, left several map-like drawings in his papers – none of his maps, however, is of the standard of Manning's map. Hahn's passion, rather, was photography (Hayes 2000).

4.2 Photographs and Texts

While the maps are the accumulated result of several expeditions, the photographs and diary entries bear witness to the personal, first-hand observations of 'explorers'. Hayes (2000) succinctly shows how visual material from northern Namibia was used to get across more subtle ideological issues such as ideas of indirect rule and identity. Colonial ideas about tribal hierarchies in the Kaokoveld were communicated in visual material and genealogy underpinning the legitimacy of these local authorities (see also Bollig 1998b).

Landscapes feature importantly in Hartmann's photography, while images of people are rare. The photographs presented by Hartmann mainly serve as an illustration of the arduous trek through the Kaokoveld's mountains towards the coast. Next to presenting illustrations of trekking, a second important motive is that of indicating the sheer scale of the landscape – a visual topic worked upon consistently since then.[9] Strangely, there are no photographs of Herero, Tjimba, or Himba, although Hartmann describes them in an empathic way in his publications.[10] This is even more surprising since in the second section of Hartmann's (1902/1903) account, photographs of Ovambo women and men are carefully staged. Clearly Hartmann's main visual topic is the intrusion of white explorers into an inaccessible but promising region.

While Hartmann's mission was mainly concerned with the exploration of the coastline,[11] Kuntz's goals, set out by the Kaoko Land- und Minengesellschaft, were more comprehensive. While his main task was to look for a potential harbour, he was also to inventory the resources of the Kaokoveld and to contact local communities. His account suggests rather populous groups, with several chiefs controlling the various communities.

Kuntz (1912b) presents two photographs of 'Owatschimba': weaponry, body adornment, and garments of both groups are strikingly

---

[9] See for example the photograph 'Grassteppe zwischen Nadas and Anabib (Kaokofeld), im Hintergrund Tafel- und Kegelgebirge' (Hartmann 1902/1903: 408).

[10] Hartmann presents an ardent racialised comment on the physical traits of the people he meets: 'They are Bantu negroes of slender build, chocolate brown colour, with oval faces and almond-shaped eyes, who are profoundly different from the Bergdamara, but are racially akin to the Ovambo in the northeast' (Hartmann 1902/1903: 136–7, my translation).

[11] Hartmann's early publications are mainly descriptions of his route and of landscape morphology; only in a fairly late article (Hartmann 1941) does he give a more detailed sketch of the subsistence economy and culture of the Kaokoveld's communities.

different (see Bollig and Heinemann 2004: 274). None of the men in the first image wear a bow, and the spear in the second photograph is of a very different type than the one in the first photograph. The hairstyles of the men in both photographs are different. If not for Kuntz's captions one would certainly think of them as being from two fairly different communities. Yet, Kuntz names the people in both photographs *Owatschimba*, and lays the groundwork for categorising the inhabitants of the Kaokoveld as representatives of ethnic units.

Vedder's contribution on 'The Herero' in *The Native Tribes of South West Africa* of 1928 was meant to satisfy the needs of the League of Nations for a credible report on the development of the native population in the mandated territory. While the photographs were probably taken in 1914, the selection of specific photographs was linked to the policies of the 1920s. Vedder had visited the Kaokoveld, searching for Herero communities 'living traditionally', and looking for opportunities to extend missionary efforts. After the Herero society had been destroyed by the onslaught of the genocide inflicted upon them by German troops in 1904–7, the missionary ethnographer saw the pastoral society of the Kaokoveld as an analogue of the Herero way of life, which might be studied as a way to learn about pre-colonial Herero society. Vedder underlined his vision of an unshattered continuity of Herero culture in Namibia's north-west in text and visual presentations. Photographs were used to portray traditional Herero. Several photographs portray women or men of different ages in a highly arranged fashion.

Obviously these were intended to portray a racial and cultural type, as well as age- and gender-specific costumes, in such a way as to fit accepted anthropological conventions at the time. Other photographs portray local people in culturally specific situations, like three elderly men 'tasting milk' at the ancestral fire, or three women sitting in front of a hut performing some kind of domestic work. Staged pictures were intended to underscore the evidence, serving as part of a scientific epistemology. It was in the Kaokoveld where the old customs of an ancient pastoral population survived according to Vedder.

During early South African rule, landscape photography was perfected. Taking photographs of trophy-hunting became the main form in which human–wildlife interaction at South African empire's last frontier was portrayed. Throughout the late 1920s and the 1930s, Carl (Cocky) Hahn ventured many times into the Kaokoveld as Native

Commissioner. Residing in Ondangwa, he initially rode on horseback to the Kaokoveld, where he visited traditional authorities during his early days in the region. Since the mid-1920s, he did so by car, and from the late 1930s even by aeroplane (Hayes 2000: 5). His diaries give detailed accounts of his travels, and he took a great number of observational notes on fauna and local populations. Although he was eager to enter into scientific discourses, Hahn did not publish much on the Kaokoveld. In the 1928 publication *The Native Tribes of South-West Africa* (Hahn et al. 1928) he contributed a chapter on 'The Ovambo', but left it to Vedder to contribute the chapter on 'The Herero', which included a great deal of data from Vedder's earlier expedition to the Kaokoveld, and left out details of more recent social and political shifts in the 1920s (which Hahn could have easily added). It was Hahn's great passion to take photographs of landscape and people in the Kaokoveld. Visually, he developed a narrative on the empty, vast savannahs of north-western Namibia and their tradition-bound pastoral inhabitants. Hahn's photographs of hunts cherished the sportsman's ideal of trophy-hunting. Rarely are African huntsmen included in his photographs. They usually portray the white hunter in a dominant position in relation to the hunted animal.

Hahn cherished the idea of making the northernmost parts of the Kaokoveld a game reserve. He himself had taken a keen interest in the Sabi game reserve of South Africa (which was later to become the Kruger Park) and at one time had applied for the job as Chief Game Warden there. In the late 1920s he turned his attention to the design of 'an ambitious plan for the development of a new reserve in the far north-west' (Hayes 1998: 183; Hayes 2000: 53f.). He designated an old Himba man, Ikandwa, as an informal warden in the area and enthused about the idea of creating a sanctuary there 'which would offer "fine opportunities for tourists and sportsmen to shoot trophies under special licences and instructions"' (quoted after Hayes 1998: 183). Hahn saw the spectacular landscape along the Kunene River as a distinct advantage, which made a sanctuary in the northern Kaokoveld superior to the Etosha Park's dull plains. Plans for a game sanctuary along the Kunene River would have fitted nicely with his idea of creating a livestock free zone along the international border to prevent livestock mobility between South West Africa and southern Angola. Hayes shows that, against modernising trends in Ovamboland, where labour migration, Christianisation, and schooling led to various forms of cultural transformation, the Kaokoveld was visualised by Hahn as the last remaining frontier of the South African colonial empire, laying the foundations for the Kaokoveld's reputation for remoteness, isolation, and backwardness. The Kaokoveld was becoming what was later dubbed 'the old South-West' – a region where ancient tribal communities were practising a sustainable form of pastoralism.

4.3 Scientific Expeditions into the Kaokoveld in South African Times

With the advent of the South African rule in Namibia the north-west became isolated from the remainder of the country. While between 1897 and 1926 about ten scientific expeditions into the Kaokoveld took place, such expeditions became rare after the late 1920s. They were replaced by the numerous tours of administrators, and of police officers, into the vastness of the Kaokoveld. With the advent of the South African administration the sheer quantity of reports and files on the Kaokoveld increased dramatically: reports, photography, and filed questionnaires added to the information about the region. The affective undertone of reports also changed: ardent comments on race and landscape gave way to supremacist, imperious, and aggressive language. Scientific knowledge of flora, fauna, and people accumulated rapidly with the increasing presence of colonial officers there. Especially arduous treks to dispersed settlements brought officers into contact with new landscapes and gave them intimate first-hand experience with local ecological conditions. Reports from the 1920s take a keen interest in geographical and hydrological conditions and vividly discuss the possibility of traces of remnant fauna (e.g. the fabled quagga, or the white rhino). It is especially the quest for the quagga, a specific sub-species of zebra, which runs like a red thread through accounts on the fauna of the Kaokoveld in the 1920s and 1930s. Many pages are filled discussing whether quaggas were still to be found, and whether quaggas allegedly seen in the Kaokoveld were just another type of mountain zebra.[12]

---

[12] The quagga (*Equus quagga quagga*), an extinct form of zebra, was one of the more common ungulates roaming the South African savannahs until the seventeenth century. By around 1850 the quagga had become extinct south of the Oranje due to excessive hunting (Shortridge 1934).

On top of the production of colonial knowledge through administrators, scientists added to the understanding of flora, fauna, and human–environment relations and 'expeditions' became a major scientific approach to knowledge production. While in German times such missions of externals were endorsed by either the companies with an interest in the Kaokoveld or by the administration, such scientific expeditions in the first three decades of South African rule were private enterprises sponsored by academic institutions, such as museums or universities or interested men of independent means. Such expeditions had to be applied for. The administration took great pains to allow only those academic endeavours which – according to their ideas – would not affect local communities negatively. The issue of whether such an expedition might raise discontent with a local population was always of importance, and a matter of discussion within administrative circles. The early and mid-1920s saw a number of scientific expeditions to the Kaokoveld; then for about two decades no further academic explorations took place in the area. The long-term native commissioner Carl (Cocky) Hahn, who dominated the Kaokoveld's politics throughout the latter part of the 1920s, through the 1930s and well into the 1940s, had scientific ambitions himself (Hayes 2000). I did not find any evidence that he was instrumental in denying scientists access to the region, but his attitude towards scientists was certainly sceptical. Only in the late 1940s and early 1950s did three further scientific expeditions (the Carp Expedition, the ethnographic expedition of South African anthropologist van Warmelo, the expedition of the German geographer Abel) take place. I will shortly delineate the expeditions being undertaken between the 1920s and the 1950s. These expeditions were mainly interested in cataloguing biodiversity, especially of fauna, the discovery of endemic species, and remnant species like the quagga.

In 1923 the director of the Kaffrarian Museum in King William's Town, South Africa, Guy Chester Shortridge organised the 'The Third Percy Sladen and Kaffrarian Museum Expedition "Ovamboland"' which ventured shortly into the eastern margins of the Kaokoveld in the Ruacana region.[13] Another expedition must have followed in the late 1920s. I did not find archival evidence of this second expedition, but in his publication Shortridge refers to observational data from

---

[13] NAN SWAA 1331/198/6/2 Shortridge, 'The Third Percy Sladen and Kaffrarian Museum Expedition "Ovamboland"'.

1928, which hints at a second expedition that took him further into the Kaokoveld. It was the aim of Shortridge's expedition to produce a complete inventory of the fauna of north-western Namibia establishing 'institutional knowledge and authority of mammals' (Witz 2015: 671). This included the scientific description of faunal species as well as the collection of specimens of each species. The expedition was jointly financed by the administration and the Kaffrarian Museum in King William's Town. Against the general prohibition on shooting game, the expedition was given rather high quotas to hunt for food and for providing specimens for museum exhibitions. The Shortridge volume contains an appendix of numerous tables specifying body size, body weight, and other features of animals. These animals were shot or killed in other ways in order to measure them. The expedition resulted in the voluminous *The Mammals of South West Africa* (Shortridge 1934). The volume contains detailed distribution maps of many faunal species.

Shortridge devoted a long chapter to the state of elephants in South West Africa. He classified the Kaokoveld's elephants as a sub-species of their own (*Loxodonta africana Zukowskyi*) and carefully scrutinised all written evidence regarding elephants in the Kaokoveld (Shortridge 1934: 358–9). This point is of considerable importance, as for a long time the conservation of the Kaokoveld's elephants, often summarily dubbed 'desert elephants', was motivated by the idea that they were a rare and highly adapted local sub-species. Only recently has genetic analysis shown that this is not the case (Leggett et al. 2003). Shortridge obtained further first-hand oral evidence from locals in order to inform his discussion of numbers and distribution.

It is only in the late 1940s that expeditions into the Kaokoveld were again conducted.[14] Van Warmelo, a government-employed anthropologist, had two rather short stays in the Kaokoveld in 1947 and 1948, with 'only few and brief interviews with some of the more important men'.[15] With additional information from Vedder and the

---

[14] I did not find evidence of a single scientific expedition to the Kaokoveld in the 1930s. Abel (1954: 13) mentions that in 1935 two German-speaking geologists, Obst and Kayser, applied in vain for a permit to do research on the geomorphology of the region.

[15] NAN Accessions 591 van Warmelo, file 15 'Manuscript on Kaoko', unpaged, here quoted from introduction. Van Warmelo also thanks Vedder in this introduction 'for kindly giving me his own views on the relation between the various Herero-speaking groups' signaling a transmission of knowledge from the early colonial period into the second half of the twentieth century.

resident Native Officer Wessels and his wife, he produced an ethnographic introduction to the Kaokoveld (van Warmelo 1951). This short volume placed an emphasis on ethnic origins and ethnic boundaries, and reified the ethnic map of the Kaokoveld, detailing the differences between Himba, Tjimba, and various Herero groups. In 1951 the Carp Expedition ventured into the Kaokoveld.[16] Bernhard Carp was a Dutch-born South African businessman with excellent relations with the academic establishment of South Africa and Southern Rhodesia. He financed a number of expeditions for various southern African museums. In 1949 the Director of the Transvaal Museum in Pretoria approached the Administrator for South West Africa[17] and advertised a joint expedition, by the museums of Transvaal, the Kaffrarian Museum at King William's Town, and the Bulawayo Museum, to the Kaokoveld 'for the purpose of collecting natural history, archaeological and ethnological material for the institutions concerned'. He also points out that the expedition was to be financed by Carp, and that 'Mr. Carp's interest in sponsoring such expeditions is in no way for personal gain but an expression of his desire to further the study of Science in South Africa'. Only three weeks later the administration forwarded a permit. While the local Native Commissioner, Eedes, complained bitterly about Carp, with whom he had had to work on a previous occasion,[18] the administrative establishment was in favour of Carp's activities and stipulated only that 'responsible scientists' should be in control of the activities. The expedition then began in June 1951, and by July of the same year Carp proudly reported to the Administrator[19] that the 'total number of mammals obtained was 650 devided [sic] over 48 species' and many thousands of different

---

[16] NAN SWAA 1336/A198/39 Carp Expedition.
[17] NAN SWAA 1336/A198/39 Carp Expedition. The Transvaal Museum, Director to the Administrator for South West Africa 3/11/1949.
[18] Native Commissioner Ovamboland Eedes to the Chief Native Commissioner Windhoek 12/1/1950; 'I am disinclined to render him any further assistance, or to give him information which I have gathered during my long period of service in the Northern Native Territories. Mr. Carp is a salesman for certain brands of liquor, and as far as I know is not a scientist.' NAN SWAA 1336 A 198/39. Native Commissioner Ovamboland Eedes to Chief Native Commissioner Windhoek 12/1/1950.
[19] Carp to Office of the Administrator 15/7/1951, NAN SWAA 1336 A198/47 Abel Expedition.

insects were collected, including 'over 100 new forms'.[20] Carp also reports on a minute '*strandloper* community' (see Chapter 2) and on rumours of 'wild tribes' in the north: 'We have been informed at the Kunene by a grandson of Oorlog, that there still live wild tribes on the Zebra and Baynes Mountains, who have never seen a white man'. It was especially the enigmatic *strandlopers* who engaged the imaginations of scientists. In the early twentieth century, scientists speculated that those communities who had left behind numerous shell middens along the South African coast had thrived by collecting food along the shores. It was assumed that they were distinct from Khoisan-speaking people and presented a distinct race of their own. The *strandlopers* were thought to represent the earliest human habitation of southern Africa (Leakey 1936: 167, 174, cited in Szalay 1983: 69). To find living remnants of *strandloper* communities on the coast of the Kaokoveld opened a window into the Pleistocene and emphasised that the 'isolated' Kaokoveld harboured keys to the prehistoric riddles of the continent. Carp's report underlines the exceptional status of the Kaokoveld as a repository of biodiversity. It emphasises the 'otherness' of the Kaokoveld's fauna and people.

In 1952 the German geographer Abel led another expedition into the Kaokoveld.[21] Abel worked for the Overseas Museum in Bremen and it was his task to fill gaps in the museum's exhibits that resulted from the devastations of the Second World War. In his application he described the Kaokoveld's fauna as largely undocumented. His specific scientific aim though was to explore the Great Escarpment in northern Namibia.[22]

---

[20] The taxidermist in Carp's team was Nicholas Arends who had also assisted as taxidermist in the Shortridge expedition. Arends had served in Shortridge's Kaffrarian Museum for many years and at the time of Carp's expedition was technical assistant in the Department of Zoology at the University College Western Cape, the precursor of University of the Western Cape. Arends described these activities in his memoirs *Trapping Safaris* (Arends and Stopforth 1967; see Figures 4.1a and 4.1b). I thank Leslie Wits for this important hint at Arends and his connection to both expeditions.

[21] NAN SWAA 1336 A198/47 Abel Expedition.

[22] Some of the participants taking part in the Carp Expedition also took part in the Abel Expedition: Eberhard von Koenen, for example, who had photographed and painted during the Carp Expedition, was also photographer in the Abel Expedition. Von Koenen (pers. comm.) himself argued that he was invited to such occasions because he had a very good knowledge of the area, and at that time owned one of the first four-wheel drive cars in the region.

4.4 The Transmission of Knowledge

How did administrators, travellers, and scientists gain their knowledge of fauna, flora, and human–environment relations? They ventured into lands about which very little prior knowledge was available. They produced maps, named places, recorded settlement patterns, and described power structures. While some information relied on observational data, interview-based information was of prominent importance for most of these scientists. They sought the testimony of locals to obtain the information they wanted; more specifically, they turned to local leaders, or better to those whom they perceived as such, to access information. During the German period Kakurukouye (alias Kasupi), residing in the western Kaokoveld in Ombepera, was a key informant of both Franke and Kuntz, while Vedder used Tjongoha, the *omuhona* ('big-man') of Kaoko Otavi, as key informant. In the 1920s and 1930s Vita Thom became the key informant for administrators like Manning and Hahn. Shortridge mentions having talked to Vita Thom, too. Both Kakurukouye and Vita Thom were established as 'chiefs' by the colonial administration, and obviously they only submitted information which would not harm their aspirations. Vita Thom therefore reported the presence of considerable numbers of elephants, indicating that poaching was not as severe as had been assumed. He also supplied Manning and Hahn with an idea of the 'traditional charter' of land use, centred upon the dominance of few 'big men' controlling major waterholes. Natural scientists (the vast majority) and social scientists both relied on interview-based data to a great extent. Most scientists visiting the region just spent a few weeks 'in the field' and during this time they travelled extensively from place to place. Usually visitors only spent a few days in any one place. In 1914 Vedder spent a few weeks in Kaoko Otavi – but this was a rare exception. Hartmann and Toennissen travelled especially in the coastal areas: they relied mostly on observational data and on the knowledge their Nama-Damara speaking guides brought along. Kuntz and Franke picked up some information on the road, asking locals questions via their guides' translations; both also visited and courted Kakurukouye – referred to as a chief in their accounts.[23] All reports and publications mention the extensive use of

---

[23] See for example NAN ADM 327; Diary entry for 12/10/1910: 'exchanges of presents confirmed our friendship'.

local informants on a diverse set of topics. Most early explorers in the region also mention that it was very difficult to obtain such informants: especially after the genocidal war of 1904–7 potential informants tended to stay away from Europeans. Kuntz writes in 1910 that he would prefer not to travel with army people, as they would make it even more difficult to obtain local informants. He speaks of the 'natives' fear and hatred of the police'.[24] Kuntz then relied on a mixed strategy: while he convinced Damara in a place called Gamgamas, using presents to help him win their favour,[25] in Kaoko Otavi he took guides by force.[26] Kuntz also reports that watering places were hidden by locals, probably in an effort to get rid of the foreign travellers as soon as possible. Vedder complains that locals ran away as soon as the expedition was sighted, and in one instance he describes how the Herero guides he had brought from central Namibia went running after fleeing locals.[27] Presents, as a form of payment for information, were common during the German era, and remained so during South African times. It is rarely specified what exactly was presented; tobacco seems to have been important, and also blankets and sugar.

Expeditions – from Shortridge's zoological enterprise to Carp's comprehensive effort to record the 'wonders' of the Kaokoveld – worked on the premise that different members of the expedition would use different methodological approaches to obtain information. In the Carp Expedition for example there were experts on entomology, mammalian species, and ethnography. One person had the task of photographing and painting what was deemed to be essential. The taxidermist Arends took part in the Shortridge Expedition of the 1920s and the Carp Expedition of the early 1950s and prepared hunted and trapped animals for museum collections (see Figures 4.1a and 4.1b).

The application of scientific methodologies (e.g. measuring the physical dimensions of individual animals killed as in Shortridge 1934, see Table 4.1), the collection of specimens (in the form of trophies, or herbariums), and the taking of photographs were essential aspects of these expeditions.

---

[24] NAN ADM 327 Kuntz Diary, entry for 25/8/1910.
[25] NAN ADM 327 Kuntz Diary, entry for 25/9/1910.
[26] NAN ADM 327 Kuntz Diary, entry for 22/10/1910.
[27] Travellers not only gave presents to locals, but also occasionally received presents from them: the standard present apparently having been a ram (e.g. Franke diary, Kuntz diary).

Figure 4.1a Taxidermist N. Arends posing with specimens of moles.
Source: Arends and Stopforth (1967)

Figure 4.1b Carp Expedition, June 1951; collected moles.
Source: Photographer H. Roth, NAN 02929

Carl (Cocky) Hahn, as an amateur scientist working on the Kaokoveld's society and nature, was exceptional in many ways. He repeatedly came back to the area, which he apparently visited at least once a year in the 1920s and 1930s. Throughout the 1920s and the early part of the 1930s Hahn relied on discussions with Vita Thom to obtain

Table 4.1 Studying the Kaokoveld fauna

The upper table shows the physical dimensions of 11 individual zebras killed mainly in the Kaokoveld; the lower table gives the measurement of 9 rhinoceros shot probably in eastern Africa, notably two by former US President Roosevelt plus one additional rhinoceros shot by the expedition in the Kaokoveld near Kaoko Otavi.

762

Quagga q. antiquorum

Field measurements of 11 out of 15 specimens collected from the Kaokoveld and the Okavango Region:

		H. & b.	Tail.	Hf.	Ear.	Locality.
(1)	♀	2460	515	555	170	Katijhuru (S. Kaokoveld).[1]
(2)	♂	2360	470	570	168	Otjitundua (C. Kaokoveld).
(3)	♂	2400	480	560	180	Otjitundua.
(4)	♀	2380	500	565	175	Otjitundua.
(5)	♀	2220	490	555	170	Otjitundua.
(6)	♂	2240	500	570	170	Tshimhaka (Cunene).
(7)	♂	2440	565	580	165	Otjimbundn (Cunene).
(8)	♂	2010	480	510	165	Otjimbundu.
(9)	♂	2220	510	610	162	Mbambi (Okavango).
(10)	♀	2170	530	592	160	Mbambi.
(11)	♀	2385	500	610	160	Mohango Drift (W. Caprivi).

Average length of *Bontequagga* skulls in the Kaffrarian Museum, 21–22 in. (S.W. Africa).

Table 4.1 (*cont.*)

Diceros bicornis

Field measurements:

		H & b.	Tail	Hf.	Ear.	
(1)	♂	13 ft. 4 in.[2]	27 in.	—	—	(Kirby).
(2)	♂	13 ft. 1 in.[3]	25 in.	—	—	(Kirby).
(3)	♂	12 ft.	24 in. (average)	—	—	(Kirby).
(4)	♀	10 ft.	24 in. (average)	—	—	(Kirby).
(5)	♂	12 ft. 1 in.	24 in.	—	—	(Jackson)
(6)	♂	10 ft.[4]	24 in.	—	—	(Neumann).
(7)	♂	9 ft.[4]	24 in.	—	—	(Neumann).
(8)	♂	12 ft. 3 in.	30 in.	$17\frac{1}{2}$ in.	$9\frac{1}{4}$ in.	(Roosevelt).
(9)	♀	11 ft. 3 in.	$26\frac{1}{2}$ in.	17 in.	$8\frac{1}{2}$ in.	(Roosevelt).

Field measurements of a male specimen of *Diceros bicornis occidentalis* from Kaoko-Otavi, N. Kaokoveld (Kaffrarian Museum):

H. & b.	Tail.	Hf.	Ear.	
2,780 mm.	520 mm.	430 mm.	215 mm.	(Kaffrarian Museum).

Source: Shortridge (1934)

information on the culture, social organisation, and social-ecological relations in the Kaokoveld. Manning had already identified Vita Thom as a reliable informant.[28] In a clever move, Vita Thom had invited Manning to set up a police station in the vicinity[29] and received preferential treatment by the authorities later on. A quarrel over rights to the natural well at Otjijandjasemo was decided in favour of Vita Thom, and in 1923 he was granted his own reserve. Hahn frequently asked Vita Thom for his opinion, and it is Vita Thom's opinions that informed the administration throughout the 1920s. Thom and Hahn communicated directly, as Thom was fluent in Afrikaans. They also communicated through letters occasionally.[30] From the early 1920s Hahn established a local support team consisting of the local chiefs and a translator, Willem Hartley.

Both Manning and Hahn relied excessively on a very few prominent locals whom they perceived as knowledgeable in order to gain their knowledge of fauna and human–environment relations. It is especially the ideas of leaders who were sustained as traditional authorities by the administration which co-produced the knowledge base on the Kaokoveld in general and its environmental infrastructure in particular. Hahn and Manning disseminated their knowledge into the wider scientific community, communicating ideas with, for example, the Royal Geographical Society and corresponding with renowned scientists of their time, and it is very likely that their knowledge informed the ideas of later generations of administrators, experts, and travellers.

During the first twenty years of the twentieth century the Kaokoveld emerged in visual representations as a colonial landscape, with key topographical features bearing the names of European explorers. Mountains and mountain ranges so crucial for orientation within a wide landscape carried European names, and still do so today. The specific blend of Europeanised landmarks and vernacular place names helped later generations of colonial intruders feel at home in a region narrativised as a true frontier district and a social-ecological system

---

[28] NAN SWAA 2516 A552/22; in his field diary Manning gives a very positive description of Vita Thom's character traits (entry for 13 June 1919).
[29] NAN SWAA 2516 A552/22; entry for 9 June 1919.
[30] NAN ADM 450 Acc. Hahn; Diary entry for 6 March 1924. Hahn notes that 'Herero native Fritz arrives with a letter from Oorlog (alias Vita Thom)'. On 16 March 1923 he notes that he interviewed Oorlog at Otjijandjasemo for three consecutive days.

with many particularities, remnant as well as endemic species, and high overall biodiversity. This narrative guided them to see the Kaokoveld as a vast natural landscape hardly impacted by humans, as a landscape different from other northern Namibian landscapes where human impact on the landscape was perceived (and construed) as being more visible (see e.g. Kreike 2013 for colonial perceptions of the heavy human impact on the vegetation of north-central Namibia).

In Chapter 5 I will depict how such knowledge was put to use in order to control the Kaokoveld's population. The drawing and enforcement of boundaries, the major resettlement of inhabitants of the southern Kaokoveld, and major veterinary campaigns were only possible with some knowledge of settlement patterns and power structures.

5 | *The Establishment of Colonial Administration and the Re-establishment of a Pastoral Livelihood*

German presence in the Kaokoveld remained ephemeral. The fact that on the one hand the German administration hardly administered the Kaokoveld, but on the other hand guaranteed that raids into the area were suppressed, made the region attractive to communities that had left the Kaokoveld two or three decades earlier fearing attacks by Fransfontein- and Sesfontein-based raiders. It held the same attraction for other 'black' communities who lived as attached groups with Dorsland Trekkers in south-western Angola in servant-like positions (Stassen 2010). North-western Namibia may have become especially attractive once the Portuguese military administration was changed to a civil administration after the Portuguese liberal revolution of 1911 and taxes and corporal punishments became regular features of the colonial administration.

5.1 Re-immigration of Pastoralists into the Kaokoveld

The re-immigration of pastoralists and stockless clients into the Kaokoveld in the early decades of the twentieth century was a major event, and had long-lasting consequences. When tracing accounts of human settlement in early German reports, we get the impression that the Kaokoveld was only very sparsely inhabited (Rizzo 2012: 91–8). Hartmann (1941), referring to information he collected between 1893 and 1900, described the local subsistence economy as reliant on three strategies: small-stock husbandry, hunting, and gathering. He emphasises that only the more prosperous homesteads possess small-stock herds of some thirty to forty heads, and mentions that only Kasupi's community was able to keep some cattle, despite the threat of Nama raids.

In stark contrast to Hartmann's and Franke's publications, in his diary Kuntz (travelling the area in October 1910, i.e. about a decade later than his predecessors) depicts the northern parts of the Kaokoveld as fairly densely settled, and inhabited by a predominantly pastoral population.[1] Kuntz found that the communities west of Kaoko Otavi acknowledged Kasupi (alias Kakurukouye) as their leader, while those people living at Kaoko Otavi acknowledged the Uukwaludhi king ruling from Tsandi on the western margins of north-central Namibia's Cuvelai basin. Other settlements are also described as being densely settled, like Otjirunda, 'where there is a big Obatschimba [sic] settlement with many goats'. In Ongango, Kuntz came across a Tjimba village of ten to twelve huts with 250 small stock. He then reports that large villages were found at Otjivise and Omangette. In the Omuhonga valley Kuntz emphatically states: 'Under high acacias in thick green grass grazed hundreds of cattle and thousands of sheep; evidently I had got to the hitherto legendary Ovatschimba paradise ... For several hours I rode up the river, finding village upon village and water everywhere in the riverbed.'[2] For some Tjimba communities the number of cattle is mentioned. Accounts of large numbers of small stock in Kuntz's report suggest a rapid repastoralisation of the region. Kuntz estimated the number of people to have reached 5,000 in 1913.[3] While it is certainly doubtful to what extent these figures represent actual population figures, the assumption that the population rapidly increased between 1900 and 1915 is also underlined by oral accounts.

There are three possible solutions to this apparent puzzle of rapidly rising population figures: either (a) Hartmann and Franke grossly underestimated the population, (b) Kuntz overestimated population numbers, or (c) between Hartmann's and Kuntz's visits to the area the population increased due to immigration. I believe that the latter hypothesis may be closest to the truth. A number of households seem to have resettled from southern Angola to northern Namibia during the first decade of the twentieth century.[4] Some Herero families fleeing the atrocities of the German colonial war looked for a safe refuge in the

---

[1] NAN ADM 327.   [2] NAN ADM 327.
[3] Colonial officers and missionaries stationed in the Outjo District to the south of the Kaokoveld noted a significant increase in population (Rizzo 2012: 97–8).
[4] A similar process of resettlement from the Portuguese-controlled side of the Kavango River across the border to the German-controlled side took place at about the same time (Fleisch and Möhlig 2002: 26).

remote areas of the Kaokoveld.[5] The immigration into the Kaokoveld continued well into the 1910s and 1920s, when it was finally restricted by increasing border controls. There are some few hints that the German administration – in this case probably Colonel Franke – actively solicited the immigration of Herero-speaking herders from southern Angola. In an oral testimony by two elders recorded in 1994, it is mentioned that Kakurukouye (alias Kasupi) was presented with a gun, which was later named Mbandururwa and gained some prominence in oral testimonies. He is given the order to go to southern Angola and convince Tjimba and Herero to settle on the southern side of the Kunene in German colonial territory (Kozongombe Tjingee, Tjikumbamba Tjambiru in Bollig 1997). There might have been ample incentives for natives to migrate from southern Angola to north-western Namibia. Between 1898 and 1906 the Portuguese conducted military expeditions against several ethnic communities in south-western Angola. While Herero-speakers were usually aiding the colonial forces, their position in southern Angola was certainly uneasy. After 1906 the Portuguese military's attitude towards the region remained predatory to say the least; taxes were often collected under the threat of violence and corporal punishment was seemingly frequent. In addition, the tense relations between Portuguese administrators and military on the one hand and Dorsland Trekkers on the other may have acted as a push factor prompting emigration to north-western Namibia, which at that time seemed to be relatively free of colonial control. After 1911 the position of the local population vis-à-vis the Portuguese administration deteriorated further. In the aftermath of the liberal revolution in Portugal, colonial control was stepped up: coercive labour extraction, tax collections under the threat of violence, and violent suppression of any form of resistance became the order of the day. In contrast to pre-1911 times, the Portuguese administration now relied more often on its own police force. The overall situation of African mercenaries became more tenuous, and in 1917, after Thom's people allegedly raided a neighbouring African community in south-western Angola, a case was brought against Vita Thom. In order to

---

[5] Communities that had taken refuge in the inaccessible mountains of the Kaokoveld at the end of the nineteenth century descended once more to the plains, where livestock husbandry was easier due to better pasture and better access to water. These mountain-dwelling communities were possibly not accounted for in earlier reports.

evade a court hearing and possible incarceration, Thom fled across the river with a considerable number of people (Gewald 2011; Stals and Otto-Reiner 1999: 34ff.).

From archival sources and older ethnography we know that several groups of immigrants entered the Kaokoveld between 1910 and 1920. Rizzo (2012: 98–110) summarises German sources, which attest to a tripling of the population, from about 1,500 to c. 5,000 people, between 1910 and 1914. The biggest influx of people took place in 1916/17 (Stals and Otto-Reiner 1999: 38). In 1916 Vita Thom entered the Kaokoveld with his group.[6] Gewald (2011) describes how Thom's highly militarised group raided several local communities and allegedly killed dozens of people when entering the Kaokoveld. Thom's military superiority and the commando-style organisation of his group made him the most powerful broker in north-western Namibia. The South African military administration urged him to present himself in Windhoek, where he was given a stern warning to cooperate with the administration and was urged to settle down. On his way back to the northern Kaokoveld he was accompanied by a South African military unit under the command of Major Manning, whom he succeeded in convincing that only he, Vita Thom, could guarantee law and order in this remote setting. Manning clearly favoured Thom, who did not have any claim to traditional leadership, against other, traditional authorities, and urged the political establishment to accept Vita Thom as the local chief. In 1917, Vita Thom settled with a group of about 200 people at the wells of Otjijandjasemo.[7] His group consisted of Herero and Himba (especially Himba who had fled the Kaokoveld; Stals and Otto-Reiner 1999: 36) as well as Nama – four of Vita Thom's wives were Nama.[8] More Himba had returned with Muhona Katiti to

---

[6] While Stals and Otto-Reiner (1999), who rely on interviews with descendants of Vita Thom, emphasise that Vita Thom was entering into a barely settled region, supporting only a few resident forager communities, Gewald (2011), who relies mostly on archival records, points out Vita Thom's rather violent strategies and the replacement of populations.

[7] His group included prominent men who became influential political figures in the Kaokoveld over the next few decades: Edward Tjipepa (Vita Thom's brother), Martin Tjiheura, Moses Ndjai, Paul Zakekua, Willem Tjireye, Ngairo Muhenye, Gabriel Cabrito, Joel Kapi, George Hartley, and Adriaan Karipose.

[8] The archival files of the 1920s address those who had lived with the Dorsland Trekkers in Humpata and who had immigrated into north-western Namibia under Vita Thom's leadership as Oorlam (Bollig and Lang 1999).

the Kaokoveld, probably only a few years earlier. During his first years in the Kaokoveld, Vita Thom resettled twice: after a short sojourn in Otjijandjasemo he lived for some time in Ongongo at the Hoarusib, possibly with the intention of continuing on to Omaruru, where he wanted to stay with his maternal relatives (Stals and Otto-Reiner 1999: 47). After being informed by the administration that such a move would be unacceptable he returned to Otjijandjasemo, a place in the wider Omuhonga basin. According to oral accounts, there he met Muhona Katiti, who also settled in the basin, but who soon retreated to Epembe (see also Stals and Otto-Reiner 1999: 43). In the early 1920s the colonial government then decided that Muhona Katiti should discard his plans to return to Omuhonga (despite his claims that his ancestors had dwelled there) and that Otjijandjasemo should become the 'headquarters' of Vita Thom's community.

Throughout the 1910s and early 1920s Herero communities settling in the Outjo region retreated to the southern Kaokoveld in an effort to avoid confrontations with the expanding settler farms (Stals and Otto-Reiner 1999: 60; see also van Warmelo 1951: 20). In several places, earlier Tjimba inhabitants were displaced by immigrating Herero families. In Kaoko Otavi, for example, the small resident Tjimba community retreated to Omuhiva after some initial conflicts with immigrant Herero (see Rizzo 2007: 257). This resulted in a situation characterised by the occupation of major natural wells in the central and southern Kaokoveld by prominent and cattle-rich Herero *ovahona* ('big men') who usually commanded ethnically mixed groups of clients. Ethnic boundaries were transient and were often redefined through intermarriage. Populations that had previously settled at the waterholes relocated to other, smaller wells in the vicinity. The western and northern parts of the Kaokoveld did not offer major water sources and were relatively uninteresting for immigrant 'big men'. Here a few immigrating families – apparently often those with smaller cattle herds and a resident population – lived in smaller settlements and displayed higher degrees of mobility. Mbwanandja, the founding father of the chiefly clan then living in the Ombuku area, resettled in the early 1920s from the northern banks of the Kunene to the southern side.

By 1917, when Manning explored the Kaokoveld, a significant shift in settlement patterns and economic organisation had taken place. Whereas previous written sources as well as oral histories emphasise the importance of hunting and gathering in the region, Manning describes the population as predominantly pastoral. In 1917 Manning reports: 'Greater proportion of Kaokoveld population is pastoral without fixed abode but wanders about with stock from one watering place to another'.[9] Only six years later Shortridge reports that 'the Kaokoveld is very sparsely inhabited by nomadic Ovashimba Herero tribes that live chiefly by raising a sufficient number of goats and sheep for their own requirements'.[10] The immigration of some wealthy pastoral 'big men' from Southern Angola brought about not only an increase in the human population (Stals and Otto-Reiner 1999: 48–9) but also a significant increase in cattle numbers. Livestock-based strategies came to rely on large household herds of cattle and small stock in some households, while the majority of households subsisted on small-stock herds and foraging strategies in the early 1920s. Stals and Otto-Reiner (1999: 62) report that in the early 1920s Vita Thom's group and Muhona Katiti's group each owned 6,000–9,000 cattle and about 14,000 heads of small stock.[11] They describe Vita Thom's huge homestead, which was c. 250 m in diameter, contained some twenty-eight houses, and had large gardens (Stals and Otto-Reiner 1999: 50–1). The huge cattle herds were distributed between numerous livestock camps (Stals and Otto-Reiner 1999: 52). In many communities that sprang up between 1910 and 1920 at the major natural wells of the region, gardens became an important feature (for example in Otjijandjasemo, Ombazu, Okorosave, Kaoko Otavi, and Oruvandjei). These gardens supplied populous semi-sedentary communities with food, and also produced goods for trade. Rizzo (2012: 95) emphasises that tobacco grown in these gardens was traded widely, and the cultivation of tobacco became a pertinent strategy for women to gain access to livestock.

The following section attempts to reconstruct patterns of pastoral land use and mobility between the 1920s and the early 1950s.

---

[9] NAN SWAA 2516 A552/22; Manning Diary, p. 2.
[10] NAN SWAA 1331/198/6/2 Shortridge 'The Third Percy Sladen and Kaffrarian Museum Expedition "Ovamboland"'.
[11] Large numbers of small stock may also be attributable to a shift in pastoral strategies: after the Rinderpest epidemic of 1897 the communities of north-western Namibia had lost up to 95 per cent of their cattle. The focus on small stock may have been a response to this disaster.

5.2 Land Use in the First Half of the Twentieth Century

While the economy of the Kaokoveld's communities was shaped by subsistence foraging and commercial hunting at the end of the nineteenth century, after 1910 the sizes of small-stock herds increased, as did the number of cattle. While around 1920 the communities of the Kaokoveld were mainly addressed as small-stock herders, by the end of the 1920s the local population was described as cattle-herding and fully pastoral.[12] Gardening was restricted to a few places that offered abundant water from wells, such as Otjijandjasemo, Kaoko Otavi, and Sesfontein.

In the following I will provide a sketch of the pastoral tenure system as it existed between the 1910s and 1940s, i.e. during a period when the local population had been repastoralised but when herding did not yet rely on a network of boreholes. The information mainly relies on oral evidence from interviews with elders who had been youths during these decades. There is very little archival evidence describing the local tenure pattern. Written sources pertaining to the 1920s, 1930s, and 1940s mainly focus on mobility restrictions imposed by the colonial administration and hence, give some information on mobility patterns.

Between the 1910s and 1940s a system of pastoral resource management developed that was shaped by environmental factors, local power structures, and an encapsulating framework consisting of mobility and trade restrictions determined by the colonial administration. Pastoral mobility was influenced by seasonality and the competition between local 'big men', and from the mid-1920s onwards by boundaries and no-go zones set by the administration. The pastoral system was characterised by a pattern of seasonal transhumance. People and herds spent the entire dry season at focal settlements which were fitted with permanent water sources. During the rainy season (and not during the dry season as today) when pans and other seasonal water sources offered enough water, livestock camps moved out to graze distant pastures. Cattle then grazed in orbits around seasonal pools. Once these rain-dependent water sources went dry, the herds had to retreat to the main settlements along seasonal river courses and around permanent wells. In the Ondjete/Okorosave area, for example,

---

[12] Rizzo (2012: 93–102) offers a historically well-documented account of the repastoralisation process.

herds moved to pastures about 10–20 km to the south, where seasonal rivers and pans provided a multitude of water sources during the rainy season. They then returned to the permanent spring of Okorosave during the dry season.

In the northernmost parts of the Kaokoveld similar patterns of livestock-related mobility were established. In the Omuramba area households from the Ombuku River migrated to Omuramba with their large cattle herds during the rainy season, and on to Ondova with their oxen-herds. Once the water sources in these areas had been used they returned to the Ombuku River, where water could easily be found in the sandy deposits throughout the long dry season.

The group of users of specific pastoral resources was clearly defined. Households held tenure rights in specific places that had permanent water, whereas rainy-season grazing areas were loosely aligned with neighbourhoods. The narratives on tenure and mobility before the 1950s depict a fairly stable transhumant system. This, of course, does away with the turbulent political history of the region. Looking at both written and oral sources for details of the competition between leading figures for appropriate places of settlement, the violent annexation of some places by militarily superior groups and the large number of immigrants during the period of time suggests that the idea of a 'traditional' tenure system, as promulgated in interviews given today, as well as those conducted by colonial officials – a system based on kinship relations and signified by ancestral graves – depoliticises access to resources. While it is perfectly possible that some immigrants sought to occupy places they knew, or where they thought their ancestors had lived, many occupied places with which they had no prior relations. Only from the mid-1920s did a stable system of tenure and transhumance become established. The 'traditional' setup came into being in the 1920s during a phase when the colonial administration established fixed external and internal boundaries and sought to inhibit extensive livestock-related mobility. The transhumant system in which livestock herds were shifted from a few semi-permanent settlements to nearby rainy-season pastures was in line with the ideas of the colonial administration on herd management. In this sense the transhumant system was as much an adaptation to local ecological conditions as to the distribution of power between livestock-owning patrons and clients, and to the ideas of the colonial administration on tenure and mobility. When asked about the history of tenure, informants highlight livestock-dependent strategies; there are only a few accounts of the history of access to gardens and foraging resources.

Places with abundant permanent water sources were often dominated by powerful leaders. Vedder in 1914 met the local leader Tjongoha at Kaoko Otavi's permanent well, and reports that Tjongoha was an acknowledged leader in the environs of the place. Remarks like 'at Khairos waterhole live two Herero chiefs, Langman and Herman, both wealthy ... for they possess hundreds of cattle and large flocks of sheep' made in Deneys Reitz's travel account (Reitz 1943: 103, travelling in the mid-1920s) are revealing in that they link waterholes with political leadership and wealth in cattle. Rizzo (2012: 103–10) describes that the repastoralisation process brought about inequality and stratification. At Okorosave, Kaoko Otavi, and Ombuku the waterholes were dominated by powerful leaders. The Ombuku waterholes were settled by the Himba leader Mbwanandja and his kin. They had resettled from southern Angola to northern Namibia in the 1910s and had selected Ombuku as 'their' place on account of several ancestral graves there. These they took as evidence of their ancestors having dwelt in the very same place before the exodus to southern Angola in the 1870s or 1880s. Leaders migrating into the Kaokoveld either from Angola or from the settler frontier in the Kamanjab/Outjo region targeted permanent waterholes in the Kaokoveld as places to settle. In many cases an acknowledged leader, wealthy in livestock, was surrounded by relatives and clients.[13] Leaders mentioned in oral traditions and archival sources for the 1920s and 1930s typically had either been mercenary leaders in Portuguese Angola (e.g. Vita Thom, Muhona Katiti), had been engaged in the Portuguese colonial economy in other ways (e.g. Adrian Karipose), had close contact with the leading clique at Sesfontein (e.g. Kakurukouye), or had their origins in prominent Herero families fleeing the genocidal war of 1904–7 (e.g. the Humu family of Kaoko Otavi). Usually these men were wealthy in cattle, and owned horses and guns. There is some evidence that leaders competed for the more bounteous wells in the area. Oral traditions vividly portray how Vita Thom and Muhona Katiti, a second 'big man' and former mercenary leader returning from Angola, competed for the

---

[13] Interview L. Bleckmann with Kephas Kuroroo, Ongongo, November 2007 in reference to Vita Thom. The informant states that 'he [Vita Thom] gave the cattle to the people that were amongst his group'.

springs of Otjijandjasemo (on the political economy and organisation of these returnees see Bollig 1998a; Gewald 2011; Stals and Otto-Reiner 1999: 42ff.). The conflict was finally settled by the incipient colonial administration in the early 1920s, in favour of Vita Thom. Similar conflicts arose around the wells of Kaoko Otavi and Okorosave. While in Otjijandjasemo two immigrant 'big men' competed for a plentiful well, in the Kaoko Otavi and Okorosave cases newcomers competed with long-time residents. In some cases the earlier residents (often referred to as Tjimba) moved out of these places: the withdrawal of the Tjimba leader Upani from Kaoko Otavi to Omuhiva is perhaps the most widely reported of these cases. Similar processes of replacement seemingly took place in Okorosave, Oruvandjei, and Ombombo.

The economy of these newly emerging settlements was peculiar. The homesteads of 'big men' were sedentary. Stals and Otto-Reiner (1999: 52f.) state that while Vita Thom's homestead at the hot spring of Otjijandjasemo was indeed large, the livestock enclosure, despite Thom's sizeable wealth, was rather small. Only a few milking cattle were kept at the homestead. The majority of the livestock were kept at a number of cattle camps in the wider region. Gardens were important assets, and were cultivated along with maize, pumpkins, and millet. Rizzo (2012: 106ff.) describes the great importance of agricultural activities and points out that 'spring and rain gardens both were used to sustain subsistence nutrition needs and enabled women and men to barter for goods they could not acquire locally'. Tobacco grown in such gardens became a major good for exchange. While homesteads before the 1920s tended to be rather small and mobile, now a few dense village-like settlements with permanent huts and more than 100 inhabitants sprang up. Unlike settlements in other parts of Namibia these villages lacked schools, mission stations, and hospitals. Applications by missionary societies to establish a station in the Kaokoveld were regularly turned down until the mid-twentieth century.

I will shortly address salient features of the pre-1950s common pool resource (CPR) management system, which was established in the 1910s and 1920s. This description relies on oral testimonies. Elders depicted the pre-1950s system as stable and resting upon an institutional framework embedded in notions of kinship and ancestral beliefs. While in some oral traditions conflicts between leaders were described at length, elders would label this category of traditions as *omapolotika* (the history of politics). When talking about tenure systems they had to rely on another type of testimony referred to as *ombazu* (tradition). These traditions typically do not take any account of political strife and conflict. They depict a uniform, non-contested, tradition-based resource tenure system: Households 'owned' specific places and a clearly defined and numerically small number of households managed pastures together. The heads of these place-owning households are addressed as *oveni vehi*, 'owners of the earth/land'. Transhumant mobility was regular and predictable during average-rainfall years. The absence of water in large tracts of land narrowed down choices for mobility during the major part of the year significantly. There were apparently two patterns of social bonding associated with tenure rights to permanent water sources. Water points were usually associated with a 'big man' (*omuhona*). Patrilineal relatives were often attached to his homestead and lived in the close vicinity of the acknowledged leader. Additionally clients joined the homesteads of 'big men' and squatted in the environs of the waterhole. Typically clients were poorer herders and/or foragers who often acted as shepherds to more endowed households. The character of the water source apparently laid the basis for political dynamics. It was relevant whether the water source was a single abundant natural well (like in Kaoko Otavi, Okorosave, or Otjijandjasemo), or a series of wells along a dry river course (like along the Hoarusib, Omuhonga, and Otjitanga rivers). In the latter case homesteads spread out along the river, while in the former, households congregated around the water source to constitute village-like structures. It is especially the larger water points which allowed for some agriculture and sedentariness, and thus became foci of conflict. For the larger wells political domination (e.g. 'many guns', 'good relations with the colonial administration') is emphasised in oral accounts, while for others (especially in the Himba context) ritual domination (e.g. 'presence of ancestral graves') is privileged in explanations of why some people had access rights to a well and others did not.

A senior male member of one of the families with a long settlement history in the area was regarded as the *omuni wehi*, the 'owner', or – perhaps better – 'guardian' of the land. This relation between a household and a place was given a historical dimension of longevity by numerous graves at which ancestors were venerated. In the Ombuku case, Mbwanandja was regarded as the *omuni wehi* and his brothers and paternal cousins gained legitimate access to land through him. He tied his status to the presence of ancestral graves in Ombuku. Access to water and pastures was inherited through different channels: the typical pattern was that a son inherited rights to a place from his father. Matrilineal channels were used to obtain access to grazing too: young men frequently herded their animals on the land of their mother's brother, the person they would possibly inherit their cattle from later on in their lives. To accept client status with a wealthier patron was another way to attain access to a place. Until the 1930s the number of stockless or near-stockless pastoralist foragers was still quite high, and it was especially individuals and households finding themselves in such circumstances who sought access to wealthier households.

We know little about rules of resource protection for the pre-1950 period. Several informants claimed that such rules were not necessary as there were very few people and even fewer livestock. The water sources in the rainy-season grazing areas were usually depleted a few months after the rains. This brought a rapid end to the exploitation of pastures. Without water these pastures could no longer be used, and of course there was no need to develop rules of protection or equality of access for such pastures. Informants also stressed that there were few conflicts over grazing, while conflicts over places with permanent water sources between leaders are prominent in oral lore. Informants did not report any specific rules governing the mode of use of water points. Access to water points was channelled through access to the community and possibly the affiliation to a local 'big man'.

There are no detailed reports on the state of pastures for the 1920s and 1930s. In the late 1920s the police officer Cogill reported some overgrazing in the central Kaokoveld around permanent waterholes,[14] but otherwise administrators rarely made comments on the state of pastures. Oral accounts, however, do make rather explicit statements about earlier states of the vegetation. Looking at recent results from pasture ecology we may deduce that the heavy impact of grazing around permanent waterholes may have led to significant changes in the structure of the bush and herb vegetation. Klintenberg and Verlinden (2008: 14) observed massive changes in the vegetation around permanent waterholes in places with high grazing intensity in the neighbouring Omusati region. They noted that the frequency of

[14] NAN PTJ Monthly Reports of Police Station Tjimhaka, Cogill in May 1928 reports that 'the reserves have been badly overstocked'. His observations were made during a drought, however.

grazing-tolerant species, mainly annual grasses, e.g. *Schmidtia kalahariensis* and *Aristida stipioides*, increases while that of the majority of palatable species, mainly perennial grasses, decreases. It is especially *Schmidtia kalahariensis*, an annual grass, which replaces perennial grasses such as *Stipagrostis uniplumis*, *Antephora pubescens*, and *Eragrostis trichophora* in areas with high grazing intensity.[15] The cover of annual grasses, however, is fairly resilient to grazing pressure. The scanty data I have on vegetation changes in the first half of the twentieth century, and the data from Klintenberg and Verlinden's study, run counter to basic assumptions of the disequilibrium model, which suggests that changes in the grass-herb cover are not attributable to grazing pressure. With Illius and O'Connor (1999, also Klintenberg and Verlinden 2008: 17) I argue that key resources such as water points and their surrounding are hotspots of vegetation change in semi-arid rangelands where herbivory does have an effect on species composition. Beyond these hotspots of vegetation change, rangelands were shaped by extensive grazing and fire management. This kind of pasture use – heavy grazing pressure over a short period of time during the growth period, followed by resting for the remainder of the year – is conducive to the growth of perennials. In many ways such a grazing pattern copies that of wild herbivores. These rangelands were apparently burned regularly. Planned veld fires burned off the old parts of perennial grasses and provided space for new growth in the rainy season. Most perennial grasses are fire-resistant, and a thick and productive pasture constituted by perennial grasses depends on regular burning (Zimmermann 2009). The first half of the twentieth century then saw the emergence of an environmental infrastructure shaped by a particular mode of grazing, transhumant mobility of domesticated and non-domesticated herbivores, and frequent burning.

---

[15] Klintenberg and Verlinden concentrated their study on wells drilled in the early 1990s, and about a decade later profound changes in grazing were already observable; i.e. the vegetation reacted rather quickly to permanent grazing pressure in the Omusati case.

6 | *The Politics of Encapsulation: Game Protection, Instituting Borders, and Controlling Mobility*

Since the first decade of the twentieth century the colonial administration tried to control the mobility of people and livestock moving within the Kaokoveld or into and out of the Kaokoveld. The South African administration effectively encapsulated the Kaokoveld, instigating strict border controls. Mobility within the Kaokoveld was also controlled. Some areas were declared no-go zones, in which any settlement was prohibited, in order to create buffer-zones between the Kaokoveld on the one hand and Portuguese Angola and the commercial ranching zone to the south on the other. Though the administration made numerous and at times harsh attempts to control mobile livestock husbandry, livestock numbers increased. Whereas at the beginning of the period in question, large cattle herds were concentrated in the hands of a few 'big men', in the early 1950s the number of cattle had more than doubled and most households were in the possession of some cattle. References to hunting and gathering, which is mentioned as an important livelihood strategy for the entire population of the Kaokoveld in the first decades of the twentieth century, are nearly absent from reports in the 1950s.

Many measures taken by the colonial administration during the first half of the twentieth century had direct impact on social-ecological relations. I will first depict the policies of the German administration and then continue to address the efforts of the South African administration to control mobility, trade, diseases, and environmental management (e.g. fires).

6.1 Game Protection and the Establishment of the Etosha Park in German Times

The major project of the German administration in the Kaokoveld was game protection. The sale of ivory from the German territory had been prohibited in 1892, and the unauthorised killing of large game was

The Politics of Encapsulation

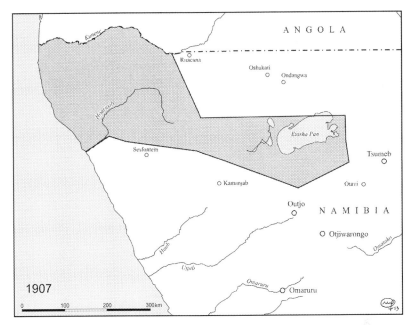

Map 6.1 Etosha Park alias Game Park No. 2 in 1907.
Source: Dieckmann (2007)

severely punished (von Francois 1899: 107). In 1902 a hunting proclamation was issued introducing a closed season and hunting licences (Dieckmann 2007: 74). In 1907 the enormous Game Park No. 2 (see Map 6.1) was established as one of three game reserves in the German colony. Governor von Lindequist announced it to comprise a massive area encompassing the entire Kaokoveld:[1]

On the basis of § 15 of the protectorate law and § 5 of the court order of the Imperial Chancellor of the 27th December 1903 it is decreed:
As game sanctuary are designated

§ 1 2.) The area south, west and north-west of the Etosha-Pan in the Districts Grootfontein and Outjo, with the following border-lines:
In the East and in the South, the western boundary of the Ovamboland from the Kunene to Osohama. From there on to Koantsab and via Ondowa, Chudob, Obab, Aigab, Vib, Chorub to Gub. From Gub

---

[1] NAN ZBU M II, C.1 Wildreservate Generalia, also quoted in Dieckmann (2007: 76).

via Otjokaware (Kowares) to Oachab. From Oachab down the Hoarusib River to the Ocean. In the West it is bordered by the Ocean. In the North from the Kunene to the Ovamboland.

§ 2 The exercise of any hunt, also on springbok and smaller game is in those game reserves described under §1 only permitted with the written consent of the Government.

§ 3 The traffic with vehicles of any kind within the game reserve is only permitted with the written consent of the next district-administration.

§ 5 The permit (to enter the area) is to be taken along and to be shown to the police on request.

§ 6 Contraventions against § 2 of this ordinance will result in a monetary penalty of 300–5000M or with imprisonment of up to 3 months or a combination of both, contraventions against § 3 will result in a monetary penalty of up to 150M or imprisonment of up to 6 weeks.

§ 7 Exempted from the regulations of § 2 are the owners of farms lying within the game reserve, if these farms are inhabited and agriculturally active. They are exempted within the boundaries of the farm, if the hunting directly contributes to the subsistence of the farming business.

This ordinance will be active from the 1st April 1907 onwards.

The game reserve covered not only the Etosha Pan, but also the entire Kaokoveld between the Kunene River in the north and the Hoarusib River in the south. Hunting was completely prohibited in this area throughout the year without the permission of the Governor. This comprised a complete ban on the hunting of giraffe, buffalo, eland, and kudu as well as springbok and other smaller gazelles. All traffic within the reserve required written permission of the district head offices. The ordinance did not preclude freehold farms being established in the park area, and existing farmers were not evicted.

The legislation first of all targeted the activities of white commercial hunters rather than subsistence hunting by Africans. Dieckmann (2007: 95–7) argues that, for example, hunting by Hai//om was hardly prosecuted by the German colonial administrators. Likewise, army officers like Franke touring the Kaokoveld did not take any notice of native hunting, but rather were trying to intercept Boer commercial hunters. In fact the German administration not only attempted to track down poachers but also dealt with requests by German hunters and travellers to shoot game in the park. In August 1914 for example, the *Kaiserlicher Bezirksamtmann* in Outjo decided that the request of the farmer-cum-hunter Steinhardt to shoot elephants which had allegedly

The Politics of Encapsulation

damaged his farm property was rejected.[2] Steinhardt was one of those 'farmers' settling at the frontier of the farm-zone, probably to take advantage of the frontier situation by venturing into hunting and smuggling, and probably trading with the local population.[3] On other occasions, however, the hunting of game was allowed. The surveyor Volkmann, for example, who surveyed parts of the Kaokoveld for the Kaoko Land- und Minengesellschaft, was allowed to shoot some game to supply his team with meat. Interestingly, in the approval the officer argues that Volkmann's request should be accepted because it would hardly be possible for him to buy small stock from the local Tjimba[4] – another hint at the small numbers of livestock in the Kaokoveld at that time. Police officers in Okaukuejo were also allowed to hunt gazelles for subsistence use, as was missionary Vedder on his expedition to the Kaokoveld. There is little evidence that the establishment of Game Park No. 2 influenced local hunting practices in any significant way. It is doubtful whether most of the local population realised at all that they were now inhabiting the world's largest protected area. They would have realised, however, that the German administration tracked down commercial elephant hunters and occasionally imprisoned them. As a consequence large-scale elephant hunting came to an end, and with it an opportunity for temporary employment for the local population. Local hunters had bartered ivory with kings of various Ovambo communities. There is no direct evidence in colonial files that German officers attempted to intercept such forms of trade. In 1914 Vedder reports that such trade was still active and an important source of income for the Kaokoveld's population. The game reserve also seems to have attracted early tourists. In 1913 the farmer Carl Schlettwein complains about the increasing number of visitors to the reserve,

---

[2] The *Kaiserlicher Bezirksamtmann* in Outjo writes: 'I do not consent to this request. Steinhardt settled in Otjikuare against the expressed wish of the administration right at the border of the game reserve. He positioned himself in a place which is not well suited to farming but may have looked promising to him due to its proximity to the game reserve. Steinhardt has been punished once before for a hunting offence. A second case connected to illegal hunting in the game reserve has been lodged against him.' NAN ZBU MII C3, my translation.

[3] Steinhardt documented his hunting adventures in the Kaokoveld in a book that contains much on his hunting exploits and very little on the people of the Kaokoveld (Steinhardt 1922).

[4] NAN ZBU 3/8/1914 Kaiserlicher Bezirksamtmann Outjo an das Kaiserliche Gouvernement Windhuk.

who – according to him – behaved badly towards the local population and apparently forced them to act as porters or scouts.[5]

6.2 The Colonial Encapsulation of the Kaokoveld during South African Rule

From 1915 to 1920 South West Africa was administered under military rule and in 1921 the former German colony was given as a mandated territory to South Africa (Emmett 1999). While during the first two years of South African rule in Namibia the Kaokoveld was not administered, in 1917 the South African Army sent Major Manning to the Kaokoveld. In 1917 Manning confiscated some seventy guns, mainly from Muhona Katiti's people, and in 1919 he took another twenty from Muhona Katiti's group and some ninety from Vita Thom's. In total some 155 guns were seized from people in the area in an effort to reduce the chances of a rebellion, to quell intercommunity conflicts, and to limit poaching (Stals and Otto-Reiner 1999: 45). Disarmament probably had some effect on social-ecological relations by reducing the rate of hunting. In fact, intensive game hunting, which had been typical before 1910, did not continue into the 1920s. Manning also tried to make sense of the political system he found during his two campaigns in 1917 and 1919. He ascertains that he was not able to find 'distinct communities or tribes there'.[6]

The South African administration immediately involved itself in local power struggles. In 1917 Manning inaugurated Vita Thom as the paramount chief of the Kaokoveld when he accompanied Thom on his return from Windhoek with an army unit and immediately proceeded to disarm local communities (Gewald 2011). While disarming Muhona Katiti's group in 1917, however, Manning decided to leave guns with Vita Thom's entourage for the time being. In early 1919 (some months before Manning's second disarmament campaign) a

---

[5] NAN MII C 1 Wildreservate Generalia. In a letter dated 28 September 1913 to the Kaiserliche Bezirksamt Outjo, the farmer Carl Schlettwein, who owned a farm near Sesfontein, complained about increasing numbers of visitors to the game reserve. He argued that they were not well accustomed to local communities and that their expeditions were not at all well-equipped. They forced people into their services according to his observations. He suggested that the number of visitors should be limited by stipulating that a deposit had to be paid to the district headquarters in Outjo.

[6] NAN SWAA 2516 A552/22 Major Manning's Report Vol. 1. p. 70.

The Politics of Encapsulation

meeting in Outjo between Vita Thom, Muhona Katiti, and Kasupi – the three of whom had been acknowledged as leaders by this time – was arranged after Muhona Katiti had handed in an official complaint against Vita Thom, who had allegedly stolen cattle from him and his followers.[7] At the meeting statements were taken disclosing Vita Thom's involvement in illicit ivory trading, and his close contacts with Portuguese traders.[8] Colonial reports from 1917 to 1923 make it very clear that local leaders tried to engage with and to manipulate the colonial administration in order to gain benefits in local power squabbles.

The South African administration subsequently enacted a policy of encapsulation, which corresponded to the policy of indirect rule (Bollig 1998a, 1998b). Proclamation No. 40 of 1920 defined the boundaries of Outjo District so as to include the entire Kaokoveld, but the Native Commissioner of Ovamboland was to administer the area. In 1923 four smaller reserves with clear-cut boundaries were delineated within the Kaokoveld:[9] the southern Sesfontein reserve and then reserves for the three acknowledged tribal leaders. In 1927 the administration tried to count the people of the Kaokoveld for the first time: of a total of 3,182 people counted, 26 per cent resided in Oorlog's reserve, 13 per cent in Muhona Katiti's reserve, and 12 per cent in that of Kahewa Nawa (the successor of Kasupi alias Kakurukouye), while about 49 per cent of the population stayed outside the reserves. While only Himba and Tjimba were counted for Muhona Katiti's reserve, Oorlog's reserve was more heterogeneous, with Himba, Tjimba, Herero, and a few Oorlam and Nama people. These figures underestimated the population. The police station at Tjimuhaka, from which the census was conducted, had just been opened, and had to survey a vast

---

[7] Vita Thom turned up with some 30 followers, Muhona Katiti with 36 followers, and Jaripo, who took part in the meeting as a representative of Kasupi, with 16 followers. The large number of people, who must all have travelled over more than 400 km on horseback and by donkey to this meeting, vividly shows that local actors were keen to involve the colonial administration in their conflicts.

[8] NAN SWAA 2516 A552/22 Office of the Military Magistrate, Windhoek to Secretary for the Protectorate, 20/3/1919.

[9] 'Oorlog's portion westwards the watering place Otjitanga, Hamalemba, Omangete and Ombakaha with Otjijandjasemo as headquarters; and (2) for Mahuna Katiti on the East side of the line his old headquarters Hondoto and other places ...'. NAN SWAA 552 Native Com. Manning to The Secretary Windhoek, 21/5/1923 'Kaokoveld: Tribal and General Affairs: Connecting Routes with Ovamboland', p. 5.

area (Bollig 2006: 71). Only two years later some 1,200 more people were counted, indicating that earlier estimates rating the population at c. 5,000 were not far from the actual numbers.

These reserves were cut much too small, and by no means described any meaningful radius of pastoral activities. The majority of the Kaokoveld's inhabitants did reside outside these reserves (Rizzo 2012: 160) and were not directly under the leadership of one of the officially recognised chiefs – despite government policies trying to institute other conditions. In 1951 van Warmelo commented that 'the setting aside of these tiny areas must have been done in complete darkness as to actual conditions and the measure was never related to reality' (van Warmelo 1951: 4) – this was shortly after those reserves had been abolished.

The pass laws of 1923 made mobility from the Kaokoveld to the south extremely difficult. People wanting to move out of or into the Kaokoveld from the Police Zone had to formally apply to the Chief Native Commissioner in Windhoek.[10] While such laws were occasionally subverted by the issuing of alternative passes through the Truppenspieler movement (see Figure 6.1), the strict enforcement of the pass laws contributed significantly to the isolation of the region (Bollig 1998a: 511). For about three decades, colonial policies in the Kaokoveld were characterised by an enforced policy of encapsulation, the control of mobility into and out of the area as well as within the region, and indirect rule through a few tribal leaders. The apparent stability of this early colonial setup was closely related to the long-term reign of Native Commissioner Carl Hahn, who structured and controlled colonial politics in northern Namibia. His political aim was to contain mobility and to isolate the communities of the Kaokoveld from communities in Ovamboland, south-western Angola and central Namibia. His motives were manifold: while on the one hand Hahn apparently believed that acculturation was negatively influencing the quality of migrant labour from the region (which remained for the Kaokoveld insignificant throughout this period anyhow), he also thought that the natural beauty of the landscape and its fauna could only be maintained as long as this 'last frontier' was kept isolated (Hayes 2000: 53ff.).

A further goal of colonial policy was to retain the Kaokoveld as a buffer-zone for future territorial politics of the colony: in the 1930s

[10] Bollig (1998a: 510) provides several quotes from archival documents showing how arduous it was to get such passes.

The Politics of Encapsulation

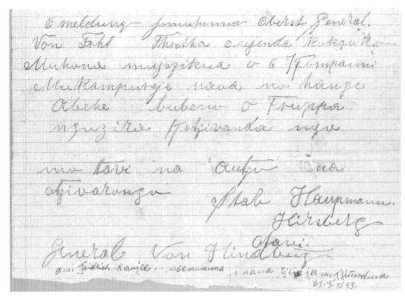

Figure 6.1 A pass created by the Truppenspieler movement. Intercepted by police in the Kaokoveld in the early 1930s, it is signed by 'Stab Hauptmann Hirsburg' and 'General von Hindburg' and recommends the 'omuhona Oberst General von Frh Trotha travelling to Otavi, Outjo and Otjivarongo'.
Source: NAN NAO 31

there were plans to annex part of the Kaokoveld for an extension of the settler zone, and in the 1940s the possibility was seriously contemplated of moving all Herero from the reserves in eastern Namibia to the Kaokoveld in order to create more space for settlers in eastern Namibia. These plans may also serve as an explanation why the reserves for African communities were cut so small in the 1920s.

Steven van Wolputte has commented on the three initial decades of South African colonial rule in the Kaokoveld and has pointed out that livestock (especially cattle) were at the intersection of colonial bureaucracy and local population (van Wolputte 2004: 153). He argued that as a consequence of a number of measures directed at the herds of Kaokovelders (control of pastoral mobility, culling of diseased livestock, culling as a punishment for transgressions of colonial laws and rules), cattle herds diminished and livestock husbandry was severely hampered. I argue here that although the policy of containment and encapsulation severely curtailed the agency of the Kaokoveld's pastoralists, it did not hinder (and perhaps even contributed to) the expansion of pastoralism in the region. While at the beginning of South African colonial rule the Kaokoveld's inhabitants were largely described as small-stock herders, and reports testify to the relevance of hunting and gathering, by the mid-1950s by far the majority of inhabitants of the Kaokoveld held significant numbers of cattle. In numerical terms: while the total number of cattle in the Kaokoveld may have been around 20,000 in the 1910s, in 1955 the number had reached about 100,000; in the same period the human population only increased from about 4,000 to 6,000. While travellers in the early 1920s reported that small stock were the main subsistence base of the Kaokoveld's communities, in the early 1950s van Warmelo commented that 'the Kaokoveld may be regarded as entirely belonging to the cattle folk' (van Warmelo 1951: 9). Already during the 1920s and 1930s most activities of the colonial government were directed at cattle, their mobility, their health, and their exchange value. Little attention was given to small stock, gardens, or foraged resources. In this way administrators were directly confronted with those locals who owned substantial numbers of cattle: these were typically male, seniors, and belonged to a wealthy stratum of the society. The administration hardly interacted with poorer people or with women, who to a much higher degree relied on small stock, on gardens, and on gathered food. Van Wolputte, however, is certainly right when pointing out that 'from this period ... stems the idea of Kaokoveld as a remote and isolated desert wilderness inhabited by traditionalist pastoralists, whereas the "isolation" and "subsistence economy" of these herders were a consequence of colonial rule rather than a "natural characteristic" of the landscape and its inhabitants' (van Wolputte 2004: 157).

While state impact on the development of environmental infrastructure was pertinent in the 1920s to the early 1950s, the factual presence of the colonial administration within the region was minimal. The Native Commissioner travelled from Ondangwa to the Kaokoveld once or twice a year. Between 1926 and 1938 there was a small police station guarding the ford at Swartboois Drift. Only during those times when administrative measures to resettle communities or to contain contagious livestock diseases were undertaken did some more administrative staff roam the Kaokoveld. In general the colonial administration was very much dependent on the collaboration of a handful of colonial chiefs whom the administration had installed. Only during the late 1930s did the colonial bureaucracy become more manifest, when a chiefly council was introduced and Opuwo was selected as an administrative centre. This council met regularly with the administration in Opuwo. While previously direct visits by police officers and native affairs officers at chiefly homesteads had been frequent and had underlined the highly personalised relations between administrator and chief, now a formal council met at the headquarters of the administration. Opuwo was founded in 1938 and a Native Officer was placed there with some administrative staff. The foundation of Opuwo as a new District headquarters, and Proclamation No. 10 of 1939, which created the new Kaokoveld District and established a court at Opuwo (van Warmelo 1951: 2), then heralded a new period in which colonial impact was much more direct.

6.3 The Control of Mobility

The German colonial government had done fairly little until 1914 to control or to contain pastoral mobility. The disappropriation of Sesfontein's herders in 1906 and of the few remaining Herero herders in the Outjo region after the German genocidal war against communities in central Namibia was not directed at the mobility of herders, but directly and wilfully destroyed the livelihood of pastoral people. Within the Kaokoveld, however, no borders were instituted and no attempts were made to control mobility. From the beginning the South African government showed that it was determined to administer the Kaokoveld in a much tighter way. In 1917 and 1919 Manning attempted to institute a colonial order: While his major task was to disarm the local population he also lectured them on the evils of fires, the unacceptability of hunting, and the governmental prohibition against crossing the Kunene River into south-western Angola. He threatened locals with severe punishments should they contravene his orders. Later the boundary between the Kaokoveld and the Ovamboland was instituted, and any migrations across this border were prohibited. At the same time the boundary to the south was proclaimed, and any movement with livestock into the Police Zone (the zone of white settler farmers) was sternly prohibited.

The Southern Boundary

By proclamation No. 40 of 1920 the boundaries of the Outjo District were defined as including the whole of the Kaokoveld. The Native Commissioner of Ovamboland, based at Ondangwa, was to administer this vast area. This government order included definitions of the southern border of the Kaokoveld, which after 1920 changed little (Government of South Africa 1963: 89). After the pass laws of 1923 had been imposed, crossing the southern boundary of the Kaokoveld in either direction meant undergoing a tiresome process of applications. It was impossible to cross this boundary with livestock. All permits had to be issued by high-ranking administrative staff in Windhoek, while district officials were only allowed to endorse these documents (see Bollig 1998a: 510).[11] Despite these major obstacles, the people of the Kaokoveld managed to stay in touch with relatives in central Namibia. Archival records show that at least since the late 1920s the Truppenspieler movement (Werner 1990) found supporters in the Kaokoveld. Delegates from Okahandja and Windhoek visited their compatriots in the Kaokoveld and spread the ideas of the movement (see Figure 6.1). However, the containment of social relations by the colonial bureaucracy contributed to the conceptualisation of the Kaokoveld as an isolated social entity.

The isolation of the Kaokoveld became more severe when between 1929 and 1931 the populations of the southern parts of the Kaokoveld were relocated to the central Kaokoveld in order to create an easily controllable no-man's land between tribal reserve and settler zone (see also Rizzo 2012: 152ff.).[12] Plans for such a move had already been discussed in the mid-1920s, when the possibilities of expanding settler farming into the Kaokoveld had been considered within the administration. In 1929 these plans were set in motion in order to create a

---

[11] Bollig (1998a: 510) reports on the ideas of containment and control guiding these strict principles of issuing travelling passes. While male workers were welcomed they had to obtain passes first. There was a general reluctance to issue any passes to women.

[12] Native Commissioner Hahn pleaded with the Secretary in Windhoek to leave the task of relocation completely to his office and to prevent the police officers in Kamanjab from taking part in the relocation. NAN NAO 28 Officer in Charge, Native Affairs Ovamboland to Secretary for South West Africa, Windhoek 23/11/1929.

'neutral zone between Kamanjab and Ombombo':[13] 393 men, 448 women, 360 children (at that time about a quarter of the Kaokoveld's population), 7,289 cattle and 22,176 sheep and goats were moved from places such as Omatendeka, Kaross, Otjovazandu, and Otjokavare in the southern Kaokoveld and were settled at Otjitunduwa, Otuzemba, Ombombo, and Kaoko Otavi in the central Kaokoveld.[14] A few boreholes were blasted by a police officer stationed for two years in the region to supervise the move. The blasting had to be partially paid for by the pastoralists themselves.[15] The shifting of about 1,200 people to the north of a line running east–west through Ombombo was one of the major planned forced relocations in Namibia's colonial history. The forced relocation was especially harsh as it was enacted in the middle of a major drought. People had congregated around the few remaining wells and were easy targets for the officers. Continued drought conditions in late 1929 and 1930 led to repeated attempts of relocated households to re-enter the neutral zone, and in 1930 Hahn had to agree to temporary permits to graze cattle in the zone. The outbreak of lungsickness in April 1930, however, hardened Hahn's stance and alarmed settlers in the Outjo District. The state veterinarian now strongly recommended the prohibition of any livestock movements in the neutral zone, and Hahn issued an order that any cattle found in the zone would be shot. Government Notice 178 of 1930 formally defined the neutral zone and laid the ground for a highly repressive colonial policy in the southern Kaokoveld, a space declared off-limits by government decrees (Rizzo 2012: 127ff.). During the next few years, waterholes in the unoccupied stretch between Ombombo and the border of the Police Zone were carefully watched to prevent

---

[13] NAN NAO 28 Officer in Charge, Native Affairs Ovamboland to Secretary for South West Africa, Windhoek 23/11/1929; 'neutral zone extending from Kamanjab to Ombombo'.

[14] There are no reports of outright violence against the local population to make them move; however, the acting police officer Hillebrand reported that locals were reluctant to move: 'I had to use some persuasion to a few natives because I could see that it was hard on some of the old boys who were so to say rooted to the places where they resided but being able to talk to them in their own language I managed to get them to see things in another light and so they shifted' (NAN NAO 28; Extract from Monthly Reports for months of May and June 1929; Post Commander SWA Police Tshimhaka).

[15] NAN NAO 28 Native Commissioner Ovamboland to Const. Cogill, Otjitunduwa Police Post, 16/9/1930. Hahn makes clear to Cogill that natives have to pay for blasting the wells.

pastoralists from secretly reoccupying such places, which they apparently did, according to the many complaints of colonial officers travelling the area. The initial plan to put all the relocated people under the authority of Chief Vita Thom was soon abandoned.[16] In April 1931 Hahn, referring to herds that had re-entered the zone, issued a threat: 'If Langman, in spite of repeated warnings has allowed this to happen through disregard of instructions then he will have to bear the consequences. I am asking the Secretary that the stock thus concerned be shot without further talk.'[17] But in 1932 another patrol of the zone gave evidence that several families had moved yet again into the area. Again people were expelled and punished.[18] The area remained contested: during the drought year 1939 several Herero families applied once more to make use of the water points at Otjovazandu and Khowarib, right within the zone – this time their application was rejected.[19] Only a small number of foragers remained in the far western parts of the Kaokoveld in the neutral zone. They were estimated to number less than 500 people and were thought to be negligible when it came to the fight against contagious bovine pleuropneumonia (CBPP).[20] The move of about 25 per cent of the Kaokoveld's human population, of about 30 per cent of its cattle, and of more than 50 per cent of its small stock aggravated stocking densities in the central Kaokoveld. In a report written in May 1929 police officer Hillebrand concludes: 'For the amount of water that is available in the northern Kaokoveld I consider the country is very much overstocked. Lions, leopards, wild dogs, wolves, etc. take a heavy toll of stock. To a great

[16] NAN NAO 28 Officer in Charge, Native Affairs Ovamboland to Secretary for South West Africa, Windhoek 31/12/1929 and NAN NAO 28 Officer in Charge, Native Affairs, Ovamboland, Ondangwa to the Secretary for South West Africa 8/3/1930.
[17] NAN NAO Native Commissioner Ovamboland to Post Commander Tshimhaka SWA Police, 24/4/1931.
[18] NAN SWAA Kaokoveld A552/1 Monthly Reports 1926–1938; reports from Post Commander Tshimhaka to Hahn, then to Secretary General in Windhoek.
[19] NAN SWAA 2513 File 552/1 Monthly Reports 1938–1952.
[20] 'These wild natives do not own stock of any consequence. They have no cattle, although here and there they have a few goats, they live principally on honey, veld kos, roots, mice, rats and such species of wildlife as they can manage to trap or hunt with bows and arrows. They have no rifles, because of their wild state it is practically impossible to get into touch with them even at the approach of more civilized natives they scatter into the ridges of the rough mountains and hills.' NAN SWAA Kaokoveld A552/1 Monthly Reports 1926–1938; 5/6/1929.

extent elephants are responsible for the shortage of water in bad years ...'.[21]

The archival sources do not say a lot about the reasons for this major move: one reason voiced by officials was the alleged danger of native stock infecting settler stock with contagious livestock diseases. The argument voiced with some fervour by Hahn and his staff was that the settler zone had to be kept free of disease. Behind this openly voiced argument two plans became tangible a few years later – neither of which materialised – and both may already have been discussed in the colonial bureaucracy at that time. In the late 1930s and early 1940s the government apparently contemplated opening up the southern Kaokoveld to white settlement. In instructions to the newly appointed officer-in-charge in the Kaokoveld in 1939, A. M. Bernard, it was explicitly stated that he had to prepare the land to be opened up for white settlement, which would have implicated further moves.[22] Some few years later again, another ambitious plan was discussed within the administration. In order to create more land for white settlement in central Namibia, the government contemplated moving all Herero from the Police Zone to the southern parts of the Kaokoveld. In the mid-1940s the government organised tours for Herero leaders from eastern Namibia to the region. The report on one of these reconnaissance tours emphasises the willingness of Herero leaders to commit themselves to this move.[23]

---

[21] NAN NAO 28 Extract from Monthly Report for the months of May and June 1929; Post Commander SWA Police Tshimhaka.

[22] His instructions read 'As it is probable that the southern portion of the Kaokoveld will eventually be parcelled out into holdings for occupation by European settlers, viz. the portion lying south of the line running due east and west through Ombombo in the Kaokoveld, it should be your steady aim and object to move the Natives gradually northwards beyond that area and to open up more water supplies in the north.' NAN SWAA Kaokoveld A522, General, 1926–54; Instructions to Mr A. M. Barnard on assuming his duty as Officer in Charge of Native Affairs, Opuwo, probably written 1939 or 1940.

[23] NAN NAO 29 Kaokoveld. Tribal Affairs. Officer in Charge, Native Affairs, Ohopoho, to Chief Native Commissioner, Windhoek, 13/12/1945; Report on a tribal meeting with Herero chiefs from the Police Zone and Herero Chiefs from Kaokoveld in order to discuss the resettlement of all Police Zone Herero to Kaokoveld. 'The Police Zone headmen were introduced to the Kaokoveld natives and it was explained to the latter that the administration intended settling all Police Zone Hereros in the Kaokoveld, if possible and if suitable country could be found for this purpose and that it was with this object in view that the leaders from the South had come up to inspect likely portions of this

Other reasons for creating a no-man's land between tribal reserve and settler farms may have been economic. Silvester (1998) has convincingly shown that poor white farmers in southern Namibia were kept in business only with state-funded subsidies in the 1920s. In a period of worldwide recession and drought they found it exceedingly difficult to survive as commercial ranchers. Dieckmann (2007, 2011) gives a comprehensive picture of the humble beginnings of commercial settler farming in the region. Competition with black livestock farmers would have seriously hampered their prospects and they were probably satisfied to see potential competitors removed: not only were the chances of infection of their herds with livestock diseases reduced, but the probability of white livestock traders buying from black farmers instead of white farmers diminished.

The Ovamboland Border

In 1926 the inhabitants of north-western Namibia were informed that it was henceforth prohibited to move cattle between the Kaokoveld and the Ovamboland.[24] This order was based on discussions between Manning, at that time Resident Commissioner in Ondangwa, and the Uukwaludhi King Mwala in the early 1920s. Manning reports that he had arranged with Mwala and other chiefs 'a broad zone between the Kaokoveld and Ovamboland in which movements of cattle or carrying firearms [was] prohibited ...'.[25] Many households had constantly shifted between the western fringes of the Cuvelai basin and the eastern sandveld of the Kaokoveld. However, for some years Manning's orders did not affect local mobility patterns much, but in 1926 Hahn set out to enforce a stock free zone between Ovamboland and the Kaokoveld more vigorously. The official reasoning here too was that the spread of CBPP could be prevented only if the cattle populations of

---

territory. Langman Tjahura says on behalf of the Kaoko Herero that the idea is nice ... as the majority of them in the Kaokoveld were either related, or had friends among the Hereros living in the South and that it would be like their own people coming to live with them. Hosea Kutako was very taken up with the Okangundumba ... flats and informed me that his forefathers had lived there ...'.

[24] NAN SWAA Kaokoveld A552/1 Monthly Reports 1926–1938; reports from Post Commander Tshimhaka to Hahn.

[25] NAN SWAA Kaokoveld A552/22 Major Manning's Report Vol. 1.

both regions were kept apart. Officers assumed that re-infection of the Kaokoveld's cattle with CBPP was likely through Ovamboland's vast herds. Hahn established that 'it is my intention to establish an unoccupied zone between the two countries'.[26]

However, not only was livestock-related mobility between both regions frequent, but trade relations, patron–client relations involving livestock exchanges, and political ties also crossed this boundary (see also Bollig 1997: 137ff.). The newly instituted border between the Kaokoveld and Ovamboland divided communities which had interacted within one economic and political system. In the late 1920s the reports from the police station at Tjimuhaka abound with hints at transgressions and punishments. The record for February 1927 reads that illegal stock movements had been observed from Okapembamba to Otjitunduwa and that a certain Tjikua was fined two oxen, two cows, and five sheep. Another Hithupu who resisted the police and tried to hide was fined nine cows, twelve oxen, fifteen sheep, and fifteen goats. In February 1928 Karuvapa, the brother of chief Muhona Katiti, brought cattle from Ovamboland to the Kaokoveld – the cattle were later culled by police who had impounded them. Throughout 1929 and 1930 the records contain stern warnings by Hahn to shoot any cattle that trespassed the boundary.[27] The sheer number of illegal border crossings that were investigated by the administrative police in the late 1920s and 1930s renders evidence of the manifold ties between the Kaokoveld and the Ovamboland. For about two decades this cordon sanitaire remained an effective barrier against exchanges between the Ovamboland and the Kaokoveld. People who had formerly made their livelihoods within a single social-ecological system were now divided and developed separately. Whereas in western Ovamboland increasing numbers of people were drawn into migrant labour, converted to Christianity, and began to seek Western-style consumer goods (Dobler 2014; McKittrick 2002), the inhabitants of the Kaokoveld were cut off from networks of trade and consumption.

---

[26] NAN NAO 28, Officer in Charge Native Affairs Ovamboland to the Secretary for SW Africa 20/9/1930 'Lungsickness Kaokoveld'.
[27] NAN SWAA Kaokoveld A552/1 Monthly Reports 1926–1938; reports from Post Commander Tshimhaka to Hahn, then to Secretary General.

The Kunene Boundary

The boundary with Portuguese Angola was even more ferociously guarded than the Ovamboland border. Migration between the Kaokoveld's arid plains and the moister foothills of the southern Angolan highlands had been frequent. Especially during drought years the Kaokoveld's pastoralists resorted to pastures north of the Kunene. Right from the inception of South African rule in the Kaokoveld the administration made it clear that moves crossing the Kunene were to be severely punished. In 1926 a Police Post was installed at Tjimuhaka, right on the banks of the Kunene River, and at one of the few major fords of the lower Kunene: its major function was to control mobility across the Kunene River. Police officers travelled up and down the river in order to detect spoors of possible trespassers. The standing order was to inhibit any move of people and livestock across the river. Notes like the following fill the pages of monthly reports from Tjimuhaka Police Post that were returned to the administrative headquarters in Ondangwa: 'Instructions received from Police Headquarters read that the border should be patrolled regularly from Tshimhaka to Erikson's Drift and that no stock, hides, skins and grain should be allowed to cross the border.'[28] In the late 1920s and throughout the 1930s and 1940s this rigid regulation was frequently put to the test. Owing to drought conditions and frequent maltreatment by Portuguese authorities, Himba households from Angola crossed the boundary on many occasions. If they were lucky, their livestock were impounded and quarantined; more often livestock were summarily culled. The culling was to be done by white officers only.[29] In September 1941 a herd of 727 sheep and goats was culled at Enyandi and their owners were detained.[30] On another occasion about 500 cattle were shot at Otjipemba because their owner had crossed the boundary illegally.[31] If we

---

[28] NAN NAO 29 Station Commander, South West Africa Police, Tshimhaka to Native Commissioner, Monthly Report December 1937.
[29] Interview L. Bleckmann with Munene Tjituri, Otwani 20/01/2008.
[30] NAN SWAA Kaokoveld A552/1 Monthly Reports 1938–1952; Police Commander, Opuwo to Native Commissioner Hahn, September 1941.
[31] NAN SWAA Kaokoveld A552/1, Monthly Reports 1938–1952; Police Commander, Tshimhaka to Native Commissioner Hahn, March 1941. More cattle were shot at the border. I briefly summarise from the police files at Tjimhaka: In June/July 1940 10 cattle shot at Onyezu, in August/September 25 cattle shot at the same place, and during the same time period 4 more cattle

imagine herds of that size being machine gunned in the presence of their owners we get a feeling for the highly confrontational character of these atrocities. The dead and putrefying corpses of these goats, sheep, and cattle signalled that the administration was to resort to any form of violence if locals did not show absolute obedience.

When in the early 1940s a number of Angolan Himba tried to escape from drought, taxation, and corporal punishment in southern Angola and shifted across the Kunene orders were given that no person was allowed to cross the Kunene.[32] Two quotes, one from 1935, the other one from 1946, make this strict handling of immigration issues clear: In 1936 an instruction reads 'I have to inform you that natives without passes from Angola should not be allowed to enter the Kaokoveld' and in 1946 officers are reminded that 'no further natives from Angola are to be allowed to settle in the Kaokoveld'.[33]

Bearing in mind that people on both sides of the river maintained close kinship links, owned livestock property on both sides, jointly managed herds, and had profited from the slightly different ecological conditions on both sides, it is hard to overestimate the result of these regulations. In 1938 the government decided to install armed guards at fords along the river.[34] The establishment of these posts apparently inflamed conflicts, as river guards and police officers shot cattle that strayed into the prohibited zone along the river regularly. After a few incidents concerning the unruly behaviour of some of these guards they were again withdrawn in 1942. After 1942 these posts were only manned during droughts, when people tried to settle closer to the river.

In order to allow the administration better control of the river basin, the Himba had been prohibited from living along the river or making use of the lush vegetation of the Kunene riparian forest since the late

near Epupa; on 25 August 1940 river guards destroyed 4 heads and were then assaulted by Angolan Himba, four of them armed with rifles; police and trespassers shot at each other and the fleeing Ovahimba took guard's rifle but send it back later; in December 1940 5 cattle were shot 'which strayed into stock-free zone'. In March 1941, 517 cattle were destroyed at Onyezu and in September that year 727 sheep and goats were shot at Enyandi and 62 natives were detained. NAN SWAA 2513 File 552/1 Monthly Reports 1938–1952.

[32] NAN NAO 29 Kaokoveld, Tribal Affairs, Officer in Charge, Native Affairs, Ohopoho to Chief Native Commissioner, Windhoek.
[33] NAN NAO Native Commissioner, Ovamboland to Post Commander, Tshimhaka 11 March 1935; NAN NAO 29 Administrator, Windhoek to Officer in Charge, Native Affairs, Ohopoho, 30 October 1946.
[34] NAN SWAA 2513 File 552/1 Monthly Reports 1938–1952.

1920s. Even during severe droughts, when the resources of the Kunene gallery forest were vital, people were generally not allowed to settle on the banks of the river. In 1937 the administration decided to stipulate a ten-mile zone along the river where no one could settle, so that 'no stock, hides, skins and grain should be allowed to cross the border'.[35] Government Notice No. 91 of 1938 then provided the establishment of a five-mile cattle-free zone along the Kunene and ordered that cattle that strayed into this zone were to be culled. During another severe drought in 1939 desperate local people sent delegations to Ondangwa, the administrative headquarters, some 350 km away, to plead with the authorities for permission to settle at the river temporarily. As a buffer-zone the riverine gallery forests had always been of tremendous importance for survival during times of extreme drought. The thick forest of palm trees (*Hyphaene ventricosa petersiana*) that were found for about 150 kilometres along the river between Ruacana and Epupa guaranteed at least some food. The numerous *Faidherbia albida* trees produced tons of pods every year. Himba herders tried again and again to gain access to the riverine forest using legal forms of application and illegal ways of slipping into the prohibited zone[36] but usually their appeals were rejected.[37]

Internal Borders

In 1923 the administration gazetted three small reserves in the northern parts of the Kaokoveld. Their boundaries were meant to become the basis for the control of internal mobility. Movements across reserve boundaries were inhibited. Several reasons were given: Confinement would mean less conflict; reduction of mobility would also lessen the risk of a spread of contagious diseases; and last but not least, less mobile people were more controllable. Stock movements outside the reserves were also controlled and made difficult. Even minor migrations within the central parts of the Kaokoveld required applications. In 1942 the headman of Okorosave for example required official

---

[35] NAN SWAA A552/1 Monthly Reports 1926–1928, Post Commander, Tshimhaka, to Native Commissioner Hahn, December 1937.
[36] NAN SWAA A552/1 Monthly Reports 1926–1928, Post Commander, Tshimhaka, to Native Commissioner Hahn, August–September 1939.
[37] NAN SWA NAO Extract from Monthly Report for February 1940 from Officer in Charge: Karuapa is fined because moving cattle to Kunene.

The Politics of Encapsulation

permission to move small stock from Otjitunduwa to Okorosave.[38] The three chiefs, who had been formally installed in 1923, were encouraged to follow up on those contravening these rules and to punish them. In 1936 a chiefs' council was installed and more chiefs were named (outside the three small tribal reserves) – they too were held responsible for controlling the mobility of 'their people'. It is likely that the chiefs were interested in maintaining the boundaries which laid the foundations of their chieftainship, and in the confinement of their subjects within those boundaries. In the end, boundaries added to their power. A letter written in 1926 makes the parallel interests of the colonial administration and the chiefs perfectly clear:

Cattle were shifted from Uaruthe, Oorlog's country, to Otjitundua ... after Oorlog had warned them that they may not shift cattle from one place to another, N. 407 Const. Cogill has gone to Otjindua to order them back to Uaruthe and I have sent Oorlog a letter that they must be severely punished and to furnish me with a report as to what action he has taken; ... cattle also shifted from Otjyandjasemo to Epembe ... Constable Cogill going to Epembe to send them back, he was defied by the Ovahimbas there, one raised his sword ... to strike Constable Cogill. These people were punished through Muhona Katiti, two being whipped by Chiparapara and one fined an ox.[39]

These strict regulations on internal mobility were maintained for some time, creating a great deal of paperwork, discontent, and confusion. However, the drastic action against trespassing apparently enjoyed a degree of success – at least in the eyes of the administration: In 1939 the Native Commissioner of Opuwo reported proudly to Hahn that 'The Natives now regard it as obligatory to obtain permission to move cattle from one post to another.'[40] However, trespassing internal boundaries remained an issue and in 1942 officials finally decided that any major stock movement within the Kaokoveld required the written permission of a colonial officer.[41] The administration became notorious for its obsession with inhibiting such moves. Stock movements into

---

[38] NAN NAO 30, Officer in Charge Ohopoho to Native Commissioner Hahn, Ovamboland, 23 June 1942.
[39] NAN PTJ Monthly Report December 1926.
[40] NAN SWAA Kaokoveld A522/1 Monthly Reports 1938–1952. Police Commander, Opuwo to Native Commissioner Hahn, December 1939.
[41] NAN SWAA A552/1 Monthly Reports 1938–1952, Police Commander Opuwo to Native Commissioner Hahn, March 1942.

the arid plains of western Kaokoveld required official approval, and in 1938 Himba were arrested 'for illegal stock movements at (or to) Sanitata'.[42]

Oral accounts make it clear that it was possible to flout the regulations to some degree. Until 1940 the Kunene fords in the inaccessible mountains of the western Kaokoveld were rarely controlled, and several elders remembered that their fathers had used hidden paths to migrate to and from south-western Angola. However, they left little doubt that migrations across the river were risky, and if it was not necessitated by drought or violence herders would not make the trip. At those times when the fords were manned by guards, migrations across the river were nearly impossible. The border to the south was even more impenetrable: not only did police patrols from Sesfontein and Kamanjab control the area but white farmers fearing the infection of their cattle reported trespassing to the authorities. The Ovamboland–Kaokoveld boundary was perhaps the most open of the three boundaries: the sheer number of cases against herders who had allegedly crossed it illegally suggests that trespassing was rather frequent. All in all, the police forces, though small in numbers, controlled far-reaching stock movements to a considerable degree; they were aided in their efforts by competing chiefs, eager to reconfirm their position vis-à-vis the government. In particular, restrictions on stock movements across the Kunene River and the prohibition on settling in the riverine forest affected the pastoral economy negatively.

A central topic of communication between various government agencies and the local population with respect to the establishment of external and internal boundaries was 'punishment'. Punishment usually entailed shooting or confiscating several head of livestock, and the colonial police did not hesitate to do so. As mentioned, occasionally entire herds of several hundred head were shot to set an example. Additionally the colonial chiefs were entitled to inflict corporal punishment. With Hahn's support, police officers and chiefs were often encouraged to punish so-called trespassers.[43] Hahn was adamant that only punishment would instil respect for governmental rules in the local population:

[42] NAN NAO 30/24-12, Post Commander, SWA Police, Tshimhaka, to Native Commissioner Ondangwa, 16 September 1926.
[43] See Hayes (1992) for an intriguing account of Hahn's authoritarian and paternalistic style of rule in Namibia's north between 1923 and 1946.

The Politics of Encapsulation

The Hereros and Ovambos have been sternly warned on many occasions and I consider it useless to waste further words. If it is found that they have moved stock without authority I would suggest that Const. Cogill be instructed to proceed to the places mentioned by him and shoot the cattle without further ado.[44]

The language of these warnings given out in instructions to field officers directly dealing with the local population is emotional. Hahn is enraged at local 'disobedience'. Again and again he urges his staff to be ruthless and to resort to violence against people and their livestock. Affect and not detached reason is informing his instructions.[45]

6.4 Controlling Trade

Trade across the newly established external borders was strictly controlled since the early 1920s. The official reasoning behind maintaining strict control over trade was the fight against contagious livestock diseases, but other reasons were mentioned as well. The administration also feared that modern guns were being sold to the Himba by Portuguese traders and that these very traders were an outlet for ivory and skins. Furthermore, Portuguese traders had been found bartering cheap alcohol for livestock along the boundary.[46]

Trade across the Kunene

Trade across the Kunene boundary remained unhampered until the mid-1920s. From 1926 onwards the police station at Tjimuhaka was not only to control the movement of livestock and people but to eradicate cross-border trade as well. The traders' activities on the other side of the river were closely scrutinised. In October 1926, shortly after the opening of the station, the police commander reported Boer hunting parties and a Portuguese trader on the other side of the river,

---

[44] NAN SWAA Kaokoveld A552/1 Monthly Reports 1926–1938, Post Commander, Tshimhaka, to Native Commissioner Hahn, July 1930.
[45] See also Stoler (2009) on affective states constituting the common sense of the governing Dutch colonial elite in Indonesia in the nineteenth century.
[46] Kreike (2009) reports on the decapitalisation of cattle husbandry in north-central Namibia under colonial rule. Whereas in pre-colonial and early colonial times cattle were sold in considerable numbers, later regulations and enforced pricing discouraged the marketing of cattle there.

whom he had probably observed for some time through his binoculars, in order to find further evidence for the malign aims of traders. Native Commissioner Hahn added his ideas to the report when handing it on to the Secretary of SWA: 'With reference to the trader ... at Hamuhenge Drift ... I would remark that these people are a constant danger on our northern borders. They trade principally in liquor, ivory, ammunition and game skins.'[47] It is remarkable that a few undercapitalised itinerant traders are depicted here as the 'danger on our northern borders'.

Several times local chiefs and notables applied for special permission to trade with Portuguese traders during severe droughts. In late 1926 the prohibition of trade had to be partially lifted to allow some emergency maize to be traded into the area. Under the supervision of the Post Commander some grain was sold for cash or in exchange for heifers.[48] For each heifer £1.10–£3 sterling was paid.[49] Within one month 285 bags (of 90 kg each) of maize had been sold – about 26,000 kg of maize was bought by a starving population, hinting at how much need there was; 151 bags were sold for heifers and 116 for cash.[50] While this maize was obviously imported from the commercial farming area, over the next years maize had to be obtained in Portuguese Angola in the case of emergencies.

In the 1930s dry seasons, Portuguese traders were allowed by both Portuguese and South African authorities to carry out some trade at the request of some local chiefs at Tjimuhaka under the auspices of the Post Commander. The Portuguese traders took grain over the river and sold each bag (90 kg) at £30 sterling, an extremely high price in those days. Initially, the Portuguese authorities did not authorise the introduction of cattle from South West Africa to Angola, and no trade in

---

[47] NAN SWAA Kaokoveld A 552/1 Monthly Reports 1926–1938, Post Commander Tshimhaka to Native Commissioner Hahn, October 1926.

[48] NAN SWAA Kaokoveld A 552/1 Monthly Reports 1926–1938, here Post Commander Tshimhaka to Native Commissioner Hahn, November 1926.

[49] The price for oxen on the major central Namibian meat markets was between 12 shillings and £2 between 1920 and 1924 and £4 in 1930 (Rawlinson 1994: 58 and 135).

[50] There were few options to obtain cash during these days: until 1926 there were still some commercial hunters in the area. They probably bought ivory from natives and paid in money for it. Furthermore there were quite a few Herero families who had good contacts in central Namibia and probably obtained cash there. NAN SWAA Kaokoveld A 552/1 Monthly Reports 1926–1938, here Post Commander Tshimhaka to Native Commissioner Hahn, December 1926.

other commodities was allowed, meaning that local herders either had to pay in cash or could not obtain grain at all.[51] However, one month later the traders were able to obtain a permit to import 500 heifers into Angola. Oxen, the main asset for exchange for the local pastoralists, were not allowed to be exported to Angola due to regulations by the Portuguese colonial government. The Post Commander of Tjimuhaka was dismayed by the restrictive handling of the trade by Portuguese authorities.[52]

Although control along the river became much stricter in the 1920s, the police in Outjo had evidence that guns and even horses were still being smuggled in from Angola as late as 1938.[53] In 1932 the administration once again felt unable to provide relief maize and asked the Portuguese authorities to allow local traders to come down to the river in order to barter maize for heifers. However, the Portuguese authorities flatly denied the request, arguing that the maize was urgently needed within southern Angola.[54] The Native Commissioner of Ovamboland, Hahn, was advised to buy the maize in the Huila district. As this was impossible given the limited funds available for famine relief, Hahn then applied for help to his superiors in Windhoek. Due to the drought conditions, the Administrator paid a hurried visit to the Kaokoveld and decided that a bit of relief maize could be paid for by the government. However, he was determined to make political use of the situation and teach his unruly subjects a lesson. Cynically, he blamed the starving population for their own misery:

---

[51] NAN PTJ Native Commissioner Ondangwa to Police Commander Tshimhaka 21/10/1930.

[52] NAN PTJ Commander Police Post Tsimhaka to Native Commissioner Ondangwa 3/11/1930.

[53] NAN NAO 30 SWA Police Outjo to the District Commandant Omaruru; n.d. probably March or April 1938.

[54] The quote from the Portuguese Governor of the Lower Kunene District to Hahn shows the difficulties of trade along the colonial borders: 'You asked this administration to authorise the import of 500 head of cattle into this territory as you wished to exchange some for Kaffir corn for the natives of your territory. We regret to state that we cannot permit you to do so as such permission would be contrary to Government notice No. 959 of the 31st March of this year ... As it is not possible to comply to your request the Administration was authorised to permit you purchase the Kaffir corn or any other food you may need in the District of Huila.' NAN NAO 28 Carlos Lino da Silva, Frontier District of Lower Kunene, Vila Pereira D'Eca to Native Commissioner Ondangwa 15/7/1932.

The Administrator blames people not to have done enough; e.g. the people at Otjitundwa and Ombathu did not plant. ... The natives of the Kaokoveld contribute nothing whatever to the labour supply of the territory at any time. They lead a particularly lazy and carefree life and they must therefore as far as it lies in their power to do so look after themselves.[55]

He then decided to deliver the ridiculous number of 26 sacks of mealies and 6 sacks of seed mealies. Rations of this relief maize were only to be given in return for labour such as road work or opening up water sources. The Kaokoveld's population had become dependent on government institutions for famine relief as their access to trade links was severely curtailed.

Trade to the South

On the southern border of the Kaokoveld communal lands were bordering upon commercial farm lands. From the early 1930s onwards the Karakul industry started booming in the commercial ranching zone. Farms there had recovered from the recession of the late 1920s and were now eagerly looking to buy sheep for interbreeding with Karakul sheep. The farmers did nothing different from what the Portuguese had done in 1930. While the Portuguese traders had demanded heifers which they wanted to sell to white farmers in the Huila highlands in need of breeding stock, the Namibian farmers wanted sheep to upgrade their Karakul enterprises. Generally the sale of livestock, livestock-based products, and for some time all other products as well (including tobacco and artefacts) was prohibited across the Police Zone boundary. Although this policy was consistent with the general aims of the government and the farmers' associations throughout the 1930s, several traders tried to find ways to conduct trade with the inhabitants of the Kaokoveld. The remote north-west offered a pool of rich pastoralists who were barred from any major markets and were eagerly looking to sell some of their livestock, even if prices were low. The Kamanjab-based trader Gärtner, for example, invented a coupon system. His agent received livestock in the Kaokoveld and gave out coupons for them. With these coupons people travelled and bought goods at Gärtner's shop in Kamanjab.

[55] NAN NAO 28 Administrator Windhoek to Native Commissioner Ondangwa 19/11/1932.

The Politics of Encapsulation

Occasionally Gärtner imported major herds of sheep observing governmental quarantine regulations.[56]

Gärtner's business had been extremely successful. At the time he was intercepted, his agent was herding about 930 sheep at Otjondeka. However, his efforts were stalled, probably due to lobbying from other livestock traders. Gärtner's efforts were obviously not an exception. Farmers, traders, and speculators were eager to buy sheep in the Kaokoveld and to sell them at much higher rates to farmers in central Namibia. In November 1935 Hahn commented on the problems involved in this trade. He argued that the major reason for the total ban on trade was the anxiety about bringing contagious livestock diseases to the commercial ranching area this way. He contended, however, that this ban brought about severe problems for the people living in the Kaokoveld.[57]

Perhaps as a reaction to this, a trader, Mr. Borchers, was allowed by the Administrator to introduce 350 sheep in 1935 and another 450 in 1936 from the Kaokoveld into the Police Zone.[58] Chief Vita Thom was apparently one of the main suppliers to Borchers – an indication of how the new tribal leaders were taking advantage of their good relations with the colonial officials. In the late 1930s the government tried several times to initiate some controlled livestock trade between the Kaokoveld and the Police Zone. Herders were allowed to import sheep through a quarantine station to the Police Zone and then had one month to dispose of their sheep among farmers. Afterwards unsold stock had to be removed back to the Kaokoveld.[59] Due to complaints from farmers who feared infection of their herds (the quarantine station was near Kamanjab), this practice had to be abandoned in 1938: '... no further stock (small stock) must be permitted to cross the Police Zone Boundary until further notice' – and further notice did not come for the next twenty years.[60] (Even today it is difficult to

---

[56] NAN NAO 31 24/23 Re.: Trading in Kaokoveld; probably 1935.
[57] NAN NAO 30 Native Commissioner Ovamboland to Secretary for SWA 9/11/1935 Re.: Introduction of Stock from the Kaokoveld.
[58] NAN NAO 30 Secretary for SWA, Courtney Clarke, to Senior Veterinary Surgeon Windhoek 2/12/1935; NAO 30 Administrator Windhoek to Veterinary Surgeon Windhoek 29/1/1936.
[59] NAN NAO 30 Magistrate Outjo to Station Commander SWA Police Kamanjab 7/5/1938.
[60] NAN NAO 30 Magistrate Outjo to Station Commander SWA Police Kamanjab 7/5/1938.

export livestock across the so-called Red Line.) Most people from the Kaokoveld were excluded from any form of trade, since on the one hand livestock sales had become impossible by then, and on the other hand no means of payment except money was accepted in transactions.[61]

The inhabitants of the Kaokoveld were not willing to accept these strict regulations. They frequently complained officially to the administration. One impressive example is Thomas Mutate's letter to the Administrator in Windhoek in 1937:

Dear Administrator, Windhoek. About one year ago your Excellency said that the borders will be opened for small stock but they have not been opened. We are facing difficulties and we are dying of hunger. Please, your Excellency, help us and open the border for small stock. If we will have to face this hunger again we will die. Surely, we are facing big problems. Your Excellency, if the borders are not opened for small stock, send us a car with food and clothes because with hunger somebody cannot live. Your Excellency, he knows [i.e. you know] that we, the Herero, are greeting you always, your Excellency. signed Thomas Mutate (original letter written in Otjiherero, my translation)[62]

Beyond the grudge Mutate is voicing here, it is interesting that he refers to the capacity and the obligation of the state to provide famine food to starving people. This indicates that the local leaders also saw the administration as a partner (if an unequal one) that could be directly negotiated with.

Another complaint, which was quoted in an inspection report in 1949, describes the disastrous situation dramatically and shows the extent of encapsulation:

We have difficulty. We cry. We are imprisoned. We do not know why we are locked up. We are in gaol. We have no place to live. This is our difficulty which we report to our Master, Nakale. Here our living is our cattle, sheep, goats, tobacco, buchu. Our donkey waggons do not fetch anything from Kamanjab. We cannot get meat from the south or even mealiemeal. Our sleeping skins cannot be sent out. We have to throw them away on the border. We enter the Police Zone with hunger. We have no money ...

[61] NAN NAO 30 Native Commissioner Ovamboland to Commander Police Post Tshimhaka. n.d. probably March or April 1938.
[62] NAN NAO 30 Thomas Mutate's complaint against livestock trading restrictions to the Administrator Windhoek 20/11/1937.

The Politics of Encapsulation

Ovamboland is closed for us. We lived on [in] Ovamboland for a long time. We want to take our cattle there, also our sheep and goats. Here in the Kaokoveld we live only on our livestock. The borders are closed. The borders press us heavily. We cannot live. We are in a kraal.[63]

Apparently affected by such claims, the Director of Agriculture, who took the statement above into his report, sketched similar problems after his inspection tour.

The administration was well aware of the problems caused by the extreme degree of the Kaokoveld's isolation.[64] In 1949 there was not a single store in the Kaokoveld and people had to travel several hundred kilometres to Kamanjab, Outjo, or Ondangwa to obtain goods. Ovambo petty traders occasionally came to the Kaokoveld with donkeys to barter tobacco from local herders in exchange for beads made from ostrich egg shells and other commodities.[65] Reacting to the complaints, the Administration proposed that SWANLA (South West African Native Labour Association), the officially gazetted labour recruitment organisation, should expand its activities into the Kaokoveld as '... the visit of a hawker to the Kaokoveld is desperately necessary in view of the fact that the Natives there are without supplies of any sort ...'.[66]

SWANLA was asked to open an office in Opuwo and send hawkers on a regular basis (twice a year) to the Kaokoveld. SWANLA started off by organising hawking trips, but showed very little interest in these activities as they turned out to be quite unprofitable. The major reason again was that SWANLA hawkers were not allowed to import livestock into the Police Zone, which precluded any form of barter or monetary exchange with local herders.[67] Although SWANLA had previously agreed on two trips per year, they completed only one trip in 1948 and 1949. The government tried to put some pressure on

---

[63] NAN SWAA 2513 A552/1 Inspection Report: Kaokoveld Native Reserve, 10/10/1949, Native Commissioner Ovamboland to Chief Native Commissioner Windhoek.
[64] NAN SWAA 2513 A552/1 Inspection Report: Report of an Inspection Tour by the Director of Agriculture, 26/10/1949.
[65] NAN NAO 29 Officer in Charge, Native Affairs, Ohopoho to Chief Native Commissioner Windhoek 22/12/1945.
[66] NAN NAO 64 17/4/ Trading in Kaokoveld Chief Native Commissioner Allen to Messrs. SWANLA 23/2/1948.
[67] NAN NAO 64 17/4 'Trading in Kaokoveld' SWANLA to Native Commissioner Ondangwa 3/7/1948 Re.: Report on Kaokoveld Hawking.

SWANLA, claiming that other white traders were eagerly looking for trading licences in the Kaokoveld.[68] Despite this pressure SWANLA was not eager to fulfil its contract – the profit margins were simply too low.

Trade was further hampered by laws prohibiting barter trade between natives and white or black traders. The legal act was advertised as an initiative to protect local producers against unfavourable trading.[69] The new law apparently had its value in trying to force even more people into waged labour in mines and on farms. Producers without any contact with the labour economy were excluded from obtaining commodities. The law stipulates that:

it is expedient to prohibit the continuance of the system of trade practised in Native areas, commonly referred to as the barter system, under which credit notes, tokens or other non-negotiable instruments, or goods, wares, merchandise or livestock are given by traders and others to natives in payment of or in exchange for livestock and produce offered for sale by the natives; ... Any person who gives or tenders any credit note, token, goods, wares, merchandise, livestock or instrument, other than cash or a negotiable instrument, in payment of or in exchange for livestock or produce offered to him for sale by any native, shall be guilty of an offence, and shall be liable, upon conviction, to a fine not exceeding 25 Pounds or, in default of payment to imprisonment for a period not exceeding three months.[70]

As SWANLA's activities in the area remained minimal, the government decided in the early 1950s to issue a few trading licences to black traders from the Police Zone and Ovamboland.[71] These traders had to guarantee that all transactions were strictly in cash or in exchange

---

[68] NAN NAO 64 17/4 'Trading in Kaokoveld' Chief Native Commissioner WDK to SWANLA Grootfontein 27/5/1950 Re.: Report on Kaokoveld Hawking.

[69] In a letter the Native Commissioner Eedes of Ovamboland comments critically on the consequences of this new law but asserts that it will help to control the flourishing barter trade of mission stations in Ovamboland – at that time there was no mission station in the Kaokoveld. NAN NAO 62 Native Commissioner Ondangwa Eedes to Chief Native Commissioner Windhoek 30/6/1948.

[70] Government Gazette 23/5/1947: Draft Proclamation: Prohibition of Barter Trade in Native Areas.

[71] NAN NAO 64 17/4 'Trading in Kaokoveld' Officer in Charge Native Affairs Ohopoho to Native Commissioner Ondangua 1/12/1951 Re.: Application for Hawker's Licence: Simon Kaatendekua. NAO 64 17/4 'Trading in Kaokoveld' Officer in Charge Native Affairs Ohopoho to Native Commissioner Ondangua 25/2/1952 Re.: Application for Hawker's Licence in the Kaokoveld: Philip Hameva.

for tobacco and *buchu*, a cosmetic powder produced from herbs and resin. Bartering for livestock was not allowed. They had to show proof of owning a vehicle and had to have a lump sum of £150 at their disposal to start the business. Until the middle of the 1950s four licences were given out, one to an Ovambo trader (whose permission was withdrawn some months later) and three to Herero traders from the Police Zone. No one from the Kaokoveld applied for a licence at that stage, as people from there were neither able to buy a car nor to save the £150 required to apply for a permit. From the beginning the Kaokoveld's traders came from the outside, a situation which was still typical for trade in the Kaokoveld in the 1990s. SWANLA's labour recruitment and hawking activities never really succeeded. Nevertheless, probably due to government pressure, SWANLA opened a first shop in Opuwo in 1954. Although the shop only operated for a few months, it is interesting to consider its 'ideological foundation' as seen by a SWANLA official:

> For your information I mention that during two-and-a-half years we recruited only 253 labourers in the Kaokoveld. This fell very far short of expectations. Ohopoho Store was opened early in May 1954, with the object of interesting the natives in better clothing, luxuries and jewellery formerly practically unknown to them and enticing them to work in order to earn money with which to buy. This device also failed. We secured fewer recruits during the last four months than during the earlier part of the recruiting experiment. The turnover in the store does not warrant the expenses involved and the small number of recruits makes recruiting prohibitively expensive.[72]

Official labour recruitment in the Kaokoveld began only in 1950, when SWANLA's recruiting officer went to Opuwo for the first time and spoke to chiefs and local men at Opuwo, Ombombo, Oruvandjei, Sesfontein, and Kaoko Otavi.[73] After discussions with the local leaders, he left the Kaokoveld under the impression that local people would flock to SWANLA's labour office; but little happened during the first year. Instead of recruiting 500 men per year plus some 300 men

---

[72] NAN SWAA 2515 A 552/18 'Native Labour' Letter of Mr Nuwe of SWANLA, Grootfontein to Native Commissioner. In the letter Nuwe announces the closing of the SWANLA shop in Opuwo and the termination of recruitment, 7/12/1954.

[73] NAN SWAA Kaokoveld A 552/1 Monthly Reports 1938–1952, here Post Commander Opuwo to Native Commissioner, September 1950.

from Angola as estimated in the beginning,[74] only about 100 labourers were recruited. In order to improve the situation the Officer-in-Charge for Native Affairs convened a meeting at Opuwo to inquire into the reasons for not going to the labour office for work.[75] Again the officer pointed out that transport to Outjo was free and that workers would be fed on the way. He pointed out to the chiefs that migrant labour was the only way to bring money to the Kaokoveld. However, he was confronted with numerous reluctant and frightened statements[76] and evasive answers that claimed that there were no young men around who were not urgently needed as herders. Furious, the officer asked every chief to hand in exact numbers of the young men in their respective areas. When the next year again brought an appalling turnout of labourers, officers were asked to look into the reasons. To make things worse, of a group of twenty-five young men recruited in late 1951, thirteen absconded in Outjo when they found that none of the contracts offered was interesting for them. Some reasons given were that returning labourers commented unfavourably on labour conditions in the Police Zone. Frequently farmers reduced wages considerably if herdsmen lost cattle, which resulted in some labourers returning without any income. Men were ordered to do menial jobs, which they regarded as below their dignity. Corporal punishment was apparently frequent and payment was bad.[77] Many potential labourers thought that contracts of a duration of twelve or eighteen months were too long; at maximum they would accept six-month contracts. The minimal response of Angolans was obviously connected to the utterly negative stance Portuguese authorities took with regard to labour migrants to South West Africa. Often families of labour migrants were summarily punished and forced to participate in compulsory road works. At the same time SWANLA was competing with farmers from

---

[74] SWAA 2515 A 552/18 'Native Labour', here Report of a visit by a SWANLA Official to the Kaokoveld 6/1/1952.

[75] NAN SWAA Kaokoveld A 552/1 Monthly Reports 1938–1952, here Native Commissioner Opuwo to Chief Native Commissioner in Windhoek 26/11/1951, Notes from a Meeting in Opuwo.

[76] 'We are afraid to go to farms to work, we will go astray and will never return. The government will never bring us back.' NAN SWAA Kaokoveld A 552/1 Monthly Reports 1938–1952, here NC Opuwo to Chief NC in Windhoek 26/11/1951, Notes from a Meeting in Opuwo, my translation.

[77] Interviews of L. Bleckmann with Christof Kavari, undated, probably 2007.

The Politics of Encapsulation

the Outjo/Kamanjab region who looked for workers privately or through their farmers' association in the Kaokoveld.[78]

The administration tried to delimit the labour recruitment activities of these private and semi-private agencies as it feared that Angolans and Ovambo could enter the Police Zone unlawfully, undermining SWANLA activities. In 1953 a SWANLA manager officially protested against private labour recruitment of farmers in Kaokoveld.[79]

The system of complete control is severely questioned from the inside. Just as some white traders tried to flout government regulations on the importing of livestock, others tried to obtain cheap labour in a way which would involve the least costs for them. SWANLA closed its Opuwo office in 1954. People from the Kaokoveld who wished to go for work had to contract via Ombalantu, some 150 km away. From the middle of the 1950s onwards there was a small but steady outlet of about 100 workers per year from the Kaokoveld. Furthermore an unknown number contracted work through farmers. Nevertheless, the Kaokoveld remained marginal as a source of labour well into the 1970s.

6.5 Fighting Contagious Bovine Pleuropneumonia – Fighting Mobility

Fighting bovine pleuropneumonia was used as another tool to extend control over the pastoral population of north-western Namibia (see also van Wolputte 2013). The control of CBPP dominated communication between various parts of the administration and the local population in the 1930s and was still important in defining state–local community relations well into the 1980s. Whereas the control of the 'neutral zone' to the south and conflicts between chiefs had previously dominated communication, it was now the threat of the uncontrolled spread of a livestock disease: the disease was dramatised and people not adhering to regulations were vilified. The disease had been introduced to southern Africa by a bull from Friesland imported to South Africa in 1854 (Schneider 1994). This highly contagious cattle disease

---

[78] NAN SWAA 2515 A 552/18 'Native Labour', here Report on a Meeting of the SWA Landbou Unie July 1954.
[79] SWAA 2515 A 552/18 'Native Labour' SWANLA Manager to Chief Native Commissioner Re: Protest against Labour Recruitment of Farmers from the Kaross Block 28/12/1953.

is hard to diagnose in its initial phase and once the first symptoms are visible in individual animals a large number of animals in the herd have been infected. Once infected, treatment is impossible. However, only 60–70 per cent of all animals die of the disease. With other animals the extent of the infection is limited to the lungs and the disease does not reoccur with them. However, these very animals can still spread the disease to other animals. CBPP is mainly spread by inhalation of droplets from the coughing of infected animals, especially if they are in the acute phase of the disease. The incubation period lasts from five days to four months.[80]

CBPP had a severe impact on the southern African cattle economy over the next decades. It caused high mortality rates all over southern Africa. While the disease had been eradicated in the commercial ranching area by about 1910 through stringent quarantine measures and simple forms of inoculation, it occurred endemically in Ovamboland and adjoining parts of southern Angola. The first outbreak was recorded in the Kaokoveld in 1925 (Schneider 1994: 130) and further outbreaks occurred in 1927 and 1928 in the Ehomba area in the Kaokoveld.[81] After Rinderpest in the 1890s this was the second time that an imported contagious livestock disease haunted the Kaokoveld. However, while in 1897/98 the losses to Rinderpest had been devastating, they were rather low this time.[82]

For the next twenty years the administration of the Kaokoveld put major efforts into controlling the disease. Cordons were cut through the land to isolate infected herds. However, the disease spread and in 1929–30 major parts of the northern Kaokoveld were affected (e.g. severe losses of cattle at Ombazu due to CBPP in 1930).[83] Fearing the

[80] www.oie.int/eng/maladies/Technical%20disease%20cards/ CONTAGIOUS%20BOVINE%20: PLEUROPNEUMONIA_FINAL.pdf.
[81] NAN SWAA Kaokoveld A552/1 Monthly Reports 1926–1938; Reports from Post Commander Tshimhaka to Hahn; March 1927 and August 1928.
[82] Van Wolputte (2013: 89) contemplates whether the pertinence of outbreaks may have been exaggerated by Native Commissioner Hahn. The low mortality rates recorded certainly speak into this direction. The CBPP infections of the 1930s certainly did not impede overall herd growth. Van Wolputte suggests that probably more animals died from measures attempting to combat the disease than from the disease itself.
[83] NAN SWAA Kaokoveld A552/1 Monthly Reports 1926–1938, Post Commander, Tshimhaka, to Native Commissioner Hahn, December 1930, addition by Hahn when sending the report on to the Secretary for South West Africa.

spread of the disease to the commercial farming area, from which CBPP had been eradicated about a decade before, the government put local herders under severe pressure to immediately report cases of infection. The local population was warned that if a herder did not report immediately, or even if he moved on with infected cattle, he would be punished. Punishment usually entailed the shooting of one or two cows from the herd in addition to the infected cattle, which were shot anyway. Examples of harsh treatment of herders who contravened Hahn's CBPP-related regulations on migration are numerous throughout the 1930s. At first, herders were partially compensated for cattle that were shot, and records from 1930 actually account for compensation payments for culled livestock.[84] However, such compensatory payments were dropped in 1931.[85] Hahn pointed out that his staff had 'standing instructions to take drastic measures when necessary to prevent the spread of lung sickness to the Outjo District'. He alleged that most Herero herders were complying with the rules, but that 'the wild Ovatjimba natives are a difficult lot'.[86] He ordered (and communicated through police officers) that any herder who had the slightest suspicion that some of his cattle were sick had to remain in his place, and that anybody who had moved had to be punished drastically. A herder who had moved some infected cattle in June 1930 was caught and all his diseased cattle were shot, and as a punishment one additional healthy cow was shot too.[87] The same herder hinted that another herdsman had moved cattle, and Hahn ordered the police officer in Tjimuhaka immediately 'I shall be glad if you would order a few of his cattle to be shot.'[88] Letters and telegrams by Hahn to his officers on the ground are emotional: Hahn's grudge against disobedient and from his point of view, irrational behaviour of local pastoralists is clearly echoed in his communication.

In April 1930 the first major inoculation campaign was launched. Infected cattle were shot, and in-contact cattle vaccinated and branded.

---

[84] NAN NAO 28 Office of the Government Veterinary Officer, Omaruru to Senior Veterinary Officer Windhoek, Lungsickness: Kaokoveld 14/4/1930. The table lists £2–£3 sterling being paid for an ox and £1 being paid for a calf.
[85] NAN NAO 28, Native Commissioner Ovamboland, to the Secretary of South-West Africa, Re.: closing of Tshimhaka Post, 5 October 1931.
[86] NAN NAO Native Commissioner Ovamboland, to the Secretary for South West Africa 26/2/1932.
[87] NAN PTJ Monthly Report June 1930.
[88] NAN PTJ Monthly Report July 1930.

Herders were shown how they themselves could inoculate their cattle with a piece of infected lung. This so-called field virus method (van Wolputte 2013: 89) was only partially successful and may, in the end, have contributed to the spread of the disease.[89] The veterinary officer ended his report on the 1930 campaign with several recommendations which were meant to contain the disease, but which were at the same time a further move to control the mobility of pastoralists.[90]

In total some 6,514 cattle were vaccinated in 1930, and several hundred were inoculated by herders themselves with pieces of infected lung. The vaccination programme was experimental to a certain degree: the glycerin vaccination, when used, was about fourteen to seventeen days old after preparation. Officers were aware that such a vaccine should be used within fourteen days if possible, and there were some doubts on the effectiveness of the programme. Many animals reacted adversely, and in 1931 the veterinarian reported that many of those animals which had been inoculated in June 1930 had lost their tails.[91] Apparently some animals also died from the vaccine. An alternative vaccination technique taught to local herders gave rise to a lot of resentment: pieces of infected lungs were rubbed into a cut on the tail of a healthy animal in order to cause a mild infection. Many locals thought that this strategy was meant to spread the

---

[89] Van Wolputte (2013: 89) describes the method as follows. 'This method consisted of infecting a calf with CBPP. After a few days, the animal was killed, the lymph collected from the chest, diluted with a saline solution and injected into the tails of the other animals to immunize the rest of the herd. Typically, this field virus method caused severe reactions in animals, often resulting in animals losing their tails or in open sores on the back.'

[90] NAN NAO 28 Office of the Government Veterinary Officer, Omaruru, to the Senior Veterinary Officer, Windhoek 14/4/1930. 'The natives should not be allowed to move from where they are at present with their cattle without permission from the police. The whole of the southern Kaokoveld should be placed under the control of the Kamanjab police, or a special police post should be established at Otjitundua. The neutral zone in the Southern Kaokoveld should be definitely fixed. Up to now the police at Kamanjab have no definite instructions and do not know the boundaries of this zone ... In my opinion, the waterholes along the 19th degree (south) latitude could be regarded as a borderline. The Ovamboland border should be closed against the movement of cattle, and no permission should be granted to bring cattle from this territory into the Kaokoveld or vice versa. I submit that if these measures are taken without unnecessary delay, and the area at present infected is strictly controlled, it should prevent the danger of the infection spreading into Outjo District.'

[91] NAN NAO 28 Office of the Government Veterinary Officer, Omaruru, to the Senior Veterinary Officer, Windhoek 10/7/1930.

The Politics of Encapsulation

disease and in later years local leaders accused the government of having contributed to the spread of the disease (see also van Wolputte 2013). The cost of this first major vaccination programme was borne by the government.[92] The forceful character of the vaccination programme contributed to strained relations between government officers and local communities.

However, these drastic measures only succeeded in keeping the disease away from the Kaokoveld for some two or three years. In 1935 outbreaks were reported in Epembe and Etengwa.[93] When in 1938 major outbreaks were noted again all over the Kaokoveld, Hahn engaged the veterinary service in a demanding campaign. It was planned to vaccinate all cattle of the Kaokoveld in order to eradicate the disease once and for all. From the very beginning the campaign was beset with problems. The administration made it clear that it would shoot cattle and punish herders who had not reported sick animals. In September 1938 a local leader (Veripaka) was imprisoned with some of his men for illegal stock movements.[94] There were rumours that Himba would try to escape to southern Angola should the vaccination programme be enforced.[95] Native Commissioner Hahn directed the campaign personally. He was determined to apply drastic measures should local people not adhere to the rules laid down by the administration. He had the message disseminated that every cow found unbranded after the 15th of September – the campaign was to start in August – would be shot.[96] In lengthy meetings he tried to persuade the chiefs at Ehomba and Etengwa to accept the inoculation. These two chiefs in particular had resented the branding of cattle, which was deemed necessary by the administration to distinguish vaccinated from unvaccinated animals.[97] In the end the chief of Ehomba grudgingly

---

[92] NAN NAO 28 Office of the Government Veterinary Officer, Omaruru, to the Senior Veterinary Officer, Windhoek 10/7/1930.
[93] NAN SWAA Kaokoveld A552/1, Monthly Reports 1926–1938, Post Commander, Opuwo to Native Commissioner Hahn, September 1935.
[94] NAN NAO 30 Stock Diseases, Post Commander SWA Police to Native Commissioner Ondangwa 16/9/1938.
[95] NAN SWAA Kaokoveld A552/1, Monthly Reports 1926–1938, Post Commander, Opuwo to Native Commissioner Hahn July 1938.
[96] NAN A450/24 Hahn Accessions, Diary 1938–1941, entry 16/8/1938.
[97] NAN NAO 30 Telegram from Native Commissioner, Ovamboland, to Secretary for South West Africa, 23/7/1938.

consented, while the other chief rejected Hahn's demands and threats.[98] Once the programme had begun, however, Hahn succeeded in putting so much pressure on hesitant herders that most cattle got vaccinated. All in all, 26,656 cattle[99] were vaccinated. After that major campaign CBPP became less of a threat in the Kaokoveld for the next decades. The decision by the Portuguese authorities to start vaccination campaigns too contributed to the improvement of the situation.[100] In a second campaign in 1939[101] more cattle were vaccinated and the administration noted decreased local resistance to the programme – perhaps due to local acceptance that the vaccinations were successful after all. Herders by that time were even coming to the station voluntarily to ask for vaccination.

The vaccination campaigns of 1930 and 1938 were the first instances in which the colonial administration launched major programmes that affected all herders in one way or another. Some cattle were culled and others inoculated, frequently against the will of local herders. The anti-CBPP campaigns put a heavy strain on the relations between the colonial government and the local communities, and in 1939 an officer wrote in a monthly report: 'The Ovahimbas are wondering why the Administration seems to be more concerned about the health of the cattle than in that of the Kaokoveld natives.'[102] The number of healthy animals culled as a punishment for trespassing or non-adherence to rules connected to anti-CBPP campaigns was probably (far) below 1,000.[103] On the whole, however, the programme

[98] NAN NAO 30 Telegram from Native Commissioner, Ovamboland, to Secretary for South West Africa, 11/8/1938. NAN NAO 30 Stock Diseases. In telegrams of Hahn to the Secretary on 11/8/1938 and 23/7/1938 resentment against the inoculation campaign by the local leaders Veripaka and Karuapa is reported.
[99] NAN NAO 30/24-12, Post Commander, South West Africa Police, Tshimhaka, to Native Commissioner, Ondangwa, 16/9/1938. Inoculation figures by State Veterinarian Tschokke, Ohohpoho, 15 October 1938.
[100] NAN SWAA Kaokoveld A552/1 Monthly Reports 1926–1938, Police Commander, Tshimhaka to Native Commissioner Hahn, January 1939.
[101] NAN SWAA Kaokoveld A552/1 Monthly Reports 1926–1938. Police Commander, Opuwo to Native Commissioner Hahn, July 1939.
[102] NAN SWAA 2513 File 552/1 Monthly Reports 1938–1952, May 1939.
[103] Steven van Wolputte (2007: 113) argues that the campaigns led 'to the indiscriminate killing of thousands of healthy and infected animals'. A thorough scrutiny of archival material did not support the claim of such high numbers but I assume that about 2,000–2,500 cattle were culled and shot as punishment.

seems to have been successful and apparently contributed to the increase of cattle in the region.

6.6 From Hunting to Poaching

The Kaokoveld had been an El Dorado for commercial hunters since the 1860s. Elephants had been shot in large numbers (see Chapter 3). Commercial hunters probably also took a heavy toll on other wildlife species. The large caravans transporting ivory to Angola mentioned by the informants of von Moltke had to be provisioned, as did the numerous smaller hunting companies roaming the area. Since 1906 the German administration had tried to keep elephant hunting at bay, and apparently succeeded in preventing hunting expeditions by Dorsland Trekkers from coming into the region. One of the first activities of the SA administration was to ban hunting by local people and commercial hunters. During the early 1920s white hunters were still occasionally roaming the area. Some of them, like de Flamingh, who had shot several elephants at Otjitambi in 1927, were prosecuted, and even forcibly removed from the Kaokoveld.[104]

Local people were disarmed not only because the government feared rebellion but because of the imminent threat of hunting. However, hunting never really came to an end in the 1920s as there was still a market for ivory and other game trophies in southern Angola. There were several major court cases due to allegations of elephant hunting, and in the late 1920s some of the Kaokoveld's leaders were accused of illegal hunting (Rizzo 2007). It became a favourite sport of the major leaders to accuse one another of poaching and bring the claims to the attention of the Native Commissioner's Office in Ondangwa. People found guilty were heavily fined, and corporally punished and/or imprisoned.[105] While local people were prohibited from hunting even for food, the local police staff and touring government employees frequently shot game for their evening meals. The absurdity of the situation becomes clear in a report of a police officer who had just found two young boys who had killed a steenbok. He warned their father rudely and threatened to force him to move to another place.

[104] NAN SWAA Kaokoveld A 552/1 Monthly Reports 1926–1938, here Post Commander Tshimhaka to Native Commissioner Hahn, September 1927.
[105] NAN PTJ Monthly Report October and November 1931 and NAO 28 Police Post Tshimhaka to Native Commissioner Ondangwa 29/10/1933.

At the same time the officer reported that some hours later he shot seven springbok for the alimentation of his entourage.[106]

The strict punishment of alleged poachers obviously had its effect. In 1935 Native Commissioner Hahn reported to the Secretary for South West Africa that hunting from the Angolan side in the Kaokoveld had ceased since the relocation of the Dorsland Trekkers to South West Africa. In 1939 the newly established Police Commander of Opuwo reported to Native Commissioner Hahn that elephants had become a menace and that it would be advisable to cull some of them.[107] He also proposed that the game reserve status of the Kaokoveld should be de-proclaimed.[108]

While commercial hunting ceased to be of importance in the 1930s, local hunting, while also declining in relevance, was still practised. Several informants indicated that especially during droughts gazelles were occasionally hunted.[109]

6.7 Combating Veld Fires

Just as the South African administration attempted to fight hunting, it also tried to combat anthropogenic veld fires, i.e. fires ignited by humans. Fire had been used by local hunters and herders alike: hunters ignited fires to hunt wildlife more efficiently, while herders at times

---

[106] NAN PTJ Monthly Report August and September 1931.
[107] NAN SWAA Kaokoveld A 552/1 Monthly Reports 1938–1952, Police Commander Opuwo to Native Commissioner Hahn, June 1939.
[108] Hahn counselled 'That portion of the Game Reserve set aside by the Government Notice No. 374/1947 as a Native Reserve be de-proclaimed as a Game Reserve, also that the small Native Reserves within the new Native Reserve, such as Oorlog's etc. be de-proclaimed. It is a well-known fact that one cannot farm with game, and it is for this reason that I suggest that that portion of the Game Reserve, which is now the Kaokoveld Native Reserve, be de-proclaimed. The elephants in this area are a danger to human life and they destroy wheatfields and are choking many of the fountains. It will be necessary to shoot a large number of these destructive animals if the Kaokoveld Native Reserve is to develop' (NAN SWAA 2513 A552/1 Inspection Report: Kaokoveld Native Reserve, 10/10/1949, Native Commissioner Ovamboland to Chief Native Commissioner Windhoek).
[109] NAN NAO 28 SWA Police Tshimhaka to Native Commissioner Ovamboland 29/10/1933 reports on the 'shooting of a giraffe in Otjitoko, 2 Tjimba imprisoned and sent to Ondangwa': 'I wish to point out that there is more game shooting going on in the Kaokoveld and it would be advisable if the Masters would take this up with a serious eye.'

burned part of the savannah just before the rainy season in order to encourage the growth of fresh grasses. While scientific accounts in the earlier part of the twentieth century demonised anthropogenic fires and described them as environmentally destructive and leading to desertification and soil degradation (Wilgen 2009: 344), contemporary range ecology has proven that on a range dominated by perennial grasses, occasional burning has beneficial results (Sheuyange et al. 2005): the dry parts of grass tufts are burned off which otherwise 'choke' the grasses (Zimmermann 2009). Sheuyange et al. (2005) report that despite the fact that anthropogenic fires account for over 70 per cent of annual fires in African savannahs, the role of such fires for vegetation dynamics is not well understood. Their research team found that frequent fires positively influence the growth and population expansion of herbaceous and tree species. Frequent burning led to the typical patch mosaics of savannahs. They found no evidence that fires led to a reduction of biodiversity (Sheuyange et al. 2005: 196). Zimmermann (2009) is the only scientific work on the role of fires in north-western Namibia. She researched the impact of fires on vegetation in the western Etosha Park and specifically researched the impact of fires on *Stipagrostis uniplumis*, a grass species which is dominant across the Kaokoveld. She found that in patches with a high fire frequency soil nutrients were low, but that burned patches were usually more productive, i.e. had a denser and better developed grass layer (Zimmermann 2009: 50). She concludes that burning, at least in the short term, leads to improved biomass production in general and is important for the population turnover of perennial grass populations. Hence, anthropogenic fires are an important part of environing and they directly contribute to an environmental infrastructure conducive to grazing. The inhibition of burning adversely affects the vitality of perennial grass populations (Zimmermann 2009: 73).[110]

Already in 1917, during his first expedition to the Kaokoveld, Manning sternly warned the local population not to ignite veld fires for the purpose of hunting or clearing off old grass stands: In his initial report Manning argues that 'during 1917 destructive fires swept over the vast

---

[110] The environmental historian Stephen Pyne has pointed out that in many colonial settings administrations made every effort to ban the burning of savannahs or forests by local herders or swidden agriculturalists. Fire became a focal topic of colonial administration in the Kaokoveld during the first half of the twentieth century.

expanse from Outjo District to the banks of the Kunene and it was often difficult to obtain grazing for the horses'. Manning's concern with fires was not purely ecological but was informed by military considerations too: if there was no grass, troops would find it very hard to move through the wide expanses of the Kaokoveld. Manning continues his treatise: 'Instructions and warnings as to severe punishments were circulated everywhere on my tour of that year and on this last journey not a single patch of burnt ground was observed. Measures taken by Oorlog and to some extent Kasupi were largely responsible for the satisfactory condition.'[111] During his second tour through the Kaokoveld in 1919 Manning again warned against veld fires:

> The general loss and destruction by veld fires, as a rule sweeping Northward over vast tracks of country as far as the Kunene, have been frequently referred to in foregoing 'Journeys'. It is hardly necessary to emphasise deplorable damage done thereby to trees, grass and veld generally, not to mention animals and birds, which if not burnt are driven about, often out of the country. As far as possible all natives were warned against this crime and drastic punishments were threatened: The people almost invariably pointed to the South as the origin of fires and generally blamed wandering Bushmen.[112]

While Manning's measures against veld fires may have been drastic, fires remained a concern for the colonial administration. The annual report for 1946 states that people found igniting fires were seriously fined. Indeed attempts to manage rangelands by fire apparently were still prominent. In 1947 a very good rain year provided the basis for extensive burning on the Kaokoland/Ovamboland boundary. The annual report states that culprits had been taken into custody and were awaiting punishment. The 1950 annual report takes a more pessimistic stand. It reports that 'practically the whole of the Kaokoveld has been burnt off' and claims that 'it is definite that the Headmen and people are not prepared to co-operate in putting a stop to the evil practice of continual grass-burning'.[113] Van Warmelo in his short ethnography of the Kaokoveld stated that the Native Council was

---

[111] NAN SWAA 2516, A552/22 Manning's Report on his Second Tour to the Kaokoveld, 1919.
[112] NAN SWAA 2516 Report of Major Manning, Second Tour Kaokoveld, Disarmament, General.
[113] NAN NAO 61 9/1, Annual Reports for the Years 1946–1952: Officer in Charge, Ohopoho to Chief Native Commissioner Windhoek.

particularly stern in meting out punishment to those causing fires (van Warmelo 1951: 26). While reports from the late 1940s still contain a number of hints towards fire-making, such remarks are absent from the records of the 1950s and 1960s. Agricultural policies had changed and rapidly rising grazing pressure led to a change from perennial to annual grasses, i.e. taking away the potential for fire-management of the savannah.

It is hard to measure the effect of this total ban of anthropogenic fires. Zimmermann (2009: 70) argues that next to rainfall and grazing, fires are a major formative force in the formation and evolution of grasslands. This formative element of environmental infrastructure was removed from the system during the first part of the twentieth century. Whether this banning of fires did also contribute to the recent replacement of perennial grasses by annual grasses, or whether this is attributable to higher grazing intensity alone is hard to say, as historical observation and ecological field experiments are lacking.

6.8 Road Construction

Roads were another feature added to the landscape since the 1920s and became an essential part of environmental infrastructure. The colonial administration required roads in order to control the vast area and its population. Road construction became essential after the administration began using motor vehicles in the middle of the 1920s. They had become necessary during the period when ox-wagons transported goods to and from the Kaokoveld. In the 1920s they became the backbone of the administration's network of chiefly places and surrounding villages. Since the mid-1920s inspection tours were regularly conducted with cars.

Right from the beginning of South African rule in northern Namibia the administration was determined to motivate and if necessary force the local population to construct roads. The three local chiefs, who had been instituted as leaders of three distinct reserves in 1923, were ordered to put teams together which could start to prepare roads. The chiefs were responsible for feeding the road gangs and for ensuring that they worked satisfactorily. In 1926, for example, Chief Oorlog worked with twenty-one men on parts of a road along the Kunene (thus enabling police patrols to control the banks of the river) while Chief Muhona Katiti was working on the same road with a group of thirty men at the other end.[114] In the 1920s the administration apparently did not contribute anything to those road construction gangs. In fact, archival notes suggest that chiefs used road construction to expand their realm of power. Vita Thom and Muhona Katiti in particular were apparently highly motivated to encourage trade and transport between their major settlements, Otjijandjasemo and Epembe, and other villages through road construction. Manning in 1923 reported that '... it may be mentioned that more recently Chief Oorlog, besides assisting on other tracks, has made a good wagon road for Government use between Epembe and Otjijandjasemo – said to have cost him 15 oxen slaughtered for the workers'.[115]

From the 1930s onwards the government occasionally contributed to the maintenance of road teams. When in 1933 roads were constructed in the central Kaokoveld by Herero work gangs the chiefs were issued £200 sterling each for distribution within their gangs – one of the very few ways of obtaining money in those days.[116] Nevertheless, road construction apparently was not meeting expectations. In 1939 a concerned official remarked: 'The Ovahimbas in the North and North-West have promised to improve the roads in their areas, but it is very doubtful whether anything will be done as they are a most indolent people and their headmen seem to have little or no influence over them.'[117] Only in 1949 did the Native Commissioner of Ovamboland decide that local people generally had to be paid when working on roads.[118] In the early 1950s a net of local roads was prepared and maintained by teams supervised by the chiefs and subsidised by the government.[119] Still progress was not meeting official expectations, and in 1952 the officer in charge urged headmen at a meeting in

---

[114] NAN SWAA Kaokoveld A 552/1 Monthly Reports 1926–1938, here Post Commander Tshimhaka to Native Commissioner Hahn, May 1926.
[115] NAN PTJ Monthly Reports Police Station Tshimhaka, May 1928.
[116] NAN NAO 278 SWA Police Post Otjitundwa to Native Commissioner Ondangwa 17/5/1933.
[117] NAN SWAA Kaokoveld A 552/1 Monthly Reports 1938–1952, here Police Commander Opuwo to Native Commissioner Hahn, June 1939.
[118] NAN SWAA 2513 A552/1 Inspection Report: Kaokoveld Native Reserve, 10/10/1949, Native Commissioner Ovamboland to Chief Native Commissioner Windhoek.
[119] NAN SWAA Kaokoveld A 552/1 Monthly Reports 1926–1938, Post Commander Tshimhaka to Native Commissioner Hahn, June/July 1936; and SWAA Kaokoveld A 552/1 Monthly Reports 1938–1952, Police Commander Tshimhaka to Native Commissioner Hahn, May 1939.

Opuwo: 'I want a network of roads connecting all inhabited areas. If any Headman intends moving his stock to another area I will require him to construct a road, if none exist to the area into which he intends moving his stock.'[120] Road construction became more intense in the 1950s and 1960s when the drilling of several hundreds of boreholes necessitated the rapid expansion of the road network.

6.9 Environmental Infrastructure in the First Half of the Twentieth Century

The environmental infrastructure acquired distinct pastoral characteristics during the first decades of the twentieth century. The period starts with significant changes: elephants as landscape architects are massively reduced in significance and only participate in environing in some few parts of the Kaokoveld after 1900. The elimination of one actant engaged in environing may have had massive effects. Comparative evidence tells us, for example, that bush encroachment along river courses may have increased and some tree species may have been hampered in their reproduction (such as the dominant tree of the Kaokoveld's gallery forests, *Faidherbia albida*). Competition for natural wells became less or ceded altogether and also gardening became an option in some areas due to the decline of elephant herds. Repastoralisation sets in rapidly in the 1910s and carries on into the 1920s. While the Kaokoveld's inhabitants are described as small-stock herders during the first two decades of the twentieth century, cattle herds dominate at least since the 1930s. This has a definite impact on the environment. Pastoralists, whether they herd goats or cattle, actively manage their environment. The management of pastures via fires is an obvious act of creating pastoral environmental infrastructure. The layer of perennial grasses and exact species composition results from edaphic and climatic factors but also from the intensity and exact timing of grazing and the use of fire. The browsing of Sanga cattle contributed progressively to the structure of the mopane bush layer and may have contributed to a gradual expansion of mopane bush as Kreike (2013: 139–50) suggests for north-central Namibia. While processes of environing via cattle herds shaped the grass layer and the mopane bush,

---

[120] NAN SWAA 2513 A552/1 Minute of Meeting held in Ohopoho from 7 to 16 April 1952.

goats actively shaped the bush layer around major settlements. The environing of cattle and goats' herds was strictly conditioned by the seasonality of water supply. Over eight to nine months of the year (from May to December/January) outlying pastures without permanent water sources were not used at all by herds of domesticated herbivores and were only grazed/browsed by sparse populations of non-domesticated ungulates. For the entire dry season people and their herds congregated around (or along) permanent water sources, natural wells, or sandy river beds where one could easily dig for water. At these places people erected major palisaded homesteads for which large amounts of wood were necessary. The effects of environing through livestock herds and humans were most severely felt around these places. The repastoralisation did provide food for a growing population and it brought the means for the accumulation of wealth and power. But repastoralisation also brought a whole set of new viruses and bacteria: without cattle there would have been no contagious bovine pleuropneumonia, no foot-and-mouth disease, and no botulism.

The colonial regime impacted local ways of environing in manifold ways. Prohibitions to light fires and to burn off pastures at the end of the dry season may have contributed to limited rejuvenation of the perennial grass cover. The most pertinent impact of colonial administrative measures resulted from the strict control of mobility. The colonial regime fostered a territorialisation of grazing areas: herders were obliged to graze their cattle within the orbit of their chief. Migrations across boundaries needed extra permits which were difficult to get. Settlements apparently were stable and lasted for many years in one place. Graveyards close to these centres of settlements attest to the longevity of inhabitation. The settlement sites themselves were profoundly transformed through palisades, dung heaps, and paths. While the majority of these sites are still inhabited, some experienced a decline in habitation since the 1950s because they were far away from roads and/or were not supplied with a borehole. Yet, even if these places were only settled in the first half of the twentieth century the traces of settlement are still well discernible today. By the late 1930s an environmental infrastructure had emerged that clearly reflected the needs and strategies of humans and domesticated livestock associated with them.

PART 4

The State, Intervention, and Local Appropriations between the 1950s and 1980s

This part comprises two chapters. Chapter 7 depicts the large-scale restructuring of social-ecological relations between the 1950s and the 1970s brought about by a comprehensive government-led modernisation programme. Chapter 8 deals with the environmental consequences of this programme, and its collapse brought about by violent conflict, rampant poaching, and drought in the 1970s and 1980s.

While the encapsulation of north-western Namibia's communities by the emergent colonial administration, the emergence of a stratified pastoral society, and the expansion of cattle-based livestock husbandry were hallmarks of the first half of the twentieth century, the three decades from the 1950s to the 1970s were characterised by state-led and state-controlled modernisation. Efforts to modernise the pastoral economy and society of the Kaokoveld were embedded in an intensification of administrative measures and an expansion of infrastructure (more staff, more vehicles, more roads, more buildings), the engagement of experts in the development and implementation of sectoral development plans, and the investment of major public funds to carry out these programmes. In contrast to prior decades this approach towards development and colonial control came about in a distinctly non-political manner reminiscent of what Ferguson has called an 'anti-politics machine', a process which he analysed as the implementation of 'an apparatus to reinforce and expand bureaucratic state power while depoliticizing both poverty and the state' (cited after van Wolputte 2007: 103). While the Native Commissioners of the previous decade had talked politics with a few chiefs and had intervened personally into local political contestations, the administrative elite of the 1950s–1970s saw themselves as modernisers. They propagated *ontwikkeling* (development) even when the locals tried to engage administrative staff in talks about justice, participation, and responsibility, and heavily criticised the administration.

7 | *A Hydrological Revolution in an African Savannah*

From the 1950s the economy of the mandated territory in South West Africa grew exponentially. Wallace states that the GDP increased from some £6.1 million sterling in 1942 to £72.3 million sterling in 1956 (Wallace 2011: 257). The economic boost in the fishing and mining industries particularly provided revenues for various government programmes.

The political setup in the Kaokoveld changed greatly during this period. The tribal council system established in the previous decade in, for example, Uukwanyama was now implemented in the Kaokoveld as well. This entailed that tribal authorities established a tribal council, held meetings regularly, and discussed issues during such meetings with administrative staff, whereas previously each tribal authority had directly negotiated with the Native Commissioner. While this did not immediately result in an improved flow of communication and more efficient decision-making,[1] by the 1950s a tribal council and court system was well established. Cases were first referred to a sub-headman or headman of the area, and then if litigants were not satisfied it was taken to the council of headmen. In the same vein the local administrative staff would first discuss forthcoming administrative measures with the tribal council. Many protocols of such meetings show that a good number of controversial measures were discussed at such meetings and at times the opposition of council members even led the administration to abandon certain policies.[2] This point

---

[1] A letter from the early 1940s from the Officer in Charge in Opuwo to the Chief Native Commissioner pleads for more patience on the side of the administration, as chiefs found it hard to get used to the new conditions. NAN SWAA Kaokoveld A522 8/5/1942 Officer-in-Charge Ohopoho to Chief Native Commissioner Botha: 'the native chiefs must have time to adapt themselves to the new conditions created by the establishment of a council of Headmen which breaks with traditions that have prevailed for many generations.'

[2] A dissident voice was also provided by Otjiherero-speakers leaving the Rhenish Mission Society for their own Oruuano congregation from 1955

notwithstanding, the council served as a means to govern and administer the local population, and in the end all major programmes were endorsed by the council. Traditional authorities were regarded as important partners in the policy of modernisation (see also Alexander 2001: 216 for similar developments in Zimbabwe). Against new elites which were regarded as potentially oppositional, traditional elites were seen as 'natural' allies of the administration. However, the decision as to how and where to start modernisation programmes was given to experts. While until then a Native Commissioner had ruled, he had now to share his powers with experts sent from the centre. Development policies and their financing were discussed and decided upon in Windhoek and Pretoria.

As the performance of chiefs was regarded as crucial for the success of the administration they were intensely scrutinised, and each annual report between 1946 and 1952 also contains detailed judgements of ten to fifteen individual chiefs. Traditional authorities gained in political stature when a tribal trust fund (*stamfonds*) to which each adult man had to contribute 50 cents per annum was inaugurated in January 1954.[3] The chiefs had control over this fund. While the *stamfonds* for the Kaokoveld always remained under-capitalised (van Wolputte 2007: 114) it provided another platform on which the government's activities could be contested. Chiefs were progressively integrated into the administration, and they were courted with a number of advantages: Chiefs were exempted from the pass laws in 1968. They also enjoyed wholesale prices at the SWANLA store in Opuwo (van Wolputte 2004:165). In September 1967 the chiefs received a salary of 120 R per year each (with a bonus of 60 R if they worked properly according to the administration's opinion).[4] By 1979 headmen's

---

(Wallace 2011: 246). As the Oruuano Church soon gained the support of senior traditional authorities like Hosea Kutako, the new native church found its way into the Kaokoveld. Religious dissent, however, was never mentioned at tribal meetings, nor did dissident chiefs deliver their arguments along religious lines or garner their speeches with quotes from the Bible – at least if we can trust the protocols of such meetings, which in no way muted dissent but often tried to portray arguments verbatim.

[3] NAN BOP 5 N1/15/6/8 Notule van Vergadering met Hoofmanne, Kaokoveld 20 tot 23 Maart 1962. The control and transparent handling of the *stamfonds* was in question at that meeting, and the officer reported that often more money was spent than accumulated during the course of a year.

[4] NAN BOB 5N1/16/6/8 Report on a Meeting in Otjondeka on 14 February 1960.

salaries had been increased to 900 R per annum.[5] In the 1970s they were also given semi-automatic attack weapons instead of the old .303 rifles which were given rather freely to commoners.[6] Throughout this period government staffing in Opuwo was expanded and government services were extended. In his autobiography Garth Owen-Smith (2010: 45–91) gives a vivid picture of the extensive administrative activities in the late 1960s: agricultural experts, veterinarians, nature conservationists, and other administrators attempted to bring about modernisation and *ontwikkeling* (development).

In November 1947 (Gov. Note 374 of 1947) the Kaokoveld was proclaimed a native reserve fusing the three small reserves gazetted in 1923 with the adjoining crown land on which the majority of the c. 6,000 people counted in 1946 were living. In 1957 the Kaokoveld became the native reserve Kaokoland under the direct authority of the Chief Native Affairs Commissioner in Windhoek.[7] The administration for this native reserve was placed in Opuwo, which gradually grew into an administrative centre. In 1970, in accord with advice given by the Odendaal Commission, the Kaokoland was degazetted as a nature reserve, and in 1978 it was placed under the Second Tier Homeland Administration of the Herero Authority.

What did these developments bring about for agricultural policies and practice? Several commissions instituted by the government were providing information and advice for the administration to establish sound environmental management and agricultural strategies geared towards a maximisation of productivity. The Long-term Agricultural Policy Commission (LAPC) of 1948 addressed pertinent environmental issues for the commercial farming sector as well as for African reserves. Soil degradation and vegetation change were addressed pointedly. The Commission found that 'the limit of carrying capacity ... has been reached' (Botha 2005: 177) and recommended soil conservation, appropriate stocking rates, and improved livestock breeds. Reports of catastrophic degradation of southern African savannahs due to overexploitation haunted the media (Botha 2005: 176). Reserve economies were to be modernised to produce enough food for a growing African population. Botha (2005: 170–1) diagnoses that 'the local administration

[5] These were about US$1,000 (www.resbank.co.za/Research/Rates/ Pages/ SelectedHistoricalExchange AndInterestRates.aspx).
[6] NAN BOB 5 N1/15/4.
[7] NAN NAO 61 9/1 Annual Reports for the years 1946 and 1947.

began greatly to expand their managerial, developmental, and research capacities ... The aim was to impose total rationality and control. Modernization theory ruled and went with disdain for any form of local, especially African, knowledge.' On a visit to SWA in 1951 Ross, a South African soil conservation expert, argued strongly in favour of more water points and rotational grazing based on a camp system.[8] Ross's recommendations became standard policy the coming years.

7.1 Sources

There are few scientific accounts on the history of the 1950s–1980s (but see van Wolputte 2007 and Friedman 2011 for the region), while there have been a number of publications on the earlier decades of colonialism (Bollig 1998a, 1998b; Gewald 2011; Hayes 2000; Miescher 2012; Rizzo 2012). Partially this lacuna can be explained by the fact that archival sources for the 1960s, 1970s, and 1980s were only made available recently in the National Archives of Namibia. A brief examination of searching aides in the Namibia National Archives, however, shows that the sheer quantity of sources increases enormously after the 1950s. The intensification of administrative activities has also brought about a rapid increase in the volume of written documentation. Government activities were carefully planned and carried out. A number of major reports (e.g. Odendaal Report 1963; Eloff Report 1976) summarise the findings of evaluation teams. These were typically manned (women are in fact absent on these commissions) by South African senior politicians, administrators, and university professors. The Odendaal Commission's visit to Opuwo and surroundings (February 1963) resulted in protocols of discussions of several hundred pages. Communication between the Native Commissioner in Opuwo and his staff and other administrative entities was also filed in large quantities. While in the previous period personal reports dominated, now rather impersonal reports were accompanied by statistical material. The documentation of borehole-drilling and the tendering for borehole equipment in the region alone fills a number of ledgers. Regular meetings with the chiefs' council are recorded in page-long abstracts detailing who said what. These records are almost all

---

[8] NAN, SWAA 1068, A138/22, C. Ross and J. C. Fick, *Report on visit to South West Africa*, Section Soil Conservation and Extension, 31/7/1951.

A Hydrological Revolution in an African Savannah 157

written in Afrikaans. The language shift from English to Afrikaans in communication within the administration and between the administration and locals happened in the early 1950s, and was pervasive. In the 1980s, when the Kaokoland was administered under the Second Tier administration of the Herero Authority, some documents were written in Otjiherero, but the main body of the communication was still written in Afrikaans. As the top levels of the local administration remained white and Afrikaans-speaking even during the 1980s, this is rather unsurprising. The tone of administrative reports also changes somewhat. In the previous chapter I reported on Carl (Cocky) Hahn's infuriated orders to his field officers when local pastoralists did not obey orders. The language of internal documents of the administration is much more cautious, sometimes even worried: especially in the 1950s and 1960s officers were careful not to confront traditional leaders and cautiously reminded each other to desist from overbearing and rash statements. The general tone of many documents is overtly paternalistic though. In contrast to this the undertone of the many reports filling the shelves since the 1950s is austere and shows the social distance and lack of interaction between planners and those being planned for (or with).

Generally speaking there is much more archival material to be organised and analysed than for the decades before. Unfortunately, some types of archival sources are lacking. While especially Native Commissioner Carl Hahn left piles of photographs and a diary, such types of material are not to be found for the later part of the colonial archives. While colonial officers certainly took photographs in this exotic environment, these were no longer regarded as sources of knowledge for administrative purposes, but rather as visual documents of leisure time – they were private rather than public. Probably there are also a few left in private archives, as access to the native reserve and then-homeland Kaokoland was strictly controlled during these periods.[9] There is another type of source which is new and abundant

---

[9] There is the private archive of Eberhard von Koenen, who visited the region repeatedly between the end of the 1940s and the mid-1950s and made a film for a German TV station on the region and its population. Von Koenen and his wife also took photographs of people, landscapes, and what they considered to be traditional subsistence techniques (e.g. the harvesting of seeds in ant-hills, von Koenen and von Koenen 1964). Beyond the von Koenens' reports from the early 1950s there are only few private accounts of travels into the Kaokoveld.

for the period under consideration: scientific reports and publications. The administration strongly believed that its approach to modernisation and intensification had to be based on scientific results. While it did not directly encourage research on social and ecological dynamics in the region, it permitted such research where it was considered necessary to put planning on a sound basis. Starting in the early 1950s with a short ethnography of the region by government anthropologist van Warmelo (1951), Stellenbosch-trained anthropologist Johan Malan published a number of papers and wrote his PhD on the kinship system of the Himba community (Malan 1972). He also published together with the then-agricultural officer, Garth Owen-Smith, on ethnobotany (Malan and Owen-Smith 1974). Government and army anthropologist Stals published on the van der Merwes of Ehomba. This Herero-speaking community had lived with Portuguese settlers in southern Angola near Lubango for many decades, and resettled to the Kaokoveld in the 1930s and 1940s (Stals 1988). Stals also wrote and published on the history of the community founded by Vita Thom (Stals and Otto-Reiner 1999). Notably, he did his ethnography in the 1980s on communities strongly allied to the South African administration and army. Philippus Jacobus (Slang) Viljoen, a biologist from the University of Pretoria, did research on elephant communities across north-western Namibia, focusing for many years on the so-called desert elephants of the arid westernmost parts of the Kaokoveld (Viljoen 1988). His research, which included a detailed study on the detrimental effects of poaching on the elephant herds of the Kaokoveld, gained worldwide attention and was taken up in some widely distributed coffee-table books (e.g. Hall-Martin et al. 1988).

A lot of research had an applied perspective to it. While much of it was geared towards learning more about the social organisation and history of potential allies or specific social-ecological issues (declining elephant herds, ethnobotany), some research seemed to have only a scientific value. Research on a Tjimba community in the remote Baynes Mountains caused some controversy between the mid-1960s and mid-1970s. MacCalman and Grobbelaar (1965) reported on an expedition of the State Museum Windhoek which had the aim to locate a fabled

The administration was very restrictive in giving permits to private people, and only in the 1970s was access to the Kaokoveld opened for private travellers. Von Koenen's archive is the only private archive I was able to locate though.

community of stone-using Tjimba foragers in the remote highlands of the northern Kaokoveld. Indeed they did meet with two small forager communities and described their material culture, especially the ways they worked with stone flakes. They described these Tjimba as speaking a dialect of Otjiherero, but as being physically clearly distinct from Himba and Herero people (smaller in stature) (MacCalman and Grobbelaar 1965: 4). At the end of the 1960s a physical anthropologist from Pretoria, H. W. Hitzeroth, revisited this community and conducted physical anthropological studies with eleven men and four women. In two articles, only published in the mid-1970s, he gave further evidence that the members of this community formed a 'separate entity' (Hitzeroth 1976: 224) and describes the physical distinctness of the Tjimba who are 'significantly shorter statured, shorter headed, with broader mandibles and lower nasal and facial heights as [sic] the Chimba/Himba'. He estimated that the Tjimba numbered at most 150 people (Hitzeroth 1976: 189). The Tjimba are stylised as a window into the Palaeolithic – an early forager population that had clung to its ancient traditions – a 'replacement' of the *strandlopers* of earlier decades so to say. It is odd that the tale of the Tjimba stops abruptly here – they do not feature in colonial records, nor are any other scientific reports produced on them after that date. The publicity given to the studies created another image of the Kaokoveld which harked back to earlier notions of remoteness and searches for the last remnants of one species or another. It also underlined the frontier character of the Kaokoveld, where far beyond the boundaries of civilisation scientific marvels still loomed. So much for the written accounts which predominantly stem from South African scientists or administrative staff of the administration. What about sources originating with the local population?

While Wallace claims that African-authored sources become more plentiful for the 1960s–1980s (Wallace 2011: 243), in north-western Namibia documents pertaining to local voices are few for the period in question. I did not find any written accounts of locals besides a few letters written to the administration. These letters are directly addressed to the Native Commissioner and usually contain some kind of protest. Local voices are captured in the protocols of numerous meetings. While such summaries or even attempts at verbatim translations are susceptible to the censorship of administrative officers, dissent over administrative measures is astonishingly well documented. In records of meetings between traditional authorities and the administration in the 1950s and 1960s, angry commentaries by Herero and Himba chiefs are quoted at length. Many of these critical comments directly touch upon social-ecological relations: land lost to the expanding Etosha Park, boreholes, and restrictions on marketing livestock.[10]

Does oral history compensate for this lack of local voices in written sources? Not to the extent that I had hoped. While for the first decades of the twentieth century the conflict between Vita Thom and Muhona Katiti, early interactions with the colonial administration, and resettlement in the southern Kaokoland all provided the material for grand tales of oral tradition, such tales are suspiciously lacking for the 1950s–1980s. The expansive borehole-drilling programme was hardly commented upon during interviews. Of course, there were personal reminiscences which would provide some local perspective on a single borehole being drilled. People also recalled how Opuwo grew and in the 1980s became a centre for the South African Defence Force and its paramilitary wing, Koevoet. However, information on these events and processes always remained highly place-specific, and specific to individual informants. I was surprised that the war of liberation into which the Kaokoveld's population was dragged between the late 1970s and 1989 left few traces in oral traditions. Many people simply said that they hardly knew what was happening and were as afraid of the South African army as they were of fighters from the Peoples Liberation Army of Namibia (PLAN). In a book on oral traditions I published in the late 1990s (Bollig 1997) oral recollections addressed the pre-colonial period highlighting the so-called Kwena Wars and detailed the conflict between 'big men' during early colonial days. There is a highly consensual presentation of these time periods. In stark contrast, the civil war and the numerous government programmes of the 1950s and 1960s are hardly mentioned in these texts – they do not form part of the collective memory. They are not regarded as part of *ombazu* (tradition) but are classified as *omapolotika* (politics). Measures to check poaching or to scrutinise the mineral resources of the region and to improve conservatory measures were hardly mentioned in interviews I conducted. The only topic consistently raised

[10] The first (and perhaps the only) longer published document written by a local is Silas Kuvare's ethnography of the Herero of the Kaokoveld, which is annexed to Sundermeier's ethnography of the Mbanderu Herero (Sundermeier 1977).

in traditions and in biographical recollections is the centennial drought of 1980/81 which killed about 95 per cent of all cattle in the region. The drought is addressed as *Otjita*, 'The Dying', and every adult person had vivid recollections on how he (or she) personally fared during this critical time and how this disaster affected the community.

7.2 A Hydrological Revolution in an African Savannah

In South Africa the report of the Tomlinson Commission laid down the concepts of 'trusteeship' and 'guardianship' as principles of administration in African reserves in the early 1950s. After its ascent to power the Apartheid government soon realised that there was very little indepth knowledge on African reserves on which a policy geared towards economic development could be based. The Commission gathered an enormous amount of data on various aspects of life in African reserves (Butler et al. 1978: 159–61). The report outlined a programme to raise rural incomes in reserves and to take measures against degradation. In South Africa the report caused a transition from a simplistic segregationist model to a segregation-with-development agenda, bringing about considerable change in the administrative framework of governance in homelands (Butler et al. 1978: 161). The infamous 'betterment' schemes of the 1950s and 1960s which transformed agriculture in many African reserves (Naumann 2014) were an immediate result of the report. In Namibia's African reserves improved planning entailed more elaborate forms of reporting and knowledge accumulation. Continuous and standardised reporting was one way to do this. However, only with the release of the Odendaal Report in 1963 was a framework for development established.

Considering Options for Development

From the late 1940s various development schemes were eagerly discussed.[11] Agricultural experts discussed the potential of improving local breeds through the import of Afrikaner bulls. A 1952 report took up the issue of water supply and suggested that a team of geologists

---

[11] NAN NAO 61 9/1 Annual Reports for the Years 1946–1952; Officer in Charge Opuwo to Chief Native Commissioner. The Annual Report for 1949 calls for the opening up of additional water supplies.

should test options to provide more boreholes. In a telling twist, agricultural development was thought to provide the basis for identity politics and a direct aid to disadvantaged communities. An agricultural officer argued that concerted development aid would help to 'uplift' the disadvantaged Ovatjimba pastoralists. More boreholes in their areas would lower stocking rates, and more numerous and better-nourished livestock would bring more money to the community, and necessarily bring about development.[12] In a parallel move, people not owning livestock were to be encouraged to look for work outside the Kaokoveld. It was alleged that more boreholes in the Kaokoveld would also help the administration to separate Herero, Himba, and Tjimba.[13]

Already these reports from the early 1950s suggest that the drilling of more boreholes would contribute significantly to the solution of a number of developmental challenges and make higher stocking numbers possible in the Kaokoveld at an ecologically sustainable level.[14] In 1949 the Annual Report had stated categorically that 'vast areas of the Kaokoveld are uninhabited due to the lack of open water'.[15] Since the mid-1950s the administration made a concerted effort to initiate water development. A first set of boreholes was drilled

---

[12] NAN SWAA 2515 A552/13-1 Allgemene inspeksieverslag – Kaokoveld, Landboubeampte J. C. du Plessis, 27/11/1952 an Die Hoefnaturellekommissaris. Allgemene inspeksieverslag – Kaokoveld, Landboubeampte J. C. du Plessis.

[13] NAN BOP5 N1/15/4/1. Native Commissioner Ovamboland to Chief Native Commissioner Windhoek, 30/4/1952 'Tribal Affairs: Kaokoveld'. Chief Native Commissioner in Windhoek, Native Commissioner Eedes, in Ovamboland, stated in April 1952: 'There is continual friction between the different groups of the same Race in the Kaokoveld. If more water supplies were opened up, it would be possible to separate the different groups, for instance, place all the Ovahimbas in the North, all the Hereros in the South and all the Ovatjimbas in the North West. In this way the Ovatjimbas would be given an opportunity to administer the portion of country allotted to them and have representatives on the Kaokoveld Tribal Council. As no water supplies have been opened up by means of boring, it will not be possible to separate the different groups at present. The Ovatjimbas will, therefore, have to continue to submit to the present system of administration – a Council of Herero and Ovahimba headmen.' Van Wolputte argues that such plans were meant to lay the basis for a later subdivision of the Kaokoveld into separate Tjimba, Herero, and Himba homelands (van Wolputte 2004: 161).

[14] This is in contrast to what happened in neighbouring Ovamboland at the same time. Kreike (2009: 88–9) reports that rapidly increasing cattle numbers were perceived as a liability there and a number of programmes were started to diminish the growth of cattle herds.

[15] NAN NAO 61 9/1 Annual Report 1949.

in 1954, to the south of Opuwo. In order to exploit existing water sources in a more rational way the capacity of natural wells at Kaoko Otavi and Sesfontein was measured.[16]

Policies for agricultural development gained even more prominence as plans for labour export from the Kaokoveld were thwarted. Trips to the Kaokoland by SWANLA officials and leading administrative staff in the late 1940s and early 1950s did not produce any major results, despite the fact that officers pressurised traditional authorities in a number of meetings.[17] In a letter to the Native Commissioner in Ondangwa the Officer in Charge in Opuwo speaks of a 'definite averseness to farm work'.[18] Since 1949 Annual Reports by the Officer in Charge in Opuwo to the Chief Native Commissioner in Windhoek contained the category 'Idle Natives' and from 1952 onwards the category 'Development'.[19] In 1954 the recruiting office for labour in Opuwo finally closed down due to lack of success:[20] The Kaokoveld was definitely no longer regarded as a labour reserve; the future lay in an improvement of livestock husbandry and a gradual expansion of agriculture. A number of measures were discussed: borehole-drilling, improvement of local breeds, encouragement of livestock sales, and gardening.

While there had been occasional reports on environmental degradation in the Kaokoveld before, now a number of studies ascertained that the problem of overstocking and degradation was grave indeed. An agricultural development plan drafted in 1957 argued that

---

[16] NAN SWAA 2514 A552/3 Water Supply.
[17] NAN SWAA 2515 A552/18 Reports on a trip to the Kaokoveld and summarising a meeting with chiefs on 21/2/1951.
[18] NAN SWAA 2515 A552/18, 14/3/1952 Officer in Charge, Opuwo to Native Commissioner Ondangwa; in prior years there had been some enrolment of labourers from immigrants from Southern Angola; the 1946 Annual Report mentions a larger group of Angolans crossing into Namibia.
[19] NAN NAO 61/9/1 Annual Reports for the Years 1946–1952, here: Reports for the Years 1949 and 1952.
[20] NAN SWAA 2515 A552/18 'Native labour' Letter dated 7/12/1954, Mr Nuwe SWANLA, Grootfontein to Native Commissioner: 'For your information I mention that during two and a half years recruited 253 labourers in the Kaokoveld. This fell very short of expectations. ... We secured fewer recruits during the last four months than during the earlier part of the recruiting experiment. ... Two hawking trips in the Kaokoveld were undertaken during the past two months; the first trip was a hopeless failure, practically nothing was sold.'

overgrazing was pertinent and that action had to be taken against degradation.[21] The report ascertained that the region had a stocking rate of some 100,000 cattle. It assumed that an absolute carrying capacity would be reached with 120,000 cattle, but emphasised that already at that time – that is, in the late 1950s – with livestock numbers nearing the carrying capacity, detrimental vegetation dynamics were clearly observable. The report recommended comprehensive measures. In contrast to other reports, this one opted for an improvement of breeds rather than an expansion of boreholes: A breeding herd of about 1,000 bulls was to be introduced in order to 'improve' the genetic material of the Kaokoveld's cattle. In a period of eighteen to twenty years all breeding bulls in the region were to be replaced from this breeding herd. This nicely circumscribes the jump in scales in developmental measures: Whereas in the early 1950s an officer thought to improve the situation by sending four breeding bulls to Sesfontein, now the input of 1,000 bulls or even a complete replacement of local bulls, was contemplated. As the scheme was to have a long-term perspective it was important to reserve grazing grounds for this huge breeding herd. The officer assumed that per head of cattle 20 morgen were sufficient, and that in total up to 24,000 morgen should be necessary (70–80 square miles). The report discussed several possible field sites for such a major scheme (the Opuwo region, the Okangundumba flats, and the Kunene Valley) and then argued strongly for the Kunene Valley option (extending from 10 miles east of Swartbooisdrift towards Epupa for 60 miles, with a width of 3–5 miles, resulting in about 180–300 square miles set aside for the scheme). The easy accessibility of water was emphasised as a particular advantage of this location. It is remarkable that in 1957 the report still says that the terrain was livestock-free – hence earlier restrictions were seemingly still in place.[22] The report also advocated that should the Kunene Valley not be considered for a large breeding scheme, it should be used as a quarantine camp.

The project never came about, however, and the administration focused its efforts on the drilling of boreholes. Already in the early

---

[21] NAN BOP 53 Landboubeampte Ondangua to Die Naturellekommissaris, Ovamboland 2/4/1957.
[22] NAN SWA/KC/7E/52 p. 658. During the hearings of the Odendaal Commission in February 1963 the Kunene Valley was described as a cattle-free zone.

A Hydrological Revolution in an African Savannah

1950s a number of boreholes had been drilled south-west of Opuwo.[23] For some thirteen successfully drilled boreholes, £19,050 sterling was spent, and another five unsuccessful drillings resulted in costs of £2,094 sterling. In 1955 the Chief Native Commissioner had made water development a priority task for the administration in communal areas in northern Namibia. He had urged officers to take account of unused lands, and asked them to consider whether such lands could be used productively if provided with boreholes. He argued:

Water provisioning will of course be the most prominent item of the development that has been considered. In this context it is only required to indicate the number of water-points, estimated 8 to 10 miles apart, which would be necessary for the normal demands of the region taking into account the number of livestock and the availability of land that has not been used yet or not used to its full capacity.[24]

Local Opposition to Ontwikkeling

This policy, oriented towards technical development, was not welcomed at all by the traditional authorities. They were highly critical of the programme and flatly rejected the proposal that the tribal trust fund should contribute to the payment of boreholes. In 1956 the Chief Native Commissioner had to telegraph to the Native Commissioner in Ondangwa that all drilling had come to a halt as chiefs were refusing to contribute.[25] In fact traditional authorities were irritated, and opposed government intervention vociferously. Van Wolputte (2004: 152) reports on a meeting of the local administration with chiefs to pacify locals who had decided to boycott government initiatives to provide water. In 1955 an inoculation campaign had been brought to a standstill by local opposition, and in the late 1950s leaders rejected the governmental donation of 25,000 R which had been meant to spur the borehole programme.[26] Apparently traditional authorities were

---

[23] NAN SWAA 2517 A552/26 1953, Secretary of SWA to Administrator.
[24] NAN BAC HN5/1/3/18 Kantoor van die Hoofnaturellekommissaris, WDK Naturellesake Omsendbrief Nr. 17 of 1955, 26/8/1955.
[25] NAN BAC HN5/1/3/18 Hoofnaturelle Kommissaris Windhoek, Telegram an Naturelle Kommissaris, Ondangwa, 17/2/1956.
[26] NAN SWA/KC/7E/52 p. 663. Reported in a meeting with the Odendaal Commission in 1963 by Native Commissioner Ben van Zyl. Van Zyl said 'They don't want anything from the government. It is being said to them like, they

afraid that they might become indebted to the government and that the government could claim further land in compensation from them later on. In the early 1960s cattle inspectors were chased away from herds, and people blatantly refused to pay taxes to the tribal trust fund (van Wolputte 2004: 163). Local leaders fiercely complained against the territorial expansion of the Etosha Park in the Otjivasandu region and bitterly reported that local livestock had been shot when transgressing the boundary into the park.[27] The Chief Bantu Commissioner Blignaut informed the leaders that the border had been established in 1947, and that it was high time that local herders accepted this boundary. He pleaded that the boundary should be fenced to prevent any misunderstanding. He also argued that the demarcation of the boundary with Ovamboland at Otjitjekwa, slightly north of the park, had been installed to prevent livestock diseases entering the Kaokoveld – so it should be regarded as a protective device for local livestock-keeping rather than as a form of confinement. Traditional authorities heavily criticised the government and rejected governmental intervention. In a meeting in January 1961 the Native Commissioner Eaton blamed the chiefs in a highly frustrated manner 'Ek verstaan julle will nie die verbeterings he nie' ('I understand you do not want any improvements') after the chiefs had rejected the proposal that a hospital be built in Kaoko Otavi. The reasoning Chief Willem Hartley gave is quite telling: 'Kaoko Otavi is the heartland of the Kaokoveld and because of that no intervention is condoned there.'[28] Traditional authorities were given an immense freedom to express their ideas and to dwell at length on their reasons for objecting to this or that governmental measure. The administrative staff members present at these meetings were rather passive and cautious, and repeatedly attempted to reassure the chiefs and their followers. In a meeting in March 1962 the administration informed the traditional authorities that any kind of insubordination against chiefs was indeed punishable, and that guilty youngsters should

---

should not accept anything. Afterwards they came with the story that they feared to be urged to pay back the money later and that they did not know where to find it' (my translation).

[27] NAN BOP 5/1/15/4/1 Vergadering met Herero hoofmanne en inwoners te Otjitjekwa op 25 Julie 1961.

[28] NAN BOP 5 N1/15/4/3 Report on a Meeting on 27/1/1961. The chief is reported saying: 'Kaoko-Otavi is die hart van ons land daarom kan daar nie gebou word nie.'

receive physical punishment and guilty elders and women should pay fines in livestock.[29] Nevertheless, despite repeated efforts by the administration to reassure the chiefs they often attacked administrative measures and the overall approach to development.

One bone of contention was the financing of development programmes: local leaders rejected financial engagements by the government. In a meeting in March 1962 a chief openly exclaimed that they did not want any money from the 'minister' and asserted: 'ons kan vir ons self sorg' ('we can look after ourselves'). He suggested that the government could help (less developed) Himba and Tjimba with its money, but should abstain from aiding Herero communities and trying to gain influence. While other Herero leaders agreed and asserted that they could provide sufficient money to drill boreholes by themselves,[30] Himba and Tjimba chiefs disagreed as to what extent monetary help by the government was acceptable. While some agreed to the flat rejection of government assistance, others, such as the main Himba leader Muinimuhoro Kapika, asserted that they still needed further boreholes. In the meeting the head of the local administration answered that the money from the *stamfonds* would not suffice to drill a single borehole. In order to prevent any diversion of resistance a Herero leader quickly asserted that despite some minor disagreements, the administration should come to regard all communities of the Kaokoveld as one nation ('ons is een nasie, ons is almal Hereros'). In 1962 the confrontation between local communities and administration came to a climax, and two letters full of serious complaints against Acting Commissioner Marais led to his removal from office (van Wolputte 2004: 163).[31] Hence, there was ample pressure on the administration to carry out development initiatives swiftly, and the

---

[29] NAN BOP 5 N1/15/4/3 Notule van Vergadering met Hoofmanne, Kaokoveld 20 Maart 1962. Referring to a decision taken by the Council on 6 May 1958: 'Strict action will be taken against all forms of contempt. Young men will then receive not more than 10 lashings with a light cane. Old men and women will be fined one head of cattle' (my translation).

[30] NAN BOP 5 N1/15/6/8 Notule van Vergadering met Hoofmanne, 20 to 23 Maart 1962. 'We have our own money and this will support us. We shall make water (i.e. drill boreholes) from the money in our account' (my translation).

[31] On the demand of Hosea Kutako, the Herero paramount chief, the Kaokoveld's Herero and Himba had also contributed cattle and money to the protest campaign against the South African occupation of Namibia by Michael Scott and a UN diplomat (de Caprio) had visited the area in 1962 to record the opinions of local leaders.

Odendaal Commission visiting Opuwo knew that it would be criticised. More letters of complaint were written in 1963. At a meeting with traditional authorities in May 1963 a long letter with complaints was read to the authorities. Disrespect for tribal authorities by the administration, the incarceration of locals without consent of the tribal council, and bodily punishments of locals were among the issues raised. However, the major point made in this letter of complaint was that the administration was attempting to administer the communities of the Kaokoveld as distinct ethnic groups, thereby subverting tribal unity. The letter asserts that while God had made the people one '*stam*', the administration had sought to create five units – 'Ovahimba, Ovatjimba, Herero, Ovambo and Damara'.[32]

In addition, the controversial issue of the vaccination of livestock was taken up again. While the government officers argued for regular vaccinations, especially to prevent further foot-and-mouth epidemics, local leaders rejected this and argued that despite the vaccinations over the previous twenty years the livestock diseases were still present, and that in fact quite a number of cattle had died because of vaccinations (see also van Wolputte 2013). They argued that enforced vaccinations had caused a lot of distrust and conflict. Chief Willem Hartley, the long-term translator of the administration, exclaimed: 'We [the local leaders] are now at war with the commissioner and the government due to the activities of the veterinarians. We plead that the veterinarians leave this place because they have killed us' (my translation).[33] In a highly frustrated manner one administrator exclaimed that whatever kind of development the administration attempted to bring, it was rejected by the local leaders. Steven van Wolputte (2007: 114) quotes a desperate Native Commissioner van Zyl reporting in the Annual Report for 1964: 'Herero have turned to a general boycott of everything, even if the development is to their advantage.'

Protests from leaders continued throughout the 1960s. In a meeting in January 1966 with the Chief Bantu Commissioner Eaton at Opuwo, further complaints were voiced. Eaton admitted that some of the government's information policy had been misguided but that on the whole he had gained the impression that local leaders would reject any form of development. He scolded the leaders and rhetorically asked

---

[32] NAN BOP 5 N1/15/6/8 Notule van Vergadering gehou 15 tot 18 Mei 1963.
[33] NAN BOP 5 N1/15/6/8 Notule van Vergadering gehou 15 tot 18 Mei 1963.

them whether 'they really want to stay behind like Bushmen who [still] live like baboons'.[34]

A report on a meeting taking place in early 1968 in Otjondeka condensed the concerns of local leaders.[35] The meeting was apparently meant to quell resistance to government programmes, but resulted in more argument directed against the government. A local chief flatly stated that while the administration was thinking about some kind of development projects, they, the leaders, were considering the loss of their land, for example to the Etosha Park. One chief from the area, Langman Tjihahuarua wondered: 'What I do not understand is that what we ask for we do not get, and we get what we do not ask for. The Government gives money while we ask for land.'[36] In the same meeting paramount chief Kephas Muzuma stated: 'we are afraid of the money of the Republic ... the government has suppressed us now for forty years'.[37] He argued that the government made a lot of money from diamonds and other resources and invested that money abroad. He wondered why it was not reinvested locally, and why now locals were being asked to contribute to school-building. Another leader exclaimed, 'We do not want to work (any longer) under the Republic'.[38] This criticism is very clear, and does not conform to images of a local population subdued by an authoritarian government and traditional leaders backing the administration.

Indeed, local leaders were afraid to provide more space for the engagement of the administration in what they perceived as internal affairs. At the meeting they carefully considered whether payments to chiefs could be interpreted as an attempt by the government to co-opt local leadership. They clearly saw that the drilling of boreholes or the building of clinics would make them inevitably dependent on the government. It would trap them in an infrastructure provided and maintained by an oppressive state. The next section will show that

[34] NAN BOP 5 N1/15/4/3 Notule van Vergadering gehou te Opohoho of 27 Januarie 1966.
[35] NAN BOP 5 N1/15/6/8 Vergadering gehou to Oseondeka (sic) op 14 Februarie 1968 (my translation).
[36] NAN BOP 5 N1/15/6/8 Vergadering gehou to Oseondeka (sic) op 14 Februarie 1968 (my translation).
[37] NAN BOP 5 N1/15/6/8 Vergadering gehou to Oseondeka (sic) op 14 Februarie 1968 (my translation).
[38] NAN BOP 5 N1/16/6/8, Vergadering at Otjondeka on 14/2/1960 (my translation).

they then gave in as they realised that boreholes could in fact be an instrument with which to cement their chiefly power as they were given the authority to decide where boreholes were to be placed.

Rolling Out the Boreholes Programme

Despite local resistance the government decided to start drilling more boreholes in the early 1960s. A major drought between 1959 and 1962 which brought about severe losses in livestock convinced the administration that immediate action was necessary. The administration also retracted its prior rule that locals should contribute to the drilling of boreholes in communal areas, thereby making the administration (at least financially) independent of the consent of local leaders. The immense bureaucratic fervour of the drilling programme which slowly got off the ground in 1962/63 was remarkable.[39] Each borehole was registered in a complex manner: Communication in the planning phase as well as data on the actual drilling and test-pumping to establish yield was all carefully filed, as was communication on the tendering for the fitting of boreholes with pipes and adequate pump systems.[40]

Money for boreholes was entered into yearly budgets of the administration from the early 1960s. For the year 1962, for example, some 20,000 R was budgeted for new boreholes (drilling plus fitting).[41] For the year 1963 the same sum was budgeted for some fourteen new boreholes. For each borehole a detailed geological evaluation was conducted – at least, this was what the regulations required. In reality, however, the process was rather swift and often did not take ecological considerations into account. After an application by a chief, the Native Commissioner decided single-handedly whether to drill the borehole. Sometimes boreholes were even drilled against the judgement of officials. In a letter written in August 1962 the Chief Bantu Commissioner in Windhoek expressed his understanding of an official's reluctance to give orders for the drilling of a borehole that Chief Muinimuhoro had applied for. Apparently the official had voiced ecological considerations as an argument against this borehole. However, his superior argued that 'in this time of unrest' it was of the greatest importance not

---

[39] NAN BAC HN5/1/3/18 has numerous files on the planning, registration, and tendering of boreholes.
[40] NAN BAC HN5/1/3/18.   [41] NAN BAC HN5/1/3/18.

to give locals any pretext to criticise the government or to use the denial of a borehole for propaganda against the government.[42]

The Odendaal Commission in Opuwo

In 1962 the South African government instituted the Odendaal Commission, a group of experts and administrators under the leadership of Frans Hendrik Odendaal, the administrator of Transvaal, to present a development plan for the commercial ranching area as well as the communal areas of Namibia (Wallace 2011: 261). J. P. Bruwer, an anthropologist, was responsible for improving the Commission's capacity to come to grips with local conditions in African reserves. Only a year later the Commission presented a comprehensive plan for how Namibia could be economically and socially developed along Apartheid lines. The Commission's recommendations have often been thought to signal the implementation of a radically new policy. Its major strategy for the agricultural development of the Kaokoveld, however, enshrined an approach that had been well tested over the previous years: the drilling of more boreholes.

I would like to take a closer look at discussions taking place in Opuwo and Orumana over two days during the course of the visit of the Commission in February 1963.[43] The consultations were organised into several sessions with each lasting between one and a half and three hours. The members of the Commission asked local experts about details of local development. In a first meeting on Monday 11 February 1963 between 10:00 a.m. and 12:00, the resident teacher and the health worker at Orumana were both consulted and asked about the health and educational status of the residents. Already in this initial meeting five salient themes were elaborated by the three white administrative staff members and the Commission:

(1) there was massive politically motivated local resistance to development measures;
(2) there was a somewhat irrational local attitude to cattle;

---

[42] NAN BAC HN5/1/3/18 Hoofbantoekommissaris van SWA an Administratiewe Beampte Ohopoho, 27/8/1962.
[43] I would like to thank Christo Botha for a hint to the files and the permission to copy part of the files from his data set. These files were listed in the Pretoria Archives under SWA/KC/7E/52.

(3) local herders were not eager to seek contracts as labour migrants;
(4) local people were easily manipulated politically;
(5) white officials were branded as culprits for development problems by local leaders.[44]

The next consultation took place in Opuwo on the same day between 2:20 p.m. and 6:30 pm. This hearing was public: in addition to four chiefs and seven councillors, the protocol says that 230 'volgelinge' were present. All four chiefs belonged to the group of traditional authorities which had collaborated with the government to some extent before. While these chiefs may have been regarded as government-friendly, they used the public hearing to voice stern criticism. Willem Hartley opened the general critique by pointing out that the Kaokoveld had been completely neglected by the government and that any kind of modern infrastructure such as schools, clinics, or markets were lacking. He especially criticised the fact that any form of livestock marketing was almost impossible due to government regulations.[45] A major thrust of the critique was directed at the loss of land due to the expansion of the Etosha Park. Kephas Muzuma openly read out a list of the places which had to be left, and pleaded that households should be allowed to return to these places. Repeatedly during the hearing he came back to the issue of land losses, and criticised the practice of shooting cattle straying into prohibited areas. The heftiness of their critique is astounding. The government was attacked as 'groot skelm' (great trickster, or even cunning thief) and scolded for cutting the ties of friendship between the local population and the administration. Chief Upani formulated the most aggressive critique:[46]

I am the headman of the Tjimbas and the Himbas. We have been together with the Government for a long time, but the whole time the Government just kept following us. It seems to be as if the Government never establishes a friendship bond with the people. He is a great trickster, because he is a white man. He is the kind of man that can never stand a poor man. That cunningness of the Government is what we have got to know now ... Now at this current moment we have nothing to do with you. If you do not know me, I am the owner of the Kaokoveld ... Rather pack and drive back. (My translation)

---

[44] NAN SWA/KC/7E/52 pp. 564–6.　[45] NAN SWA/KC/7E/52 pp. 594–5.
[46] NAN SWA/KC/7E/52 pp. 623–4.

However, again and again the official chairing the meeting returned to the issue of boreholes. He voiced his opinion that the grazing in most parts of the Kaokoveld was not in a good state and that more boreholes would solve the overgrazing problem. Repeatedly he asked the audience to name stretches of land which did not have adequate water supply.[47] He advocated development (*ontwikkeling*) and proclaimed: 'The government will now come; it will build schools, it will build hospitals, and it will help to make roads and boreholes ... the government will pay for [all this] by itself' (my translation).

In two evening sessions on that same day a geologist and an agriculturalist were interviewed in detail: again the inquiry focused mainly on boreholes.[48] Technical issues were discussed and the management of boreholes detailed. It was undisputed that the entire responsibility for management of the boreholes would lie with the administration and that all costs would be carried by the government. In discussions with the geologist it was pointed out that more boreholes were technically feasible and unproblematic from a hydrological point of view. The hydrological expert also advised the Commission that the natural wells of the Kaokoveld should be developed as well.

The finalised Odendaal Report (Government of South Africa 1963) then recommended boreholes as the key to economic development in the Kaokoveld:[49] 'It may be expected, however, that, when better use is made of the underground water resources by means of boreholes, it will be possible to extend the utilization of grazing in order to increase the livestock population to the benefit of the economy of the Kaokoveld.' Great hopes were placed on technical innovation – many South African officers had witnessed the hydrological development of the South African landscape through extensive borehole-drilling. There the number of windmill-driven boreholes increased from 44,000 in 1926, to 101,000 in 1946, to 151,000 in 1955, and a considerable local industry manufacturing borehole equipment had developed (Archer 2003: 122). In 1963 the administration also gazetted a team of experts to evaluate the development of rural water supply and to judge the potential for a further expansion of the system of boreholes.

[47] NAN SWA/KC/7E/52 pp. 594–5.   [48] NAN SWA/KC/7E/52 pp. 641ff.
[49] In 1963 a first scientific report on boreholes was compiled (Blom, L. Horn J. K. Linning, P. Meyer n.d. [probably 1963] Boorplekke Kaokoveld). The report is accessible at the Namibian National Archive NAN BAC HN5/1/3/18.

It is likely that this was done as an immediate follow-up of the Odendaal Commission's findings. The team was constituted by water engineers and geologists. Evidently it submitted a report arguing for a further development of boreholes.[50]

Throughout the latter part of the 1960s, 1970s, and 1980s boreholes were drilled in large numbers in the Kaokoveld. The ideal process ran as follows: At the beginning of the year the agricultural office in Windhoek detailed how many boreholes could be drilled with the funds available. The actual decision about where boreholes were drilled was left to local administrative staff in Opuwo. There was never a comprehensive plan detailing where boreholes should strategically be drilled to provide maximum grazing at a sustainable level. Local chiefs applied to the Department of Water Affairs for the placement of a borehole in their area and were then consulted by local officials to identify an optimal placement (Garth Owen-Smith, former Agricultural Officer, personal communication). Usually chiefs brought up their wishes in the meetings with the administration.

The chiefs usually tried to convince the administration to fit the borehole with an engine. However, often the administration opted for wind-pumps, which was the cheaper and the less troublesome solution for them. In the 1960s and 1970s often the pleas for more boreholes took up considerable time during the formal meetings of the administration with the local chiefs. Chiefs often competed with each other for boreholes, and an administrator in the late 1970s voiced his concern that the development of water was indeed what the traditional leaders were after: 'It is obvious that "water" is the central concern of the chiefs and all ask for "water" [development] ... The development of boreholes and the maintenance of water supply infrastructure is of the utmost importance to gain the trust of local inhabitants'[51] (my translation).

The Water Affairs officer in Opuwo tried to match a list of applications for boreholes handed in by chiefs to his budget, and finally decided which applications were to be approved. The geological section of the Water Affairs section then established exactly where a borehole was to be drilled. The Department of Water Affairs tendered the drilling

---

[50] NAN BAC HN5/1/3/18 Report of Blom, L. Horn J. K. Linning, P. Meyer n.d. (probably 1963) Boorplekke Kaokoveld, MS.
[51] NAN BOP 5 N1/15/4/1 Notes of a meeting on 13 November 1978.

and a contractor came to drill the boreholes. The administrative section dealing with boreholes employed a white superintendent and sixty black local workers who earned 50–80 R per month. A modest local labour market gradually developed through labour-intensive government projects. While the drilling of a borehole and the fitting of equipment were tendered out on behalf of the Ministry for Agriculture, the later maintenance of boreholes was completely run by the Department of Water Affairs, and borehole maintenance became one of the major activities of the administration.

Boreholes were carefully registered and fully maintained by the Department of Water Affairs (see Figure 7.1). For all boreholes a brief estimate of their hydrological potential and their agricultural use was noted down. Figure 7.1 shows such a summary for a borehole drilled in the Marienfluss area. It was especially these boreholes in the Marienfluss Valley which were later thought to be responsible for an ecological disaster.

Ecological concerns did not really matter. The suitability of wells was judged not only by looking at their potential contribution to livestock husbandry but also from a local political perspective. Loyal chiefs were rewarded with boreholes and could thereby show their followers that indeed they could influence the administration in a beneficial way.

In the 1950s some forty-three boreholes were drilled in total; these were all around Opuwo or to the south-east of Opuwo. During the 1960s another 136 boreholes were drilled, and in the 1970s 128 more boreholes were put in place. The Kaokoveld was now covered with a network of boreholes, some of them equipped with wind-pumps, some with motor-driven pumps, and some with hand-pumps. In the 1980s another fifty-seven boreholes were added. Drilling continued well into the 1990s (see Map 7.1). While in the 1960s boreholes were negotiated and then drilled with little environmental concern, in the late 1970s the damage done by too many boreholes and high stocking rates was clearly visible and chiefs were advised to consider the arid nature of the Kaokoveld and encouraged to sell more livestock. Apparently a regulation was implemented that boreholes had to be set at least 11 km apart.[52]

---

[52] NAN BOP 5 N1/15/4/1 Notes of a meeting on 13 November 1978.

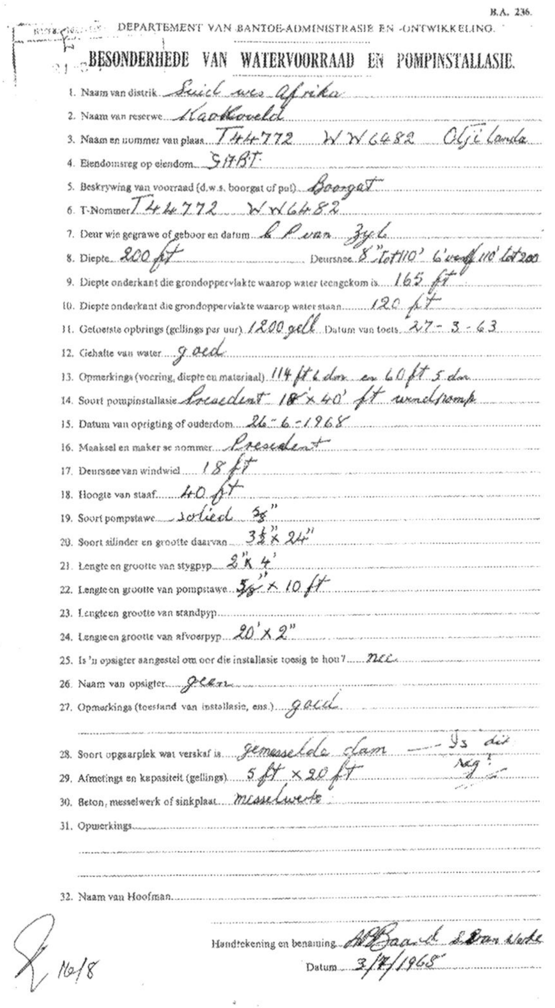

176   *The State, Intervention, and Local Appropriations*

Figure 7.1 Registration sheet of a borehole.
Source: NAN BOP 5 N1/15/4/1

A report in 1975 summarises the successes of borehole-drilling campaigns.[53] In total some 268 wells had been drilled, 189 of them successfully. Of these, 40 were equipped with wind-pumps, 24 with animal-powered mechanisms (*dierekragpompe*), 43 with engines, and

---
[53] NAN BOP 7 N1/15/6 Memorandum: Feite Posisie van die Kaokoland 1975.

A Hydrological Revolution in an African Savannah

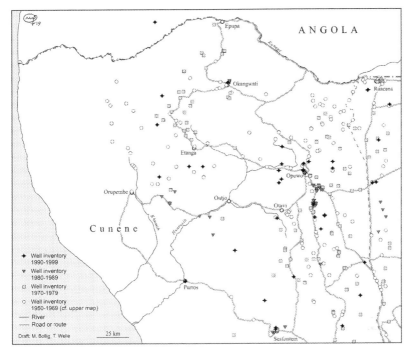

Map 7.1 Map of boreholes established until 1999.
Source: Department of Water Affairs, Opuwo

22 with hand-pumps. Some 60 were not yet developed at that time.[54] Besides boreholes a number of dams had been built. These were so-called sand dams. Behind a storage wall silt and sand built up to establish a body which could store water during periods of high flood. The checks in the layout of the dam were based on methods developed by the US Bureau of Reclamation. They were built along the 'Standard Design Procedure – Arch Dam Design – Small Dams' which specified the proportions of the arch and the amount of cement needed.[55] A report in 1975 says that six dams had been erected in

---

[54] A second comprehensive report is handed in 1976. D. Page, 1975, *Evaluasie van die Hulpbronne van Kaokoland en Ontwikkelingsvoorstelle* (Stellenbosch: Universiteit van Stellenbosch). This report gives a list of 44 boreholes which are apparently meant to be developed in the near future.
[55] NAN BAC HN5/1/3/18 Director of Water Affairs Windhoek to Chief Bantu Affairs Commissioner, Windhoek 'Storage Dams in Kaokoveld' September 1967.

the recent past and asserted that more dams were being requested by local leaders.[56]

Boreholes and dams were the first enduring physical infrastructure of the state in much of the Kaokoveld landscape. They had a lasting impact on the region's environmental infrastructure. Borehole-drilling was inextricably linked to the extension of a network of bush roads. In order to drill a borehole new roads had to be bulldozed into the bush, and in order to maintain these boreholes the roads also had to be maintained. At the end of the 1970s more or less all settled places were connected by roads and were accessible by the administration. This rhizomatic expansion of the state penetrated the local environmental infrastructure effectively and irrevocably. At the same time it provided an entirely new infrastructure to this social-ecological system, an infrastructure that on the one hand facilitated the coupling of more subsystems than before and on the other hand tied mobile livestock producers to a man-made and state-controlled hydrological system.

7.3 Other Development Projects: Modernising a Rural Economy

While the drilling of boreholes was certainly the biggest development project aimed at the intensification of livestock husbandry, other projects were envisioned and carried out as well – all of them had considerable social-ecological implications. New livestock breeds were introduced, and various options for increasing livestock sales were considered. Gardening was intensified in specific places. In the mid-1970s the development of specific agricultural growth-points was considered, which would be based on extensive irrigated agriculture. The following paragraphs outline these development projects and programmes.

Breeding and Increasing Livestock Sales

In the early 1950s the import of 'improved' livestock breeds was considered. In 1951 agricultural officers gave the immediate instruction that four such bulls should be bought for the Sesfontein reserve. They argued that 'by using improved breeding methods' the best could be made of local cattle, which arguably had a number of advantages in

[56] NAN BOP 7 N1/15/6 Memorandum: Feite Posisie van die Kaokoland 1975.

an arid environment.[57] Their suggestion that a breeding herd constituted by thirty head of selected local cows and breeding bulls should be started near Opuwo was never realised. A year later, in 1952, the visiting agricultural expert devoted his attention to an improvement of small stock through the import of cattle of the South African Boerbok breed.[58] The 'improvement' of local breeds remained a salient topic. An agricultural development plan in 1957 proposed a scheme in which breeding bulls would be kept and would breed with selected stock from the region. Furthermore, 'improved' bulls were to be sold to locals in order to rapidly improve parameters of the regional herd. In a fine-grained manner it was budgeted that per year some sixty-six new bulls had to be introduced into the Kaokoveld's cattle herds to influence local herds sustainably.[59] In 1962 a plan for the improvement of the local sheep breed was submitted, and an initial batch of sheep was bought. It was diagnosed that the local breed 'is not strong and rapidly loses shape ... an improvement is urgently recommended' (my translation).[60] In 1966 it was again established that the local cattle breed urgently needed to be improved[61] and in the early 1970s a fairly comprehensive programme developed in which individual 'progressive' farmers could buy improved livestock at subsidised prices. The Bantu Trust sold many Afrikaner bulls to local farmers since the early 1970s. Seemingly it was mainly local businessmen and occasionally chiefs who took advantage of the government's offer.[62] The sale of subsidised cattle, goats, and sheep was practised throughout the 1970s.[63] The import of breeding stock impacted the herds of Herero communities living around Opuwo and in the south-western parts of the Kaokoveld

---

[57] NAN SWAA 2515 A552/13-1 Inspection of the Kaokoveld by Agricultural Officer; Inspection of the Kaokoveld by Agricultural Officer, tour 10/12/1951–18/12/1951.
[58] NAN SWAA 2515 A552/13-1 Allgemene inspeksieverslag – Kaokoveld, Landboubeampte J. C. du Plessis. 27/11/1952 an Die Hoefnaturellekommissoaris.
[59] NAN BOP 53 Kaokoveld Teel Stasie. Landboubeampte Ondangwa to Naturellekommissaris Ondangwa 2/4/1957.
[60] NAN BOP 53 N8/4/5 Administrasie Beampte Kaokoveld Ohopoho an die Hoofbantoesakekommissaris 14/5/1962.
[61] NAN BOP 53 N8/412 Kantor van die Hoofbantoekommissaris to Bantoesakekommissaris Ohopho 13/4/1966.
[62] NAN BOP 53 N8/4/3 lists for example Nangoro Tom, Chief in Okangwati and Pineas Puriza, a businessman in Opuwo, as recipients.
[63] NAN BOP 53 N8/4/2 documents the sale of subsidised animals in 1978.

more than it influenced the herds of Himba communities in the northern parts. Informants alleged that the influence of Afrikaner bulls on local herds was clearly visible in cattle herds in the southern parts of the Kaokoveld. They held that this change also had detrimental consequences. The offspring of this breeding stock were much bigger in physical stature and less capable of climbing steep mountains than the local breeds. Some alleged that the very high losses of livestock in the 1980/81 drought were also attributable to crossbreeding with alien breeds which were thought to be less capable of coping with extreme stress. It is difficult to exactly ascertain the impact of the breeding programmes. It is, however, important to note that the administration's development projects not only shaped environmental conditions by changing the hydrological conditions but also impacted local herds by changing the gene-pool, thereby influencing parameters like mobility (less capacity to graze steep mountain pastures), milk yield (possibly higher yields), and weight.

The logic of the development paradigm linked an expanding system of boreholes, improved breeds, and increased marketing. However, it was especially the last of these developments which was beset with internal contradictions. The situation was somewhat paradoxical: The government had taken major measures to increase the numbers of livestock. Now that numbers had actually increased the area was regarded by many as overstocked, and administrative staff campaigned for more livestock sales. Yet, it was still very difficult to sell any livestock within the Kaokoveld, let alone to buyers beyond the Red Line. The boundaries to the south were still firmly closed. Neither cattle nor small stock could be transported across the Red Line. Throughout the 1940s and 1950s the strict laws on livestock marketing were kept in place. At the same time sales of livestock across the border to southern Angola were illegal. However, while the southern boundary was still closely controlled, the administration apparently turned a blind eye to sales to southern Angola. A report in the late 1960s estimated that about 7,000 cattle and 200 heads of small stock were sold to Angola and the Ovamboland per year (see also von Wolputte 2004: 161).[64] Also trade with the Ovamboland apparently became easier and the government's stand on livestock trade across the Kaokoland–Ovamboland border was more relaxed since the late 1940s. Already

---

[64] NAN BOP 7 N1/15/6.

in 1947 the Annual Report notes that 'hundreds of Ovambos visited the Kaokoveld with articles of clothing, sugar, coffee, hoes etc. and money to barter and purchase tobacco from the Hereros'.[65]

In the 1960s the government made some tentative attempts to improve the situation and to set up a livestock-marketing system. In the late 1960s the government reconsidered its regulations with regard to the Red Line and ruled that cattle could be traded to the south after a long quarantine. The idea was that the government would buy the cattle from herders and then quarantine them in a camp, and finally facilitate their transportation south of the Red Line. In his memoirs Garth Owen-Smith, who as young man was employed as an agricultural officer to institute this system, describes in a detailed manner the approach he took to convince locals to sell livestock. Owen-Smith had initially succeeded in convincing two chiefs in the south-western Kaokoveld to encourage their people to bring cattle to a government-sponsored auction. Both chiefs were of a section of Herero who had come to the Kaokoveld from the Outjo area and were in opposition to the majority of chiefs, who claimed an indigenous status. The livestock-selling project was catalysing this split even further and the two chiefs were strongly opposed by other chiefs when accepting the government's offer. At the very first auction, however, the administration made very low offers for the cattle presented. The officers in charge had been given a very conservative estimate of the value of livestock, and had fully budgeted for the quarantining and transport costs. Hence they only offered a fraction of the money which was usually paid at livestock auctions in the commercial ranching area. Local herders felt cheated, and rejected the offers the administration was prepared to make, and the entire livestock auctioning/quarantining project failed at a very early stage.

When in 1974 the Angolan livestock market collapsed and the issue of an internal market became ever more pressing, livestock inspectors and other officers in charge came up with more ideas as to how to sell cattle, and submitted these ideas to their superiors in Windhoek. In 1978 an officer propagated a small-stock breeding project. He wanted to produce lambs for sale. His idea was to start with 100 local ewes, which were to be kept in stables. In order to feed

[65] NAN NAO 61/9/1 Annual Reports for the years 1946–1952. Here report on the year 1947.

them, about 20 ha of irrigated land were necessary. On this land lucernes, maize, and sunflower were to be produced as feed. The officer planned to produce some 6,600 kg of maize per annum, to be fed to the sheep alone. Each year some 300 lambs were to be produced, of which some 280 were to be sold locally to schools, clinics, and to whites living in Opuwo. The officer admitted that the project was not really viable financially. Per year he assumed gains of c. 8,000 R, with initial input costs at 12,500 R and considerable running costs which he did not specify. He argued that the project would have economic significance once expanded after a successful initial phase.[66] The project never came about. The difficulties involved in selling livestock remained a topic throughout the 1970s, but then two events changed the conditions of livestock marketing considerably. In the early 1980s a major percentage of livestock were killed during a centennial drought and there were few animals left to sell. Furthermore, the army units which were stationed at Opuwo, Okangwati, and Ehomba since the late 1970s bought livestock at very good prices, and a number of informants ascertained that all saleable livestock were actually sold at Opuwo.

Gardening Projects

In contrast to discussions in administrative communications about boreholes, livestock sales, and veterinary issues, gardening projects featured rather modestly. Local communities practised traditional irrigation agriculture in three localities: Ehomba, Kaoko Otavi, and Sesfontein. In these locations the administration conducted studies on the productivity of the natural wells in the early 1950s. Van Warmelo had added a section on Sesfontein in his ethnography of the Kaokoveld, and in the 1980s army anthropologist Stals produced a small ethnography of the Ehomba community in which several families traced their distant origins to Zululand and their more recent origins to the Humpata area in southern Angola. Stals focused especially on agricultural practices, and reported that irrigated agriculture and orchards had been brought from Humpata in the 1940s and had successfully been practised in Ehomba since then (Stals 1988: 21). Stals and,

[66] NAN BOP 83 N8/2/3 Sekretaris van Plurale Betrekkenige en – ontwikklening and Hoofbantorsakekommissaris 24/5/1978.

earlier, van Warmelo (1951: 20), had described local agriculture as highly diversified, with maize, wheat, potatoes, pumpkins, and beans as major crops.

A report in 1975 developed the idea of irrigated farming to a new level. Page (1975) elaborated the idea of rural growth points (*groeipunte*) and detailed that the Omuhonga Valley, the area between Opuwo, Orumana, Omutambo Maowe, and the Etosha border and the area from Opuwo to Kaoko Otavi[67] should be developed in such growth points. The report also calculates the potential for a dam near Okanguati. If the c. 30 million cubic metres of water which were calculated to be the total runoff water of the basin could be captured in a dam, then about 30,000 cubic metres could be made available for irrigation (Page 1975: 39). I did not find any documents which further developed the idea of rural growth points; nor did I find any administrative measures furthering this idea.

Other ideas on systematic natural resource-harvesting were brought in from outside entrepreneurs and were positively reviewed by the administration. In 1977 for example the SWA Teufelskralle Exporters Ltd. applied for a permit to enter Bantu areas and, *inter alia*, also the Kaokoland. The application argues that the hand-picking of Devil's Claw was usually done by local people, often in a manner leading to losses in quantity and value. For that reason the company intended to send two employees to the harvesting areas in order to introduce sound handling methods and to induce 'Bantu in areas where herbs are not being collected to start this as a money earner for the respective district'.[68] It was noted that the company was in direct contact with overseas pharmaceutical industries and that agents of these industries would also like to visit the original areas of the plant. It was argued that Namibia was in direct competition with Botswana in this respect, and that only free access to the areas where Devil's Claw was harvested would help Namibian companies.[69] According to my reading of the

---

[67] The Page report added that the third growth point continued to Ombombo, which seems erroneous if the village referred to is Ombombo in the southern part of the Kaokoveld, since this would create a very large area – very different from the idea of growth points advocated here.

[68] NAN BOP 83 SWA Teufelskralle Exporters to The Secretary of Bantu Administration and Development, Pretoria 16/8/1977.

[69] NAN BOP 83 SWA Teufelskralle Exporters to The Secretary of Bantu Administration and Development, Pretoria 16/8/1977.

archival files the permit was given but in fact the harvesting of Devil's Claw did not get off the ground until the 1990s.

Roads, Township Development, and the Growth of Infrastructure

Throughout the period under consideration modernity was inscribed into the landscape through the establishment of a road network and the building up of Opuwo as a central place. Certainly road construction started way back in the 1920s at a moderate level. In the 1920s and 1930s roads were made by local road gangs under the supervision of a chief who also fed the group 'volunteering' to cut trees and smooth the terrain. Cars were consistently used by the administration from the late 1930s. Roads were intended to connect settlements,[70] and a SWANLA manager remarked that the lack of accessibility was a major hindrance to further development. He reasoned: 'many kraals are inaccessible for want of roads. So, for example, there is no road along the Kunene from Swartbooisdrift to Epupa, a stretch of country some 60 miles along fairly well populated [lands]. Here a road should be made ... It will be essential to have roads to those and other settlements made. I have been informed that headmen in these areas have been instructed or requested to make roads to their kraals or to move their kraals on to existing roads.'[71] There is some evidence that locals actually resettled closer to the roads and left more remote settlement places. In particular chiefs and elders sought to be accessible along the road network. Indeed, the Annual Reports from the late 1940s and early 1950s document that while in the past it was necessary to send out native constables to control road maintenance and road-making, by 1947 the work was 'done entirely alone by Ovahimba under control of their headmen'. Road gangs were furnished by the administration with confiscated cattle.[72]

From the 1950s these road gangs became professionalised. By the mid-1970s about 1,280 km of road had been built, of which 1,003 km

---

[70] NAN SWAA 2515 A552/13-1 Allgemene inspeksieverslag – Kaokoveld, Landboubeampte J. C. du Plessis. 27/11/1952 an die Hoefnaturellekommissaris.
[71] NAN SWAA 2515 A552/18 Report on a trip to Kaokoveld 6/1/1952; Vlok, SWANLA Manager, hoped to recruit 500 natives in Opuwo per annum; this report also hints at the necessity of building roads.
[72] NAN NAO 61 9/1, Annual Reports for the Years 1946–1952.

were *egte bospad* ('real bush roads'). By that time a professional team of 64 black workers headed by a white superintendent had been established. They earned between 50 and 80 R per month, plus 1 R per day when staying out of town.[73]

7.4 Changing Patterns of Pastoral Mobility, Tenure, and Wealth

The impact of the borehole-drilling programme on environmental infrastructure was profound. The development of a network of boreholes in former dry-season grazing areas between the 1960s and the 1970s led to a reversal of the mobility pattern.[74] Herds could now stay in the former rainy-season areas during the dry season as they were no longer dependent on rainwater. Much wider areas than before were now accessible for permanent grazing. A new set of rules had to be developed to address questions pertaining to the regulation of access to these newly-won pastures and to sustainability. The net effect was that herds stayed at the permanent water points along the rivers during the rainy season and then moved to outlying pastures during the dry season where water was now provided by a borehole. It is tempting to relate borehole-drilling and rising livestock numbers.[75]

Also in the wider Epupa area, in the northernmost area of the Kaokoveld, the situation changed with the development of water resources in the area: boreholes were drilled at Omuramba, Otjikango, and Omuhandja in the 1960s and 1970s and a dam was built at Okombanga, near Omuramba. At the same time further boreholes were installed at other places in the region (Omuhonga Valley, Ominyandi). Places that had been rainy-season pastures in the past now became dry-season pastures. The major focus of chief Muinimuhoro's settlement became Omuramba, a place close to the road, which

---

[73] NAN BOP 7 N1/15/6 Memorandum: Feite Posisie van die Kaokoland 1975.
[74] Kreike (2009: 92) describes major changes in the mobility pattern of cattle herding in neighbouring Ovamboland. There large-scale fencing, e.g. on the Angolan/Namibian border, on the Etosha National Park border, and on the border to Kaokoland had a severe impact on the management of cattle.
[75] Kreike (2009: 89) describes the impressive growth of cattle numbers in neighbouring Ovamboland; from 1925 to 1975 cattle numbers rose from 60,000 to 530,000 there. He also reports on high off-take rates there and assumes that between 1966 and 1975 about 20–30 per cent of the total herd was slaughtered annually.

replaced Ombuku as the major settlement site. In a meeting in 1962 the chief reported that the grazing had become *swak* ('weak') in the former area.[76] His decision to move to Omuramba prompted a number of other households to resettle there. As far as I can reconstruct, the borehole at Omuramba was drilled in the same year. Only during the height of the dry season would people fall back to the Ombuku Valley, where in previous years they had dwelt for the entire dry season. The change of the grazing regime probably took place as a consequence of borehole-drilling in the area.[77]

Similar processes of concentration of households in the vicinity of boreholes were common in the 1960s and 1970s. Boreholes contributed to the territorialisation of chieftaincy areas. In contrast to the prior state, a clear link between individual households and specific grazing areas was replaced by a clearer specification of the group dealing with a resource. Increasingly chiefs and their councillors, acting as paid semi-officials and intermediaries between local community and the state, became prominently involved in allocating access rights. Membership of a resource-managing community was still established via kinship links. Graves, and rituals conducted at these graves, gave proof of the legitimacy of tenure rights in a specific place. Relations of patronage and clientelism were transformed: while in the earlier years of the twentieth century patronage was based on the control over access rights to water, now access to pasture was the more prominent topic. Also, while patronage had been built on factual militaristic power and good relations with the incipient colonial administration, now it was more based on wealth in livestock. Good relations with the colonial administration still counted for a lot, but now chiefs were firmly established in chiefly councils and they had accepted certain channels for expressing dissent. Chiefs profited from cordial relations with the administration and enjoyed a number of privileges. The status and economic potential of clients also changed: while they had been impoverished or even cattleless before, with the overall spread of livestock wealth they were wealthier and economically more independent.

---

[76] NAN BOP 5 N1/15/4/3. Meeting 20–23/3/1962.
[77] There were other reasons for moving the major settlements from Ombuku to Omuramba: a newly built road was nearby and Omuramba lay in the midst of splendid grazing whereas Ombuku was placed at the edge of it.

The rules of good grazing (*ozondunino yomaryo*) evolved as a reaction to the implementation of the borehole programme. When I recorded these rules in the mid-1990s, local herders reflected upon them with some pride and portrayed them as the traditional rules of grazing in the region, something that had been imbued and embellished by *ombazu*, tradition. Only when I was working on changes within this setup and focused on the demise of the rules of grazing in the first decade of the twenty-first century did some of the elders contemplate that also these rules had not been there forever. They had come with the boreholes, as previously – so many elders said – there was no necessity for rules. I then began to understand that the norms addressed as being brought about by this hydrological revolution necessitated the development of a set of rules to guarantee equal access and some degree of sustainability. The development of rules for proper conduct of grazing was an attempt to minimise the chances of conflict (Bollig 2006: 330 gives these rules in detail, here a summary is presented).

Grazing in the dry-season grazing areas is prohibited during the rainy season.
Cattle camps must move a considerable distance away from the main settlement areas.
Livestock camps must move together in a group.
Herders must look for dry-season grazing near to their major settlement.
Once settling in a specific place cattle camp owners must decide in which 'direction' each herd is herded; i.e. in the morning each herder takes out his herd from the camp in a specific direction.
Too much movement to and fro (*okukandakanda*) is not appreciated.
Special areas should only be used during droughts and not during normal dry seasons.

What challenges did people want to address when developing these rules? The prohibition to settle ahead of others, for example, ensured that all herders had the same chance to exploit a pasture area (Behnke 1998: 15). Rules narrowed down the options for cattle camps and made moves of highly mobile cattle camps more predictable. A reason for moving cattle away from the main homestead early on in the dry season was the necessity to maintain grazing near the main settlements to ensure the supply of milk to elderly folks and children during the dry season when the majority of cattle were taken to outlying pastures.

Grazing guards (*ovatjevere vomaryo*) were nominated by neighbourhoods. These were instituted into their office by a meeting of the community. The fact that these men were also addressed as *ovapolise vomaryo* (grazing police) shows that they were regarded as an extension of the homeland bureaucracy. The *ovapolise vomaryo* were entitled to screen the area for homesteads and camps which did not adhere to the rules. However, everybody could bring up complaints against a neighbour or herder he thought was behaving contrary to the rules. Cases were first negotiated at the neighbourhood level and if no decision was reached there, the case was heard at the chief's court. The colonial administration encouraged chiefs to punish wrongdoers 'according to tradition'. Habitually trespassers had to pay a fine, usually an ox. When several oxen had come together these were driven to the Native Commissioner's compound in Opuwo.

Changes to the Vegetation Structure

The change of the original mobility pattern brought about a shift in the vegetation structure. The pre-1950s system, with intense grazing on outlying pastures only during the rainy season (i.e. for only three to four months during the growth period) favoured perennial grasses. In contrast, the new mobility pattern, which implied intense stress through grazing during the dry season, disadvantaged perennial grasses and advantaged annual grasses. The new rules stipulated that outlying pastures should not be grazed during the rainy season, thereby ensuring that annual grasses were not disturbed during their main vegetation period. Annual grasses were protected until they had developed seeds and their reproductive success was granted. In contrast, perennial grasses were massively disturbed during a period of time when, due to the lack of soil moisture, they could not sufficiently recuperate. This led to a rather rapid change from a pasture dominated by perennial grasses to a pasture dominated by annual grasses.

Owen-Smith (2010: 464) points to two other causal chains that contributed to the degradation of rangelands. He argues that the issuing of strychnine and .303 rifles to headmen in the 1960s and 1970s resulted in rapidly declining numbers of predators. Stock owners could now leave their cattle to roam freely. Cattle were not herded rigorously anymore and could selectively graze out preferred grasses. Indeed, when I observed grazing in the northern parts of the Kaokoveld in the mid-1990s herders of one locality would lead their cattle in the morning towards the pastures they then wanted to graze that day. They gave the herd a direction, as they would say, and then left the animals alone. In the evening the herd would habitually come back on its own. The changes in herding style contributed directly to the demise of highly valued grasses as cattle were left time and space to graze highly selectively. Furthermore, Owen-Smith points out that many Herero households became progressively more sedentary and cattle increasingly stayed close to permanent waterholes for several months.

There is other evidence that the change in the grazing style had been comprehensive. Until the 1940s there were repeated warnings from the administration that any intentional igniting of veld fires would be severely punished. However, throughout the 1930s and 1940s and well into the 1950s veld fires regularly occurred. After the 1950s I did not hear about any major veld fires – clear evidence that a grass layer of perennial grasses had been replaced by a grass layer of annual grasses. These built up much less biomass and hence were much less susceptible to fires.

The Expansion of Livestock-Based Exchange Networks

Livestock exchange networks have certainly been of significance among Otjiherero-speaking livestock keepers for a very long time. Concepts like *ovahona*, designating 'big men' who give out cattle on a loan basis to clients and thereby gain political influence, are undoubtedly pre-colonial and have defined relations between cattle-owning herders and foragers for a long time. While the institution of livestock loaning is an old one, networks of livestock loans increased in size, as did the numbers of heads of livestock transferred with rapidly growing livestock numbers. Increasing overall wealth in livestock and the tremendous accumulation of cattle with some individual herders increased opportunities for livestock exchanges. Such networks have been extensively described in an earlier publication on the basis of data procured with Himba communities in the mid-1990s (Bollig 2006: 294–309).

Rules of inheritance guaranteed (a) a coordinated and unambiguous transmission of property from the testator to one heir and (b) the concentration of property rights in livestock in the hands of a few. Household herds were inherited within the matriline (*eanda*), first from the deceased to a brother (of one mother) and then to a sister's son (ZS), or any equivalent in the matriline (like ZDS or ZDDS), if a sister's son was non-existent. It was only among the Himba of the northern parts of the Kaokoveld that all livestock were inherited along the matrilineal line. In most Herero groups (Crandall 1992; Irle 1906; Viehe 1902) and, in fact, among the western Himba too, ancestral cattle were inherited patrilineally while non-ancestral cattle are transferred in the matriline. As matrilineal relatives tend not to live together, inheritance usually implied a major shift of the entire household. As it is well known who has inherited from whom in the past and who will do so in the future, inheritance transfers are often laid out as chains. One such inheritance chain which I recorded in the 1990s may serve as an example for the spatial scope of inheritance transfers. The example highlights the rules of inheritance as well as the spatial character of transactions.

Tjandero, an extremely wealthy herder owning about 800–1,000 cattle, will pass on the entire herd to his sister's son (*omusyia*) Kasorere. Kasorere, who is already in his sixties and not much younger than his uncle, will in turn pass on the herd to his next younger brother, Mbatjanani. Mbatjanani will once again pass it on to a younger brother, Karenda. Then the herd will be transferred to their sisters' sons' lines. The first heir of the herd will be Wezuzura, the eldest son of Kasorere's, Mbatjanani's, and Karenda's oldest sister, Watundwa. Wezuzura will hand on the herd to his younger brother, Maaesuva. If Maaesuva should die, then the sons of Kasorere's, Mbatjanani's, and Karenda's second eldest sister (Mungerinyeu and Manuele) will inherit, and when the herd has been handed down the brotherly line, the herd will fall to the sons of Kasorere's, Mbatjanani's, and Karenda's third and youngest sister.[78]

The household herd in question will cross the Namibian/Angolan border several times. Within a period of about thirty to fifty years residential changes of the household may take place eight times. Inheritance leads to a continuous redistribution of the regional herd. At each inheritance transfer, several herders, closely related to the deceased matrilineally, may take out a few head of livestock from the herd (*okuramberia*). The night before the inheritance is finally allotted to

---

[78] When this inheritance chain was first written down this was a future projection. Now that Tjandero and Kasorere have died the cattle are with Mbatjanani.

the heir by the elders of the clan, they pick out single animals and leave quietly. Referring to this rather clandestine means of livestock appropriation, these secondary heirs are referred to as *ovarumata*, 'the biters'. While inheritance on the one hand guarantees a concentration of property rights it also leads to a continuous redistribution of use rights in large numbers of livestock.

There is something very special about the Himba inheritance system, which combines a concentration of property rights and, at the same time, facilitates the distribution of livestock. Many inheritance transfers listed above include a transfer of property rights from a deceased man to his brother. Frequently the brother is roughly the same age as the deceased person. Even transfers from a deceased man to his sister's son do not always bridge a generation. Many sisters' sons who were enlisted as heirs were only slightly younger than their mothers' brother. In fact, cases in which an entire herd is transferred from a deceased elder to a very young man are rare. Most men who had inherited a herd had done so when they were older than 45. While only 1.5 per cent of all the animals obtained via exchange by herders under the age of 45 originated from inheritance transfers, herders between 45 and 59 years of age obtained 16.5 per cent of all animals through inheritance, and herders of 60 years and above even obtained 27.9 per cent through inheritance transfers. Of all the animals transferred in inheritance, herders of 60 years and above obtained 52 per cent, people between 45 and 59 years obtained 44.9 per cent, while herders under the age of 45 received just 2.6 per cent. Himba rules of inheritance constitute a system in which many men have a vague chance of becoming owners of larger herds at some indefinite time in the future. The practice of inheritance guarantees that most herders will only become wealthy herd-owners when they are already quite aged. Property is moved within the matriline from household to household through generations. This 'rotating pot' works like a trans-generational, matriline-bound savings association: everybody contributes (livestock and/or labour) and has the hope of being the sole owner of the herd one day.

Livestock Loans

Loans of single animals, and also of entire herds, as well as livestock transfers at inheritance were the major institutions for distributing and transferring use rights and property rights in livestock. Bridewealth was low (only two to three head of cattle) and did not play a major role in exchange relations. Livestock exchanges between friends, which are so prominent among East African herders (Bollig 1998c), were virtually absent in the Himba pastoral economy. Almost a quarter of the off-take from cattle herds went to livestock transfers in the form of loans and presents (the remainder being sales, cases of premature death, etc.). When transferring livestock the Himba differentiated clearly between loans and outright shifts of ownership rights. Only in the case of inheritance and livestock gifts did ownership rights change alongside use rights. In most cases, however, when livestock were transferred, only use rights were exchanged while ownership rights stayed with the original possessor. Many herders relied almost completely on loaned cattle. For young herders this was the normal situation: They started off with a herd which consisted mainly of borrowed livestock and gradually expanded their own property. For impoverished herders their dependence on borrowed stock was a lifelong problem.

Himba differentiated two major forms of livestock loans. Many herders, even poorer ones, occasionally shared out single animals and loaned them to relatives. These animals were addressed as *ozondisa* – herded animals. Next to single animals, wealthy people allocated entire livestock camps to young and poor herders. However, the difference between livestock loans (*ozondisa*) and an allocated livestock camp (*ohambo*) was not always clear. If livestock loans were repeatedly taken from one wealthy relative, the receiving household would gradually lose its independence and become a livestock camp of the wealthy household. Exchanges were not conditioned so much by social structures as they relied on personal considerations on the access to livestock; nevertheless, they were always clad in the discourse of kinship solidarity. Himba tried to strengthen ties to potential heirs, to offspring of one's mother's brother (whose herd one will inherit) and to people with whom one had a common inheritance claim towards one herd through the donation of animals. Livestock loans were governed by a fusing of matri-clan solidarity and personal interest: they supported individual inheritance claims and enforced clan solidarity at the same time.

Usually only heifers were exchanged on a loan basis, while male stock were given as presents more often. The recipient kept the borrowed livestock; he drank their milk and could, after some time, even take out a male animal for sale or slaughter. If he wanted to barter an animal for maize or to slaughter it at a celebration, he had to wait until the animal that he had initially borrowed had given birth to several calves. He did not have to ask the owner of these animals beforehand, but had to tell him about the fate of the animal afterwards. All animals descended from the borrowed heifer – no matter how long ago the animal was borrowed – still belonged to the original owner of that heifer or to his legal heir. Occasionally the owner could present an animal to the borrower as a gift, thereby enabling him to gradually build up his own herd. Although property rights in loaned animals stayed with the original owner, livestock loans were a relatively safe form of capital. Kinship morality prevented the owner of the cattle asking for a large number of his cattle back all at once. Conditions were different for livestock camps. Only if the person who had borrowed the animals neglected them was the donor entitled to ask for his cattle back. Although this possibility was considered theoretically, I never heard of a case in which an owner had taken back all his animals at once. While borrowed cattle were safe capital, it was deemed appropriate to obtain borrowed animals from many different recipients. To spread one's benefactors was seen as the only way to prevent dependence on one wealthy patron.

Of course, it was preferable to obtain livestock gifts instead of livestock loans. About a third of all livestock exchanges (excluding the transmission of livestock camps) were presents, while two-thirds were loans. Herders clearly had a better chance of obtaining livestock gifts after they had reached a specific age. While of the animals obtained by herders younger than 40 only 5.8 per cent were gifts, the percentage of animals given as gifts grows to more than 25 per cent for people between 40 and 50 years of age.

7.5 Hydrological Revolution and Changing Environmental Infrastructure in North-West Namibia's Savannah

State-led policies and programmes led to profound changes in the environmental infrastructure between the 1950s and the 1970s. While a number of development options were scrutinised in the 1950s it was only the borehole programme which was then forcefully developed. Notably all planned interventions aimed at major impact on the environmental infrastructure. If ideas on crossbreeding and the introduction of large breeding herds for cattle, goats, and sheep had been followed up systematically, the entire gene-pool of domesticated livestock of the Kaokoveld would have been transformed within a decade or two. This did not happen though and cattle are still predominantly of the original Sanga stock. If plans for irrigation and the development of agricultural growth points had been developed, the Kaokoveld would have had a number of sizeable farm areas today. The Omuhonga Valley was at one time seen as a major irrigation area with an artificial lake as the source for irrigation water. Also this did not come about. Only the idea of a transformation of the hydrology of the landscape was developed and was financed over three decades. The presence of many new boreholes created very different hydrological conditions and contributed to a sizeable increase of the regional livestock herd. Boreholes were usually drilled some 50–100 metres deep expanding the environmental infrastructure subterraneously. Boreholes were placed habitually in areas that were deemed to have good grazing but no reliable water sources beyond the few months of rainy season. The boreholes expanded the grazing range profoundly and allowed for the grazing of these pastures during the dry season. Cattle numbers rose fourfold within two decades. Pastures across the region were used much more intensively than ever before and they were used differently than before. Cattle herds stayed at dry-season camps for eight to nine months a year throughout the dry season whereas before they had stayed at a perennial water point for that period. Grasses were now intensely used during the dry season when they could not compensate for grazing damage by regrowth. In many places this contributed to a near-complete change from perennial grasses to annual grasses – a change that had taken place around the perennial water sources four or five decades earlier. As a consequence veld fires became rare and ceased to be a method of environing. While droughts occasionally caused a reduction of herds, on the whole, pastoral wealth increased tremendously. In the 1970s the cattle tycoons of the Kaokoveld were said to have owned several thousand cattle spread out over a number of livestock camps. Via exchange networks pastoral wealth was spread widely throughout the population. The peculiarity of the local inheritance system guaranteed a frequent shift of major herds of cattle. A wealthy pastoral population highly specialised in nomadic livestock husbandry developed in this period. Forager traditions became extinct, and remote livestock-poor communities also expanded their herds. The politics of intensification had major ecological repercussions.

This expansive system of livestock loaning and inheriting was certainly tied to older patterns of distribution. The tremendous increase of livestock wealth fuelled this system of transfers and obligations and created the material basis for a number of social institutions. It was this complex system of livestock transfers that I had the chance to describe ethnographically in the mid-1990s. In the form I observed it then, this system emerged in the 1960s and 1970s. It was closely coupled with the changing hydrological infrastructure and rapidly growing livestock herds.

8 | Conservation and Poaching in the 1970s and 1980s

The intensification of livestock production had been the major governmental project of the 1950s and 1960s. By the late 1960s, and more so throughout the 1970s, detrimental environmental consequences of this intensification programme were observed. This certainly contributed to the increasing presence of conservationist voices criticising the intensification paradigm and outlining alternative paths of development: the Kaokoveld became progressively seen more as a large conservation area and an attraction for tourists. From the mid-1970s environmentalist NGOs began financing zoological research and also some small environmentalist projects in the region. While the modernisation-cum-intensification paradigm remained dominant and was the main project of the administration well into the 1970s, when it was followed by a focus on securitisation and anti-SWAPO measures, from the late 1960s alternative projects of natural resource management were envisioned. The re-emergence of conservation thinking was paralleled by a period of intense poaching. While more and more plans for the conservation of natural resources in general and wildlife in particular were made, wildlife was nearly hunted out in the 1970s and 1980s. The period under consideration here is also marked by the expansion of the Namibian civil war into the Kaokoveld in the 1970s, and the centennial drought of 1980–2, with stock losses of up to 90 per cent.

In the next section I will delineate the emergence of conservationist thinking since the late 1960s, outline some of the more prominent plans, detail some aspects of increasing research on wildlife in the Kaokoveld, and finally turn to the rapid and detrimental increase in poaching and the collapse of pastoral herds in the early 1980s.

Before detailing the development of human–environment relations in the 1970s and 1980s I will briefly provide a sketch of Namibia's history during this time period. Unlike the decades before, which were marked by the build-up of administration, infrastructure, and encapsulation, the decades in focus now were more turbulent and more marked by political strife. Even if the Kaokoland remained rather isolated from political agitation and war, these ground-breaking events which finally led to Namibia's independence in March 1990 had significant influence on processes in north-western Namibia.

In mid-1971 the International Court of Justice declared that South Africa's occupation of Namibia was illegal, and urged the government of South Africa to withdraw from Namibia immediately. Later that year a general strike by contract workers broke out and spread across the country (Wallace 2011: 274–5). The Apartheid government reacted strongly, virtually imposing a state of martial law in the Ovamboland, banning public meetings and allowing imprisonment without trial. The international border with Angola now became controlled by the army instead of the police, more troops were stationed in northern Namibia, and traditional leaders were given arms. At the same time the South African government sought to conform to international opinion, allowing Namibia a shallow type of autonomy while maintaining control over essential resources and the population. The South African government propagated itself through an ethnicised political structure allowing semi- or pseudo-independence for the ten ethnic homelands in the near or distant future. The Advisory Council, created in 1973, instituted the political representation of the governmentally defined 'ethnic communities' of Namibia. Ministers and officers from Bantustan administrations featured prominently in the council. The Advisory Council was followed by the so-called Turnhalle constitutional conference in 1976. About 150 delegates selected from the various population groups attended the conference. In 1977 the Turnhalle delegates proposed that Namibia should become independent as a federal state on 31 December 1978. The constitution thus envisioned enshrined the homeland setup, and gave local ethnic governments significant powers. Tribal councils were established locally; the Nama council in 1976 and the Damara council in 1977. These steps were meant to show a degree of self-governance. The Turnhalle proposal did not gain international acknowledgement and was not carried out, however, but a so-called three-tier administration was installed. The first-tier national administration was still very much dominated by South Africa; the second tier authorities were progressively built up in the homelands, with more fervour in some than in others. However, throughout the 1980s the majority of officials in Opuwo were still white South Africans or Namibians. At least in the

Kaokoland, the institution of a tribal council never worked. At the same time South Africa stepped up military activities in the north, with violent raids far into southern Angola. The vicious raid on the Cassinga camp in 1978, leaving more than 600 people dead, became a significant rallying point for local and international opposition to South Africa's occupation of Namibia.

During the latter part of the 1970s northern Namibia was transformed into a war zone. In 1974 the Portuguese government formally granted Angola independence, and Portuguese authorities left the country in the middle of a bloody civil war in which pro-Western UNITA forces were pitched against pro-socialist MPLA and FNLA forces (Wallace 2011: 279). The border between Namibia and Angola became increasingly uncontrollable, and PLAN fighters took advantage of this situation by infiltrating northern Namibia. The major battle zone, however, was the Ovamboland. PLAN fighters infiltrated the Kaokoland in small numbers only from the early 1980s (Reardon 1986: 136). By the end of the 1970s between 15,000 and 45,000 South African troops were stationed in northern Namibia (Wallace 2011: 285). Namibian auxiliary forces were progressively recruited, and in 1980 the South West Africa Territorial Force (SWATF) was founded – a Namibian branch of the South African Defence Force (SADF). In 1988 SWATF employed 9,277 Namibians across the north of the country (34 per cent of all jobs in formal employment) (all data from Wallace 2011: 292–5). In 1979 the counter-insurgency Koevoet (crowbar) organisation was founded as a section of the South West African Police – it went on to employ up to 3,000 black Namibians in the following decade. Koevoet actively recruited in the Kaokoland. The paramilitary unit was heavily involved in the man-hunting of 'terrorists'. Each 'kill' was honoured with an individual bounty. Additionally, huge numbers of guns were given out to the local population in order to enable them to defend themselves against so-called terrorists. Throughout the earlier part of the 1980s South Africa, emboldened by the support of the Reagan administration in the US, waged its war against PLAN soldiers in northern Namibia and southern Angola and established Bantustan administrative structures throughout the north. The massive engagement of the Soviet Union and Cuba on the side of the Angolan MPLA government and SWAPO, and of South Africa and the US on the other side, led to an escalation of violence in southern Angola. In the end the terribly high costs of the war, the military stalemate in southern Angola, and the political and economic depression in South Africa itself convinced the South African government to give in to negotiations along the lines of the UN Resolution 435/1978, which led to Namibia's independence in 1990 and the engagement of the international UN-legitimated UNTAG forces in the transition process in 1988 and 1989.

Due to the war-torn conditions there was little to no developmental work taking place in north-western Namibia. Modest efforts at conservation came to a near-standstill: The Namibia Wildlife Trust withdrew from activities in the Kaokoveld in 1984, and the Endangered Wildlife Trust did so about a year later (Reardon 1986: 84–5). It was only in the early 1990s that such programmes were taken up again.

8.1 Conservationist Planning and Anti-Conservationist Practices between the 1950s and the 1970s

In contrast to earlier decades, the 1950s and 1960s were anti-conservationist: Many administrators held the idea that the intensification of livestock husbandry was incompatible with conservation. Commercial farmers were allowed to destroy animals defined as 'vermin' (jackal, hyena, wild cats, leopards, wild dogs, and lynx). There were also 'jackal-hunting clubs' and jackal-proof fencing subsidies for farmers. Ambitious jackal hunters were remunerated with a bounty for bringing in jackal skins (pers. com. Rob Gordon). Botha (2013) reports that in 1960 alone some 6,000 jackals were killed on commercial farms. Lions could also be killed by farmers if they had preyed on their livestock, and even elephants were shot at times for destroying fences. Administrators in the north tried to help the local population to control 'vermin'. In the late 1940s elephant damage to gardens was repeatedly dealt with in annual reports, and the administration saw it as its duty to protect locals against damage caused by wildlife. An annual report for 1950 referred to vermin traps being given out on payment.[1] During the hearing of the Odendaal Commission in Opuwo in 1963 the 'olifante pla'[2] ('elephant plague') was made a topic by the locals, and in stark contrast to earlier times the white official heading the meeting simply agreed, and emphasised 'Ons stem

---

[1] NAN NAO 61 9/1, Annual Reports for the Years 1946–52.
[2] NAN SWA/KC/7E/52 p. 630.

saam die olifante moet doodgeskiet word' ('We agree that the elephants have to be shot dead'). Rules for wildlife protection were now interpreted more loosely in communal areas. In the 1960s especially locals were given poison, and later even guns were handed out.

Some of the administrators in Namibia's north took a strongly anti-conservationist stand. In 1976 the commissioner in Opuwo claimed that wild animals were often a severe liability for local farmers, and reported that officials were frequently asked to help with the eradication of so-called problem animals. He suggested reconsidering the hunting ban, and advocated that locals should be allowed to hunt, or that it should be investigated as to what extent trophy-hunting could be used to lower the number of 'problem animals' in the Kaokoveld to an acceptable level.[3] Most administrative staff apparently agreed that local herders rightfully complained about predators and wildlife damage and that the state was obliged to aid them. In 1976 an officer anxiously reported that even local supporters of the government complained that some regulations privileged animals over humans.[4] The Odendaal Commission had recommended a massive reduction of the extent of the Etosha Game Reserve and had advocated that the entire Kaokoveld be de-gazetted to pave the way for agricultural development. The Commission's advice was put into practice in the late 1960s (Hall-Martin et al. 1988: 61).

This process was somewhat contrary to what was happening in the commercial ranching area. There wildlife was increasingly valued as a commercial resource from the mid-1960s. Apparently, it was especially farmers of German descent who became interested in the commercial exploitation of wildlife, whereas Afrikaans-speaking farmers rather opted for an intensification of livestock husbandry. The Department of Bantu Administration, however, was dominated by Afrikaners who did not feel inclined towards an environmental ethic at that time (pers. comm. Rob Gordon). In 1967 an official proclamation granted

---

[3] NAN BOP 83 N21/1/2, Naturbewaring in die Kaokoland; Bantoesakekommissaris and Hoofbantoesakekommissaris, 10/11/1976.

[4] NAN BOP 83 N21/1/2, Naturbewaring in die Kaokoland; Bantoesakekommissaris and Hoofbantoesakekommissaris, 3/12/1976. On the other hand, in the same report increasing rates of poaching were bemoaned, and it was argued that a conservation officer should be posted at Opuwo to ensure a better harmonisation of some conservation goals. In addition, an anthropologist (*volkekundige*) was requested to improve the understanding of pastoralism.

ownership of wildlife on farms to farm owners. Farmers were given the right to sell wildlife, to advertise it for commercial hunting purposes, and to dispose of wildlife products. These legal changes proved effective in providing a pathway for the commercialisation of wildlife hunting. Trophy-hunting tourism developed well throughout the 1960s. By the mid-1970s some 92 wildlife farms had already been established, and by 1985 the expanding Namibian trophy-hunting market accounted for about 12 per cent of the total African market, signalling a gradual transition from cattle ranching to wildlife farming and touristic activities. Southern Africa was seen as the future destination within an emergent global tourism market. A glossy book published by the Republic of the Transkei (1976: 109) reports that in 1971 alone the percentage growth of tourism for Africa was 25 per cent, while it was 7 per cent for the rest of the world. The government publication goes on to contemplate how much single African states earned through tourism, and argues that the South African homelands had a huge potential for attracting tourists. A similar publication by the Ciskei government mentions that tourist numbers climbed from 460,000 in 1971 to 730,000 in 1975, and that more than one million tourists per annum were expected in the 1980s (Ciskei n.d.). Touristic activities were to be mainly geared towards international tourists, though would also cater for internal tourists. Notably, the citizens of Bantustans were also viewed as potential clients, and the construction of a number of hotels catering exclusively to 'Bantu' is mentioned (Republic of Transkei 1976: 115). A Transkeian government publication claimed that:

The potential for tourism in the homelands of South Africa, areas which will eventually be independent states, is indeed great. Apart from the wonderful, sunny and unspoiled natural beauty, there are also few parts of the world that can offer such a large variety of interesting and virtually untouched tribal traditions and modes of living as the Bantu homelands of South Africa. (Republic of Transkei 1976: 109)

The argument presented here resonates with considerations by administrators of the emergent homelands of northern Namibia, where tourist numbers were also increasing, from 100,000 in 1966 to 144,000 in 1968.[5]

---

[5] NAN BOP 83 21 An die Minister van Bantu Administrasie en – ontwickeling en die Administatreur, Report of the Komitee van Ondersoek na Naturbewaring en Tourisme-probleme in Bantoegebiede van Suidwes Afrika, p. 6. I did not find figures specifying how many tourists went to the Kaokoland at that time.

The 1960s saw organisations like International Union for Conservation of Nature (IUCN) and World Wildlife Fund (WWF) establishing their leading role in the planning of conservation in sub-Saharan Africa. Both organisations were firmly focused upon extending and safeguarding a system of national parks and exclusive conservation zones. Since the early 1970s the South African WWF affiliate SANF (South African Nature Foundation) directly influenced research and planning in north-western Namibia. The re-emergent conservation paradigm competed and at times was in open confrontation with the development paradigm, which had become ever more questionable due to ecological degradation and the failure to encourage the participation of increasingly livestock-rich communal farmers in larger markets. While the government had invested much energy in the expansion of boreholes, and the regional cattle herd had more than tripled, the Kaokoveld's farmers were still barred from any export of cattle to the commercial ranching area by the infamous Red Line.

While a modernist and anti-conservationist stance had been dominant throughout the 1950s and 1960s, nature conservation was put back on the agenda in the northern communal areas in the 1970s. The successful commercialisation of wildlife hunting through trophy-hunting, and the immense increase in tourism both contributed to the reconsideration of conservation in northern Namibia. In addition to economic arguments, environmentalist concerns also entered into the debate: rare large wildlife species, unique adaptations of wildlife to an arid habitat, and an immense wealth in biodiversity were all at risk. Conservationist thinking in South Africa and Namibia was linked to and informed by increasing environmentalist activities on a global scale. A major point of concern for a wider audience – which was protested against by South African conservationists as well as by international organisations (Reardon 1986: 16) – was the revocation of the game park status for the Kaokoveld instigated at the recommendation of the Odendaal Commission. The revocation of game park status and the endorsement of homeland status resulted in a situation in which the emergent homeland Kaokoland, had no applicable legislation on conservation whatsoever. Formally, homeland authorities would have to establish a new legislation for the Kaokoland in the long run, but for the time being conservation was transferred to the Department of Bantu

Administration and Development.[6] In the early 1970s a number of South African homelands did indeed establish legislation on conservation[7] but in northern Namibia this did not happen (Lenggenhager 2018).

The emergence of a conservationist perspective in the late 1960s and 1970s was rather a matter of grand-scale planning and research, and did not result in immediate action in north-western Namibia.[8] On the contrary: The 1970s were characterised by a rapid decline of wildlife. Both stories need to be told here: that of ambitious plans to safeguard wildlife and environment through the establishment of reserves and a major restructuring of environmental infrastructure, as well as that of the catastrophic demise of wildlife during the same period. Grand plans for game parks and wildlife corridors, rampant poaching, and continued efforts towards agricultural modernisation mark a period of ambiguous political planning.

This period of administrative malfunctioning and hesitation ended in disaster. The centennial drought of 1980–2 resulted in an almost complete breakdown of livestock herds, the nearly complete demise of elephant and rhino populations, and a rapid decline of other wildlife species. By 1980 many Himba and Herero survived in famine camps outside Opuwo, where they were fed by the army.

I will first delineate the basics of four separately drafted conservation plans of this time period, and then deal with the decline of wildlife populations and finally address the catastrophe of the early 1980s.

The de la Bat Commission

The government foresaw that the revocation of the Kaokoland's game reserve status would attract some national and international critique.

---

[6] NAN BOP 83 21 Aan die Minister van Bantu Administrasie en –ontwikkeling en die Administatreur, Rapport van die Komitee van Ondersoek na Natuurbewaring en Tourisme-probleme in Bantoegebiede van Suidwes Afrika, p. 10.

[7] In the Transkei, the Nature Conservation Act in 1976 followed the inauguration of its first nature reserve in 1974 (Dwessa/Cwebe); and in Bophuthatswana the Nature Conservation Act of 1973 was followed by the establishment of a Nature Conservation Division shortly after that and the inauguration of a reserve in 1977.

[8] One may be tempted to interpret conservationist planning as a consequence of large-scale poaching. This is not so as far as I can see. Major conservationist plans were drawn up in the end 1960s and early 1970s while poaching became a major issue from the mid-1970s onwards.

Already in the late 1960s a commission was mandated to conduct research into the potential for nature conservation in the two emergent homelands of Kaokoland and Ovamboland, to consider new legal arrangements for conservation in the Bantustans of northern Namibia, and to explore the tourism potential of those areas.[9] The committee consisting of high-ranking administrators (including authorities like de la Bat, the director of nature conservation, Greyvenstein, the under-secretary for tourism, and Klopper, the Secretary for South West Africa) carried some bureaucratic clout. It strongly argued for the inclusion of the northern homelands within a wider tourism and conservation strategy for South West Africa. It highlighted the immense potential of these areas, which still had abundant wildlife and comparatively low population numbers. But here too – as in other regions – the human population was growing and needed more space for subsistence herding and agriculture. Hence some kind of action was required to conserve wildlife and at the same time provide space for agricultural intensification.

As the Odendaal Commission's recommendations concerning wildlife legislation were only applicable to the commercial ranching area, the Commission stressed the need to develop and enforce some kind of conservation legislation for the northern communal areas. The basic principles of such legislation were shortly delineated. It was stipulated that it should provide protection for the conservation of wildlife and flora and at the same time preserve local traditions 'and other issues of scientific concern' for the benefit of local inhabitants.[10] This, of course, was a very vague stance, which did not directly contribute to the search for new legislative measures. A number of potential problems were outlined: What was to happen with the existing wildlife which had been living in a game park, and now, after de-gazettement, found itself in an agricultural landscape geared towards modernisation and intensification? How could the administration deal with poachers, since no poaching laws were actually in place? How should one deal with large migratory wildlife which would move from the park to areas

---

[9] NAN BOP 83 21 Aan die Minister van Bantu Administrasie en –ontwikkeling en die Administarateur, rapport van die Komitee van Ondersoek na Natuurbewaring en Tourisme-probleme in Bantoegebiede van Suidwes Afrika.
[10] NAN BOP 83 21 Aan die Minister van Bantu Administrasie en –ontwikkeling en die Administarateur, rapport van die Komitee van Ondersoek na Natuurbewaring en Tourisme-probleme in Bantoegebiede van Suidwes Afrika.

outside the park?[11] In accordance with the modernisation (and anti-conservation) paradigm dominant in the 1960s, the Commission established that elephants were causing substantial damage in some northern areas. It stated that 'mense en olifante nie kan saamlewe nie'[12] ('people and elephants cannot live together') and recommended 'dat olifantengewere teen betaling aan verantwoordelike persone verskaf word'[13] ('that elephant guns should be given to responsible people on payment'). It considered in some detail the possibility of granting hunting rights in the area, especially to trophy hunters. It also proposed that the sale of ivory should be legalised and that the income from such sales should benefit the Bantu *stamfonds*.[14] A specific idea propagated in the report was the plan to create game parks for Bantustans (*Bantuwildtuine*) – something which had been put in practice in South Africa. Reardon (1986: 16) quotes a ministerial statement stating that the government intended to create 'Bantu-Wildtuine', and rated it as an attempt to mollify critical conservationists. The report argued that for educational purposes such parks in Bantustans were important, and proposed that they could have separate rest-camps for white and black visitors. Black visitors would learn to appreciate the beauty of nature, and white visitors could learn more about the black population inhabiting the area. The Kaokoland seemed to be of particular interest in this respect, and the Commission detailed that the inhabitants of the Kaokoveld were in favour of wildlife conservation in their homeland. It was proposed that such *Bantuwildtuine* could directly border Etosha and could be developed together with the Etosha Park.[15] The committee

[11] NAN BOP 83 21 Aan die Minister van Bantu Administrasie en –ontwikkeling en die Administarateur, rapport van die Komitee van Ondersoek na Natuurbewaring en Tourisme-probleme in Bantoegebiede van Suidwes Afrika, p. 13.
[12] NAN BOP 83 21 Aan die Minister van Bantu Administrasie en –ontwikkeling en die Administarateur, rapport van die Komitee van Ondersoek na Natuurbewaring en Tourisme-probleme in Bantoegebiede van Suidwes Afrika, p. 14.
[13] NAN BOP 83 21 An die Minister van Bantu Administrasie en –ontwickeling en die Administatreur, report oft he Komitee van Ondersoek na Naturbewaring en Tourisme-probleme in Bantoegebiede van Suidwes Afrika, pp. 10 and 14.
[14] NAN BOP 83 21 An die Minister van Bantu Administrasie en –ontwikkeling en die Administatreur, report oft he Komitee van Ondersoek na Naturbewaring en Tourisme-probleme in Bantoegebiede van Suidwes Afrika, p. 11.
[15] NAN BOP 83 21 An die Minister van Bantu Administrasie en –ontwickeling en die Administatreur, report oft he Komitee van Ondersoek na Naturbewaring en Tourisme-probleme in Bantoegebiede van Suidwes Afrika. The Andoni Plains

outlined broad prospects for trophy-hunting in the area and the general increase of tourists visiting the region. The report depicts the Kaokoveld as of particular touristic potential. Here the Marienfluss Valley, the Epupa Waterfalls, and parts of the Kunene River were emphasised as tourism highlights, and it was proposed that these areas should be developed as tourist destinations.

The report had no immediate consequences. No Bantustan game reserve was established, nor did any touristic development take place in the Epupa Falls area or in the Marienfluss Valley. In contrast to South Africa, where Bophuthatswana, Ciskei, and Transkei gazetted conservation legislation in the 1970s, there were no efforts made to establish any conservation legislation for the northern communal areas. Perhaps due to the lack of government activities, further criticism fomented and resulted in a number of additional reports.

The Tinley Report

A report published in 1971 in the journal *African Wildlife* as a supplement titled 'Etosha and the Kaokoveld' developed the idea of additional national parks further. Ken Tinley, the author, had been biologist in Etosha in the mid-1960s and he had been asked by the Wildlife Society (not the government!) to review the potential consequences of the revocation of game reserve status for the Kaokoveld. Tinley's input was the first scientific report on the Kaokoveld endorsed and paid for by a non-governmental organisation. The report foreshadowed an era in which NGOs increasingly compiled their own information on social-ecological relations, devised development policies independently, and attempted to influence governmental action in north-western Namibia. While previously the government had compiled, systematised, and archived information on the region alongside the work of a few independent researchers, now NGOs became key sources of environmental knowledge – a process that has continued into the present.

Tinley's account began with the observation that especially the western Kaokoveld was extremely rich in endemic species and offered unique landscapes. He saw species diversity, large game, and natural landscapes under threat, and proposed a number of measures to conserve them.

 in the Eastern Etosha Park were outlined as another such area and could serve as a *Bantuwildtuin* for Ovamboland, p. 19.

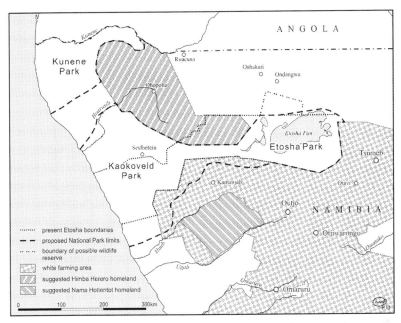

Map 8.1 Tinley's plan for two additional game parks in north-western Namibia.
Source: Tinley (1971)

Tinley advocated two new national parks for north-western Namibia: The first was the Kaokoveld National Park in the Hoarusib, Hoanib, and Uniab river catchments, with a narrow strip of land connecting this protected area with the Etosha National Park. This park was to be completely livestock-free and would be used as buffer-zone for veterinary considerations. The second park proposed, the Kunene National Park, stretched from the Epupa Falls downriver to the Marienfluss Valley.[16] Tinley wanted both parks to be linked to each other and to the Etosha Park by corridors which would allow large wildlife populations (especially elephants) to move freely (see Map 8.1). No Himba and Herero livestock herds were to be allowed west of the 100 mm isohyet. This geo-meteorological boundary definition implied that Sesfontein, a major village, would have to be relocated.

---

[16] Tinley's Kunene National Park strongly resembles Cocky Hahn's ideas for a game sanctuary in the Kunene Valley formulated in the 1930s, though Tinley does not refer to Hahn's plans directly.

The Tinley report also argued that more farmland should be bought in the southern parts of the Kaokoveld to be included into Etosha and the Kaokoveld National Park. However, Tinley was not only arguing for an expansion of the Etosha Park: he also pointed out that some parts of the western Etosha Park should be cut off to be included in the Kaokoland homeland, and should thereby be opened to grazing by local livestock herds.

The most comprehensive and far-reaching consequences of the implementation of the Tinley plan would have impacted the Sesfontein community. Tinley had argued that large-scale degradation proved that human use of the Sesfontein Valley was inadequate, and he advocated that Nama people at Sesfontein and in the adjacent lands should be removed to the Fransfontein area where a Nama reserve should be opened and widened through the purchasing of more farmland. The implementation of the Tinley plan would have halved the settlement area of the Kaokoland.

The Tinley report was submitted by the Wildlife Society of South Africa to the Office of the Prime Minister in late 1969. It earned a stern rebuttal. The government stated that the report's recommendations were completely out of line with the administration's planning based on the Odendaal Report, and that local people's ideas and wishes for development had to be balanced against the need for conservation. The government's answer strongly underlined the vision of agricultural development for the Kaokoveld, and in a somewhat ambiguous manner emphasised that the local people's wishes for development had priority. Tinley's report was presented in the journal *African Wildlife*. However, the publishers of the journal also directly annexed the minister's reply and a press statement issued by the Department of Information at the request of the Department of Bantu Administration and Development. The press statement clarified the context from a government perspective:

> The Minister of Bantu Administration and Development will, on behalf of the Government, at a time convenient to both parties, negotiate with the Natives concerned with regard to the establishment of a game park in their homeland. In the meantime, conservation of fauna and flora will be carried out according to the existing SWA legislation and, if necessary, special steps will also be taken.[17]

---

[17] Issued by the Department of Information at the request of the Department of Bantu Administration and Development. Tinley (1971: 15).

Two other reports confirmed some and criticised other aspects of the Tinley report – in essence, however, they pointed in the same direction. Environmental degradation due to high stocking rates and the decline of wildlife threatened the touristic potential of the Kaokoveld, and protected areas were a good way to cope with these problems. Game parks would also have filled the legal vacuum with regard to conservation in homelands. Game parks such as those that Tinley's report and also subsequent reports recommended would have been organised and governed under the national legislation.

The Owen-Smith Report

Garth Owen-Smith, who had been agricultural officer in the Kaokoveld in the second half of the 1960s for two and a half years and had then been transferred to South Africa by the administration because of his criticism of certain governmental measures (Owen-Smith 2010: 133), felt challenged by the Tinley report. In accordance with the overall Odendaal policy he argued that 'the requirements of the human population should take precedence in any conflict of interests' (Owen-Smith 1972: 36). Unlike the other reports, he stressed that the major threat to wildlife at that time did not come from a growing African population but rather from large numbers of white officials prone to poaching. He also surmised that the intensification of livestock husbandry in the area had led to major detrimental changes in the grass-cover and that in many intensely grazed areas perennial grasses had been lost altogether. Like Tinley, Owen-Smith viewed Sesfontein and Warmquelle as hotspots of degradation, and concluded that intense grazing had turned the environment into a dustbowl. At the same time grazing on the arid pre-Namib plains around Orupembe and Onjuva had led to the destruction of the perennial grass layer in these areas. There a number of boreholes had made grazing possible even during the dry season. In this case a maladapted government initiative had directly contributed to degradation.

Although Owen-Smith agreed with Tinley on a number of points he strongly disagreed on other issues. He submitted his report to the government in 1971 and later published a version of his report in the *South African Journal of Science* (Owen-Smith 1972). The major point of disagreement was that he did not see any need to dislocate people for the sake of conservation. While Owen-Smith agreed on the necessity of

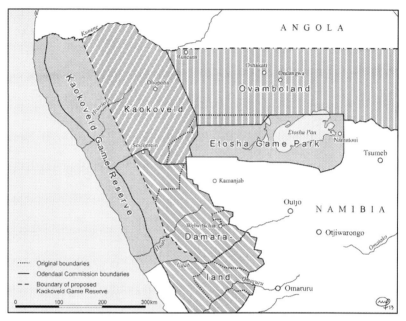

Map 8.2 Owen-Smith's plan for the Kaokoveld Game Reserve in north-western Namibia.
Source: Owen-Smith (1972)

improving wildlife conservation in the region and also saw game reserves as a means to that end, unlike Tinley he envisioned game parks where people also lived. He argued that the game parks Tinley proposed would necessitate the removal of a large number of people. This would disenfranchise three of the region's most influential headmen and would significantly compromise the relations between the administration and local community (Owen-Smith 2010: 151). While Owen-Smith did not propose two game reserves as Tinley did, he suggested an expansion of the Skeleton Coast Park (see Map 8.2). In contrast to Tinley, Owen-Smith also did not plan for a wildlife corridor between Etosha and the Skeleton Coast Park (Owen-Smith 1972: 36). He argued that there was no evidence of any large-scale migrations between the Etosha ecosystem and the coastal areas that would warrant such a corridor.[18]

---

[18] Recent research on the migratory behaviour of the elephants in the Kaokoveld has shown that there is some exchange between Etosha-bound elephant populations and Namib-bound populations. The interaction between both

Owen-Smith pointed out the great tourism potential of the Kaokoveld and insisted that income from tourism could become a major economic asset for the local population. He also argued for a number of land use changes: the entire pre-Namib area should be put under protection, basically expanding the Skeleton Coast Park boundaries some 50–100 km eastwards; while he did not see any need to remove herders from this area forcibly, he argued that a number of boreholes drilled further east would certainly motivate herders to leave the pre-Namib plains. The hardly used and unoccupied escarpment zone would create a natural buffer between the pre-Namib conservation area and more intensively used savannah stretches further inland. Owen-Smith (1972: 36) argued forcefully for the participatory inclusion of local communities in the planning process, and reasoned that income from tourism could become a major source of revenue for the bankrupt tribal trust fund.

One hundred copies of the Owen-Smith report were privately disseminated and distributed to government departments, NGOs, universities, and conservationists (Owen-Smith 2010: 161) and a year later the report was published. The report was (apparently) ignored by the government, and in his memoirs Owen-Smith said that he received some criticism from conservationists because he had gone against the Tinley plan, thereby complicating the picture for outsiders and obscuring the environmentalists' point of view (Owen-Smith 2010: 156–8).

The Eloff Report

Little happened on the ground: although the South African minister responsible issued a press release stating that the government was committed to expanding and establishing appropriate game reserves, no legislation for conservation was passed nor was any conservation area for a Namibian Bantu Homeland gazetted in the early 1970s (Hall-Martin et al. 1988: 62). Whereas reports on poaching were rare until the late 1960s, such reports were frequent throughout the 1970s. This put more pressure on the government to act. As in other instances of indecision, the government installed another commission, which was formally endorsed by the SANF, to draw up a master plan for

communities, however, seems rare and rather a matter of single bulls walking very long distances (Leggett 2006).

conservation and tourism for the Kaokoland and the Damaraland, to provide a report on the state of wildlife, and to advise the government on conservation in the region. It is interesting that in this case the government allied itself with a large and well-connected NGO, the SANF, probably to show conservationists worldwide that it was prepared to accept their input. The SANF was South Africa's branch of the WWF. Stephen Ellis (1994) has pointed out the close relations between the Apartheid government, the SANF, and the WWF. The South African business magnate Anton Rupert co-founded the WWF, and was the dominant figure in the SANF in the 1970s (Ramutsindela et al. 2011).

In October 1974 three Pretoria-based university professors, Fritz Eloff, Guillaume Theron, and Koos Bothma, travelled the region for two weeks (Owen-Smith 2010: 349). Eloff was a highly influential academic, well connected in the Broederbond, and President of the Northern Transvaal Rugby Union (pers. comm. Rob Gordon). In early 1975 Professor Eloff handed in a report with a number of recommendations to the government in Pretoria.[19] In a targeted manner the Eloff report elaborated the 'bewaring, bestuur en benutting van natuurreservate in Damaraland en Kaokoland' ('conservation, management and use of the nature reserves in Damaraland and Kaokoland'), gave evidence of the 'omvang van erosie en habitatvernietiging as gevolg van onoordeelkundige grondgebruik' ('quality and quantity of erosion and habitat destruction as a consequence of uninformed land use'), and advised on the protection of wildlife species. In an introductory preamble Eloff emphasised that a convincing conservation strategy was a 'status symbol' in the world community and that such a strategy would pay off in the long run because the tourism potential of the region was immense.[20] He detailed that good conservation measures in Namibia were the more necessary as the mandated status of the territory placed South Africa under even more scrutiny. To a much greater extent than the reports by Tinley and Owen-Smith, this report portrayed conservation in the Kaokoveld from a nationalist and global perspective. The Kaokoveld and Damaraland were depicted as ideal due to their spectacular landscapes and their high degrees of endemism, and hence were

---

[19] NAN BOP83 21/2/2. Meesterplan vir die Bewaring, Bestuur en Benutting van Natuurreservate in Damaraland en Kaokoland.
[20] NAN BOP83 21/2/2. Meesterplan vir die Bewaring, Bestuur en Benutting van Natuurreservate in Damaraland en Kaokoland, p. 5.

lauded as being of global value. The report listed seventeen tree species, nine bush species, four mammal species, nine species of bird, and an unspecified number of reptiles and invertebrates as endemic to Namibia's north-west. A number of unique species or species features were listed; the uniqueness of the Kaokoveld's elephants was especially highlighted: (1) According to the three professors, the elephants were likely to be the biggest in Africa; (2) the lions of the region were possibly a specific sub-species; and (3) the long-ranging migrations of elephants and rhinos into the desert and into inaccessible mountain areas were unique in the world.[21] However, the ecology of the Kaokoveld was under immediate threat. Degradation (*aftakelingsproses*) was observable in many fields. Unique habitats, such as in the Marienfluss Valley and the Khowarib Gorge, were being destroyed, partly because of borehole-drilling in inappropriate locations. According to Eloff these areas were not suitable for even sporadic grazing. The report also detailed the decrease of wildlife numbers in the region, and an interim report by Eloff pointed to massive poaching (Hall-Martin et al. 1988: 62). According to the report the expansion of pastoralism to the arid western parts of the Kaokoveld, made possible by borehole-drilling in the 1960s (a fact not mentioned by the report!), was responsible for this decrease in wildlife. The increase in poaching linked to the illegal trade of skins and ivory further contributed to the demise of wildlife. Eloff lamented that there was in fact no law controlling hunting in these areas.[22] This, the report surmised, resulted in irrevocable damage to South Africa's international reputation.[23] Eloff proposed that a nature reserve should be erected west of the 150 mm isohyet (in accordance with Owen-Smith's proposal) thereby adding a substantial stretch of land to the Skeleton Coast Park (see Map 8.3). Any permanent settlements west of this line were to be prohibited – in complete disagreement with Owen-Smith, and rather along the lines of the Tinley report. In a true professorial manner Eloff advised that more research should be done on specific species and on hydrological conditions before proper plans could be made. He also advised that no

---

[21] As far as I know, none of these points have become substantiated by later research.
[22] NAN BOP83 21/2/2. Meesterplan vir die Bewaring, Bestuur en Benutting van Natuurreservate in Damaraland en Kaokoland.
[23] NAN BOP83 21/2/2. Meesterplan vir die Bewaring, Bestuur en Benutting van Natuurreservate in Damaraland en Kaokoland.

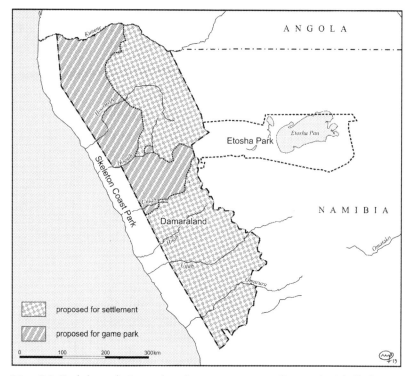

Map 8.3 Park boundaries and settlement areas according to the Eloff plan.
Source: NAN BOP83 21/2/2. Meesterplan vir die Bewaring, Bestuur en Benutting van Natuurreservate in Damaraland en Kaokoland

hunting should be allowed and that pot-licences for local administrative staff should also be revoked. Game wardens should be employed to combat poaching. These wardens were to be directly linked to specialists in the Department of Bantu Administration in Windhoek. The report recommended that for the time being tourists should only be allowed into Damaraland but that in the long run the Kaokoland should be included in touristic planning.

The territorial reorganisation of the Kaokoland under the banner of conservation was the major project proposed by the Eloff report. The report suggested two conservation areas, and broadly followed the Tinley report in their delimitations: (1) The first, in the southern Kaokoveld, was to connect the Etosha Park to the Skeleton Coast Park; this area was to be combined with a conservation area in northern Damaraland. Together both areas would provide a significant corridor for wildlife migration between Etosha National Park and the coast. The report argued that such a corridor was necessary for the survival of species such as elephants. (2) The second conservation area was proposed for the western stretch of the Kaokoveld. Principally it was to include the area west of the 150 mm isohyet. It was also to include the entire Kunene River Valley west of Epupa. The report argued that the entire Kunene Valley should be regarded as an area for conservation, but as the area east of Epupa was settled more densely it was not realistic to enforce conservation there. The area was also to include the Baynes and Otjihipa Mountains. While some sporadic herding in the major part of this area was to be allowed, other areas such as the Marienfluss Valley were to be completely closed to herding. It was argued that the valley's scenery would be more profitably put to use for tourism than for herding. The environmental destruction brought by herders lured to these places by the presence of boreholes was highlighted in strong words. The report recommended that some boreholes in the prospective conservation area should be closed down.

The major obstacle to the implementation of conservation measures, according to the report, was the presence of the Himba pastoralists. It was argued that these herders would only desist from moving into the proposed conservation area if further boreholes were developed in the eastern part of the then-remaining settlement area.[24] These massive land use changes would also demand more staff for conservation, and the report argued for the setting up of a department of conservation in the area. In a report for the *World Wildlife Yearbook 1976–77* (Jackson 1977) Eloff emphasised that it was the pastoralists and their ever-increasing cattle herds that had changed the situation. He alleged that 'the last grazing and waterholes available to the game are now being utilised by man. Water can no longer be spared for the use of game. At Sanitatas and Oropembe [sic] ... the waterholes are fenced and fires are lit at night to drive off the game' (Jackson 1977: 89, in which Eloff contributed a part). There is no mention in Eloff's text that most of these boreholes had been drilled by the South African administration only about a decade earlier.

---

[24] NAN BOP83 21/2/2. Meesterplan vir die Bewaring, Bestuur en Benutting van Natuurreservate in Damaraland en Kaokoland, pp. 10–11.

A South African Empire of Nature?

The two publications (published in two renowned South African scientific journals), together with the report of the de la Bat Commission and the Eloff report and other journalistic reports on the demise of wildlife, were well circulated in South Africa's elite circles. Anton Rupert, the South African business magnate who co-founded the WWF in the early 1960s and who had installed a South African at the head of the organisation in the early 1970s (Ramutsindela et al. 2011), involved himself personally in issues concerning conservation in the Kaokoveld. Ellis (1994) and Ramutsindela et al. (2011) have shown how closely the South African establishment in the 1970s was connected to the WWF. Ellis particularly pointed out the close relations between top South African conservationists, NGOs, government politicians, and the army. Ramutsindela et al. (2011) depict the ideological underpinnings of the close liaison between top South African capitalists and conservation in the 1960s and 1970s. It would certainly be too easy to simply label pro-conservation elite members as extensions of the government – the field of conservation also offered some space for a moderate critique of some of the measures of the Apartheid government – but the leading South African conservationist organisations were certainly close to high-ranking politicians. The Broederbond offered a close-knit network through which Eloff and Rupert were connected to prominent Apartheid politicians. Leading South African conservationists also found conservation to be an important means by which to circumvent South Africa's political isolation. During a period in which the South African Apartheid government was sidelined worldwide and faced considerable pressure from international bodies, international conservation was a field in which South Africans were still accepted, and in which they even dominated discourses. Contemplating conservation plans at the highest level and launching them on the international scene ameliorated South Africa's tarnished reputation, gave its allies something to point to in international meetings, and painted a rosier picture in internal press releases. The project of conservation was also followed up in the South African homelands of Transkei, Bophuthatswana, and Ciskei, with small conservation areas emerging there in the 1970s. Hence, motions to support conservation in Namibia fit well within the homeland paradigm, with just one significant difference: whereas the conservation areas in the South African homelands were minuscule due to high population densities, at the borders of the South African empire large-scale conservation areas seemed feasible. Such giant conservation areas would have framed the outer borders of a rapidly growing South African economy, and could have sheltered – perhaps more in symbolic than in military terms – a white-dominated South African society from the rest of the continent.[25]

In 1976 the President of the SANF, Anton Rupert, communicated that the Prime Minister of South Africa, B. J. Vorster, had commissioned the planning of the world's largest conservation area, to be established in northern Namibia. It would include substantial stretches of land in the Kaokoveld and in Damaraland. The announcement was made in an *African Wildlife* issue of 1976 (introduced as 'the most exciting, tantalizing statement', *African Wildlife* 1976: 19):

'As President of the S.A. Nature Foundation I am glad to be able to tell you that the Prime Minister of South Africa has just informed me of one of the most important events in the history of nature conservation,' said Dr. Anton Rupert. 'A contiguous nature conservation area covering 72,000 square kilometres is being planned for the northern part of South West Africa. This allays many fears which scientists of the International Union for the Conservation of Nature and Natural Resources and the World Wildlife Fund have had, as regards the future of this important habitat. This conservation area will include the existing Etosha Game Reserve as well as the Skeleton Coast Park, and will be more than three times the size of the Kruger National Park, and indeed one of the largest in the world.'

Rupert also suggested that the foundation of this enormous park would have global significance. The new park would have been the world's largest park area. It would have been a flagship project for the WWF, in which Rupert was active, and would have given the Apartheid regime some positive press worldwide. However, none of the plans envisioning major transformations of environmental infrastructure was carried out and during the latter part of the 1970s the Kaokoland became a battlefield. PLAN soldiers infiltrated the area from southern Angola, three SADF army units were placed in the

---

[25] In his PhD Lenggenhager gives a very detailed account of the close collaboration between conservationists and the military in Namibia's north-east in the 1970s and 1980s. Here two smaller game parks, Mudumu and Mamili (now Nkasa Rupara) were actually gazetted in 1989 after a long period of administrative contemplation, a number of commissions, and several scientific reports (see Lenggenhager 2018).

Kaokoveld, and for a decade military considerations overruled other development efforts.

8.2 Scientific Explorations and the Elephant Question

Since the late 1960s, planning for conservation in the Kaokoveld was accompanied by scientific research. The Eloff report sparked off research on the Kaokoveld's elephants, which had become the key topic of conservationists (Hall-Martin et al. 1988: 62). The number of elephants at the end of the 1960s may have been slightly above 1,000.[26]

The SANF financed a comprehensive ecological survey of the Kaokoveld in the aftermath of the Eloff report. Viljoen, a biology graduate student from Pretoria University under Professor Eloff, was commissioned to do this research. His research on elephants documented the various aspects of their demography, feeding habits, and herding behaviour. It also detailed the rapid decline of the species due to poaching. Viljoen's research was jointly financed by the SANF, the newly founded Endangered Wildlife Trust,[27] and the Eugene Marais Chair of Wildlife Management of the University of Pretoria (Reardon 1986: 84). There was a lot of speculation about desert elephants, and it was increasingly suggested that they were a separate sub-species (Owen-Smith 2010: 378). Viljoen did not support these speculations, but according to Owen-Smith he believed that 'the elephants had made behavioural adaptations to their arid environment that, combined with their intimate knowledge of the area, made them ecologically unique

---

[26] Owen-Smith (2010: 370) asserted that in the early 1970s the elephant population was probably around 1,200. Initial aerial surveys with the explicit aim of counting elephants were run in 1968 and 1969 by the then Department of Nature Conservation and Tourism. In 1969 out of a total of 279 elephants counted, 145 were observed in the west of the Kaokoveld, 86 in the northern drainage basin at Omuhonga, and 52 in the eastern regions. Viljoen suggests that both aerial surveys were grossly inaccurate because each was conducted in under 15 hours' flying time (Viljoen 1988: 51). In the mid-1970s, on the basis of numerous on-the-ground surveys, Owen-Smith estimated elephant numbers to be between 700 and 800 in total, of which 200 roamed the eastern Sandveld, 100–160 the northern drainage system, and 200–300 the pre-Namib region, the Beesvlakte, and the mountains south of Sesfontein (Viljoen 1988: 51).

[27] The Johannesburg-based NGO began its involvement in the Kaokoveld in 1978 after its chairman, Clive Walker, visited the region together with Professor Eloff (Reardon 1986: 83).

and, therefore, irreplaceable' (Owen-Smith 2010: 378). From 1981 the IUCN gave top priority to the elephants of the Kaokoveld and they progressively gained the status of flagships of conservation.

I will present some of Viljoen's research efforts in detail. It was the first in-depth and long-term ecological study in the Kaokoveld. It had a tremendous impact on the further development of conservation and contributed to the fact that elephant protection became the major project of nature conservationists for the following two decades. The report also documents a new level of surveillance of social-ecological relations through external actors in the area. Until then single rangers had tracked game and occasionally poachers in a vast area by foot or on horseback, or occasionally by car. Now wildlife movements as well as the activities of poachers were surveyed from the air, and at the same time controlled in extensive ground-truth studies – walks and drives along carefully planned transects. There is yet another important difference between Viljoen's research and earlier research on wildlife. While previously local informants and interpreters had played a dominant role in provisioning researchers with information, now 'hard' data was to be gathered through more technical methods. Local informants apparently did not feature importantly in Viljoen's research on elephants.

In October 1976 Viljoen conducted a comprehensive air survey covering much of the Kaokoveld.[28] With a four-seater Cessna Skylane, two wildlife researchers were flown over the territory, one of them being Viljoen. From a height of 100–200 m they counted wildlife and livestock for 40 hours, the most comprehensive survey of wildlife up to that date, and also the most expensive. The costs were covered by the Wildlife Society of South Africa.[29] In an exact manner the coverage of the survey was estimated: with 40 hours' flying time at a speed of 160 km/h, and with a coverage of 800 m on each side of the route about 10,240 km^2 were covered – about a fifth of the entire Kaokoveld. The findings were presented in a detailed manner: for each stretch of land observed, a quantified summary was given (see Map 8.4).

---

[28] NAN BOP 83 21-2-2 Kaokoland Wildsensus, 17–23 October 1976.
[29] WESSA (the Wildlife and Environment Society of South Africa) is one of South Africa's oldest and largest non-governmental environmental organisations. Founded in 1926 the organisation has been in continuous existence since that year.

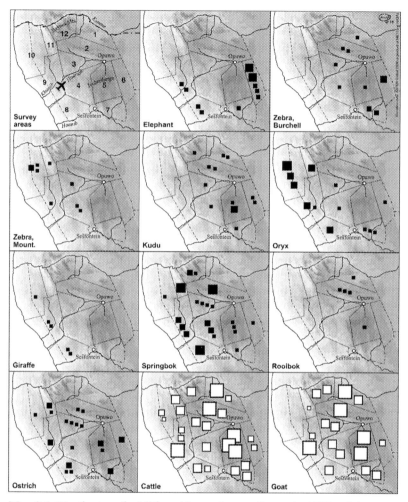

Map 8.4 Distribution of wildlife and livestock according to the 1976 aerial census. Note: The archival file contains a map with the survey areas. The numbers of specific species are given in statistics. Cartographer M. Feinen plotted these figures onto the map of survey areas in order to visualise wildlife and livestock distribution.
Source: NAN BOP 83 21-2-2 Kaokoland Wildsensus, 17–23 October 1976

The survey showed where wildlife was concentrated in the mid-1970s. Wildlife was particularly found in the western Sandveld near the Etosha Game Park and in the westernmost stretches of the Kaokoveld. Livestock was concentrated in the north-eastern, central, and south-western

Table 8.1 *Wildlife counts between 1969 and 1976 based on aerial photography*

	1969	1975	1976
Burchell zebra	1,476	323	137
Kudu	336	13	118
Elephant	434	190	162
Mountain zebra	735	803	117
Oryx	637	590	593
Springbok	1,060	1,528	974
Giraffe	58	79	40

Source: NAN BOP 83 21/2/2 Kaokoland Wildsensus. 17–23 October 1976.

parts of the region. High stocking numbers and wildlife were apparently compatible.

The census also gives a good idea where certain wildlife species were concentrated. While elephants, Burchell zebra, kudu, and ostriches were predominantly found in the eastern Sandveld, giraffe and oryx concentrated in the western pre-Namib stretches. The northernmost stretches 1, 2, and 12 had hardly any wildlife.

The overall results, however, were depressing: wildlife numbers had decreased massively when compared to the figures from the first aerial census in 1969 (see Table 8.1). The decline in elephant numbers was catastrophic. Whereas in 1969, 434 elephants were counted, this number being extrapolated to give a total population of c. 1,200, in 1976 only 162 elephants were counted, 126 of these in the eastern Sandveld bordering (and north of) Etosha Park. For the Hoanib River, nineteen elephants were indicated, and for the Hoarusib-Khumib-Orupembe area some thirteen elephants. The authors of the census attributed the decline in numbers to the migratory behaviour of elephants and – in accordance with the Eloff study done during the same year – the fact that the Himba herders were occupying many of the better wells in the area.[30] In contrast to this, a number of other reports gave strong evidence that elephants in particular were being poached in considerable numbers since the early 1970s (Owen-Smith 2010: 367ff.).

[30] NAN BOP 83 21/2/2 Kaokoland Wildsensus, 17–23 October 1976. 'The small number of elephants living in the west can be explained as most elephants had left for Damaraland and Angola as their normal drinking places were occupied by Himba and their livestock' (my translation).

In the mid-1970s the remaining elephants were living in three clearly separate populations: (1) The northern population of the central Kunene drainage basin mainly dwelt in the Omuhonga Valley; it then consisted of only eight cows, with no bulls (in 1969, eighty animals were counted). Only a few years later in 1983, these last animals had also disappeared or had been killed. (2) The eastern population was counted at 134 animals in 1977, and in the more exact survey some six years later at 207 animals. Viljoen stressed that this population displayed a marked seasonal fluctuation in numbers. Interestingly, the highest concentration of animals was found in the area which also displayed the highest density of human population. (3) The western population numbered sixty-five animals; as no calves survived between 1975 and 1978 this population was also under extreme threat (Viljoen 1988: 53–62). Between 1980 and 1983 Viljoen continued his study on the elephant population of the Kaokoveld. On the basis of a number of ground surveys, supplemented by twelve 10-hour aerial surveys, three 25-hour aerial surveys, and one 85-hour aerial count, he found a total of 357 elephants in the Kaokoveld in 1983. The intensive and very costly surveys also found 123 elephant carcasses, of which 107 showed clear signs of having been shot. In two cases elephants had been chased to death by vehicles.

The overall trend was clear. After a massive decrease in numbers between 1880 and 1910 the elephant population apparently remained stable until the early 1970s. Throughout the 1970s the onslaught faced by elephants was massive, and it was local poachers and soldiers as well as politicians who participated in the hunt. In 1978 viable herds were only to be found on the Ovamboland border and along the Ombonde River. The northern population was completely wiped out between 1970 and 1980. At the same time the western population declined from 300 animals in 1970 to 65 in 1977, then to 39 animals in 1983 (Viljoen 1988: 67). The elephant population of the Kaokoveld had collapsed within a decade and by 1980 was close to annihilation.

8.3 Poaching and the Failure of the Homeland Development Paradigm

While Viljoen is exact and detailed when describing the demise of the Kaokoveld's elephant population, he remains vague when discussing possible causes for this decline. In his PhD thesis he briefly deals with such causes in a single paragraph (Viljoen 1988: 67). He first alleges that the accessibility of 4x4 vehicles had brought even remote wildlife populations within the reach of poachers. Who these poachers were is not discussed, though Viljoen's account leaves little doubt that they were not local herders. He further suggests that local people had been provided abundantly with guns by traders in Angola in exchange for ivory. In a final point he lists 'more and more outsiders, who are inclined to poach and who possess the necessary arms and ammunition' (Viljoen 1988: 67) as a cause of increased poaching, but again does not specify who these outsiders were. It is strange indeed that a man who had stayed in the region for a good number of years was not able to identify poachers in a more lucid manner. He may have been reminded of the fate of Owen-Smith, who was transferred from the civil service for accusing administrative staff of poaching (Owen-Smith 2010: 133). Given the involvement of high-ranking South African politicians and military men, the threat may have been even more obvious.

Poaching had been kept at a low level for a number of decades. From the mid-1970s, however, reports of poaching became ever more pressing. Hall-Martin et al. (1988: 63) describe the illegal hunting of elephant, rhino, and black-faced impala as having become 'epidemic'. Two major reasons for this were openly discussed at the time: On the one hand the price for ivory and rhino horn was climbing to astronomical levels, and on the other the political destabilisation and ensuing militarisation of southern Angola since 1974 were given as major causes. While cross-border trading of weapons may have contributed to the increase in poaching in northern Namibia, there were other more salient reasons which were less frequently voiced. As SWAPO insurgents had opened a western front in the Kaokoveld with repeated forays into the territory from strongholds in south-western Angola, a panicked local administration had handed out between 2,000 and 3,000 rifles, most of them unregistered, along with about 200,000 rounds of ammunition to local residents, allegedly with which to protect themselves against the PLAN fighters (Owen-Smith 2010: 377). There was little need for trans-border weapons trading as suggested by Viljoen, as the South African military itself equipped locals with guns and ammunition. Furthermore, the centennial drought of 1980/81, with losses of cattle of around 95 per cent, certainly led to an increase in poaching – quite a number of impoverished herders saw poaching as a last resort to gain some income. Yet another cause was not talked about at all: top-level South African politicians as well as the local white administrative and military staff contributed significantly to poaching (Owen-Smith 2010: 367–406). While anti-poaching efforts were put in place by the political elite, it was often the very same persons responsible for the rules who took the liberty of breaking them. The Kaokoveld was regarded as a haven for passionate (white) hunters, and hunting there was a prerogative for high-ranking politicians, army officers, and local administrative staff. Mitch Reardon (1986: 13), a South African journalist accompanying Owen-Smith in the late 1970s, observed: 'Let loose in a wildlife treasure house the majority of men appointed to safeguard the Kaokoveld embarked on a hunting frenzy, the profligacy of which astonished the resident tribes who bore witness to it.'

Wildlife was not only poached but also legally shot by white administrative staff in Opuwo. It was one of the prerogatives of white staff stationed at Opuwo to acquire private hunting quotas in order to provide themselves, their families, and their staff with meat regularly. The issuing of so-called pot-licences had been a standard administrative practice to allow subsistence hunting for white officers. In 1971 the Native Commissioner in Opuwo, Jooste, wrote a letter to the Chief Bantu Commissioner in Windhoek to ask for higher hunting quotas for white staff. He argued that twenty white staff were then living in Opuwo with their families and that a school and a hospital had to be maintained. He recounted that Opuwo, the administrative headquarters, was isolated, and that shop-bought fresh food was hard to get. He then pointed out that wildlife was plentiful in the region, and asked for an annual quota of 200 springbok, 30 kudu, 20 oryx, and 25 zebra. He proposed a scheme in which a hunter would have to pay 4 R for large game and 2 R for small game.[31] Apparently the issue was seen as problematic in Windhoek, and was handed on to Pretoria, where officers questioned the high demand for wildlife meat. About a year later Jooste again felt it necessary to argue for a high quota, and reasoned that there was a 'redelike oorvloed van wild' ('an abundance of wildlife'). He then asked for a more moderate quota of 100 springbok, 20 kudu, and 20 oryx. Additionally, he argued that chiefs should also be given their own hunting quotas, and quotes chiefs pleading for

---

[31] NAN BOP 83 21/1/2. Bantu Commissioner, Jooste Opuwo to Chief Bantu Commissioner Windhoek, 28/5/1971.

a right to hunt wildlife.[32] Later that year the administrator became involved, and sent a letter to all Bantu Commissioners saying that pot-licences were legal but that hunted wildlife should be paid for. He proposed fees far higher than the prices Jooste had envisioned, and asked, for example, for 20 R for a kudu and 25 R for an oryx. In 1973 the Chief Bantu Commissioner attempted to regulate the highly opaque commissioning of pot-licences and gave quotas to white officers resident in reserve areas. The quota was given to each Bantu Commissioner, who could then further distribute hunting rights amongst his staff members. The quota put out for the Bantu Commissioner in Kaokoland was indeed very high – much higher than any other quota in the country: he was allowed to shoot eighty springbok, ten kudus, ten oryx, and twenty zebra per year. The letter indicated that more zebra could be shot if meat was needed for schools, hospitals, and local chiefs. In contrast, the Bantu Commissioner in Damaraland was given a quota of only one springbok per week and one springbok per person employed in the household per year.[33] The idea of special pot-licences for chiefs was not taken up.

Legal hunting and poaching took a heavy toll. A report by Clive Walker to the IUCN, the SA government, and the SADF in 1978 rang the alarm bells and drew attention to the catastrophic state of affairs. Walker's report was widely disseminated and also read in international conservationist circles. As a consequence of the report a further study was commissioned by the SANF on the state of rhinos and elephants. The Endangered Wildlife Trust, a small South African NGO founded in the early 1970s, supported the study and sponsored a number of aerial surveys. These surveys found evidence of a large number of elephant and rhino carcasses. By the early 1980s black rhino had been wiped out in the Kaokoveld, and only a few elephants were left (Reardon 1986: 55).

The situation was equally dramatic in adjoining parts of southern Angola. However, while there is quite widespread reporting on the demise of wildlife in the Kaokoveld, I found only a single hint at the scale of poaching in south-western Angola. Brian Huntley, game warden in Iona National Park in the early 1970s, reported in a short

[32] NAN BOP 83 21/1/2. Bantu Commissioner, Jooste Opuwo to Chief Bantu Commissioner Windhoek, 6/6/1972.
[33] NAN BOP 21/1/2 Hoofbantoeskekommissaris van SWA, 'Pot-lisensies vir die skiet van wild', 10/7/1973.

contribution to *African Wildlife* that hunting within the confines of Iona National Park had become rampant. In his memoirs (Huntley 2017) he gives a detailed account on the causes and practice of poaching in the Iona Park area.[34] The situation seems to have been similar to that in northern Namibia. Huntley reports that in Iona, too, police and military personnel regularly hunted oryx, and that their activities paralleled the efforts of well-organised teams of poachers killing hundreds of mountain zebra, black-faced impala, and black rhinoceros. In south-western Angola poaching had escalated after 1974 when the region became embroiled in the multi-decadal Angolan civil war (Huntley 1976: 13–14).

By the early 1980s the once-abundant wildlife resources of the Kaokoveld had been depleted. An important part of the environmental infrastructure had been violently eliminated. While the drought of the early 1980s certainly contributed to the demise of wildlife, the major reason for the collapse was the rapid increase in poaching. But governmentally legalised killing of so-called problem animals also contributed to the collapse. During the drought of 1980/81 predators became a problem for local livestock farmers. They received permission to kill predators vying for their herds: within two years seventy-six lions and thirty-three cheetahs were killed with traps (Reardon 1986: 34). As yet we know very little about the effects of the collapse of wildlife. Today, more than thirty years later, we know that this demise was not final, as wildlife numbers have increased considerably since the mid-1990s. For the 1980s and 1990s however the near-absence of wildlife had important consequences for other sectors of the economy. The near-collapse led to increased attention from national and international media and organisations. Despite governmental attempts to mute efforts to deal with poaching publicly, there was reportage on these issues. In March 1979 *Die Republikein* asked: 'Gaan Kaokoland se wildlewe dié aanslag oorleef?' ('Can Kaokoland's wildlife survive the attack?') The newspaper article clearly points out the international dimensions of the issue, referring to statements by Prince Bernhard of the Netherlands, who had been president of the WWF for some time, and by Anton Rupert, the South African industrial tycoon and head of the SANF, who both expressed deep concern

---

[34] Huntley (2017: 66–7) reports that mainly zebra were poached in Iona for their skins which were then traded on to Namibia and sold to tourists there.

over the situation in the Kaokoveld.[35] The demise of wildlife in the Kaokoveld became a topic in the international media, and preliminary efforts to cope with the situation were widely publicised. The catastrophic decline of wildlife brought global conservationists to the region. While in the 1980s funds to improve conservation were still moderate, in the 1990s major donors like USAID paid for participatory conservation efforts, and today the conservation programme launched in the Kunene Region is lauded as one of the most successful programmes in the world. This change will be part and parcel of the next chapter. This chapter, however, will end with a description of the parallel collapse of the pastoral economy in the early 1980s.

8.4 *Otjita*: The Drought of 'The Dying'

The catastrophic decline of wildlife was paralleled by a centennial drought between 1980 and 1982, and by the increase of violent interaction between the South African army and PLAN soldiers. The drought of 1980–2 is named *Otjita*, 'The Dying', by local herders. There is one other year that the Himba and Herero of the Kaokoveld refer to as 'The Dying' – the year 1897, when Rinderpest swept away c. 90 per cent of the herds in the region. The name *Otjita* was chosen to draw a link to this primordial year of collapse in local traditions. To call a year 'The Dying' indicates a complete breakdown of herding and stands for outright starvation and social disintegration. The personal experiences of such a year are appalling: herds one has cared for over decades crumble and are lost within a year or two; lines of ancestral cattle one's forebears have carefully tended suddenly come to an end. Rituals necessary to link the living to their ancestors are no longer feasible, because oxen that must be slaughtered at such rituals are lacking. There are more parallels: with the demise of cattle herds in 1897 the Himba and Herero – many of them at that time living in south-western Angola – were forced to resort to other activities. Many worked as mercenaries for the Portuguese colonial army and were actively involved in the suppression of anti-colonial revolts among the Nkumbi, Ngambwe, and Angolan Kwanyama (see Chapter 2). Similarly, in 1981, many Himba and Herero had to resort to non-pastoral activities and again soldiering offered itself as resort strategy.

[35] *Die Republikein* 14/3/1979, 'Gaan Kaokoland se wildlewe dié aanslag oorleef?'

The disaster was locally perceived and interpreted as a complete breakdown of the entire social-ecological system. We have heard that wildlife had been poached intensely throughout the 1970s, and yet more wildlife died during the drought, so by the early 1980s the landscape was devoid of any wildlife, which previously had been a highly visible feature of the social-ecological system. The intensification of the pastoral system envisioned by the administration in the 1950s and 1960s had failed miserably. While it had certainly contributed to a rapid increase in livestock numbers, a number of measures taken by the government had ostensibly contributed to grave ecological problems. The degradation of the ecological system seemingly climaxed, and resulted in what was seen as a total collapse of the system. Retrospectively, outside commentators blamed the revocation of the game reserve status in 1970 – a consequence of the Odendaal planning – as a major cause of the catastrophe. They also blamed the rapid infrastructural development of the region, the extension of the road network, the hundreds of newly drilled boreholes, and the expansion of the veterinary services without any parallel intensification of conservation measures (Hall-Martin et al. 1988: 61). Internal perceptions and presentations of the early 1980s as a collapse are echoed and reinforced by outsiders' impressions. Hall-Martin describes these years in an apocalyptic way, and states that the 'balanced co-existence of pastoral man with nomadic wildlife was to be gradually, but irredeemably, disrupted' (Hall-Martin et al. 1988: 61). While there is well-founded doubt as to the 'balanced co-existence of pastoral man with nomadic wildlife' there is no doubt about the severity of disruption.

Within a period of two years Kaokoland's regional herd had been diminished from 110,000 to 16,000 cattle – a loss of about 90 per cent. Since the great Rinderpest epidemic of 1897 no other disaster had depleted the regional herd so severely. The sense of complete annihilation can be clearly seen from the informants' statements. Not only had an individual herd been erased: the 'cattle of the Himba had been vanquished', and 'the Himba had been destroyed', as one old man put it. The Himba were portrayed as a starving nation in the national newspapers – although, due to political circumstances, the full extent of the catastrophe was not revealed to the public.

The combination of climatic drought and violence ushered in the catastrophe. Climatic conditions changed during the middle of the 1970s: since the rainy season of 1976/77, nine consecutive years were recorded with below-average rainfall. The prolonged drought started with two consecutive bad rainy seasons from 1976/77 (minus 27.9 per cent) and 1977/78 (minus 32.1 per cent). The drought is remembered as *Ourumbu Wonde* – the 'Drought of the Fly'. The name of the drought is derived from obstinate flies, thought to transmit disease. Precipitation in the late 1970s did not return to normal, and all years between 1976 and 1984 are recorded as having had precipitation below the average. A climax of adverse conditions was reached in 1981.

Climatic perturbations were exacerbated by political conflict. The armed wing of SWAPO (South West Africa People's Organisation), PLAN, stepped up its efforts along the Kunene border. While military conflict had been prominent in north-central Namibia since the early 1970s and in the Caprivi and Kavango region since the mid-1970s, PLAN opened its front in the Kaokoland only in the early 1980s. Allegedly they maintained several guerrilla camps in the areas immediately bordering the Kaokoland to the north. In order to check advances by the guerrillas, the South African administration established three major military camps in the Kaokoland in the second half of the 1970s: Opuwo, Okangwati, and Ehomba. Paramilitary units (Koevoet), which were placed alongside regular army units, recruited heavily among the Himba. Many young men tried to cope with stock losses by joining Koevoet units. The army administration was determined to make use of the local population against the rebels. Locally the war was portrayed as an ethnic conflict in which the Oshiwambo-speaking rebels were pitched against the Herero-speakers. Locals were outfitted with guns. In the preceding section I outlined how the distribution of many .303 rifles and enormous numbers of cartridges contributed to poaching in the Kaokoveld. Communities became heavily militarised and people were given the feeling that militarily preparedness was necessary. This shift had enormous consequences. An article by the *Rand Daily Mail* in December 1981 argues that 'AK-47s bring the ways of the West to the Himba'.[36]

As yet it is difficult to access the archival files of the SADF in Pretoria in order to find out exactly how many locals joined the SADF or Koevoet. Hundreds of young Himba men joined the army or police

---

[36] *Rand Daily Mail* 10/12/1981, 'AK-47s bring the ways of the West to the Himbas'.

forces. The sizeable incomes offered lured many men into the army, as this seemed to be the only way to compensate for drought losses (Owen-Smith 2010: 406). In February 1981 the *Rand Daily Mail* reported 'ethnic training camps operated by the police in the SWA operational area, where hundreds of tribesmen are being recruited to become policemen'. A base camp geared towards training local Himba recruits in Opuwo is specifically mentioned. The article asserts that such a transition from 'relatively undisturbed lives' could be 'traumatic', but argues that the lure of a payment of 6 R per day is so tempting that many young men opt for it.[37] The article reports that 'almost every adult male carries the new symbol of manhood, the rifle' in Opuwo.

Fighting in the Kaokoveld never reached the dimensions of the war in southern Angola, where the South African army launched a number of offensives against the joined forces of MPLA and PLAN, which were supported by Cuban air forces. In the Kaokoland, PLAN insurgents repeatedly planted land mines on roads to interrupt army supplies or simply to threaten a pending large-scale infiltration. While smaller groups of PLAN combatants were apparently fairly active in the Kaokoveld, operating from some strongholds in south-western Angola, there were hardly any outright battles in which larger groups of soldiers opposed one another. What spread horror in the local population was that local leaders who were deemed to be close to the South African administration were targeted and occasionally killed. Repeatedly young people were also abducted from the Kaokoveld and brought to PLAN camps in southern Angola. Attacks on Ehomba and Ombaka in the northern Kaokoveld in the early 1980s were widely reported upon. During a raid three members of the chiefly van der Merwe family were killed in Ehomba (Owen-Smith 2010: 406)[38] and two alleged collaborators were killed in Ombaka (Menestrey-Schwieger 2017: 209). PLAN activity was apparently most intense close to the few fords of the Kunene River: in the far west PLAN soldiers entered the Kaokoveld through fords at Otjinungwa and Otjomborombonga. In order to suppress PLAN forays into the western Kaokoveld, the long-term chief of the westernmost arid stretches of the

---

[37] *Rand Daily Mail* 4/2/1981, 'Politics and war change the way of life in SWA'.
[38] *Rand Daily Mail* 10/12/1981, 'AK-47s bring the ways of the West to the Himbas'.

Kaokoveld Vetamuna Tjambiru 'invented' a ritual fire meant to ward off aggressors magically (Warnloef 2000). PLAN soldiers also intruded into Kaokoveld at Swartbooisdrift repeatedly making their way into the inaccessible Zebra Mountains. Some people described their situation as dramatic: in the night guerrillas came and punished herders for working too closely together with the South Africans, and during the day South African soldiers came and, seeing the spoors of the guerrillas from the previous night, punished the herders for hosting PLAN fighters. In order to check on the infiltration of guerrillas, Himba households in the Kunene Valley were forced to resettle in the Omuhonga Valley near Okangwati in 1979. From 1978 to about 1985 mobility was frequently conditioned more by considerations of personal safety than by the requirements of grazing. Opuwo, the capital of the Kaokoland, was fenced in with barbed wire. Transports into and out of Opuwo were only acceptable in convoy, and the few children of white officials in Opuwo were flown to and from school.

Drought Aid in the Homeland Context

The Kaokoland became an emergency zone. The starving population of the Kaokoveld was to be given food-aid. Such aid was provided by the International Red Cross and distributed by the SADF (Owen-Smith 2010: 405). In the middle of 1981, thousands of people flocked to the relief camps around Opuwo (Jacobsohn 1990: 16), where government institutions and the Red Cross were handing out famine food. Private donors also sought to aid the local population. By mid-1981 the first donations were received by local leaders: 13,000 R were presented to local leaders to buy famine-relief food.[39] The parastatal FNDC (First National Development Corporation) donated further food-aid.[40]

By May 1981 the South African government had set up a comprehensive drought aid and relief plan: A total of 55,252,000 R was to be donated to Namibia to help the people to cope with the disaster. Of these funds, 20 million were reserved for the administration of the whites; i.e. more than a third of the money was to be given to less than 10 per cent of the population, in an effort to keep up commercial farming. The remainder of the money was to be divided between the various population groups organised in separate Bantustans. The amount of money

[39] *Allgemeine Zeitung* 11/6/1981, p. 1.   [40] *ENOK Bulletin* 26/6/1981.

allocated for infrastructural measures (such as the drilling of further boreholes) to the Herero, Kavango, and Ovambo administrations differed: for the Herero administration, 1.75 million; the Kavango administration, 3.75 million; and for the Ovambo administration, 3.93 million. For each group it was worked out how many livestock had actually been affected by the drought. For the Herero administration, including the Kaokoveld, Himba, and Herero, some 375,163 animals were counted, and of these, 214,371 were directly affected by the drought. A total of 5,387,313 R were transferred to the Herero administration, 5,039,744 to the Ovambo Administration, and 1,644,074 to the Damara administration. While the money for infrastructural measures went directly into the coffers of, for example, Water Affairs and Veterinary Services, the money attached to livestock numbers was given to the Bantustan Administration. For the first three months after their allocation, such funds could be used for example for the transport of slaughter animals. Meat factories were given further financial support to subsidise the buying of emaciated livestock.[41]

Personal Recollections

Personal recollections of the disaster and the turbulent years preceding it convey a strong doomsday sentiment. A pastoral lifeworld was on the brink of annihilation. Often the situation is circumscribed with phrases like 'we were destroyed'. Interestingly the drought aid programme, which according to government reports was of considerable scale, was rarely mentioned in oral accounts. Vahikura, an elderly man in his seventies in 1995, recollects the disastrous consequences of the 'Drought of the Dying':

> That one totally destroyed us. Some people came out of it with a few cattle and others came out with no cattle at all, and yet others came out with just one cow, and that single cow gave birth again (and formed the basis of a new herd). We were eager to obtain sacks of maize until the rains came; some went to beg for livestock from paternal relatives; you asked those who still owned cattle for help ... goats died too, but most of the small stock survived. The people lived off the remaining goats. Those that survived were enough for the people to live on. (Vahikura Kapika, July 1994)

---

[41] NAN AHR 59 12/8/1 Droogtehulpmaatreels, Administrator General and Sekretaris: Landbou, 18/5/1981.

Increased mobility was one key strategy used by local herders to cope with drought conditions. As a first reaction to the onset of the drought, some households shifted to the Kunene River or to its tributaries, despite the war. There they hoped to supplement their food with palm nuts. The goats and some lactating cattle could feed on the seeds of *Faidherbia albida*. However, it soon transpired that the drought was so serious that it exceeded the perturbations of a normal dry year. Especially young families then crossed the Kunene and set off to Angola. Many went as far as Otjandjou (about 100 km north of the Kunene) leaving the Himba area at its north-eastern edge. Others migrated towards the Kuvale area at the north-western rim of the Himba area. At the height of the drought some Himba herders even moved close to Lubango (pers. comm. Samuel Aço). The situation was aggravated by the fact that due to the Angolan civil war, very little food could be bought in south-western Angola. It was mainly young mobile families who risked the long migration, taking with them the cattle of less mobile households, while the old, the children, and many women stayed behind. However, herders claim that although losses in Angola were also very high, those herders who went to southern Angola were at least able to save two or three oxen.

The following case study gives an idea of the hardship people underwent to save the lives of a few animals during the Drought of the Dying.

This land has seen many droughts. During one drought I lived in Omuhonga, I migrated with my cattle to the hill of Tutu in the Omavanda Mountains. There I stayed. My wife remained behind at our small garden in Omuhonga. Later I asked her to come and join the cattle camp and we moved to Osia together. There I stayed with some friends for a short while and then migrated close to Etengwa to a place called Okotuhama. My wife was pregnant and I brought her to her mother. A little time later she gave birth.

I returned to my herds and drove them back to Omuhonga. There I stayed with my hunger. I rested until there was nothing left to eat anymore. I asked Vahenuna's father for a big ram which I slaughtered immediately. I ate and ate and ate, I ate with great hunger. That year was a serious drought. Then I moved again. I left my goats with my mother's younger sister, the mother of Karambongenda. I drove my cattle to Oyomiwore; the next day I set off to Okahamwanda, where I settled together with some friends. When the grass was finished we moved on via Oviyere to Okayere and then to the hill of Muzema. We stayed there for some time. But the cattle became too weak to climb the hill. There was still water in the waterhole but the hole was far from where we settled. I wondered, 'What shall I do?' I moved again and migrated to Otjisoko; finally I stayed in Otjitamutenya. I fetched my wife from her mother's place and brought her to Omuhonga. There our newborn died in the midst of the drought. I brought my mourning wife to her father in Omuramba. Then I set off to shift my goats. I slept one night at Ombandaondu; the next day I drove them and I stayed in Ombaka. From Ombaka I went to the camps of my friends who had migrated from Omuhonga. Then it started raining. Our starved cattle died of the sudden cold. I returned to Omuhonga, but still cattle died from the cold brought by the rains. The calves died in great numbers. The women skinned them to take the hides and make them into clothing. They died and only some survived. Nearly all the calves died.

When I returned to my homestead I found that many of my cattle had died. Many more had died in my herd than in the herd of the others. Yes, cattle do it that way, some cattle struggle to survive and some just give in and die. I set off again and migrated with all my livestock; goats, cattle and sheep. I stayed in Oromutati. One night my calves escaped and ran back to the old homestead. One calf was killed by a hyena that night. In that place, Oromutati, several female cattle died. All pregnant cows had died by now, one cow after the other was skinned. The cattle just died of drought. One cow I lost there, and I never saw it again. Then I sold one heifer and I got some maize meal and sugar for it, on which I lived for some time ...

Now the big drought came. I stayed here in Ombuku until *oruteni* [Oct.–Dec.], then I moved beyond that hill to where it is called Okomwangwei. There another cow died. Then I divided the goats herd. Some I gave to my sister's son and some I left with another herd of goats. I was all alone as my wife was still with her parents. I had to do everything by myself: I watered the cows and calves and milked the goats. At that time I heard that it had rained in Otjitanga. I tried to move there. The cattle moved well the first day. We slept at Ohamukuta. But the next morning they did not want to get up. However, in the end we arrived at Otjitanga. The rain had not been good and we had to move on, but this time the cattle were too weak and many died. I divided the cattle: the stronger ones I gave to a Tjimba herdsman, the weaker ones I took. Now the cattle started dying all over the country. Entire herds were finished. The people became sad; their hearts were red. And during this disaster the war of Ozoteri made things worse. The remaining cattle fled.

People looked for straying cattle in the bush around Okangwati. If they saw an animal they just shot it and sold the meat at Okangwati. I decided to climb the hills of Omazorowa with the remaining animals. After we arrived there all my cattle died, one by one, finished. Yes, finished, nothing was left. I said to myself 'Now I will join the army'. I sent a child with the remaining goats to my wife and told her to slaughter one for meat and sell the other ones for maize. I left to join the army. But suddenly the spirit of my mother's brother started to speak to me. And it told me not to join the army. It told me to return. And so I did. I went to Ombuku and took some of the cows I had given to the Tjimba shepherd, and some animals which had been lost previously I found in the bush, until I had about 10 cattle. ... But the cattle still went on dying. When the cattle died in our land of the Himba, many people went to the town to look for food. A person who died was not mourned anymore. The person was just buried and the people went back to their homes shortly afterwards. They did not stay at the funeral, not even a day. (Tako Hunga, June 1995)

For Tako spatial mobility was the key to saving some cattle. Tako shifted his cattle camp many times during the drought in order to save a few head of cattle. The places he visited were about 60 kilometres apart. While Tako occasionally moved together with friends, he usually moved alone. In other accounts of drought-related migrations, three or four households moved together and coordinated their labour. Drought-related migrations were a continuous fight against adverse conditions: hunger, tiredness, and heat. The military situation in northern Namibia and southern Angola brought about additional stress.

I conducted interviews on the drought and coping strategies with a community living close to the Namibian/Angolan boundary. Communities living in the central and southern parts of the Kaokoveld found it much harder to move on. Despite the drought, the Red Line remained impassable: as drought conditions also prevailed south of the fence, the lure was not great in any case. At the climax of the drought Herero herders settling adjacent to the Etosha Park's western fence received a special permit to move cattle herds into the western sections of the park. Movements into Ovamboland were apparently rare: as war-conditions were much more pressing there, and since the drought also had a significant impact on the grazing in Western Ovamboland, again the motivation to move east may have been low.

By the end of the drought in 1982 the Kaokoland's cattle herd had been reduced to 15,000 heads of cattle. For sure, a good number of cattle owned by Himba and Herero from the Kaokoland may still have been in Angola in 1982, but there is no doubt that losses were catastrophic. Outsiders as well as local people contemplated the end of pastoralism. Reardon (1986), who visited the area soon after the drought, describes a depressed situation, with famine relief camps around Opuwo, and depressed herders taking to alcohol.

The next chapter deals with the resurgence of a pastoral social-ecological system. Repastoralisation and reorganisation of environmental governance, however, took place under altered circumstances: Namibia became independent in 1990. This led to a complete reorganisation of the administration, the setting of new developmental goals, and the institution of new developmental projects. NGO activities in the field of conservation became of immense importance.

PART 5

Dynamics of Social-Ecological Relations between the 1990s and the Present

Since 1990 many parameters of the social-ecological system have changed. Most obvious are political parameters: Namibia became independent and the entire regional administration was reorganised. While principal land use patterns did not change greatly, with pastoralism still being the most important component of the rural economy, some significant changes in social-ecological coupling did occur. Most visible perhaps is the spectacular expansion of agriculture in riverine valleys and in the peri-urban area of Opuwo. Roads have become more common and since 2008 a tar road connects Opuwo to other Namibian centres. Also new boreholes have been drilled in considerable numbers. Opuwo and other sub-centres have expanded often with government buildings like schools and clinics making for the core of new settlement nuclei (with teachers' houses or housing for nurses attached to them). These new infrastructures provide the material base for a more intense and more diverse use of space.

Wildlife increased in numbers, and new laws on wildlife management reopened venues for the local population to make use of wildlife. In many places elephants have again significant impact on the environment and on land use. Predators, notably lions, again take a significant toll on livestock herds.

Other changes are less visible: population growth is high throughout the region, and especially the last two decades have been marked by rapid growth, a dynamic that will probably unfold its effect fully only in the next two decades. Much of the natural resource management system has also changed: while traditional authorities are still relevant, institutions like elected conservancy committees and water management committees organise day-to-day resource use and frame resource management plans often in conjunction with traditional authorities. The impact of the state and also of international NGOs on local social-ecological dynamics has been significant, with conservation-minded donors pouring millions of dollars into the region. While the Kaokoveld is framed by a number of local, national, and international actors as a conservation area par excellence, a place where wildlife and human livelihoods (potentially) harmonise, lately large companies have become interested in the mineral riches of the Kaokoveld, and the government is planning major new infrastructures along the Kunene River.

This part takes up the story in the 1980s and then follows social-ecological dynamics into the present. After depicting the political ramifications of these dynamics Chapter 9 will be devoted to an ethnography of contemporary herding practices and the political ecology of pastoralism at the end of the twentieth/beginning of the twenty-first century. Chapter 10 deals with the comprehensive reorganisation of natural resource management notably in the wildlife sector in the first two decades of the twenty-first century. Chapter 11 attempts to cast a glance into future social-ecological dynamics, many of which are ambitiously planned for in the present.

A Glance at the Sources

The history of northern Namibia in the 1980s and 1990s still remains to be written. There are a number of reasons for this. The most important reason certainly is that archival files on the decade are still – by and large – inaccessible. This pertains to files stored in the National Archives in Windhoek, where files for the 1980s are not yet fully fitted with finding aids and are still stored in inaccessible boxes. This pertains even more to the numerous files originating with the SADF administration in northern Namibia during the war years. Archival files for the 1990s have generally not been accessible for this book. I have repeatedly spent time in north-western Namibia since 1992 and since then myriad semi-official publications, papers, and plans have filled the shelves. A bird's eye look at the production of knowledge, and specifically knowledge on human–environment relations, would probably identify the early 1990s as a turning point. While previously most information was produced by governmentally endorsed officials or scientists, since then knowledge has been produced by a multitude of information-producers. While in the 1980s there was a very moderate production of knowledge on the region due to war conditions, since the early and more forcefully since the mid-1990s there is a flood of publications on the region. First of all these emanate from different ministerial offices and projects connected to them. The large IFAD-funded NOLIDEP programme (Northern Livestock Development Project), which had one project base in Opuwo, produced many papers. Then NGOs, and here particularly IRDNC[1] and the umbrella organisation for community-based natural resource management in Namibia (NACSO)[2] produced an enormous amount of information which since the early 2000s has been accessible online. The US-financed Millennium Challenge Account invested intensively in community-based tourism activities, livestock marketing, and pasture management between 2010 and 2014. The project left a great number of documents on the Web.[3]

Since the early 2000s the Internet started to store pieces of information on the region and its people. A short Google exploration reveals the sheer amount of data available on different aspects of life in the region. With the 1990s the media used to disseminate information on the Kaokoveld, its landscapes and the people dwelling in them became more diversified. While until the mid-1990s written information in published and unpublished texts dominated, since then a great number of films have been broadcast on the region. Warnloef (2000) reflects on the making of one such film by a BBC team in the late 1990s. Craig Matthew has been working on a number of documentaries on the region and his price-winning film *Ochre and Water* (2001) has been broadcasted in numerous countries worldwide. The film *Authenticized: Authenticity Comes at a Price* (Kraak et al. 2013) reflects local efforts to live up to images cast of locals by international filmmakers, photographers, and tourists. The South African-French filmmaker Rina Sherman has contributed a number of films on cultural dynamics in the region.[4] Lately the Kaokoveld has also been discovered for reality shows (Meyer 2007): Westerners, sometimes as singles and sometimes as families, are 'dropped' in pseudo-remote

---

[1] www.irdnc.org.na/history.html.   [2] www.nacso.org.na/index.php.
[3] www.mcanamibia.org/files/files/KuneneFactsheetFinal.pdf.
[4] For an anthology of Rina Sherman's films see: www.rinasherman.com/indexcine.html.

places and the documentary captures how they cope with the customs and constrains of primitive life. Very recently, i.e. in the 2010s, a great number of YouTube videos, e.g. on protests against the hydroelectric dam, on a chief's enthronement or another chief's shift to the SWAPO Party, have appeared online, adding to the complexity.

9 | *Pastoralism, Environmental Infrastructures, and State–Local Society Relations in the Late Twentieth and Early Twenty-First Century*

While the Kaokoland formally became a semi-independent homeland in 1979 and was to be administered through the 2nd Tier Herero authority from its administrative headquarters in Okahandja (du Pisani 2010), on the ground there was little change. The pertinent changes actually taking place were linked to the escalating civil war and the presence of large numbers of soldiers. For a period of about five to eight years settlement patterns became seriously disrupted. When relocating to their original homes in the latter part of the 1980s often newcomers mixed with old-time settlers.[1] The disruptions of the early 1980s also led to more permanent shifts in settlement. Quite a number of households that had been pressurised to resettle to the Omuhonga basin in the early 1980s, for example, remained there after independence, and the Omuhonga basin became one of the most densely settled areas in the entire Kaokoveld (Sander et al. 1998).

While the Kaokoveld became a militarised zone and military activities became habitual, no major battles took place in the region. The front line never extended into north-western Namibia, and besides some minor forays of PLAN soldiers with a limited number of casualties attached to them, the Kaokoveld was firmly controlled by the South African army. Opuwo was developed as a headquarters for the region. Here the major part of the army was stationed, and civil infrastructure (schools, hospitals) developed. A black residential area was constructed close to a small town centre, and the obligatory white residential area was constructed at a distance from both black living quarters and town centre (Müller-Friedman 2005: 57). The white residential area was minuscule, as in other towns in the northern

---

[1] Menestrey-Schwieger describes how – when the inhabitants of Ombaka village in the northern Kaokoveld finally went back from Okangwati to their erstwhile home – they found the place already occupied by a number of homesteads. Finally old-time settlers and newcomers amalgamated to form a larger community (Menestrey-Schwieger 2017: 210).

homelands, and black residents have greatly outnumbered white residents since the 1970s. The army was closely connected to the hospital (army doctors) and the school, where army officers, and also their wives, taught.[2]

Herding went on despite the ever-present threat of violence and the relocation of people. From the local perspective the 1980s were not only shaped by violence and military threat but also characterised by efforts to restock depleted herds. Only in 1984 were the rains back to normal: the year itself is called the year of calves. Both Himba and Herero emphasise the great care invested in each and every calf throughout the 1980s. They also describe travels to Angola, Uukwanyama[3] in north-central Namibia, and Okakarara in eastern Namibia (Bollig 2006: 302ff. on various restocking strategies after the centennial drought of 1981; Ohta 2000) to buy and/or exchange heifers. By the end of the 1980s the regional cattle herd was back to c. 80,000 heads of cattle.

The 1980s were also the time of an emergent grassroots initiative to ensure basic conservation measures. In 1982 Garth Owen-Smith initiated an NGO that sought to adopt a new approach to wildlife conservation (Endangered Wildlife Trust). In close correspondence with local chiefs a handful of community game guards were nominated in some communities in the western parts of the Kaokoveld. These game guards were selected by local chiefs and were to patrol the area and to look out for poachers and record wildlife sightings. In return they were given food rations (Owen-Smith 2010: 418). Owen-Smith based this initiative on the close relations he had developed with chiefs especially in the southern and western Kaokoveld during the period he had worked for the Ministry of Agriculture in the 1960s. Throughout the 1980s a number of poaching cases were attended to by courts, of these the

---

[2] *Paratus*, the official journal of SADF, published a Special Issue on the army in the Kaokoland, emphasising the humanitarian character of military intervention and the close linkage of the army to the local population. Soldiers are depicted as devoted development workers defending Africa against communism (Paratus 1982). The journal claims that 'men as hard as the untamed terrain over which they watch, [are] protecting land and its people', that the 'Kaokoland is a beautiful area of good people and honourable soldiers', and finally that the 'Himbas are still "children of nature"'.

[3] Kreike (2009: 90) reports much lower mortality figures for neighbouring Ovamboland, especially for Uukwanyama and estimates losses of 10 per cent there for the years 1979–80 and no major losses for 1980–1.

majority were brought to the attention of the authorities by game guards (Owen-Smith 2010: 425). The activities of the NGO were not aligned with conservationist efforts of the government. In fact, the local game warden for the Kaokoveld was directly opposed to the NGO's activities, not least because he was alleged to be one of the major poachers in the region (Owen-Smith 2010: 447–8). In 1990 the piloting community game guard programme became the NGO Integrated Rural Development and Nature Conservation (IRDNC), which gained significant international funding for its community-based conservation programmes in the 1990s and early 2000s.[4] It is hard to reconstruct exactly how much money went into the establishment of conservation measures connected to the widespread community-based natural resource management (CBNRM) programmes financed by diverse donors in the Kaokoveld in the 1990s and early 2000s. The End of Project Report of the Living in a Finite Environment Programme summarises the financial input of USAID funds into the programme on a national basis: it is reported that USAID/Namibia invested a total of US$39,934,006 in the CBNRM programme between 1993 and 2007 and that the majority of these funds flowed through WWF cooperative agreements with Namibian NGOs. It is also reported that donors invested a total of N$802 million into Namibia's CBNRM programme between 1990 and 2007 (LIFE 2008: VII–VIII). The greater proportion of these funds was spent on measures at the national level and on programmes in the Kunene, Erongo, and Zambezi (formerly Caprivi) regions. Never before had the Kaokoveld experienced such a sustained financial input from the outside to influence environmental infrastructure in specific ways; Chapter 10 will show to what ends it did so.[5]

[4] Since the early 1990s Garth Owen-Smith led the NGO together with his partner Margie Jacobsohn, who had done ethnoarchaeological fieldwork in the western Kaokoveld throughout the 1980s.
[5] Sullivan (2012: 198–9) speaks of a 'spectacular investment frontier in conservation' and shows 'how business and finance sectors, in collaboration with conservation organisations, conservation biologists and environmental economists, are engaging in an intensified financialisation of discourses and endeavours associated with environmental conservation and sustainability'. Although Sian Sullivan did research in Kunene Region she does not directly refer to the Kunene case. A deeper look into the case study may have revealed that next to this move towards financialisation other factors contributed to the rapid expansion of conservationist projects in the region. The goal to implement participatory approaches in conservation and to provide income-earning

South African rule as well as 2nd Tier government through Herero administration came to an end in 1989. UN peacekeepers, the UNTAG troops, came to the Kaokoveld in 1989[6] and South African troops withdrew from their bases in the latter part of that year. UNTAG troops settled in Opuwo and Okangwati for a number of months to facilitate the transition period. The removal of SWATF and Koevoet troops and their short-term replacement by UN soldiers brought about several major changes for the economy of the area. Quite a large number of young men had been employed by the army or by Koevoet in the 1980s.[7] Most of them left the army during the course of 1989.[8] The South African army and its military wing had played a major role for local businesses, bars, and bottle-stores for about a decade. They all had to look for new customers and a number of businesses apparently went out of operation in the early 1990s.

In March 1990 a new government was elected (Wallace 2011: 306; see Figure 9.1). Herero and Himba had been labelled as anti-SWAPO by the media, and in fact DTA, SWANU, and NPF – parties that felt oppositional to the dominant SWAPO party – were voted in for the region in 1990. Party alliances in the Kaokoveld still reflected older alliances to traditional leaders and Herero royal houses. While DTA alliances reflected the close relations between many Herero and Himba with the Maharero Royal House based in Okahandja, SWANU support was frequent among those in alliance with the Mbanderu Royal House and those voting for the NPF associated with the Zerauua Royal House based in Omaruru. All three Herero royal houses had supporters in the Kaokoveld, although Maharero affiliated supporters were clearly in the majority. Since the late 1980s the situation was becoming even more complex as people in the Kaokoveld established a fourth Herero royal house, the Otjikaoko Royal House (Friedman

---

opportunities for a marginalised rural population were certainly further motives of planners in the 1990s and in the early twenty-first century. Sullivan's observation that international capital flows are directed towards the globe's conservation areas is certainly valuable and of much relevance in this context.

[6] http://archives/un.org/sites/archives.un.org: 'Summary of AG-038 United Nations Transition Assistance Group (UNTAG)' (1989–90).

[7] Until now I could not find any conclusive hint as to the exact numbers. These figures should be obtainable from the SADF archive in Pretoria.

[8] I know of only a handful of locals who returned to South Africa with the South African troops. In general the participation of people from the Kaokoveld is not well documented and awaits archival studies in the SADF archives in Pretoria.

State–Local Society Relations   245

Figure 9.1 Young Himba children demonstrating for the coming elections for the NPF, a political party in Namibia, 17 April 1989.
Source: Bundesarchiv NAN 11602

2011: 203) to which especially all Himba, and also those previously associating with Tjimba ancestry, rallied. The Otjikaoko Royal House was also an effort to define an autochthonous in-group (those who have deep ancestry in the Kaokoveld) vis-à-vis outsiders (those who came to settle in the Kaokoveld in the twentieth century).

Namibia's independence brought about several path-breaking changes for north-western Namibia. In 1992 the administrative unit Kaokoland was abolished and the former homeland was integrated into the wider Kunene Region, which included commercial farmland in the Outjo-Kamanjab region.[9] The administrative capital of the region was moved to Opuwo, the Kaokoveld's only town-like place,

---

[9] The former Bantustan Kaokoland is roughly equivalent to the two constituencies Epupa and Opuwo.

bringing numerous government offices, banks, and shops there during the course of the following two decades (Müller-Friedman 2005). The population of the town grew from some 2,000 inhabitants in 1990 to about 6,000–7,000 inhabitants in the 2010s. This shift was gradual, however, and the build-up of infrastructure has continued until today. The main road is lined with numerous shops, quite a number of them now with Chinese owners or renters. Chinese traders started to come to Opuwo, as to other northern Namibian towns (Dobler 2008, 2014) after 2005. In 2008 a Chinese company won the tender to comprehensively refurbish Opuwo hospital, and perhaps about 100 Chinese workers stayed in Opuwo for many months. Many local informants claimed that Chinese traders first came to Opuwo at that time.

The development of the town has accelerated since a tar road was completed in 2008. Opuwo is now well connected to the outside world. While in the 1990s telephone land lines were often defunct, nowadays cell phones are in plenty. The rural population is also well connected to the Namibian networks through thousands of cell phones. The National Census for 2011 reported that in Opuwo constituency 45.6 per cent (of 5,178 households) possessed at least one mobile phone, and in Epupa constituency 17.3 per cent (of 2,781 households) owned such a device (Republic of Namibia 2014: 38). A household survey conducted in 2018 suggests that the involvement in cell phone based communication networks is expanding rapidly: out of 235 households only 46 had no mobile; the other 189 households owned together 549 mobiles (amounting to a per household ownership of mobiles of 2.3). This significantly widened options for local pastoralists, for example to find good information about livestock marketing, but, of course, also contributed to more communication across large distances among kin and non-kin. However, the major obstacle for livestock trade, the Red Line, separating the Kaokoveld from central Namibia with its ruling that no livestock may cross the line, remained in place – despite ongoing debates in Parliament and action plans to remove it.[10]

---

[10] *The Namibian* 21/6/2004 'Government moves to eliminate veterinary cordon fence' reports the minister saying that the fence would be removed by 2010 (www.namibian.com.na/index.php?id=6381&page=archive-read), but until now nothing has happened in this direction.

Throughout the 1990s and early 2000s Opuwo's significance for pastoralists from the surrounding rural areas increased. The hospital attracts thousands of people every year. Patients are brought to Opuwo by family members or friends, and while patients are treated indoors, those accompanying them seek shelter in the township. A number of wealthy pastoralists have rented or even own houses in town. Unlike in Anders Hjort's case though – 'Savannah Town' on Isiolo in northern Kenya (Hjort 1979) – rich herders did not invest heavily in trade or housing, i.e. they did not transfer wealth in cattle into other economic enterprises. The wealthy traders and bar-owners in town are often Oshiwambo speakers or originate from southern Angola. Otjiherero-speakers dominate the administration and – if in formal employment – are habitually working in or connected to governmental offices. Pastoralists also visit Opuwo to obtain medical drugs for themselves and for their animals. They go there in order to buy maize or other commodities. Local businesses cater for the needs of pastoral customers and sell, for example, herbs for traditional perfumes, crushed haematite stones for the production of ochre with which women anoint themselves, and veterinary drugs. Visiting herders also participate in political meetings and religious ceremonies there and lately have used Opuwo's urban environment to stage protests against the government. Opuwo has grown from a minute administrative outpost into a true economic, social, and political hub of the Kaokoveld.

In sum, the past twenty-five years have seen revolutionary changes in the Kaokoveld in many respects. The once isolated region was opened up to national and global flows of ideas, finances, and institutional designs. New infrastructures are creating new options for land use and mobility. Human settlements are expanding and enforcing a trend towards more sedentariness. Economic sectors other than pastoralism, such as tourism and mining (both linking local resources to global markets), have gained in significance. Certainly, livestock husbandry is still of major importance. The National Census for 2011 gives rough numbers: in Epupa constituency 77.7 per cent (of 2,781 households) claimed that farming was their major source of income, while in Opuwo constituency only 46.6 per cent (of 5,178 households) depended primarily on farming. There wages were the major source of income for 27 per cent of all households and business activities for another 11.6 per cent (for Epupa wages accounted for only 6.2 per cent and business for 5.1 per cent). Old-age pensions featured significantly in both constituencies (Epupa 7.6 per cent, Opuwo 9.2 per cent) (all data Republic of Namibia 2014: 37).[11]

According to the Namibia Poverty Mapping Report (Republic of Namibia 2015) the Kunene Region was the fourth poorest region of Namibia in 2011 (after Kavango, Oshikoto, and Zambezi). While rates of poverty have declined significantly since an earlier survey in 2001 they are still at a high level compared to figures from elsewhere in Namibia. According to the 2015 Namibia Poverty Mapping Report, Epupa Constituency had a poverty rate of 69 per cent which is the highest in Namibia (Opuwo of 44 per cent and Sesfontein of 40 per cent). This poverty rating takes into account access to money as its major yardstick, and it is here that the pastoralists of north-western Namibia do particularly badly. The northern parts of the Kaokoveld have become the poorhouse of Namibia and at the same time the country's major target for anthropo-tourism and conservation.

9.1 The Pastoral Household Economy

The rest of this chapter seeks to sketch the local livestock-based economy in the present. I mainly rely here on information I gathered during the mid-1990s during a two-year period of fieldwork. Much of the information has been updated during later periods of fieldwork between 1999 and 2018. Some of the data on pastoral adaptation and household economy were published in a monograph in 2006 (Bollig 2006). In this chapter I will first sketch the pastoral economy as I experienced it in the 1990s and 2000s. A final section will highlight pertinent changes of pastoral land tenure and mobility in the present.

After the collapse of livestock herds in the early 1980s, the regional herd had fully recovered and even surpassed previous figures by the mid-1990s. A further expansion of the network of boreholes in the 1990s and in the first decade of the twenty-first century and some good rain years between 2000 and 2010 allowed the cattle population to increase to over 200,000 animals by the mid-2000s. Elements of crises were observable towards the end of the 1990s: pasture degradation, failing institutions of common-pool resource management, pertinent

---

[11] Yet, according to these census figures the northern Kunene Region is less dependent on social transfers than other northern Namibian regions: in the Zambezi Region up to 20 per cent of households depended on income derived from social transfers.

conflict on access to grazing, a defunct livestock marketing system, and new forms of mobility signified growing frustrations.

Pastoral Land Use in the 1990s and Early 2000s

In 1994 I conducted a survey of some ninety-four pastoral Himba households in the wider Okangwati/Epupa area. I repeated this survey in 2004/5 and in 2018. In 1995 I also recorded c. 4,400 cattle progeny histories: I noted down all individual cows in the herds of twenty-six households, listed all calves, and took a short account of their life histories, i.e. I recorded whether each calf had been sold, gifted, or borrowed; if it died prematurely I noted down the herders' ideas about the causes of death. In 2004/5 I repeated this exercise with a smaller sample of cattle. This resulted in excellent information on mortality rates and causes of mortality, on exchange networks, property rights in livestock, etc. spanning two decades. Furthermore I conducted plenty of interviews on and directly partook in herding work. Most livestock-related data pertain to Himba communities in the northern Kaokoveld. Data on herding among Herero communities in the areas south of Opuwo were obtained from Ziess (2004), Tönsjost (2013), and from recent ethnographic work by Elsemi Olwage.

The Herd

During the mid-1990s I spent some time researching the productivity of herds: The Sanga cattle breed herded by Himba pastoralists was well adapted to the arid conditions of north-western Namibia.[12] Kreike (2009: 95–7) gives a good summary on the browsing qualities of the Sanga breed and Schoeman (1989) highlights its favourable productivity characteristics. When in the dry season grasses become scarce and lose grazing quality, trees and bush emerge as the major source of cattle feed. Kreike (2009: 96) refers to trials done in the late 1960s and 1970s which showed that the bush and tree leaves in the Ovamboland retained high nutritional values much longer than grasses and contained higher concentrations of essential minerals, e.g. phosphate and copper. Due to their browsing capacity the Sanga can make use of

---

[12] Herero herds have more crossbreeds. After the collapse of livestock herds in the centennial drought of 1981 Herero went to Okakarara to buy cattle and they picked up quite a number of crossbreeds there (Ohta 2000).

northern Namibia's bush savannah in a much better way than other cattle breeds.[13] The Sanga can subsist for months on browsing without losing body weight (Kreike 2013: 145). Large herds of Sanga contribute to the vegetation structure and the expansion of mopane bushland (Kreike 2013: 147).

The age at first calving established on the basis of progeny histories in 1995 was four rather than three years (mean: 50.31 months, median 48 months).[14] Inter-calving intervals were quite long (mean: 20.37 months; median: 15 months). On both counts Schoeman (1989) gives diverging data: he reports an inter-calving interval of 372 days, i.e. of 12.2 months and an age at first calving lower at c. 24.7 months (753 days) (Schoeman 1989: 56–7). Schoeman gained his data mainly from herds held at Omatjenne research station in northern Namibia and comparative literature on Sanga and Nguni cattle. The divergence of data may indicate that under the precarious circumstances of a highly arid environment as found in the Kaokoveld the Sanga is able to adjust its reproductive behaviours significantly. During dry years cows did not get pregnant easily and annual calving rates differed quite a lot according to fodder availability. It was not uncommon that cows did not calve for three or four years in a row. There are slight differences in the cattle breeds herded in the Kaokoveld in the early twenty-first century. Himba herds rarely have crossbreeds with 'alien' stock. The Himba are very fond of cattle colours and reckon that, for example, crossbreeds with Brahman or Afrikaner tend to be mono-coloured. Another reason that speaks against crossbreeding with heavier stock is more compelling. Himba herders said that their breed of cattle, smaller in build and tremendously resilient, are superior at climbing mountainous ridges and exploiting rocky pastures and browse on hillsides effectively. They reckon that they have observed that crossbreeds with Brahman and Afrikaner tend to stumble more often on rocky pastures. This is especially so when animals become weak at the height of the dry season. They also proudly emphasise that their cattle breed is more colourful and simply more beautiful than any other breed of cattle. Schoeman's contribution (Schoeman 1989: 56–8)

---

[13] Kreike (2013: 136–73) gives a highly interesting account of the browsing quality of northern Namibia's Sanga cattle and of research done in South African times on this topic.

[14] This data is based on the statistical analysis of a survey of about 4,600 cattle from 36 households.

suggests very material advantages of the indigenous Sanga breed: their fertility is exceptionally high and they consume less feed than other cattle breeds attaining the same and even better productivity results. The feed conversion ratio exceeded that of other high performing breeds significantly.

Most calves in the herds I scrutinised were born from November to January at the beginning of the rainy season, providing new-born calves with good environmental conditions. Milk production peaked some weeks after the first heavy rains when more grasses became available (usually January to April). The lactation peak was quite short and with the onset of dry conditions in May lactation decreased considerably. Cattle were sometimes milked for more than twelve months, even if they produced minimal amounts of milk in the end (Figure 9.2).

Goats had three kidding peaks per year (November, March, June). While milk production from goats varied over the year, some goats' milk was always available – even in poorer households.

Three different types of cattle herds were discernible. Herds kept at distant livestock camps consisted predominantly of oxen, non-lactating

Figure 9.2 Himba woman milking; the milker takes milk from two teats while the calf is drinking from the other two other teats at the same time.
Source: Photo courtesy of Lambro Tsiliyiannis, Cape Town

females, tollies (castrated calves), and heifers. In those herds kept close to the household lactating females and calves were dominant. During the dry season there is a constant shifting between both herds while during the rainy season both herds are joined for some few months. While wealthy herders often have two or more oxen herds kept in different camps, in poor households such camps are lacking as there are too few oxen to warrant labour invested in an independent camp.

The size of cattle herds varied greatly. Cattle herds numbered anything between 3 and 500 cattle and there were a few herders (not staying within the sampled community) who were said to possess more than 1,000 cattle distributed over several camps. In a survey of cattle progeny histories of 36 households (comprising altogether the progeny histories of some 4,634 cattle), rich households (n = 7, 19.4 per cent) herded some 35.6 per cent of all cattle, medium-wealth households (n = 13, 36.1 per cent) herded 43.2 per cent, while poor households (n = 16, 44.4 per cent) herded only 21.3 per cent of the total herd. These figures do not yet give a clear idea of the distribution of wealth. In those herds kept by poor and medium-wealth households there were numerous animals which had been borrowed from rich herders, who distributed their wealth over several widely spread cattle camps.

The distribution of ownership rights in cattle herds is highly complex. Most herds consist of a sizeable number of animals borrowed from different but always closely related matrilineal kin. This was corroborated by the survey of progeny histories conducted in 2004/5: out of 367 cows listed, 60 per cent were borrowed animals. The situation is made more complex when looking at the ritual status of cattle: Himba differentiate between ancestral cattle (*ozondumehupa*) and normal cattle (*ozondukwa*). Ancestral cattle fall into roughly twenty-five families, some of them of higher sacral value than others. Those of highest ritual importance may not be milked by those who have borrowed them. All milk must be left to the calves of these ancestral cattle. The 2004/5 survey showed that nearly 40 per cent of all cows accounted for were ancestral cattle. However, very strict ritual taboos would apply for only about 10 per cent of these animals.

Among the Herero, livestock wealth is also distributed unequally. The pattern seems to be slightly different though. Informed estimates reckoned that wealthy Herero herders in the Omao/Otjomatemba/ Epunguhe region owned 400–500 cattle (pers. comm. Elsemi Olwage). A larger number of households than among the Himba have very few livestock there. Even stockless households maintain independent homesteads as long as there is some kind of income. Social transfers, especially monthly pensions to the elderly, also make stockless households viable. Tönsjost (2013: 85) offers some figures on 11 (Herero) household herds for the village Okazorongua. There all households owned cattle herds, the largest counting 178 animals and the smallest only 22 animals. The richest household in Okazorongua owned c. 19 per cent of all cattle herded by the villagers.[15] As in Himba cattle herds a little less than 50 per cent of the herd is actually owned by the head of the household (Tönsjost 2013: 89). All other animals were owned by other members of the household. Cattle ownership is gender biased: only 26 per cent of all cattle in Okazorongua were owned by women (Tönsjost 2013: 98–9).[16] The number of borrowed animals is considerably less than among the Himba. Based on progeny histories Tönsjost (2013: 91) and Bollig (2006: 91) claim that in Herero herds only 1.6 per cent are borrowed, while in Himba herds nearly 14 per cent of all cattle left the herd as animals lent to somebody else. Tönsjost (2013: 92) assumes that a higher degree of commodification of cattle among the Herero does make the investment of cattle in social networks less attractive.

Small-stock herds varied in size as did cattle herds. However, differences were not as dramatic as in cattle herds. While rich Himba herders possessed up to 400 heads of small stock (approximately two-thirds being goats, one-third sheep) poor households owned around 100 heads of small stock. Among Herero herders small-stock herds are somewhat smaller than among the Himba. In an analysis of small-stock herd sizes in the Herero village Okazorongua in the south-western Kaokoveld Tönsjost (2013: 116) found an average small-stock herd size of only 46 animals and a maximum herd size (in nine households) of 115 animals. Altogether the nine households in Okazorongua herded some 410 heads of small stock. The number of small stock recorded by Tönsjost is low. She explains this low number with the fact that Okazorongua is a cattle post and that some of Okazorongua's

---

[15] Schnegg and Bolten (2007: 234) report even higher degrees of inequality in the southern Kunene Region: in Fransfontein 65 per cent of all livestock were owned by just 7 per cent of all cattle owners.
[16] Tönsjost (2013: 99) asserts that cattle ownership by women among the Herero is very high in a comparative perspective. Among East African herders women rarely formally own cattle.

households may have more small stock herded in other units of the household. Interestingly Okazorongua's small-stock herds suffered from high losses: while only 3.7 per cent of small stock produced in the homesteads was sold, a staggering 12 per cent was lost, killed by predators, or stolen. Only 1.7 per cent of the small stock was slaughtered – Tönsjost takes this as further evidence for the fact that most consumer goods as well as food items are bought with cash and are not exchanged with traders as among the Himba. Income from salaried work featured far more importantly in Herero households than in Himba households.

Wealth is clearly correlated with gender and with age: the wealthy are habitually elderly men; in contrast to many other pastoral communities women do own wealth in livestock, but this is rare. In a household survey among 95 Himba households these discrepancies surfaced clearly. These households were wealth-ranked by 5 informants. Among these 53 households, 23 were classified as rich or very rich. Their household heads were all male. Twenty-two households were classified as well-to-do; among these were 21 male-headed and 1 female-headed. Thirty-six households were regarded as poor or very poor; of these, 29 household heads were male and 7 female. Only among the 14 very poor households were female household heads present in some numbers: of these, 9 were male-headed and 5 female-headed.

Increasing Livestock Numbers

Cattle numbers in the Kaokoveld have increased over the past twenty years: while by the end of the 1990s cattle numbers exceeded 160,000 animals, by 2006 for the first time more than 200,000 heads of cattle were counted (Figure 9.3). However, this number has not subsequently been exceeded. The drought of 2012–15 brought numbers down again substantially and the 2018–19 drought again cut numbers substantially.[17]

It is harder to get any reliable figures on the dynamics of the regional small-stock herd. The small-stock numbers diverge quite a lot between years. A first count connected with the resettlement of Herero in 1929 in the southern Kaokoveld counted or estimated some 38,876 heads of

---

[17] I did not find numbers for the regional cattle herd for the past few years that would reflect this decrease adequately. Numbers are possibly between 120,000 and 150,000 heads of cattle in 2019.

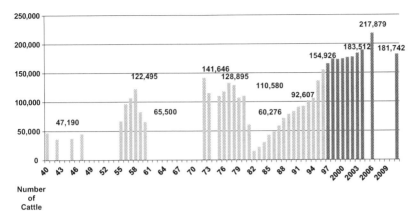

Figure 9.3 Dynamics of the regional cattle herd.
Sources: van Warmelo (1951); Page (1975); Veterinary Extension Service at Ministry of Agriculture

small stock. Another count in 1957 gives 190,000 as an estimate, and a count ten years later in 1967 gives 207,500 as the number for small stock.[18] Figures for the years 1970 to 1996 collected by the Veterinary Department suggest that small-stock numbers were more frequently prone to miscounts. Numbers jump repeatedly in an unpredictable manner. For 1975, documents give the number of 150,739 heads of small stock without giving any reasoning on the demise of the regional small-stock herd from 1967.[19] The data, however, suggest a number of observations on the small-stock herd. For many years the number of goats hovers at around 120,000; only after 1990 does it exceed 200,000, and in 1996 even climbs higher than 300,000. Also the number of sheep is remarkably consistent, remaining between 20,000 and 30,000 in most years, and only in the late twentieth century jumps to 40,000 and more. Small-stock herds recovered rapidly from the centennial drought of 1981. Within only five years small-stock herds had recuperated while it took the cattle herd some fifteen years to

---

[18] NAN BOP 7 N1/15/6 gives a figure of 207,500 small stock, of which 59,500 are sheep and 148,000 goats. The same file gives for 1975 the figures 25,901 sheep and 102,739 goats. These divergences point rather to grave problems in accounting for numbers than to real trends.

[19] The figure for 1929 is from NAN NAO 28 Officer in Charge to Native Commissioner Windhoek, the figure for 1957 from NAN BOP N1/15/2, the figure for 1967 from NAN BOP 7/N1/15/6. The figure for 1975 also comes from NAN BOP 7 N1/15/6.

recuperate. Overall the trend of the small-stock herd suggests that goat and sheep numbers have been fairly stable in the second half of the twentieth century, while goat numbers rapidly increased after the mid-1980s. This increase is linked to the increasing relevance of goats for purchasing maize meal and other consumer goods.

Small-stock marketing reached a height in the early 2000s. Vigne (2001) reports on estimates that up to 142,000 to 180,000 heads of small stock are sold per annum. Vigne assumes that there may have been about 580,000 heads of small stock in the area in 2000. These numbers are enormous, and shed an important light on the dynamics of livestock husbandry. Small stock are used as the currency to engage with the market and cattle are progressively relegated to a class of property which is there to store wealth. This trend was also reflected in a household survey conducted in 2018. We asked how many livestock were sold during a period of six months prior to the survey: while only 42 households (out of 236) sold any cattle at all (62 in total), 74 households sold a total of 675 goats in the same period.[20]

9.2 Changing Demographic Parameters: From a Slow-Growth Pattern to Exponential Growth Parameters

The total population of the Kaokoveld[21] increased gradually during most parts of the twentieth century and more rapidly over the past twenty years (see Figure 9.4). While the Odendaal Report of 1963 gives a population number of 9,234 people for the Kaokoveld, archival files for 1967 give a population number of 14,637 people.[22] For the year 1981 the population figure given is 15,570, and for 1991 the figure is 26,176 (Bollig 2006: 72). In 2001 the figure was 34,021, and in 2011 it was 44,968.

The population increase is likely to stay at a high level. The National Census of 2011 gives an annual growth rate for Epupa constituency at

---

[20] The number of households not selling anything is astounding though. Here social transfers like state pensions are important. I will comment on the relevance of social transfers in Chapter 11.
[21] Nowadays the Epupa and Opuwo constituencies of Kunene Region equal the former homeland Kaokoland. Demographic figures for these two constituencies can be compared with older figures on the colonial administrative unit Kaokoland. Kaokoveld is used as a general reference to the north-western Namibian landscape.
[22] NAN BOP N1/15/6.

State–Local Society Relations 257

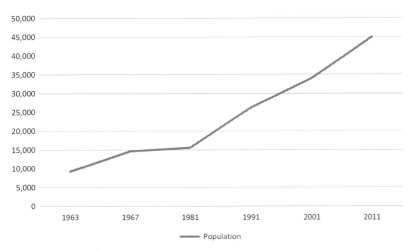

Figure 9.4 Population increase 1963–2011.
Sources: Republic of Namibia (2014); Namibia Statistics Agency, NAN BOP N1/15/6

3.0 per cent and for Opuwo constituency at 2.7 per cent (Republic of Namibia 2014: 12); both numbers are extremely high, and far above the regional average (2.3 per cent). These figures also hint at the fact that the growth rates in the Himba community (the main community of Epupa constituency) may indeed be very high. In the 1990s I took a demographic profile there on the basis of life history accounts of post-reproductive women and came up with low growth rates (at that time lower than 1 per cent p.a., Bollig 2006: 74). I reasoned that high infection rates with STDs caused low fertility rates and contributed to low growth. In the 1990s the administration expanded the net of clinics and ran a programme directly targeting STDs. The programme was meant as a measure to lower HIV/AIDS infection rates. By the end of the 1990s STD infections were under control and obviously did not have an effect on demographic parameters any longer.[23] There are other indicators pointing at rapid growth rates. A look at age pyramids for Epupa and Opuwo constituencies (Republic of Namibia 2014: 56–7) shows that the majority of the population are very young

---

[23] Other factors apparently do not vary much among communities in the Kunene Region: the average age of mother at first birth is given at 20.8 years for Epupa constituency and 20.6 for Opuwo constituency, while the regional average is 20.7 years (Republic of Namibia 2014: 13).

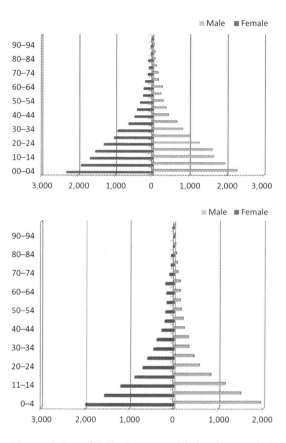

Figures 9.5a and 9.5b Age pyramids for the populations of Epupa and Opuwo constituencies according to the 2011 National Census

(see Figures 9.5a and 9.5b): in Epupa constituency 52.8 per cent and in Opuwo constituency 43.4 per cent are below the age of 15 (Republic of Namibia 2014: 3).

The differences between both age pyramids are striking. In Opuwo constituency 31 per cent are below 10 years of age while in Epupa constituency 39 per cent are under 10. This very clearly shows that the Himba population is growing at a much quicker pace than the Herero population. In the long run this has, of course, a great number of consequences. Children working as herders are abundant among the Himba, but rarer among the Herero, an effect that is exacerbated by much higher school attendance rates among the Herero.

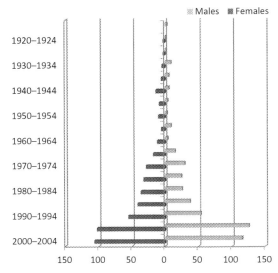

Figure 9.5c Age pyramid, data from a household survey from 2004–5.
Source: author's data

This extreme bias is even more prominent in a sample taken from a survey of eighty-five Himba households in 2004 (see Figure 9.5c).

In this sample 46.7 per cent were younger than 10 years, and 58 per cent younger than 15 years. There is a very obvious gap between those born in the early 1990s (or before) and those born since the mid-1990s. The age-cohorts 2000–4 and 1995–9 have double the size than the age-cohort 1990–4.

9.3 Land Tenure and Spatial Mobility in the Twenty-First Century

This section will give a short overview of current settlement and land use patterns and aims to depict how people access and make use of resources in the present. In the early twenty-first century centres of population have developed in the form of a quickly urbanising capital town (Opuwo) and also in the form of progressively dense, village-like settlements. A number of settlements have developed into true villages with some infrastructure such as schools and clinics over the past twenty years.

Among the Himba semi-permanent settlements were concentrated along seasonal river courses or at permanent wells and boreholes.

260   *Dynamics of Social-Ecological Relations*

Semi-permanence here means that parts of the household stayed in the place the entire year while camps would branch off with the household's herds to distant dry-season grazing areas. Households were preferably located in places where there was good access to water, pasture, and arable land all at the same time. The spatial organisation of the Himba pastoral community was characterised by four utilisation zones:

1. Population centres with more than ten to fifteen sedentary households in the vicinity. Opportunities for gardening were found in these places and reliable water resources were habitually nearby. The Omuhonga Valley community, with several hundred households, was extraordinary in this respect (see Map 9.1). Such dense settlements only came about during the last thirty years. Aerial photographs from the early 1970s show only a little more than a dozen households in the Omuhonga basin where today more than 200 households are located. There are various reasons for this densification of settlement: next to population growth and a growing emphasis on agricultural activities the final demise of elephant herds roaming the river valleys in the 1970s, and the enforced policy of SADF to settle people near army barracks have contributed to this process.

   Map 9.1 shows in an exemplary manner the settlement on a 5 km stretch between Okangwati village and a randomly chosen

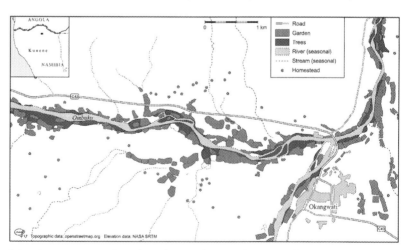

Map 9.1 Homesteads and gardens in the Omuhonga Valley.
Source: Google Maps (2017)

point 5 km upstream. The dense settlement and gardening of the river banks continue for another 10 km upstream of the Omuhonga basin.

These population centres – an estimated number of 1,000–1,500 people live in Omuhonga's households – do not amalgamate into village-like structures. While a school has been built in Omuhonga, shops and other infrastructure are absent. Drinking water is obtainable from a number of boreholes drilled along the river banks, and in the dry season a number of wells are dug into the deep sands of the river. Even during the rainy season large numbers of cattle are rarely found in the valley as the grass layer is flimsy. Sander et al. (1998) give an idea of the very high degree of soil erosion in the settlement zone along the river. There 30 cm or more of topsoil has been removed. Not only has the soil layer been degraded; as homesteads use a substantial amount of wood for stockades around their inner and outer enclosures, a great number of mopane trees have been cut down. Regularly a homestead is surrounded by a ring of several hundred square metres of completely denuded land. Households own rights to specific gardening land near the homestead. More specifically such land is owned by a woman from the homestead. For the erection of the massive fences around homesteads and gardens, usually experts originating from Angola are hired. They work on a fence for several weeks and are then paid in cash or in kind. The rapidly growing Omuhonga basin community is also multi-ethnic: there are nowadays a number of Hakaona and Zemba households mixing with the numerically dominant Himba households.

2. Villages with five to fifteen permanent households. These places frequently had good, but limited gardening opportunities and long-lasting water resources. A specific hallmark of settlements of types 1 and 2 was that they had graveyards in close proximity, which marked them as permanently occupied places. Ombaka, a place about 120 km from Opuwo, is settled by thirteen households, most of them closely related. The Ombaka settlement is spread across an area of c. 12 km^2 and is inhabited by c. 280 inhabitants who all categorise themselves as Ovahimba. During a survey by the LINGS project in the wider Epupa region it became clear that this type of settlement prevailed. While perhaps the majority of inhabitants today live in agglomerations like the Omuhonga Valley or in

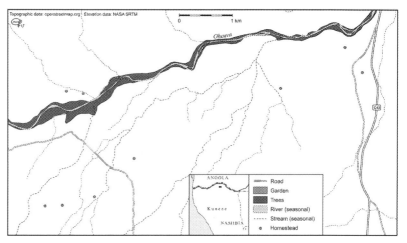

Map 9.2 The dry-season grazing area of Oheuva showing dispersed cattle camps in the vicinity of the seasonal Oheuva River.
Source: Google Maps (2017)

village-like places like Okangwati and Ehomba, settlements of this type are probably the most widespread type of settlement.
3. A major part of the land was used by mobile cattle posts (*ozohambo*) only. There were usually no gardening opportunities in these areas and water resources were limited. Typically such camps are smaller than the homesteads. Often two or three such camps are close to each other and there is ample space between such small clusters which spread out over dry-season pastures. Cattle camps also do not have the elaborate spatial structure of homesteads, and ancestral fires are regularly absent (see Map 9.2).

Map 9.2 shows the dry-season grazing of Oheuva. On a stretch of c. 6 km in length and 5 km in width only nine homesteads or cattle camp structures were visible. At least three of them were ancient (and at that time unused) structures. The homesteads are all placed at a distance of 0.5–1.5 km from the course of the seasonal river.

4. Grazing reserves (like the Baynes Mountains) were used during periods of intense stress when other pastures were depleted. In the 1990s these grazing reserves were used only every other year. Only a few cattle camps went there as life in these remote areas was strenuous. There are no boreholes in, for example, the Baynes

Mountains and cattle have to be driven to wells far away. When I visited a cattle camp there in 1996 dry season cattle were only watered every third day, which the herders commented upon as suboptimal. Since the end of the 1990s these grazing reserves were more regularly used during each dry season and not only in exceptionally dry years.

Settlement Patterns in Herero Communities

In Herero-dominated areas in the southern and central Kaokoveld, the settlement pattern is somewhat different. Here central villages have been established with a larger number of homesteads. Each homestead still has the typical layout of a Herero homestead, with a central livestock enclosure and an ancestral fire placed between the livestock enclosure's entrance at its eastern edge and the homestead's main hut.[24] Often such villages have basic public infrastructures such as a school and a health clinic and some shops. Map 9.3 shows Ombombo, one of the older Herero villages. Map 9.3 suggests that there are some eight large homesteads constituting the centre of Ombombo village, each homestead consisting of a number of huts and being organised along the typical east–west orientation. Beyond these homesteads there are a number of houses that are not integrated into typical homesteads. These are often the houses of teachers, traders, and labour migrants (habitually coming from south-western Angola) who work seasonally in one of the homesteads.

Herero villages have one or two dry-season camp areas, and a number of them also have rainy-season camps. In such dry-season grazing areas cattle camps cluster together and are not dispersed as among the Himba. Sometimes such a cluster of cattle camps gradually turns into a village. Only for short periods of time are cattle kept at the main homestead. Many informants claimed that the Herero style of nomadism is different from the Himba style. Mobility patterns are more predictable and have a transhumant character. Ideally there is a consensual decision, formulated by the headman and his elders, when such dry-season grazing areas can begin to be used. Some villages also

---

[24] 'Main hut' here refers to the fact that this hut is occupied by the most senior wife of the household head. The hut does not look different from the other huts in any way.

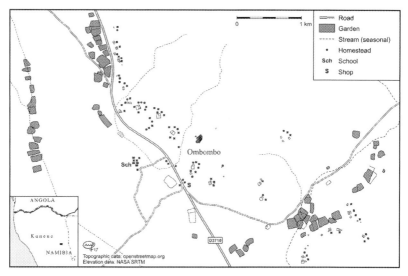

Map 9.3 Ombombo village.
Note: The map shows a dense cluster of houses with governmental infrastructure such as school and clinic; huts are clustered in homesteads around livestock enclosures. Gardens are found in large numbers adjacent to the village.
Source: Google Maps (2017)

maintain rainy-season camp areas, i.e. cattle are not brought back to the main homestead during the dry season, but taken to a place with ideal rainy-season conditions.

Ziess (2004) gives a neat description of a typical Herero village, Omuramba. The place had been used as a cattle post by a number of Herero households until the mid-1960s, and only when a borehole was drilled in the late 1960s were permanent homesteads erected in Omuramba. Due to favourable grazing conditions in the proximity of the village along with good gardening opportunities there, the village grew rapidly. At the time of her research in the early 2000s Ziess counted nineteen households with a total population of 468 people. Some households were populous, and six counted more than thirty people, the biggest being a home with eighty people. The households together owned some 6,300 cattle, 4,500 goats, and 1,200 sheep. Thirty-nine adults received salaries/wages, twenty-four of them as migrant workers. Twenty-eight elderly people received pensions. Hence, most households received a monetary income and in fact only one household out of nineteen had to rely solely on livestock. During the rainy season cattle were herded in the immediate vicinity of Omuramba village. As soon as these pastures are grazed, most cattle, and at a later time in the year also goats and sheep, are transferred to the cattle posts. In the dry season of the year 2003 Ziess counted sixteen cattle camps. The distance from village to camp was about 6–9 kilometres. Two dry-season grazing areas which were apparently used in other years (Outjete and Otjandawe) could not be used in 2003 because the boreholes there were defunct. In comparison to the mobility data on Himba cattle posts, the mobility pattern Ziess describes is more confined and more centred on the village – the major cattle posts were less than 10 kilometres away from the village. Cattle camps move and act less individualistically than cattle posts among the Himba.

The Urban Situation: Opuwo

The Kaokoveld has just one urban area: Opuwo. The development of Opuwo town, founded in the late 1930s as an administrative outpost, has been described in previous sections. Müller-Friedman (2005) has given an in-depth account of the increasing urban agglomeration. In 2011 the town had a population of c. 7,500 people. A major percentage of the population lives in the two informal settlements Katutura and Otuzemba. It is not easy to maintain a town in an arid landscape. Water supply is a constant problem in Opuwo, and the town made it into the newspapers a number of times during the past twenty years because water supply was low in quantity or in quality. The town is currently supplied with water mainly from a well-field located in the north-west of the town (Moilanen 2015: 22). This well-field is constituted by five boreholes ranging from 90 to 130 m in depth located in an alluvial plain c. 1–3 km north-west of the town centre. After being pumped to the surface, the water passes through a modern filtration system and is then pumped into two storage tanks.[25] Unlike the boreholes in the surrounding areas, the water designated for Opuwo town is managed by the parastatal NamWater, and the installations in town by Opuwo's municipal council, thereby creating a sharp divide

---

[25] Moilanen (2015) reports that the water derived from the well-field is abundant (i.e. it could be used sustainably even with a growing population) but of a low quality.

between hydraulic management systems: while water-point associations managed water in the rural areas, here the town council and the parastatal NamWater were in charge of water provision. Most households in town need wood and charcoal to do their daily cooking. I did not find any figures on the energy consumption of town dwellers: at the informal town markets wood is always on sale and every morning women carry headloads of firewood into town to sell at the roadside. While the growing town Opuwo (current growth rate c. 3 per cent) imports most of its food and fuel, it also draws heavily on resources from the surrounding landscape.

9.4 Access to Pastures

Among both Himba and Herero places were associated with an 'owner of the land' (*omuni wehi*). He and his immediate patrilineal and also matrilineal kin would claim hereditary rights to this land. In order to claim such rights reference to the longevity of inhabitation was central. The 'owner of the land' had to be consulted if somebody without hereditary rights to this land sought to settle there. Such rights included the right to establish a homestead in that place, to use water there, to access gardening land if available, and to use pastures in the vicinity. Land beyond the zone of settled permanent households was managed jointly by the men of a neighbourhood. While these pastures were used by herders from one or from a few villages among the Herero, among the Himba such pastures were more freely accessed by people from other settlements. They habitually found good reasons to legitimate their access to these pastures: they were closely related to some of the residents, they themselves or their fathers (or their maternal uncles or their fathers' maternal uncles) had previously stayed there, or they were simply in dire need of pastures. In this way pastures temporarily turned into open-access resources; for these, certain rules concerning how to graze herds appropriately and in cooperation with others were still of practical value, but the number of users could not be delimited effectively.

Traditional authorities in Himba and Herero communities had a different grasp on access rights. While in Himba communities I found that preferably the 'owner of the land' was consulted and chiefs or their councillors only came in in conflicting cases, among the Herero chiefs were involved at an earlier stage. The picture was complicated here as habitually two or three men were competing for chieftaincy in Herero communities and were entertaining competing groups of councillors.

Himba pastoralism in the mid-1990s depended on independent movements of livestock camps (*ozohambo*) and households (*ozonganda*). After a few weeks of heavy rain (usually January–March) the entire household herd gathered at the main homestead. In an average year they stayed together for three to four months while the major gardening work was done. However, a cattle camp for oxen, tollies, heifers, and non-lactating stock would be established long before grazing became depleted around the homestead in May or June. If a household had enough herders oxen were herded separately from young stock (tollies, heifers), as both types of cattle have different grazing requirements. Later, in July or August, male goats and sheep were separated from the household and either a separate small-stock camp was established or the small-stock herd joined the cattle camp. During the drier parts of the year small numbers of livestock were constantly shifted from the main household to the various livestock camps and vice versa. At the height of the dry season, between September and December, a number of households shifted all their remaining cattle to their cattle camp to ensure that the cows had enough fodder when calving started towards the end of the year. During these latter parts of the year, the household often also changed its place. These moves of the main household, however, rarely covered large distances.

In Herero communities the mobility of cattle herds adheres to a transhumant pattern. As shown in the case study on Omuramba South, the places for cattle camps are rarely more than 10–15 km away from the main homestead. Villages like Ombombo, Okorosave and Kaoko Otavi maintain satellite places that they safeguard as dry-season grazing. Dry-season grazing areas are thought to 'belong' to a village. In Ombombo I saw in the early 2010s that the chief personally removed the engine from a borehole and stored it away for months in order to prevent any grazing in the dry-season grazing area of his village. Especially Herero small-stock herds are often herded by employed shepherds. The larger number of these shepherds come from Angola and are prepared to take over herding work for very low salaries. Cattle herds were rarely entrusted to shepherds from the outside. Typically cattle herds are walked for an hour or so into the direction they are meant to graze during the day. Then the herd is left on its own for the remainder of the day and often returns home in the late afternoon independently. Herding labour is then mainly focused on watering animals at the well during the dry season.[26]

Dynamics of Communal Management in Himba and Herero Communities since the Late 1990s

In interviews conducted in 2001, 2004, and again in 2014/15 Himba informants claimed that the local system of pasture management had virtually crumbled. In 2015 massive conflicts over grazing rights in Herero-occupied areas abounded. Some of these conflicts made it into court rooms: land rights conflicts were no longer solved by traditional authorities and their councils satisfactorily, but by lawyers and courts. Indeed, the past ten to fifteen years have been characterised by conflict and negotiations around pasture access. Several factors were apparently contributing to these institutional dilemmas. The number of cattle of the total regional herd had nearly reached the 200,000 level by 2010, an all-time high. This put additional stress on grazing resources and made the management of livestock herds more difficult (in the sense of increased transaction costs for reaching agreements on pasture management). Grazing became even more precarious as most years of the 2010s had sub-normal precipitation and for the years 2012–15 and 2018–19 severe droughts impacted livestock husbandry. Several indicators for the demise of grazing control were given by Himba informants:

In several grazing areas disputes concerned who was allowed to make use of specific pastures. While on the one hand politically dominant figures succeeded in reserving pastures for their own herds (even without fencing them), in other areas young herders moved onto pastures which were far away from their regular settlements and thereby turned commons into open-access resources. All informants stated that the sanctioning of misbehaviour had virtually been abandoned. Several reasons were given: difficulties in pressing for sanctions for contraventions of grazing rules; the deaths of some elders who had dominated the local community as wealthy cattle patrons and who had been central for the handling of cases; and widespread doubts about the applicability and contents of some rules. Notably chiefs wielded

---

[26] This mode of 'loose herding' is seen as a consequence of the decrease of predators in the 1970s, 1980s, and 1990s by some. As pointed out before, this style of grazing has particular consequences for the grasses.

little influence in this respect. The demise of chiefly control over resources corresponded with increasing political competition from within and lack of recognition for the large number of traditional authorities by the state.

Conflicts over grazing lands in Herero communities often circled around contested chieftaincy and the rights of newcomers to use grazing permanently. In many Herero chieftaincies three or more would-be chiefs contested the power of the original chief. Incumbents would try to bring in followers granting them settlement rights in the villages under their control. In this way the number of Himba migrants settling in Herero communities rose.

Himba and Herero herders reported on a great number of meetings which had taken place to find new institutional solutions to the grazing problem. Herders were contemplating how to revive the former institutional setup, strengthening the position of traditional authorities and/or increasing sanctions. They also discussed whether the local police could be co-opted and urged to supervise measures of resource control. In one instance the local chief actually pleaded with the police to control the chopping of palms for palm wine production along the Kunene River and in another instance police were called upon to enforce the relocation of households that were deemed to 'settle in the wrong place'.[27]

Especially Himba herders commented negatively on the state of pastures. They summarised their observations in a claim that the land had become weak, meaning that even with good rains, pastures did not produce sufficient grass. As a consequence calf mortality increased. Himba herders framed their observation, 'the land has become weak', explaining this concept with a number of concrete observations on the replacement of, for example, perennial grasses with annual grasses, and of high-yielding annual species with low-yielding species. Quantitative data from 1995 and 2005[28] suggest that livestock mortality

---

[27] Jean Ensminger (1992) reported that the Kenyan Orma in the 1980s brought in police to solve internal grazing conflicts. They thereby shifted – so her argument goes – the costs of sanctioning to the administration. Himba and Herero traditional authorities resort to similar means at the moment and wherever possible try to engage the state apparatus on their behalf.

[28] Both data sets originate from progeny histories; i.e. they reflect accumulated trends over a number of years. Most of the calves reported as having died in the 1995 sample had died between 1985 and 1995, while those reported as having died in 2005 had died between 1995 and 2005.

indeed increased and that increasingly livestock died from emaciation, but also from diseases and predators and/or got lost more often.

Next to internal local problems of resource allocation two further dynamics of mobility were frequently commented upon by locals as threats to sustainable resource management: the immigration of Oshiwambo-speaking farmers along the eastern boundary of the Kunene Region, and the migration of Himba herders from the northernmost stretches of the Kunene Region to the Anabeb, Omatendeka, and Sesfontein areas in the southern Kaokoveld.

The immigration of farmers from the Omusati Region into the eastern border areas of the Kunene Region is a major issue of concern for many herders in the eastern regions of the Kaokoveld. In interviews with members of communities bordering Omusati Region this issue was consistently raised. Over the past decade immigration into the Kunene Region, i.e. into lands west of the Kamanjab–Ruacana road has been considerable. A traditional authority residing in Okongoro Conservancy estimated that the number of Oshiwambo-speaking households in this area had increased from about 30–40 in 2004 to 60–80 in 2012. In some places a replacement of the former Otjiherero-speaking population had taken place. He also asserted that most newcomers fenced their farms, impacting negatively on herding routines in the region.

The second 'mobility issue' is of even more concern as it is not restricted to the borderlands of the Kaokoveld but brings strife right into the core Herero grazing lands. A sizeable number of Himba households from the northern parts of the Kunene Region migrated to the wider Sesfontein area over the past twenty years. I interviewed some of the household heads on the reasons for their decision to move south and in 2012 conducted a survey on Himba households having moved to the southern Kaokoveld. In total an estimated number of c. 800 people, mainly Himba, left the northern rangelands of the Kaokoveld to search for better pastures in the southern Kaokoveld. There an increasing number of Himba households co-resided with Herero households and sought more permanent grazing rights. In some places they constituted village enclaves of four or more Himba households within Herero chieftaincy areas. I will briefly portray the history of M., who migrated from Omuramba to Sesfontein in c. 2008.

M., at that time about 50 years old, according to Himba standards moderately wealthy and married thrice, had considered moving out of his established grazing range for several years. For two decades at least he had maintained a semi-permanent dwelling in the Omuhonga basin, where his two wives had gardens and where his old mother resided. He would spend the rainy season there and then leave with the major portion of his livestock during the early dry season towards Ondova. He realised that his cattle were frequently sick and that more calves had been dying than in the past. On top of these problems he attributed his occasional fits of ill health to the witchcraft of a close relative also living in the area. A very close friend of his had left the region some three years earlier and had proven – according to M.'s analysis – that cattle herds actually did much better in the southern and western parts of the Kaokoveld. M. then first visited potential grazing places in the far west, in the Onyuva plains at the fringes of the Namib Desert in the mid-2000s. The Himba community there, however, made it very clear that they were not at all keen to accept another herder. M. then decided to scrutinise the situation around Sesfontein in the southern Kaokoveld and went into direct negotiations with one Herero chief whom he had known for some time. That chief advised him to wait for some time until the community had decided on the issue. When this did not happen for a period of some months, M. turned to another competing chief and finally secured an agreement to settle in the chief's village near Sesfontein.[29] In two moves M. brought first cattle and then small stock to Sesfontein. The migration, across over 350 km of barren land, was arduous and took him more than two weeks in each instance (in 2007). In the place he settled he joined three other Himba households who had already been settled there for some few years under the supervision of the same Herero chief M. had also negotiated with. M. brought most of his livestock to Sesfontein and left only a few animals in the cattle camps of close relatives in his former home area. The homestead of his mother, where his younger brother and his sister also resided, was still regarded as 'his', and through his siblings and his mother he retained rights in the Omuhonga/Omuramba community. In his new place M. did not reside with his whole family. At least during the planting and harvesting season two of his three wives lived at their gardening places near Opuwo, halfway between the original home at Omuhonga and the new home at Sesfontein.

---

[29] M. apparently paid about N$5,000 to the chief. This sum was reported by others on hearsay. I found the sum realistic. Also other Himba herders alleged that they had to pay Herero chiefs for their grazing rights.

In 2015 M. was caught up in the conflict with the Herero majority in the Sesfontein area, like many other Himba herders. Together with six other Himba household heads he was ordered by the chief to leave his place of residence close to Sesfontein and to move back to Omuhonga where he had first come from. Apparently the chief who had facilitated his migratory shift could no longer support him against the majority vote of his community. M. moved his homestead, but only shifted some 60 km further north to a place called Otjerunda. He had convinced a local chief to grant him temporary residence there as long as drought conditions lasted. He promised to then move his cattle for good once rains had set in.

In this way M.'s homestead was not simply relocated to a new home area, but virtually spread over a much larger area. I observed such a strategic spread of household members linked to similar long-distance moves in many instances. Expanding rhizomatically Himba herders thereby created a number of new options for their homesteads. The scattering of household members also offered the advantage that different development initiatives could be tapped into. M., like many other respondents, thought it worthwhile to involve himself in, for example, a conservancy in his former home area and also in the local water-point committee in the new place.

The intrusion of Himba households into areas previously settled by Herero households led to a number of counter-reactions. Himba immigrants were usually not accepted as formal members of their new communities, and their settlement is described as transient and framed in a discourse on drought and the necessity to shift to distant pastures during periods of hardship. In some instances later Himba migrants were barred access from Herero communities, and even the fact that they could claim that local Herero were in fact close matrilineal or patrilineal relatives did not help. Those who successfully took up settlement in Herero communities usually worked through the allegiance to a Herero chief. They took full advantage of competition between Herero chiefs (and would-be chiefs) and that occasionally Herero chiefs were interested in broadening their base of clients in such a conflict. Often Himba herders also bought themselves into new grazing lands, paying a 'fee' to a local traditional authority.

Many Herero herders viewed these moves with considerable scepticism and alleged that migrant Himba herders contributed to the demise of grazing by adding substantial numbers of cattle to the regional herd and by not adhering strictly to grazing rules. In 2015 conflicts climaxed. Threatened by a drought and more Himba migrants seeking refuge in rangelands in the southern Kaokoveld, some Herero traditional authorities convened and instigated a legal process. In early 2015 a number of Himba households were threatened with a court order to leave their places of residence and some left.

The question of who can legally and legitimately access pastures is still a much-discussed topic and a likely point of severe intercommunity conflict in the future. The legitimacy of herders moving freely over the landscape is strongly contested in the early twenty-first century, and many local actors prefer a neater definition of grazing territories. There is a remarkable move towards village grazing territories in all Herero communities. These are still communally managed but attempts are made to delimit access to pastures to inhabitants of the village.

9.5 The Expansion of Agricultural Activities

Agricultural activities over the entire Kaokoveld increased significantly during the 1980s and 1990s. Welle (2009) gives a detailed account of the spatial expansion of gardening in the Omuhonga basin between 1975 and 2006. The positions and sizes of gardens in 1975 were reconstructed on the basis of aerial photographs, while LandSAT imagery was used to pinpoint gardens in 1996 and 2006 (Welle 2007).

Map 9.4a–c shows the expansion of gardens between 1976 and 2006. The map shows that gardening has changed profoundly: first, intensification took place along the major river course; second, an expansion towards tributary rivers can be observed; and third, even off-river places came to be progressively used, and agricultural use along the river's banks became denser throughout the period so that today garden borders upon garden. In summary, the number of individual gardens between 1976, 1996, and 2006 had risen from 79 to 176 and up to 339. The total garden area had also risen from 87 ha to 165 ha and up to 260 ha in 2006. On the other hand the mean garden size has decreased over the last thirty years from 1.1 ha in 1976 to 0.94 ha in 1996 and 0.77 ha in 2006. While mean garden size is not directly linked to wealth, total gardening area of one household corresponds strongly with wealth. While the eleven wealthy households commanded a total garden size of 33.92 ha, twenty-six poor households

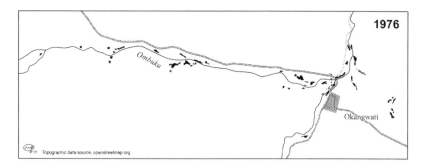
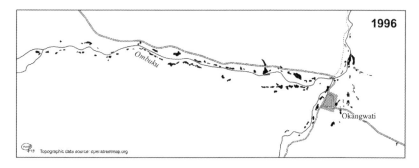
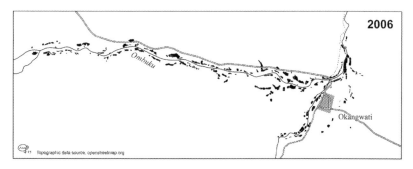

Map 9.4a–c Expanding agriculture in the Omuhonga basin between 1975 and 2006.
Source: Welle (2007)

only managed a garden size of c. 28 ha. While wealthy households maintained on average three separate gardens each, poor households only commanded some two gardens each at most.

In a survey of Himba households in 2018, fifty households had no garden, sixty-two maintained one garden, eighty-two households

State–Local Society Relations 275

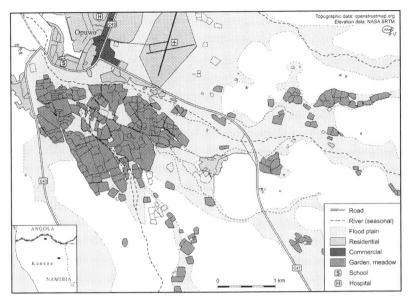

Map 9.5 Gardens bordering Opuwo town in the south-west.
Source: Google Maps (2017)

cultivated two gardens, and thirty households even had three gardens. There were five households running four gardens, three having five gardens, two having six gardens, and one household having seven gardens. The great majority of Himba households nowadays combine agricultural activities with herding.

Agricultural activities also expanded significantly in other areas. A look at Google Maps shows that there are hundreds of gardens around Opuwo today. Many Himba and Herero migrants[30] cultivate there near the town in either Okapare or Ovinyange, both extensive gardening areas within a 2–6 km reach (Okapare) or 5–10 km reach (Ovinyange, Oukongo) of Opuwo (see Map 9.5 for Okapare). What people plant in these fields does not differ much: in most fields maize dominates. Millet and sorghum are occasionally planted. Map 9.5 shows the western part of Opuwo and a significant gardening area to the west of the town. Hundreds of gardens have been established there

---

[30] Many people who gardened in the vicinity of Opuwo had their main homestead somewhere else in the Kaokoveld and after the harvest returned to this homestead. They stayed close to Opuwo only during the gardening season.

by people living in Opuwo, and also by people coming to Opuwo's peri-urban areas from other places and just staying in Opuwo for the gardening season. While some of the produce from these gardens is sold in Opuwo's informal markets, most of it is consumed by the gardening households themselves (Thuening 2018). Map 9.5 only captures a part of this agricultural expansion area to the west of Opuwo. There is a second agricultural expansion area to the northeast of Opuwo at a distance of c. 5 km from town (Oukongo), where large gardens tilled by tractors are also found. More space than ever before is intensively used and transformed by humans.

The expansion of gardening has changed environmental infrastructure in one major way. Nearly all riverine patches that receive annual inundations are now used for gardening. Previously these sections of the landscape were only extensively used. Occasionally goats' enclosures were erected in the shadow of *Faidherbia albida* trees at the height of the dry season. Cattle used these riverine gallery forests mainly for resting after being watered in the shallow wells that were dug into the river sands. This extensive pastoral use of the riverine oasis is still possible despite intense agricultural use. Pastoral activities have decreased in intensity though and are restricted to smaller areas in the river basin's gallery forest for much of the year. Only after harvest, at the beginning of the dry season, will livestock use the entire terrain once again: the stubble and remains on agricultural fields are browsed after harvest and the dung left behind is welcome manure before the next agricultural season begins.

9.6 Changing Environmental Infrastructure

While some aspects of the environmental infrastructure did not change much during the past three decades a number of important features did change profoundly. Let me first turn to these features that stayed stable. Pastoralists are still farming predominantly with the same breeds of livestock their fathers and their forefathers have made use of. The Sanga breed is still the dominant type of cattle used. Due to its capacity to subsist on browsing for a number of months, its qualities have become even more salient than before given that the grazing has diminished with a turn from high yielding annuals to annuals of a lower quality on many pastures. Pastoralists in north-western Namibia favour the Sanga over other breeds for its hardiness and its productivity despite detrimental conditions. Only in the southern Kaokoveld has some crossbreeding with other cattle breeds taken place. While many herders would put forward the beauty of their Sanga as a major reason for favouring them, in longer talks on the quality of the Sanga they are adamant in emphasising its endurance and the capacity to recover weight after drought. Also goat breeds have been maintained and little inbreeding has taken place. The local goat breed has very high fertility rates and two to three kids per year are habitual. Twinning is frequent. What did change, though, is the size of the regional herd. The cattle herd reached the 200,000 level in the early 2000s. Since then it has not increased again significantly and the droughts in 2012–14 and 2018–19 have brought cattle numbers again below 200,000. Still, cattle numbers are very high and to feed such large numbers of cattle the entire range has to be grazed intensely. Goat numbers increased rapidly: while c. 200,000 goats were counted around 1990, in 2000 (Vigne 2001) estimates this number to be at almost 600,000. Goats are generally kept closer to the main homestead, i.e. browsing intensity around the main settlements has increased massively. Kreike (2013: 150–6) documents and historicises the impact of goat browsing on the vegetation in north-central Namibia. There goat numbers apparently fluctuated as they did in the Kaokoveld. Intense goat browsing is thought to be responsible for the delimitation of bush encroachment. Whereas bush encroachment is a key environmental problem on commercial farms south of the Red Line it is no problem in north-central Namibia. Also in north-western Namibia the absence of bush encroachment (despite intense use of pastures by cattle) as an ecological problem may be linked to the high numbers of goats.

The human population of the Kaokoveld more than doubled within thirty years. Settlements expanded and new settlements were founded. The provision of more boreholes facilitated the expansion of human settlements. More households than before seek to combine agricultural activities with pastoral ones. Such expansion of settlement and intensification of land use has significant environmental consequences. Homesteads are equipped with palisades and also gardens are well fenced. Habitually mopane wood is used for palisades and often also for fences. Hence, mopane trees are heavily used around settlements. Mopane is an extremely hardy tree species and even heavily used and cut trees re-sprout. Often, however, their growth is severely limited and distorted. Almost all settlements in the Kaokoveld are heavily dependent on firewood. This necessitates the use of even more wood. In Opuwo firewood is a sought-after commodity and is regularly sold in large quantities in the open air market.

Especially river valleys have become densely settled during the past thirty years. The building of governmental infrastructure (schools, hospitals, roads) contributed to this densification of settlement and certainly encouraged sedentariness. Humans and their livestock use natural resources more intensely than ever before. Environmental infrastructure reflects intense use: a sparse coverage of annual grasses (of low quality) is hard to overgraze as long as the seed bank is intact; preferred bushes are browsed out by goats and only the hardy mopane trees withstand intense browsing by cattle and goats. Humans and their livestock are in need of constant water supply and only the tapping of subterranean aquifers provides sufficient water for both. Chapter 10 will show how the resurgence of wildlife and changing institutions of resource governance diversify and change this heavily used landscape.

10 | *The Establishment of 'New Commons' by Government Decree*

Many aspects of natural resource governance have been dramatically reshaped in northern Namibia during the past twenty-five years. The communal management of pastures, water, forests and wildlife was reorganised according to models for efficient commons management implemented by different ministries and their extension staff as well as NGOs active in the area. Hence the history of the commons of north-western Namibia differs from comparable histories in eastern and southern Africa. In north-western Namibia the commons were not dismantled and fragmented by privatisation and state projects, but rather were reorganised along the lines laid out by the state and by international donors.

Since the mid-1990s the Namibian state sought to reorganise natural resource management in the northern communal areas. Community-based natural resource management (CBNRM) became the umbrella term for a variety of efforts to reshape the governance of natural resources in communal areas. The aim of legal transformations and organisational changes was to decentralise resource management, to give local users a stronger voice in the management of resources and to establish local institutions within a democratic setup, and, perhaps most importantly, to valorise natural resources and wherever possible open them to commodity markets. Many of these initiatives were launched in the spirit of the seminal Rio 1992 Earth Summit (Agrawal 2001). CBNRM was designed as an effort to co-manage natural resources between the state and local communities by establishing formalised 'new commons' (see Bollig and Lesorogol 2016).[1] In terms of epistemological background these legal changes were on the one

---

[1] I use the term 'new commons' here to describe commons that are defined within the context of government programmes and state legislation. The 'new commons' are characterised by continuous negotiations between state agents and other externals fostering new ideas about social institutions, and locals holding on to and furthering older institutions of resource management.

hand close to Elinor Ostrom's design principles and were based on the assumption that the devolvement of rights and duties from state institutions to local actors would bring about more participation, ownership and sustainability. On the other hand the neo-liberal approach to conservation and resource management via market principles was salient. Environmental and social challenges were to be solved through market-based solutions (Sullivan et al. 2016: 14) and financed through international donors and businesses (Fairhead et al. 2012: 243–4; Sullivan 2012). Büscher and Dressler (2012: 367) address the emergent form of conservation as hybrid, referring to a process 'whereby multiple fields of reality are co-constituted to produce new organizational forms, motives, behaviours and actions over time and space'.

The establishment of CBNRM in different fields came with a number of implications. In the case of wildlife – a resource completely appropriated by the state since early colonial times – the state administration was to give back entitlements to the community. In the case of water it was less rights that were to be handed down to communities than obligations and costs: while boreholes had been completely government-run throughout the late colonial period, now such boreholes were to be handed over to communities on the proviso that they established waterpoint associations steered by elected committees that would charge community members for water use, and with this money could run the water point sustainably. The Communal Land Reform Act of 2003 resulted in further changes – though with a ten-year delay in the Kunene Region. A land board, as the body steering the governance of the communal land reform, was only established in 2008 and became active in the early/mid-2010s. Its main activity was the registration of informal land rights and the endorsement of 99-year leaseholds – both processes will be commented upon later in this chapter.

10.1 Conservancies: Development, Governance, Economic and Ecological Dynamics

When Namibia became independent, the handling of wildlife in communal areas was a significant challenge. While the colonial administration had ceded rights in wildlife on commercial farms to farm owners in the 1960s, the rights to wildlife in communal areas were retained by the state and anxiously guarded by government officials. Since 1996 rural communities in Namibia's communal areas could apply to the Namibian Ministry of Environment and Tourism (MET) for conservancy status in order to further their claims to wildlife and other natural resources. The new legislation stipulated that under specific conditions use-rights in wildlife and other natural resources linked to tourism were to be devolved to local communities (Jones and Murphree 2001; Jones and Weaver 2009). CBNRM was motivated by the aim to further rural development, address rural poverty, enhance participatory planning, and to ensure the conservation of wildlife at the same time. The Promulgation of Nature Conservation Amendment Act, 1996, defined conservancies and stipulated the way in which they were to be structured. Local communities were encouraged to establish corporate community-based organisations with a formalised membership, a well-defined territory of 'jurisdiction', representative forms of internal leadership, and detailed management plans including the zoning of core conservation areas in which no farming activities were allowed. In return, the MET delegated rights of wildlife management to conservancies (Republic of Namibia 1996; Jones 1999; Owen-Smith 2010: 540) on an annual basis (and since 2015 on a three-yearly basis) and the MET allots a game quota to a conservancy. With the gazetting of the conservancy a community also receives the right to tender land for rent through private investors.[2] There are no clear-cut regulations on how conservancies must deal with their incomes. The monetary gains of a conservancy were to be invested first of all in its upkeep (e.g. salaries for staff members, financing of meetings, transport). The remainder could be distributed to conservancy members (as a few conservancies do) or be spent on communal projects (as a majority of conservancies do). A significant number of conservancies, however, do not yet generate any substantial income.

The Rapid Expansion of Conservancies in the Kunene Region

Since 1998 the number of conservancies in the Kunene Region has increased rapidly (see Map 10.1). Map 10.1 shows a clear pattern: in an initial phase, conservancies in the wildlife-rich areas along the desert

---

[2] Before this legislation was put in place a private investor could obtain permission to occupy (PTO) through a local chief. Usually money or other forms of remuneration were paid for the concession of a PTO. With the new legislation, private investors have to address the conservancy committee, and any rents paid must go to the conservancy coffers.

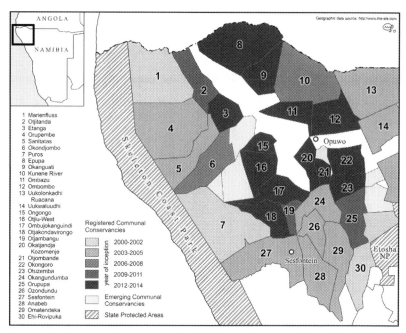

Map 10.1 Communal conservancies in north-western Namibia.
Source: NACSO (2018)

rim, along the boundary of Etosha Park and in areas linking both wildlife-rich zones were gazetted as conservancies. Their establishment clearly shows the input of conservationists interested in the protection of wildlife in those few areas where wildlife was still to be found. Then in two later phases, conservancies with less wildlife and in more densely populated areas in the central Kaokoveld were gazetted. By 2015 almost the entire Kaokoveld was covered by conservancies. These figures suggest that after an initial push motivated by the activities of environmentalist NGOs (notably IRDNC in the Namibian context) and donors, actors in other communities with lesser conservation potential realised that the move towards conservancy status conferred a number of benefits on individuals (e.g. employment, education, linkages) and the community (e.g. income diversification, clear-cut and legitimised boundaries) (see also Jones and Murphree 2001).[3]

---

[3] Silva and Mosimane (2012: 38) show for the Zambezi Region that many communities hoped to benefit from income from tourism in the long run and

This, of course, is the view of experts on the beneficial effects of these changes. Local informants emphasised the positive effects of clearly fixed boundaries and potential future incomes from tourism. They also hinted at increased access to game meat in some conservancies. In interviews the future benefits of clear and governmentally acknowledged community boundaries were raised first of all. Such clear-cut boundaries were to prevent encroachment on lands by outsiders but also to lessen the probability of intra-community conflicts. This also involved the idea that officially endorsed boundaries opened options to engage the state apparatus should such boundaries be infringed, i.e. to call upon the police to remove intruders.

Although legally the state did not cede land ownership rights to local communities when a conservancy was established, but only devolved specific management and transfer rights to them, the delimitation of territorial boundaries fostered the idea held by local people that they had in fact wrenched land rights from the government (see also Bollig 2013) and that the new setup made lands more governable. The establishment of a conservancy also allowed rural people to express belonging, ownership and allegiance to a traditional authority. This is also something Silva and Mosimane (2014) found prominent among the residents of Mayuni conservancy in the Zambezi Region. Although frustrated with the economic achievements of the conservancy, local people were still in support of it as it fostered social cohesion and supported local institutions like chieftaincy and group boundaries.

Many conservancies were gazetted along the boundaries of chieftaincies, i.e. when defining the boundaries of a conservancy apparently those discussing the issue with neighbouring communities adopted boundaries officially endorsed in the 1970s or 1980s (or even before that time). Such boundaries were convenient and did not require extensive discussion. However, in a good number of cases the establishment of a conservancy and its boundaries was linked to the breaking away of an area from one chieftaincy and the establishment of a new one; i.e. it was linked more with local divisive chieftaincy politics than to considerations of development or conservation. The Ozondundu conservancy area (see Map 10.1, conservancy 26) had previously been under the

> direct aid and support from NGOs in the short run. Only conservancy status allowed access to those benefits. Like Silva and Mosimane (2014) I did not find any hint that coercion by the state mattered as e.g. Igoe and Croucher (2007) have shown for Tanzania.

authority of a chief residing in Ombombo, the main place in Okangundumba conservancy (see Map 10.1, conservancy 24). Only when local actors succeeded in negotiating the boundaries of Ozondundu conservancy as separate from Okangundumba conservancy could a new chief establish himself, making the newly established conservancy the area of his chieftaincy (pers. comm. E. Olwage).

In many ways conservancy boundary making has led to a new type of territorialisation. On the one hand these newly gazetted territorial entities conformed to the ideas and strategies of traditional and newly established leaders alike; in their view, bounded territories precluded unwanted immigration, (re)legitimised and (re)territorialised traditional leadership, reconfirmed communal ownership of pastures and other natural resources, and also opened venues for investment from the outside. On the other hand conservationists and administrative staff advocated spatial entities with clear-cut boundaries in order to facilitate their programmes. The procedural rules of the MET stipulated that it was mandatory to submit proof of the consent of the traditional authority together with the application for conservancy status. Both NGOs and local administration were keen to involve those authorities. Hence, traditional authorities actively took part in this reterritorialisation, reifying their chieftaincies' boundaries or establishing their claims to a chieftaincy by showing that they were in command of an area. Integrating traditional authorities into the process, however, proved ambiguous. Why did NGOs like IRDNC put so much emphasis on engaging traditional authorities in the making and the governance of conservancies? The independent Namibian SWAPO-led government had only acknowledged two traditional authorities and had left more than thirty unacknowledged. This meant that traditional authorities – undisputed intermediaries of power in the 1970s and 1980s – were now struggling for influence themselves and were often keen to involve themselves. The official conservancy legislation, however, only gave them a peripheral role in these new bodies of natural resource management: they were to endorse boundaries. But the question then became one of how to get local acceptance for the manifold interventions. Only traditional authorities could serve as intermediaries between community and the implementing NGO and hence got involved more intensely than the original legislation had stipulated.

The twenty-eight conservancies in the northern Kunene Region range in size from some few hundred to a few thousand hectares.

Conservancies gazetted in 2012 and later were notably smaller and less populous than those gazetted earlier on. While the smallest conservancy has only around 100 members, the largest has about 3,500 members. Eighteen conservancies have less than 1,500 members, and eleven have between 2,000 and 3,500 members. Membership in a conservancy is easy to attain. Most conservancies stipulate that any adult can become member who has lived more than five years in a given area. A few conservancies allow for members who do not presently reside within the conservancy but are politically aligned with the traditional authority residing there (here membership comes very close to affiliation to a chief) or who have resided in the conservancy area for a long period in the past and whose absence is rated as only temporary.

Governing the New Commons

Conservancies are governed by elected committees. Traditional authorities who have an important voice in all matters pertaining to access to natural resources in communal areas are excluded from being members of such committees. With some hindsight the legislator made a decided effort to implement democratic conditions in the governance of the new commons. The legal act did not specify the structure of committees clearly but stipulated that committee members should represent the resident population, should be capable of handling its finances and should contribute to sustainable wildlife management.[4] All committees adhere to one formula: a chairperson, a secretary, and a treasurer, along with their respective deputies are necessary to establish a committee. Next to this mandatory core group other committee members can be co-opted. Committee members are elected at fixed intervals (between yearly and three-yearly). Committees are accountable to a general assembly which is organised in the greater proportion of Kunene's conservancies on an annual basis. At the annual general

---

[4] Government of Namibia 1996: '(a) the relevant committee is representative of the community residing in the area to which the application relates; (b) the constitution of such committee provides for the sustainable management and utilization of game in such area; (c) such committee has the ability to manage funds and has an appropriate method for the equitable distribution, to members of the community, of benefits derived from the consumptive and non-consumptive use of game in such area.'

meeting committee members report on their activities and present the annual budget. When electing committee members many conservancies make some effort to ensure that each village or territorial unit within the conservancy is represented; i.e. according to population size, each village is allowed to vote one or more people into the committee. The ten conservancy committees that were analysed in more detail consisted of ten to fifteen people. For these ten conservancies data on age, gender, educational status and employment status of current committee members were obtained. There is a clear dominance of male (73.5 per cent) over female committee members. However, women make up roughly a quarter of all committee members – in traditional authority structures women were hardly represented at all. Interestingly, and in startling contrast to prevailing authority structures, the majority of committee members (70.7 per cent) are younger than 40 years. Only a dwindling minority of 4 per cent are older than 50 years: conservancy committees are not constituted by seniors. Roughly 50 per cent of all committee members fall within the age bracket of 31–40 years, and 25.1 per cent are even younger than 30 years; i.e. more than three-quarters of committee members are below 40 years. A number of the twenty-five committee members younger than 30 years are women. Committee members stand out from the rural population in that they are fairly well educated. Roughly 40 per cent had some secondary school education, many of them having finished grade 12, i.e. having successfully completed secondary school. Less than a third do not have any school education. Good school education, however, did not help these young people into reliable jobs. Many failed to establish themselves in permanent employment: while many committee members had good school education, nearly 70 per cent did not have a job (some, however, had had a job in the past). About a third were employed, and some 8.5 per cent combined employment outside the conservancy with local engagement.

These organisational structures were certainly new to the area. While the involvement of traditional authorities gave conservancies some legitimacy, there is little doubt that the rules and procedures of conservancies were an entirely new way to organise the management of natural resources. I have pointed out above that the conservancy model is a globally circulated model which had been adopted by Namibian legislation. While the South African colonial government had ruled through local chiefs, i.e. had co-opted existing governance structures and had altered them according to the needs of a colonial administration, the Namibian government now implemented entirely new structures. Perhaps for the first time the state deeply infiltrated institutions of local resource management. Local governance structures are now closer to the state apparatus than before. While the traditional political systems of north-central and north-eastern Namibia were entirely different from the political system of Himba and Herero in the Kaokoveld, the newly implemented structures of resource governance were very similar if not identical to one another. Hence, in many ways the implementation of conservancies is tantamount to an expansion of the state, though in other ways it is not. Conservancy committees also step up local action against the state (e.g. organise protests and seek national alliances against state projects) and follow their own logics. Boundary making of conservancies in the eastern Kaokoveld is directed against Oshiwambo-speaking farmers and elites. Conservancies also have the potential to bypass state organs: the NGOs dealing with conservancies are better equipped, sometimes better salaried, and strategise in a more efficient way than ministerial offices.

Conservancy committees are intermediaries of power between global and national environmental agencies, market interests in wildlife and wilderness areas, and local agents. All committee members interviewed were actively involved in livestock husbandry and sought to sustain and increase their herds. At the same time they sought to gain access to benefits from development programmes and/or formal employment, i.e. they were keenly interested in livelihood options beyond livestock husbandry. Especially the young and fairly well-educated male members of the committees sought to establish themselves as brokers between development organisations, governmental institutions and local communities and to reap status and benefits from such a position. The writing and reading skills of most committee members are necessary (or perhaps just make it easier) to communicate with NGOs, donors, extension workers of ministerial offices, trophy hunters and tourism operators – and occasionally also with lawyers, who are increasingly made use of to settle conflicts. Many committee members are typical gatekeepers for their communities, capable of translating the ideas of donors, ministerial staff and NGO workers to other community members, knowledgeable about the motivations of extension workers of different organisations (who are often their age-cohorts and former schoolmates), and mobile enough to attend a great number of meetings and workshops. Many committee members state that, first of all, they want to be active in the development of their area and that they feel that their specific capabilities can add to such a development perspective best in the context of conservancies.

Committee members and local NGO workers are aware that wildlife and wilderness are distinct assets in the global setup. Partially commoditised, they are tradable, and there is lots of interest from the outside world to buy options to access wilderness areas and/or to view and hunt wildlife. Within a period of twenty years the natural resources of the Kaokoveld have been re-valorised. Many millions of Namibian dollars are spent in the Kaokoveld by tourist companies on leaseholds for hotels and salaries for local employees and by trophy hunters to shoot antelopes, gazelles, birds of prey, and even lions and elephants.

The age structure of committees has a number of implications. Among Himba and to a large extent also the Herero livestock property is concentrated in the seniors' age group, while younger men frequently do not own large herds of livestock. Among the Himba it was found that household heads younger than 40 years owned only a very small percentage of the cattle they herded. The vast majority of animals in their household herds were borrowed (Bollig 2006: 294–301). Hence, many of the committee members will not feature among the wealthy in their respective communities. They are also not prominent in local politics, where wealthy elders (some of them with the status of traditional authorities) dominate. These *ovahona* control access to resources, own a large percentage of the livestock, and formulate local consensus. In order to form new institutions, committees have to exert some power and it is clear that this power will rarely emanate from their role as livestock-rich 'big men'. It is rather connected to their capacity to link remote rural communities to a wider national and international resourceful framework. Conservancy committees establish a new arena of local politics in management, and can channel substantial benefit flows. They also propose game species for the quota hunting list and thereby contribute to the process of valorisation and commodification of natural resources.

Do committee members profit financially from being engaged in the conservancy? Officially they are not allowed to receive any direct salaries. They may, however, receive allowances (and in most settings in which I conducted interviews such allowances were paid) for attending meetings and undertaking trips, e.g. to Windhoek, for the conservancy.[5] Committee members enjoy other privileges: they are well informed about activities planned within their conservancy, and may directly profit from these. I found very little evidence for systematic elite capture, as De Vette et al. (2012) attest for conservancies for example in the Omusati region. First of all there is no clear evidence for the presence of an elite.[6] Wealthy and powerful people are tied into kinship networks, and often compete with each other for influence. Patronage is the form of dominance within these networks not elite status. Instead of systematic enrichment, I found that influence is used to allocate benefits to relatives and friends in the form of small salaries. Rather than accumulating wealth, conservancy members create and deepen social relationships. They create influence and patronage by channelling benefits in certain directions.

Environmental Governance through Conservancies

How do conservancies govern social-ecological relations, and what fields of human–environment relations do committees address? What visions and practices are there to distribute the benefits accruing from this common-pool resource?

Boundary Making

Let us first shed some light on the boundaries a conservancy has to establish in order to become gazetted. Day-to-day herding takes place mainly within these boundaries. In a survey of ninety-five households in twenty conservancies in 2012 I found that in normal rainfall years most of the grazing takes place within a conservancy. This is a strong hint that many if not most conservancies – while mandated to manage wildlife – also define grazing territories, and by implication stipulate

---

[5] In two instances we found committee members who were also employed with the conservancy, i.e. who directly decided upon their own salaries and job descriptions.

[6] Julia Pauli (2019) shows in her ethnography of marriage practices in Fransfontein that a rural elite established itself during the 1980s and 1990s. This elite has a clear idea of its dominant status, is economically well off and shelters its wealth through elite marriages. In Fransfontein elite strategies are aligned with kinship and religious beliefs. I do not see that the same mechanisms of elite formation have been of significance in the Kaokoveld. Strong kinship bonds and patron–client relationships embedded in the traditional context of subsistence orientated pastoralism have prevented the emergence of an easily definable elite.

boundaries around these grazing territories. The boundaries of these grazing territories are still porous though: A third of the households surveyed in 2012 said that they would have access to pastures beyond the boundaries of their conservancy through kinship ties in times of need. Schnegg and Bollig (2016) showed that during the drought in 2013/14 a number of households crossed conservancy boundaries in their search for pasture. This, however, rather underlines that the conservancy is the grazing management area in normal years. The establishment of conservancies reifies such grazing areas and formalises them. Events occurring in 2015 hint at progressive exclusionary practices: Himba who had migrated south of Opuwo and had settled there with Herero communities were denied access to conservancy membership. Some Himba households had gained access to grazing by seeking refuge with a relative, living with him for some time, and only then establishing an independent household. Some had directly paid money to chiefs and would-be chiefs to gain grazing rights. Legitimacy of tenure can only be achieved if a traditional authority concedes permanent rights of residence and often he does so in relation to the conservancy he is residing in. When the conflict heated up in 2015, court orders were directed (or threatened to be directed) against Himba living in Herero-dominated areas in the southern parts of the Kaokoveld. A number of Himba families then left, but only some of them did so permanently. This move, however, shows that conservancies and their boundaries are increasingly emphasised, leading to the emergence of a kind of village territory. Himba and Herero interviewed on the matter presented slightly different reasoning regarding the relation between migratory shift, climatic conditions and legitimacy of such moves. Herero alleged that Himba households came during a drought (*ourumbu*) and asked for temporary acceptance. Himba alleged that the state of *ourumbu* in their home areas was permanent (*ehi raswaka*, 'the land has become weak') and that their sojourn in the southern Kaokoveld would (and should) be protracted.

Zonation
The zonation of a conservancy is an instrument to differentiate conservation zones from zones for touristic use, for commercial hunting, and for subsistence herding and/or farming (see Map 10.2). Such zonation planning usually results in management maps. Resource management planning takes place at the interface between committees, and NGO

The Establishment of 'New Commons' by Government

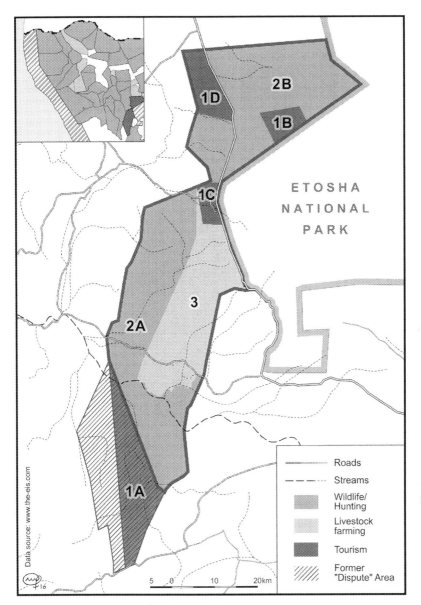

Map 10.2 Zonation map for Ehirovipuka conservancy.
Source: NACSO

and governmental organisation staff, who give advice on the topic. Committees do know that a rough categorisation of the conservancy area is needed in order to be governmentally acknowledged – so wildlife areas and settlement areas should be singled out. Conservation areas were often placed at the margins of conservancies, typically dry-season grazing areas that were not regularly used. Often conservancies hope to lure a tourist campsite or even a lodge to such exclusive areas.

Table 10.1 details the zonation plan for Ehirovipuka conservancy, and Map 10.2 shows the zonation plans of Ehirovipuka conservancy. Four different types of tourism areas were established: in some of them the grazing of livestock is minimised or totally forbidden (though emergency grazing is allowed everywhere). Furthermore, hunting areas and multi-use livestock farming areas are designated.

Table 10.2 shows how much space is devoted to a specific type of usage. It is significant that in the five conservancies analysed here management plans devoted substantial areas to wildlife and hunting, in many ways foreclosing substantial land use change: about a third of the land is given to conservation, with the hope of reaping communal benefits later on. Brooks et al. (2011) qualify this creation of commodified wilderness areas as 'third nature landscapes', landscapes that are shaped by the demands of wildlife-based tourism in pursuit of future gains.

In many ways the zonation of conservancies acknowledges earlier pastoral land use patterns. Habitually drought-resort grazing areas, or areas that were rarely grazed, were declared hunting and wildlife areas. As all management plans contain the clause that during very dry years these zones may also be grazed with the consent of the conservancy committee, at face value not much has changed. However, recent cases show that factually land use patterns and their governance have changed. The wildlife conservation areas are probably the clearest spatial expression of the new commons. In many ways these new commons prepare for a commodification of land without privatising it and without fragmenting it into freehold farms. Whether they can be addressed as 'commoditized land', as Büscher and Dressler (2012: 374) imply, is doubtful: these authors claim that 'new property relations "sever" customary ties and institutions by placing both under the auspices of self-regulating capitalist markets'. In north-western Namibia local forces, e.g. the competition between chiefs, and the quest for internal institutions of tenure rights within a pastoral system, certainly influence social-ecological relations as much as the capitalist

Table 10.1 *Zonation of Ehirovipuka conservancy*

Zone	Activities Allowed	Activities Discouraged
1A Core wildlife & tourism area & 'Dispute Triangle': Otokatorwa/Ombonde south	Wildlife, tourism, lodges, campsite (Ombonde river lodge, Palmfontein lodge); camp sites; craft centre Emergency grazing with TA (traditional authority) and CC (conservancy committee) authorisation	Commercial consumptive use (shoot & sell) Hunting Further settlement
1B Tourism areas: Okonjota	Wildlife, camp sites (Okonjota, Okatjovasandu, Okomutati), Okonjota Herero traditional village, craft centre Existing settlements; emergency grazing with TA and CC authorisation	Further settlement Hunting (trophy and own-use)
1C Tourism areas: Otjokavare	Wildlife, tourism, Otjokavare camp site, joint-venture tourist lodges, craft centre Grazing, settlement, crop farming	Hunting (trophy and own-use)
1D Exclusive Tourism Zone	Lodge Wildlife & upmarket tourism	Settlement, grazing, hunting (trophy and own-use), camp sites
2A Hunting area: Ehirovipuka west	Wildlife, trophy & own-use hunting, shoot & sell, live capture, limited tourism (Ombonde north camp site), hunting camp Emergency grazing with TA and CC authorisation	Tourist lodges, high-density tourism Unauthorised harvesting of natural resources; grazing Further settlements
2B Mixed-use area: Onaisohoek	Wildlife, existing settlement, own-use hunting, limited tourism Livestock, grazing, farming & gardening	Trophy-hunting Further settlement
3 Livestock farming: Onguta/Otjokavare north	Wildlife, settlement, own-use hunting, limited tourism; camp site; livestock, grazing, crop farming & gardening	Trophy-hunting

Source: Management Plan Ehirovipuka, NACSO.

Table 10.2 Spatial extent of zones in five conservancies

Conservancy	Anabeb km²	%	Puros km²	%	Omatendeka (+ 'dispute area') km²	%	km²	%	Ehirovipuka (+ 'dispute area') km²	%	km²	%	Epupa km²	%
Wildlife/hunting	504	32	1,292	36	453	28	694	37	704	35	939	42	575	20
Farming/	480	31	1,770	50	1,139	70	1,153	61	451	23	451	20	1,559	53
tourism/settlement	589	37	504	14	31	2	31	2	195	10	195	9	794	27
Mixed (all of above)									635	32	635	29		
	1,573		3,566		1,623		1,878		1,984		2,219		2,928	

Source: NACSO.

market. 'Customary ties' are 'alive and kicking'; they are resistant and vital and are co-producing social-ecological formations (see also Silva and Mosimane 2014 for Namibia's Zambezi Region).

Apart from the core conservation zone, all other zones allow pastoral land use as well, implying that the same space is regulated by different institutions – conservancy committees on the one hand and traditional authorities on the other. Committee members in fact had a very good knowledge of the boundaries of zones. Information about these boundaries was communicated to a wider public in formal meetings. We found only one conservancy (Ehirovipuka) which actually marked zone boundaries in the landscape itself with marks on trees or piles of stones. In the wider pastoral population knowledge of zonation boundaries was not yet widespread in 2012, as a number of interviews showed.

The conservation zones are a clear expression of the close linkage between conservation and the commodification of landscapes. The tourism sector specifically looks for such wilderness areas and is prepared to pay sizeable prizes for them. Conservation areas and hunting grounds are no longer near waterless stretches of land but are now highly valorised and can be traded in a market.

Increase in Wildlife Numbers

The conservation measures taken since the early 1990s (but also very good rainfall years) contributed to a sizeable increase in wildlife. A number of informants both from the pastoral population and officials had pointed to such an increase. The following figures are from a NACSO data set, which takes sightings of wildlife species (which are painstakingly recorded in event books) and then extrapolates to larger areas. The trend lines clearly show that the numbers for all wildlife species have been increasing (Figure 10.1), in the case of gemsbok and zebra greatly so, in the case of kudu and giraffe more slowly. The spikes in the curves are more likely to be attributable to different numbers sighted and probably do not reflect true demographic changes. The trend lines are more indicative. The steep decline of wildlife since 2014 is connected to a severe multi-year drought.

While there are data on the increase of some wildlife species, the number of elephants is hard to establish. Chapter 8 has shown that they were nearly exterminated by the mid-1980s. Since then the

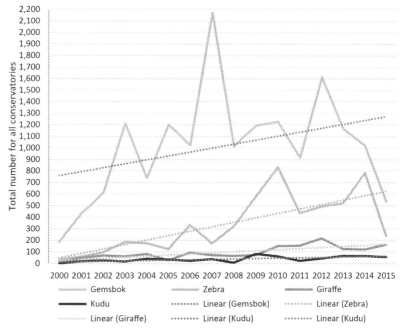

Figure 10.1 Dynamics of specific wildlife populations between 2000 and 2015.
Source: NACSO

increase in their numbers has been sizeable. Most people agree on this observation, that total numbers have starkly increased and that elephants are again populating areas from which they had been absent for many decades. Elephant counts, however, are never published, probably in an attempt to temper the lust to put too many elephants on the quota list. In recent years three elephants ended up on the quota list, which prompted stern criticism among national and international conservationists. A stable increase in numbers would suggest that many more could be put on the list. Given that per elephant US$25,000 (and usually more) can be made, this idea certainly makes sense from the local point of view.

Wildlife has also been reintroduced into the area. The most spectacular reintroduction programme was the transferral of seven rhinos from Etosha to the western Kaokoveld; but black-faced impala and other antelopes have also been reintroduced into the area and contributed to increasing wildlife numbers (Green and Rothstein 1998). The Kaokoveld resembles other parts of southern Africa in this respect: Schröder (2015) showed that in South Africa the numbers of wildlife animals on private lands increased tremendously over the past three decades, probably from some 0.5 million head in 1965 to more than 15 million head in the present. As in Namibia, about a fifth of the freehold farms are game farms and make their profits from trophy-hunting, game meat and live animal sales in the early twenty-first century.

Increasing Human–Wildlife Conflicts

Increasing protection through conservancies has contributed to an increase in wildlife. This in turn is linked to more human–wildlife conflicts (HWC). The recent expansion of lions and other predators, and perhaps most significantly the increase in elephants, have contributed to a sizeable increase in 'damage' brought about by wild animals. A report by Chris Brown on human–wildlife conflict in conservancies (Brown 2011) clearly established this link.

The figures indicate substantial costs of HWC in some conservancies, and that conservancies in the Kaokoveld were particularly prone to such damage. In Ehirovipuka conservancy the costs were as high as N$350,000 p.a., and in Sanitatas more than N$250,000 according to Brown.[7] This is more than both conservancies earn per annum. Brown took into account damages resulting, for example, from elephants destroying pipes at boreholes, as well as losses of livestock to predators. Within conservancies damages were unequally distributed, and people living close to core conservation areas lost considerably more livestock. Brown also observed a great deal of inter-annual variation in respect to losses. The very high costs of HWC in Ehirovipuka are closely connected to its proximity to Etosha National Park and Hobatere concession area. To some extent small-scale farmers are (partially) paying the conservation costs of a national park and a large wildlife concession. The ministry in charge, and also IRDNC, as the lead NGO in the region, addressed the issue of HWC through the Human–Animal Conflict Conservancy Self-Insurance Scheme (HACCSIS) for some years. Within the HACCSIS programme affected conservancy members are paid fixed rates in compensation for losses due to certain wildlife species that have collective value for conservancies. HACCSIS has two

---

[7] Also Silva and Mosimane (2014:1 87) report on sizeable losses due to human–wildlife conflict particularly in Mayuni conservancy.

components: (1) compensation of stock losses for registered conservancy members, (2) a funeral benefit of N$5,000 in the event of the death of a conservancy member (or his/her minor child) due to any of the listed wildlife species. An affected conservancy member has to apply through his/her respective traditional authority to get an assessment of claims and also pay-outs. HACCSIS was started in early 2003 and ran until 2010. The HACCSIS scheme was stopped in 2010 on the instruction of the MET when it introduced its new compensation scheme (Human Wildlife Conflict Self-Reliance Scheme) and the MET started to give a fixed sum of N$60,000 to each conservancy (on the provision that the conservancy tops up this sum with another N$60,000) to organise compensatory payments. The claims are now handled by a committee constituted by a few MET delegates and some conservancy committee members. Inquiries in 2018 showed that this compensation scheme is beset with flaws and works very slowly to the disadvantage of the damaged party. The lack of a true compensation mechanism in the face of high losses is endangering the entire conservancy programme, as wildlife damage is almost stereotypically connected to the conservancy.

Since 2009 a human–wildlife management policy is in place which focuses on minimising HWC by technical means: e.g. establishing elephant-proof water points (by building walls around them) and fencing fields (Republic of Namibia 2009). In fact, many wells in the western Kaokoveld have been equipped with elephant-proof walls in recent years making this infrastructure fit for the cohabitation of elephants, livestock and humans.

General Income Situation of Conservancies

Unlike resources held in private ownership commons must not only produce sustainably, but must also facilitate the just distribution of benefits. Agrawal (2001) sees unpredictable benefit flows and unfair allocation as having adverse effects on the durability of institutions of common-pool resource management. The allocation of specific communal rights in wildlife and land to conservancies by government decree requires private business partners to turn these communal assets into a benefit. I will first of all address the question of income in general before touching upon intra-community benefit flows. The total income of Namibian conservancies increased from N$600,000 in 1998 to N$39.5 million in 2010 (NACSO 2012: 4). In 2013 the total income was as high

Table 10.3 *Sources of income of conservancies*

Source of income	% of total 2007	% of total 2010	% of total 2013	% of total 2016
Joint venture tourism	51.9	47.3	43	54.3
Trophy-hunting	26.1	28.2	31	28.0
Game meat distribution	7.0	7.0	9	6.1
Own-use game	6.8	4.0	5	3.3
Veld products	2.7	1.9	4	?
Shoot and sell	2.0	4.0	1	0.9
Campsites and CBTEs	1.3	2.6	3	2.5
Live game sales	1.0	1.0	<1	0.1
Craft sales	0.8	3.4	2	1.3
Premium hunting	0.2	0	0	0
Bank interest	–	0.2	–	?
Miscellaneous	0.1	0.2	<1	?

Sources: NACSO (2008, 2012, 2014, 2016); Suich (2009:18).

as N$68 million (NACSO 2014), in 2016 it was at N$111 million (NACSO 2017) and in 2017 at N$132 million (NACSO 2018). The income of single conservancies differed greatly. In 2010 some 45 out of 59 gazetted conservancies had some kind of cash income, and some 23 conservancies operated independently of donor support, i.e. paying salaries and operations from their income. In 2013, 65 out of 80 conservancies generated returns, 36 covered their operational costs from own income, and 38 distributed cash or in-kind benefits to members or were able to invest in community projects (NACSO 2014: 31).

Where does conservancy income (i.e. the return on common-pool resources) come from? Table 10.3 gives an overview of various sources of income in Namibian conservancies for the years 2007, 2010, 2013 and 2016.

Table 10.3 shows that about half of the income in cash and in kind is generated from joint ventures in the tourism sector (i.e. mainly rents from lodges, and wages paid to conservancy members in such enterprises). A substantial amount of income is earned through trophy-hunting; in 2010 some 28.2 per cent resulted from this activity, in 2013 some 31 per cent and in 2016 28 per cent. Data presented by Naidoo et al. (2016) strongly hint in this direction. In 2010 trophy-hunting generated some N$13.9 million. The meat of the wildlife hunted by trophy hunters in conservancies is distributed locally and game meat distributions were consistently named as one tangible benefit.[8] While own-use hunting remained limited,[9] other marketable veld products, and incomes from camping sites and craft sales, very slowly gained in relevance. Profits result from the offer of local natural resources, landscapes and wildlife. They are generally not worked upon or modified but sold and leased in their 'raw state'. Büscher and Dressler (2012: 369) claim that such forms of CBNRM eventually result in 'a loss of local means of (re-)production through incorporation often [reinforcing] marginalization'. While access rights to some resources are lost or curtailed (e.g. to core conservation areas within conservancies) other resources are gained (e.g. wildlife, income from employment for some).[10] I do not see any evidence for marginalisation resulting from such programmes: a formerly encapsulated population interacts with actors beyond the regional level and they offer products on a fairly abstract market. They also compete with conservancies, e.g. in Namibia's Zambezi Region, which are wildlife-rich and close to areas with large herds of elephants. This, however, seems to be of more concern to the professional hunters offering wildlife on the international market than to conservancy committees in the Kaokoveld.[11]

---

[8] Trophy hunters, or more often their helpers, usually only cut off the 'trophy part' of the animal that has been shot. The meat is left with the community for distribution.

[9] Olwage even observed that own-use hunting was regarded as wasteful (Bollig and Olwage 2016).

[10] Fairhead et al. (2012) report on a 'veritable explosion of scholarship examining neoliberalization of environments' in their influential article on 'green grabbing'. The emergence of conservancies in Namibia can certainly be connected to neo-liberal policies: a resource that had previously been appropriated by the state is now liberalised and made into a commodity. While the academic focus may help us to understand the legal and political conditions of wildlife management in north-western Namibia in the early twenty-first century, it does not help us to understand the material consequences of such policies nor its social ramifications. Namibia's conservancies also cannot be classified as 'green-grabs' easily as local agency was often the driving force behind their being gazetted. This may also be due to the fact that 'the tourism industry' which is certainly interested in gaining access to wilderness areas and wildlife factually is constituted by a great number of highly diverse actors.

[11] Conditions within the value chain are not entirely favourable though. In a study of a conservancy in southern Kunene Schnegg and Kiaka (2018) estimate that the conservancy gets about 20 per cent of the total gains made in the trophy-hunting sector (see also Fairhead et al. 2012: 247 for other cases of skewed benefit distribution in conservation projects).

Conservancies in north-western Namibia 'produce' commodities jointly: wildlife and wilderness areas. They need external operators, commercial hunters and clients to turn both these resources into income – to transform wildlife into huntable wildlife, and landscapes into marketable wildernesses. Both commodities are peculiar in many ways. Conservancies receive annual game quotas, which are set in annual meetings in which conservancy members, officers of the MET, NGO staff, and also trophy-hunting companies participate. About 20 per cent of the quota is designated for trophy-hunting, whereas 80 per cent is kept for own-use hunting. The latter category consists of animals assigned to traditional authorities to furnish meetings with meat, animals traded in shoot-and-sell contracts to butchers from the wider region, and animals exchanged with local agencies for their services. Bollig and Olwage (2016) report that animals from this part of the quota were also given to the local police in payment for some services, to road contractors for extending a road, and to traditional authorities to host meetings.

For those animals assigned for trophy-hunting and for shoot-and-sell hunting a buyer has to be found. Conservancies compete for trophy hunters, and a number of them do not find anybody interested in their quotas. Currently only three trophy-hunting companies share the Kaokoveld's conservancies' trophy-hunting quotas: one dealing with eight conservancies, another with just two, and a third with an unspecified small number. While in theory trophy-hunting quotas should be publicly advertised, in practice conservancies are directly approached by trophy hunters. The exact contract between hunter and conservancy is negotiated between various stakeholders. The trophy-hunting company may only buy part of the designated trophy-hunting quota. They usually then guarantee a fixed number of game animals which will be hunted, and an optional number which will be paid for per individual animal hunted. The designated quota is paid in several instalments over the course of the year, directly to the conservancy account. A number of conservancies complained that they had not managed to attract a trophy-hunting company yet, i.e. they had failed to reap any benefits from wildlife. In an interview the director of one such company remarked that trophy-hunting quotas in some conservancies are too small, or simply have the wrong set of animals on offer to make it worthwhile to contract them.

Much of the remainder of the quota is given to shoot-and-sell contracts. Here local butchers come and buy large numbers of game from the quota. They drive into the area with a cooler truck and then often shoot large numbers of animals. Due to the Red Line regulations they are not allowed to export game meat south of the Red Line. Hence, lucrative game-meat markets in Namibia's centre are not accessible to them. The main market for game meat from Kunene is the rapidly growing urban area of Oshakati/Ondangwa, where an urban middle class distinguishes itself through the consumption of game meat. There is a conflict of interest between trophy hunters and shoot-and-sell hunters. The trophy-hunting companies advocate that shoot-and-sell hunting is taking place at times and in places where their clients are not present. In the past few years shoot-and-sell hunting has come under criticism because of alleged over-hunting and excessive cruelty (Bollig and Olwage 2016) and was put on hold in 2015.

Table 10.4 shows that a wide range of game has been put on the quota of conservancies in the Kunene Region.[12] From baboon to crocodile, elephant, gemsbok, and kudu, many species are present on the list. Conservancy hunting quotas are tendered to registered Big Game Hunters in Namibia.[13] Table 10.4 sums up the quotas for all conservancies in Opuwo and Epupa constituencies for the year 2013. Some animals have sizeable quotas: springbok with c. 2,000 animals, or gemsbok with almost 1,000 animals. These are enormous numbers but, astonishingly, most of the quota is not hunted at all, as the table shows – there are apparently hindrances to the full commodification as well as local utilisation of wildlife. The quota is only fully utilised for some species like elephants, lions or crocodiles. In other cases it is not used at all: of some 113 baboons offered on the list, only 6 were actually hunted; or, perhaps more astonishingly, of some 236 ostriches,

---

[12] It is basically the conservancies themselves that first propose what game should be put on the quota list. This explains why a number of game that are unlikely to be sold to trophy hunters end up on the quota list.

[13] Professional hunters are hierarchically ordered. The entry level is called a Hunting Guide. A Hunting Guide has passed his/her hunting examinations and may guide clients on his/her farm or within a company. After two years of successful hunting operations and at least twelve hunting safaris a Hunting Guide may apply for the status of a Master Hunter, which allows him/her to hunt on different properties (and not just on his/her farm). After another two years and a theoretical and practical examination the Master Hunter may apply for the status of a Professional Hunter. The final category is Big Game Hunter. One can only become a Big Game Hunter after two years of employment with a registered Big Game Hunter and passing another exam successfully (Weaver and Petersen 2008).

Table 10.4 *Wildlife put on wildlife quotas of conservancies in Kunene Region and their use (conservancies located in Epupa and Opuwo constituencies) for 2013*

Animal	Quota total	Actually used
Baboon	113	6
Black-faced Impala	9	4
Burchell Zebra	2	0
Caracal	15	1
Cheetah	12	2
Crocodile	4	3
Dik-dik	7	0
Duiker	13	0
Eland	2	0
Elephant	5	5
Gemsbok	974	421
Giraffe	14	9
Hyena	9	2
Jackal	142	5
Klipspringer	27	5
Kori bustard	5	0
Kudu	163	92
Leopard	13	4
Lion	2	2
Mtn Zebra	381	150
Ostrich	236	28
Springbok	2,002	869
Steenbok	55	6
Warthog	3	0
Wildcat	0	1

only 28 were hunted. Conservancy committee members alleged that hunting companies are only after some specific game: elephant is clearly the most cherished type of game, a view that was corroborated by the director of one hunting company. He also explained that some wildlife listed on the quota does not have any market at all.

Trophy-hunting and shoot-and-sell hunting have become income generators only for some conservancies. Commercial hunting is hardly relevant to the larger number of wildlife-poor conservancies (and will probably remain so for a number of years). Nevertheless, about 1,500 head of game were hunted in one year alone bringing profit and also meat to conservancies and their members. Liaising with private business partners in trophy-hunting is a complicated issue, though. There is little knowledge within conservancy committees about exactly how beneficial contracts with trophy-hunting enterprises are made. Conservancies are very much dependent on advice from IRDNC and MET staff, or officers from the WWF. Practically, these advisers formulate all details of a contract and supervise to ensure that such contracts are drawn up in a fair manner.

Distribution of Incomes
Quite a number of conservancies in Kunene Region achieve sizeable incomes these days. While the income situation is well documented, the way conservancies distribute incomes is less transparent and thus also more complicated to describe. Both within Kunene and at a national level there has been very limited analysis or documentation of benefit distribution. In fact, in our 2012 household survey most people interviewed said that they had no clue as to how conservancy income was distributed. Also, committee members could rarely give a precise account of how income was distributed. This is due to several factors: (a) Income distribution is complex as sources of income are highly diverse; contract conditions differ and hence are not easy to portray; (b) income distribution is a touchy subject, as most internal conflicts (and they seem to be frequent) hinge around this issue; (c) some non-transparency leaves space for committees to manoeuvre. While financial reports are compiled they are not scrutinised by the committee. Despite this, committee members were well prepared to talk about how they distributed funds.

A major part of conservancy incomes is invested into salaries. A NACSO report on the year 2010 establishes that conservancies all over Namibia covered the majority of the costs of 619 conservancy management jobs using income generated through conservancy related activities (NACSO 2012: 25). In Kunene North (i.e. Epupa and Opuwo constituency) in 28 conservancies some 100–50 people were employed, making conservancies, after the government, the most important employer in the region. Unfortunately I do not have exact figures on those employed: a majority of them, however, are male and aged between 30 and 50. In interviews with committee members in some ten conservancies we found a tendency to employ more staff when income generated by the conservancy increased. Typically game guards were employed first. In the past decade, if a conservancy had not generated sufficient funds, the IRDNC stepped in and supplied limited funds to pay game guards during an initial phase. These payments were then phased out once a conservancy proved to be financially viable. Most conservancies had at least four game guards. Additional staff positions are created when the income of a conservancy increases: usually a programme officer, a field officer (coordinating the activities of game guards), and a financial administrator are employed. The salaries of these positions varied. Usually the programme officer was the best-paid position (with some N$2,500 to 3,000 per month, c. €220–320 in 2012); game guards were found to earn between N$500 and 1,000 per month in 2012. These salaries are very moderate according to Namibian standards, and the salaries for game guards were usually below the minimum wage fixed by law (N$722 in the agricultural sector in 2014; SACAU 2014).

Commoditising Plants

While wildlife has been commoditised through commercial hunting and the quota system, non-domesticated plants were for a long time not considered comoditisable. Since late 2004 the NGO IRDNC explored how Himba people used specific plants to produce perfume with the intention of exploiting such plants commercially and thereby widening the environmental infrastructure. This explorative research indicated that *omumbiri* (*Commiphora wildii*) was the most important single species used for perfume by Himba women. A feasibility study ascertained that the harvest of *omumbiri* was sustainable, since it is only resin that is naturally exuded that is harvested. It was also shown that about 50 tons of resin are produced naturally every year in the five conservancies where this investigation was conducted (Puros, Orupembe, Marienfluss, Sanitatas, Okondjombo). The resin was first commercially harvested in October 2007 and a total of 5 tons, worth US$50,000, was harvested by 319 conservancy members (206 were women and girls) – a gain of N$250,000 was distributed among these harvesters. These gains increased in 2008/9 when the harvest could be pre-purchased due to funds obtained from WWF and ICEMA (Integrated Community Ecosystem Management).

By virtue of this approach plant resources that previously were not used commercially came to be associated with a monetary value. The sale of resin added to the incomes of women in these five conservancies. The average income per annum was modest but significant in a remote rural context (roughly N$1,100 per annum per harvester). The highest-earning individuals, however, earned up to N$7,000 in a year (which almost amounts to a year's minimum salary according to Namibian standards). In total some 150–250 people participated in the sale of resin. Harvesters are paid immediately when resin is delivered to the buying point.

The marketing of *Commiphora* resin is complex and propels local producers into global commodity chains. IRDNC negotiated with a number of internationally active partners in the perfume industry. An Access and Benefit Sharing contract (ABS) has been signed between the five *Commiphora* resin-producing conservancies and the company Afriplex. According to this contract Afriplex agrees to pay an additional 10 per cent to a conservancy, acknowledging that local traditional knowledge has contributed significantly to the commodification of the product. Despite these pertinent efforts, international marketing still presents a major problem for resin production.

Currently the plant-harvesting programme ambitiously tries to broaden its portfolio. Promising attempts have been made with gathering *Ximenia* kernels, mopane seed kernels, Devil's Claw, and various other *Commiphora* species' resin. With capital and technical assistance from ICEMA a processing plant has been set up in Opuwo. The essential oil from mopane seeds, and *Commiphora* resin, are going to be distilled there, lowering the costs of transportation and adding value to the product locally.

10.2 Communal Water Management through Water-Point Associations

Water management in the Kunene Region has been profoundly transformed over the past two decades by legal reform. While until the 1990s the state was responsible for water supply based on drilled boreholes fitted with appropriate pipes and energy-providing machinery (e.g. wind-pumps, diesel pumps, solar driven pumps; see Chapter 7), these responsibilities have now been delegated to rural communities. These transformations were linked to global reconsiderations of water management: while for decades the hydraulic mission of the state dominated planning and development practice (bring more water to water-scarce areas in order to encourage development), now community ownership and responsibility and the consideration of water as an economic good are salient topics of the discourse (Schnegg et al. 2016; Linke 2017). The whole mindset connected to that change was a product of trends in water management in the Global South in the 1980s and 1990s. It was fomented at international meetings, controversially discussed by international experts, and in the end put into an agenda then signed by a great number of nations; from there on it was translated into national legislation and finally brought to the local level by ministerial extension staff (Kelbert 2016). Community participation in development planning as well as community ownership of resources was put high on the agenda. Far from the situation depicted in Hardin's 'tragedy of the commons', here communities were depicted in an Ostromian manner as the stewards of natural resources. It was specifically the 1992 Dublin Accord which then impacted the water policies of many states in the Global South.[14] The Dublin Accord established that water was an economic good that needed to be valorised; hence it should be paid for according to the quantities used. This was a significant step: from water access as a fundamental right and a core value, to water as a valued, quantifiable good. It was also stipulated that rural communities were themselves best qualified to cater for their own water management and that the state should at best acknowledge local capacities for sound resource management. If the communities were able to define clear rules of access and exclusion, and develop monitoring skills and sanctioning capacities, they were better able than the state to provide equitable, sustainable and economically efficient supplies of water. A number of international bodies and notably a great number of UN membership states endorsed the Dublin Accord. But how did the agenda then come to Namibia? It certainly did not come to the remote north-western parts of Namibia first of all: again, the content and the consequences of the agenda were intensively discussed in the mid-1990s, in Namibia's parliament, amongst national experts and in civil society at large (Kelbert 2016).

---

[14] Thekla Kelbert's PhD (2016) focuses on the translation of global blueprints for rural water governance to the Namibian national level and subsequently to the regional level of the Kunene Region.

In 1997 the Directorate of Rural Water Supply (DRWS) launched a strategy for Community-Based Water Management (CBWM) (Bollig and Menestrey-Schwieger 2014). This plan prescribed that rural communities should become responsible (over a period of ten years) for the operation and maintenance of the water infrastructure (diesel pumps, hand pumps, pipes, water tanks, etc.) in a staged and planned process (Republic of Namibia 2004a). The reform stipulated that members of a community using a common water point should form water-point associations (WPAs). Each adult community member was meant to become a member of their respective community's association. They were also to develop regulations governing access to and usage of their boreholes, as well as means of recovery of maintenance costs. These rules were to be laid out in a constitution, which needed to be endorsed by ministerial staff in the Directorate of Water Affairs head-office in Opuwo. These regulations include the power to establish and impose sanctions on persons not complying with the stipulated conventions. For the day-to-day management of the borehole a governing body called a water-point committee was to be elected. The role of traditional authorities within the WPAs was not mentioned explicitly in the legislation. However, the extension staff of DRWS held (according to Menestrey-Schwieger 2017: 246–8) that chiefs and councillors should directly take part in the formulation of management plans, but should not hold office within the committee.

The process of establishing WPAs (water-point associations), the election of the committees, and the development of water-point management plans were supported by the extension staff from the DRWS in Opuwo (or by NGOs acting on behalf of and/or in coordination with them). The formal handing-over of the borehole from the state to the community was habitually carried out within the framework of a community meeting between the DRWS staff (and possibly involved NGO staff) and the users of that water point. At such meetings, which often lasted a number of days, the DRWS staff explained again the principles of fairness and equity according to which the water point should be managed.[15] The extension staff also gave advice as to

---

[15] These principles are given to the communities in written form and in a standardised way; they are the basis of the 'water-point constitution'.

which rules were to be included in the management plan, oversaw the election of a first water-point committee, and supervised the registration of the users as a WPA. Menestrey-Schwieger (2017), Kelbert (2016) and Linke (2017 for southern Kunene) found that DRWS extension staff workers had very clear ideas about which rules should be adopted. They directly involved themselves in the making of the constitution, and Menestrey-Schwieger (2017: 231ff.) reports that in a meeting in Ombaka in northern Kunene the DRWS extension staff also recommended several strategies for funding the water point: to collect the contributions according to the number of animals each household owns (e.g. N$1 per head of cattle and 50 cents per goat/sheep, both per household per month); to introduce a water-point membership fee (N$20 per adult per year to acquire the right to have a voice in the WPC meetings); a household levy (N$10 per household per month for the human consumption of water); and special conditions for external users (i.e. that they would have to pay more than the permanent settlers for using the water point: N$2 per head of cattle and N$1 per head of small stock). Furthermore, the extension officers recommended that penalties be established for whenever rules were breached. After the management plan for the water point was discussed and decided upon, the corresponding rules were jotted down by DRWS staff. Hence, the newly established commons are very much a product of negotiation, and in many ways water-point constitutions do reflect the ideas of extension staff rather than those of the locals themselves.

In relation to the establishment of the water-point committee, extension officers openly advocated the inclusion of young men and women on the board – often people of their own age and educational background. Table 10.5 shows that this advice certainly had impact. Within the context of the LINGS project we analysed demographic characteristics of members of water-point committees in forty-two WPAs in communities in the northern Kaokoveld: c. 30 per cent of the committee members are women and about 10 per cent are women below the age of 30. In total 37 per cent of the committee members are younger than 30 and c. 65 per cent are below 40.

This shows that just like in conservancy committees the administration-inspired institutions pave the way for an engagement of younger people in the day-to-day management of resources. This move brings with it a problem also encountered in conservancies:

Table 10.5 Water-point contributions rules in the communities immediately surrounding Okanguati

Community	Type of water pump	Date of WPC establishment	Contribution rule
Etengwa	Diesel pump	1997	**Rotation system**: each month a different household (HH) provides 25 litres of diesel (or N$200)
Ohamaremba	Hand pump (2)	2007	**Flat rate**: N$5 per adult per month
Ohavatje	Solar pump, Hand pump	2010	**Individualised**: N$1 per head of cattle per HH per month + N$30 per HH per month + N$50 per HH per year
Ohayua	Solar pump	2008	Government pays costs of operation and maintenance
Okapara	Solar pump, Wind-pump	2010	**Individualised**: N$1 per head of cattle + 50 cents per goat per HH per month N$20 per month per HH N$10 registration fee per year
Ombaka	Diesel pump	2003	**Stratified flat rate**: richer HHs pay more (N$200) than less wealthy ones (N$100 or N$50)
Omuhonga	Solar pump, Hand pump	2008	**Individualised**: N$1 per head of cattle per HH per month, N$30 per HH per month, N$50 per HH per year
Oruhona	Solar pump, Diesel pump, Hand pump	1994	**Rotation system + Flat rate**: each month a different HH provides 25 litres of diesel (or N$200) + N$30 per HH per month for the caretaker + N$10–15 per HH per month in case the solar pump gets broken
Otjozombinda	Solar pump, Hand pump	2009	**Individualised**: N$1 per head of cattle + 50 cents per goat per HH per month + N$2 per hut within the homestead + N$20 per adult per year
Ovijere	Diesel pump	2002	**Rotation system**: each month a different HH provides 25 litres of diesel (or N$200)
Owomiwore	Solar pump, Hand pump	2010	**Individualised**: N$2 per head of cattle per HH per month + 20 cents per goat/ sheep per HH per month + N$20 per HH per year.

Note: Due to lack of space only 11 of the 25 communities surveyed are displayed here.
Source: data collected and analysed by D. Menestrey-Schwieger.

decisions made in the committee have to be negotiated again with the resourceful elders of the community.[16]

According to the blueprint designed by administrative staff, committees were meant to consist of a chairman, a secretary, a treasurer, and a pumper/caretaker, together with their respective substitutes (Republic of Namibia 2004a). In a similar way as in conservancies, extension staff members persuaded traditional authorities not to become part of committees, in order to foster participation as well as gender equity, and to allow for free nomination or even election within the committee. In the cases we observed, committee members were not elected but rather named in a meeting. Membership of committees also often changed. Water-point committee membership has none of the privileges that membership in a conservancy committee has. There are no funds to be distributed, and no interesting economic options are negotiated. Committee members are responsible for handling the day-to-day management of the well, for motivating people to pay their shares, for administering such money, for reporting to the administration whenever severe technical problems arise, and for solving smaller problems by themselves.

The elected committee members receive some training in their respective roles (some days or weeks later) together with members of other water-point committees. The caretaker and treasurer are given guidelines on how to monitor water-point users and how to control for the timely payment of contributions. The treasurer is supposed to keep a written record of all payments, and the caretaker is obliged to safeguard the water point and to be present when the water point is used intensively (for his or her continued presence the individual is entitled to receive a small monetary remuneration). The treasurer is supposed to collect the fees, to keep a part of the fees collected in his/her house, and to deposit the rest in a bank account in Opuwo, the regional capital. The DRWS extension staff supply the treasurers with a simple ledger in which to note down contributions and unpaid fees.

The first water-point committee is inaugurated in a formal session in the presence of administrative staff. Then the chairperson of the WPC, his or her deputy and two witnesses sign the constitution (in many cases with an 'X' or a thumbprint) as a gesture that its contents will be

---

[16] Diego Menestrey-Schwieger (2017) describes in his PhD thesis a number of such conflicts and negotiations.

followed. At the end of this inauguration, the users of the common water points are registered as a WPA at the DRWS office in Opuwo (Republic of Namibia 2004a). Later changes in committee membership are informal.

According to the register of the DRWS (last updated in November 2011), there were fifty-eight active WPAs in the wider region of Okangwati, i.e. the northern Kaokoveld. All were responsible for the basic maintenance and operation of the water infrastructure (e.g. the replacement of spare parts, and buying diesel). Major repairs (such as pipe replacement or re-drilling) remained the responsibility of the government. In other parts of the Kaokoveld too the reform has been comprehensive, and nearly all water points are nowadays controlled by committees. At water points with a diesel engine they contribute significantly to the upkeep of the water point. This is different in water points equipped with solar cells (since the end of the 2000s c. 30 per cent of the water points have been equipped with solar cells) and those water points equipped with wind-powered pumps, of which there are only a few left in the region. Neither solar power driven nor wind driven boreholes need much input and maintenance work especially on solar cell driven wells needs to be done by technical experts.

Governance

WPAs are advised and mentored by the same group of extension workers from DRWS in Opuwo. Hence, their water-management plans are similar to one another in structure and content. In practice, however, the comparative studies conducted under the LINGS programme showed that many communities governed their water resources in ways not corresponding to the DRWS principles (see Table 10.5). For instance, the recommendation that contributions should be collected according to the number of animals that a household owned and the quantity of water it used accordingly was often not followed up. Many communities implemented flat-rate solutions which stipulate that every household should pay exactly the same amount of money; others implemented stratified flat rates in which richer households pay more (N$200) than less wealthy ones (N$100 or N$50). Also simple rotational systems were practised (each month a different household provides 25 litres of diesel or N$200 for the operation of the pump). Finally, there were still a few communities where the government remained responsible for the operation and maintenance of the water infrastructure.

Schnegg et al. (2016) looked at the institutional outcome of the implementation of WPAs in fifty-six communities in the Kunene Region: of these twenty-five (44.6 per cent) agreed that individual members should pay fees proportional to the number of livestock they owned (e.g. N$2 per head of cattle and N$1 per goat/sheep per month). They practise a payment system based on proportional equality. Seven communities (12.5 per cent) used a simplified form of proportional equality in which the rich paid more, but not exactly in proportion to the number of their livestock. Communities then applied rough proportionate rates and classified households as wealthy or poor. In twenty-four communities (42.9 per cent) we found flat-rate payment systems, i.e. all households paid the same amount as a contribution fee (e.g. N$100 per household per month). These payment models are based on the principle of numerical equality. In contrast to what theoretical literature predicts (Ostrom 1990: 90; Pomeroy et al. 2001; Trawick 2001; Cox et al. 2010), proportional equality does not regularly emerge. There was also no clear-cut relation between technological infrastructure (solar pumps vs. diesel pumps) and cost distribution as Anderies had proposed (Anderies et al. 2004) and Ostrom's hypothesis that institutions tend to develop in ways that serve the majority (Ostrom 1990: 193) could not be corroborated. A test of Ostrom's hypothesis showed that in most communities (88.9 per cent), the majority of households would have profited financially from a proportional rule. Instead we found that only communities in which the state had protracted impact – with extension workers frequently visiting the community, repeatedly arguing in favour of the proportional equality model and actively supporting the poor and their interests – did models based on proportionate equality emerge. In all other cases, the social dynamics worked in favour of flat-rate solutions.

We modelled the consequences of non-proportional payment schemes in order to find out to what extent such a payment rule would foster inequality (see Schnegg and Bollig 2016 for extended argument). For eighty households we made detailed counts of small stock and cattle and later figured out the livestock unit held by each household. We stereotypically assumed that herds grow by 2 per cent per year and that under a regime of numerical equality a household has to pay a monthly fee of N$200. The only way to procure money is to sell livestock. For each livestock unit (LSU) some N$4,000 can be obtained. In order to model the effects of numerical payment modes households were sorted into three categories: the poor (less than 20 LSU), those moderately well-off (20 LSU to 100 LSU), and the rich (more than 100 LSU). We based this ranking on wealth rankings by local people: out of the eighty households, twenty-one were regarded as poor, thirty-five were moderately well-off, and twenty-four were rich. The simulation (Schnegg et al. 2016) tries to predict wealth dynamics over a period of 100 months. According to the rule of numerical equality all households pay an equal amount to use the water; the amount actually used, however, varies significantly between groups. Already at the beginning the wealthy households used fifteen times more than the poor for the same monetary amount contributed. After 100 months this figure is eighteen times what the poor consumed. The numerical equality model directly forces the poor and intermediate groups to subsidise the increasing water consumption of the wealthy. It is mainly the poor who lose out. Of course, one may interject that such a simulation is far from reality: livestock diseases, drought-related deaths, inheritance transfers and livestock loans interfere. Also we have come across a number of communities, like Ombaka, which experiment for some years with one model and then switch to another one. However, the overall trend indicated by the simulation is so strong that one may safely assume that in some communities inequality will increase.

In many ways, the newly emerging common-pool resource management system is different from traditional commons. The 'new commons' are complex judicial entities inspired by and launched by the state, and often fuelled by donor funding: i.e. the formulas on which new institutions are founded derive from global and national discourses on sound resource management. These new commons are partial and fragmented, and their use is monitored by the state.[17] Despite these restrictions, conservancies and water-point committees have spread rapidly in north-western Namibia. Obviously they not only play a role in defining and facilitating the use of a (new)

---

[17] In this way, however, they are no different e.g. from Acheson's lobster fisheries in Maine: here too the usage of a single resource is defined conjointly between the community of users and an administrative body (Acheson 2006).

common-pool resource; their innate structures (membership, boundaries) can also be used for local political purposes: they provide a mechanism for territorialising political ambitions and for defining inclusion and exclusion via newly made or reified boundaries. At the same time they serve as a platform to negotiate the commodification of nature. Environmental infrastructure is compartmentalised and valuable (or better tradable) elements are made accessible for markets. Meant as a vehicle for nature conservation and sustainable natural resource management, they are used as a tool to legitimise the emergence of village territories under the joint guidance of elected committees and traditional authorities and at the same time for the financing of conservation measures through international organisations. Hence, the new commons are firmly embedded in markets. The valorisation and commodification of resources is essential. Price tags are attached to entities which were previously non-negotiable and did not have a market. I have shown that this commodification process is ongoing and incomplete. While the income in some conservancies is sizeable and way above N$1 million per annum, in many conservancies there is as yet little income from the new commons. The distribution of benefits from these new commons is still problematic, and a point of concern not only for those planning and facilitating conservancies but also for local activists. How can income meaningfully be distributed, what is a just and equitable mode of benefit dispersal, and how should costs accruing from the rising number of wildlife and the establishment of core conservation areas as no-go zones be handled? Similar questions arise regarding water use. How can the costs of water management be handled in a just and sustainable manner? These are open questions that are ambitiously discussed in the local context.

To what extent have new communal institutions been developed, and what do these new commons look like? This chapter has detailed three salient processes linked to the establishment of the new commons. The emergent institutions of conservancies and water management are deeply intertwined with existing institutions and organisational patterns of decision-making regarding access to and management of natural resources. Traditional authorities have considerable influence on the development of conservancy programmes and also a significant say in water management. In fact, they used the implementation of CBNRM projects to reinvigorate their positions within the local context. Committees do, however, create a new platform for young, educated males and females. Just as traditional authorities were intermediaries of power between colonial administration and local population, committees are intermediaries between international and national organisations focusing on conservation, private business partners, and local communities.

11 | *Into the Future: Envisioning, Planning, and Negotiating Environmental Infrastructures*

What kind of future awaits the Kaokoveld over the course of the twenty-first century? How will human–environment relations change? What kind of social-ecological transformations do actors on the ground aspire to? The social sciences have lately dealt extensively with future-making as a particular brand of cultural practice. Arjun Appadurai (2013) differentiated between a future of *probabilities*, which is based on formalised and often quantified practices of prognosis, and a future of *possibilities* that rests on aspirations for a brighter future (however that may be defined).

Beckert (2013) argues that economic action is often motivated by fictional expectations. This nexus between fictional expectations (pertaining to future ecology, future economic structures, and future social transformations), design fantasies (Beckert 2013: 225) and contemporary social-ecological dynamics is at the core of this chapter.[1] Here I will deal with fictional expectations – mental representations that are highlighted in plans, scenarios, and prognoses – of a diverse set of actors, scientists, politicians, environmentalists, investors, and donors, to attempt to peer into the future, and show that mutually contradictory approaches to future-making are being taken. Only a few of these expectations are point predictions (such as projections of precipitation decline). Most are narratives of various sorts: scientific texts, the scenarios of political planners, and the projections of entrepreneurs. Some narratives are more explicit than others. The point projection on climatological change is narrativised with longer accounts on the possible consequences of such changes. These narratives talk about a multi-decadal to centennial temporal scale, and projections depict

[1] Beckert (2013: 219) defines fictionality in economic action as 'the inhabitation in the mind of an imagined future state of the world and the beliefs in causal mechanisms leading to this future state. Actors are motivated in their actions by the imagined future and organize their activities based on these mental representations.'

possible future situations in the second half of the twenty-first century. Narratives of economic scenarios habitually refer to the next one or two decades, and only occasionally talk about longer timescales. Namibia's Vision 2030 (www.gov.na/vision-2030) has a timeframe of some three decades. Some economic scenarios are more explicit than others. A mining-based future, characterised by intensive mining and the exploitation of hydrological resources, is depicted with some confidence. A future in which the region becomes an 'Arid Eden' which harvests wealth from its highly ranked conservation status and international tourists is also well delineated. Namibia's ambitious governmental plan for sustainability and wealth, Namibia Vision 2030 (Republic of Namibia 2004b), embellishes the potential of community-based eco-tourism. It argues that 'land-use for tourism in parts of Namibia, outside protected areas, has extremely high economic potential', and also predicts that 'in a few years tourism will become the leading economic sector in our country' (Republic of Namibia 2004b: 151). The governmental prognosis emphasises that spectacular scenery, wide-open spaces, and wildlife are singular selling points in the global tourism economy and become 'sought after commodities that must be regarded as valuable natural assets' (Republic of Namibia 2004b: 151). The preservation and development of these assets is crucial in governmental plans 'to maintain a comparative advantage within the global market'. Consequently Vision 2030 argues for the recovering of wildlife populations on land outside state-owned parks, and lauds the founding of conservancies.[2]

In contrast to that, an economic future in which the incomes of many are based on social transfers (pensions, grants) and the local population is made progressively more independent from their immediate environment, has an implicit future-making component: welfare and poverty alleviation will only come about if the state increasingly caters for its citizens' needs. Citizens derive a rightful share of the nation's wealth through such unconditional transfers. Interestingly, the future-making perspective that envisions more rural people gaining incomes from social transfers is not spelled out in either Vision 2030 or other agendas. It is also not part and parcel of conservationist arguments,

[2] Vision 2030 was published in 2004 when only around 23 conservancies were registered. The governmental strategy to foster these community-based tourism activities has been successful, with some 86 registered conservancies country-wide in 2019.

though in principle both narratives would harmonise. James Ferguson (2015: 38–9) observed that arguments based on a productionist agenda – production of minerals and ores or wildlife and other commodities from the wild for the world market, in the Kaokoveld's case – are politically more acceptable in southern Africa than arguments based on a distributionist agenda. Even if social transfers do not feature importantly in future plans of social-ecological development, I will deal with them here, as their relevance is demonstrably increasing. Where are local voices in this? Recently voiced local ideas demanding more cultural autonomy depict an alternative path. Resting on a broad understanding of indigenous rights, a modernity is envisaged in which strong traditional leaders and custodians of local customs govern natural resource management.

The sources for this chapter are somewhat different from those used for the previous chapters. There is little local consideration for climate-change projections, while the recent drought, however, is connected to the narrative on global climatic change. There are also local voices commenting upon the exploration activities of mining companies and plans for a hydroelectric dam at the Kunene. There are very audible and widely broadcast voices presenting opinions on the prospects of a broadened cultural autonomy and the future relevance of traditional leaders in social-ecological governance. A lot of the information assembled in this chapter originates from web-based presentations, published scenarios, newspaper articles, and government plans.

I will first deal briefly with ecological projections, then detail some economic fictional narratives, and finally depict scenarios of socio-political development.

11.1 Ecological Scenarios: Global Climatic Change, Species Dynamics, and the Future of Pastures

According to the projections of climate-change specialists, northern Namibia will suffer substantially from the effects of global warming, and by 2080 conditions will have become substantially drier than they are today. It is tempting to connect contemporary drought conditions like those that prevailed between 2011 and 2019 with these projections (Schnegg and Bollig 2016). The recent multi-year drought gives an impression of the conditions that may prevail from the mid-twenty-first century onwards. This rather dull scenario stands in stark contrast to a second scenario, which I will refer to here as the 'Arid Eden' scenario. Wildlife numbers are growing and local communities progressively make a living from wildlife-based tourism. While projections of climate change rather pertain to the second part of the twenty-first century, 'Arid Eden' scenarios deal with the coming two decades.

Climate Change and its Effects on Social-Ecological Dynamics

In climate-change maps,[3] north-western Namibia is designated as a hotspot of climate change. Throughout south-western Africa average temperatures are likely to increase by 1–3.5°C by 2046–2065. Reid et al. (2007: 8) even allege that 'by the 2070–2099 period maximum warming in Southern Africa is expected to be up to 7°C'. Due to increasing temperatures and a weakening of the southern African monsoon, decreasing rainfalls are predicted, resulting in a sharply diminished growing season. In the northern parts of Namibia the rainy season is likely to begin later and to end earlier, while rainfall intensity may increase. Predictions leave little doubt that annual rainfall will become even more variable and drought may occur more frequently. Evaporation and evapotranspiration will increase by 5–15 per cent. Flows in perennial rivers will decrease up to 25 per cent and the recharging of aquifers will be reduced by 30–70 per cent. This may render a large number of boreholes in the region uneconomical or unusable. Reid et al. (2007: iii) assume that 'even under the best-case scenarios ... subsistence farming will fall sharply' in much of northern Namibia. In fact Map 11.1, a snapshot from a map showing the consequences of global climatic change for agricultural production by 2080 for the entire African continent produced by the United Nations Environment Programme (UNEP), shows that agriculture in central and north-western Namibia will become unviable and that adjoining areas in northern Namibia and southern Angola may suffer from decreases of up to 50 per cent in agricultural productivity. The website of the German International Development Cooperation office in Windhoek alleges that by 2050 'it is anticipated that it will only be possible

---

[3] See for example the UNEP-produced map of projections of changing cereal output: https://reliefweb.int/map/world/africa-change-potential-cereal-output-2080. The map is based on *HadCM3*, a coupled atmosphere-ocean general circulation model (AOGCM) developed at the Hadley Centre in the UK. It was one of the major models used in the IPCC Third Assessment Report in 2001.

Into the Future: Environmental Infrastructures 321

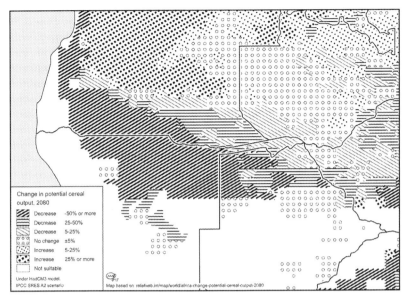

Map 11.1 Consequences of global climatic change for agricultural production by 2080.
Source: https://reliefweb.int/map/world/africa-change-potential-cereal-output-2080

to practice rainfed agriculture using current methods in Kavango East and Zambesi'.[4]

These projections are of considerable significance for north-western Namibia. Already at this stage the Kaokoveld is deemed as not suitable for agricultural production; but also in neighbouring areas agriculture will no longer be possible. Many aquifers will fall dry in the second half of the twenty-first century. Possibly the vegetation will change accordingly all over north-western and north-central Namibia. This will have grave consequences for local subsistence economy: farming along river courses may vanish altogether and livestock husbandry may diminish significantly. In fact, when viewed in the context of a centennial timescale, rain-fed agriculture along the Kaokoveld's

---

[4] Possibly this website draws directly from the UNEP map, but for unexplained reasons changes the decades somewhat: grave transformations are here already anticipated for the mid-twenty-first century. www.giz.de/projektdaten/projects.action;jsessionid=9EC46B946DA3031ED92281FCE2402D04?request_locale=en_GB&pn=201397678.

seasonal rivers may eventually turn out to have been only a short-lived interlude of some five decades.

Recent droughts are interpreted as precursors of harsher climatic conditions in the second half of the twenty-first century,[5] and strict political measures are demanded. They are essential ingredients of fictional expectations of a changing climate and its broad ecological consequences. In 2016 the Namibian president declared a state of emergency due to drought, and a number of compulsory measures were introduced in Windhoek, the country's capital. Social pressure to provide safe water was established via virtual platforms and other media.[6] When writing the final pages of this book in spring 2019 again news on a disastrous drought and high livestock losses haunt the media and yet another national emergency was declared in May 2019.[7] Those who are casting alternative economic futures for north-western Namibia often allude to the fact that climate change sets an invariable frame that influences any other economic development. The prospects for agriculture and livestock husbandry appear to be poor, and incentives to invest into the long-term sustainability of the rural livestock-based economy may decrease: if boreholes are going to run dry in the second half of the twenty-first century, why invest in extensive improvement of livestock husbandry in the region?

Who talks about climate change and its local effects? At this stage it is mainly governmental and non-governmental planners and external development agencies who put climate change high on the agenda. Lately I have heard some local staff of NGOs and local politicians reasoning about climate change. In contrast to land conflicts and

---

[5] *The Namibian*, 14/8/2007, 'Namibia feels effects of climate change', by Absalom Shigwedha.

[6] www.theguardian.com/sustainable-business/2016/jul/13/namibia-drought-coca-cola-meat-construction-industry-water-crisis-climate-change: 'Two weeks ago, the President of Namibia officially declared the country to be in a state of emergency. The country is facing its most severe drought in more than 25 years. ... In Windhoek, authorities have ordered businesses to cut water use by 30%, a move affecting small and micro businesses along with big companies. ... Social media has been particularly effective in targeting companies seen to be using water irresponsibly. Any wasting of water is promptly reported to online local groups such as Facebook group Water Wise Windhoek, run by environmental scientist Theo Wassenaar.'

[7] *The Namibian*, 26/4/2019, 'Drought kills about 64.000 animals in six months'; *The Namibian*, 6/5/2019, 'Drought declared National Emergency'.

contestations with the state over land and resource management, climate change did not feature prominently in local discourses.

The 'Arid Eden' Scenario: Increase in Wildlife and Sustainably Managed Pastures

The 'Arid Eden' scenario entails a narrative that suggests that sustainable and highly resilient social-ecological relations can be achieved, if local communities benefit from species diversity and high wildlife numbers, local institutions ensure an equitable distribution of costs and benefits, governmental institutions guarantee a high degree of co-management, and – perhaps most importantly – private business partners invest in and reap sufficient profit from such a 'healed' landscape. The 'Arid Eden' scenario is a fictional expectation that pertains to ecological trends as much as to social dynamics. I will here first look at the ecological aspects and deal with political, economic, and social ramifications later in the chapter.

While the idea of wildlife conservation has been repeatedly promulgated during the Kaokoveld's history, the 'Arid Eden' scenario, hypothesising a future in which pastoral land users live in harmony with and profit from a high density of wildlife, and in a true sense become the custodians of Eden's natural abundance, is a product of the late 1980s and 1990s. Namibia's Vision 2030 expresses this scenario in a clear way and sets a target: 'healthy, diverse and productive wildlife populations of economically important species on land outside State-owned parks, integrated into economic activities on farmland, and making a significant contribution to the national economy' (Republic of Namibia 2004b: 153). The Vision 2030 plan embellishes a Third Nature in which a commodified wilderness contributes to rural livelihoods. Not direct exploitation of natural resources but the remodelling of the landscape as an accessible wilderness with appropriate tourism infrastructure will guarantee future wealth (see Brooks et al. 2011: 263 for the emergence of Third Nature wilderness landscapes in South Africa).

In Chapter 10 I outlined the pertinent increase of wildlife over the past two decades. I have also outlined the problems involved in finding good quantitative evidence, for example of the increase in elephant numbers. There is no doubt, however, that their numbers have increased substantially. Possibly, numbers are again around 1,000 animals, and have

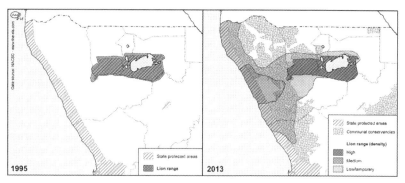

Map 11.2 Expansion of lions in north-western Namibia, 1995–2015.
Source: Heydinger et al. (2019)

reached figures that prevailed in the mid-twentieth century. Maps published by NACSO also contain data on the increasing number of lions in the area. While lions were almost exterminated by the early 1990s and restricted to the Etosha Park area, now large areas of the Kaokoveld are once more populated by these predators (Map 11.2).

The Kaokoveld is home to much more wildlife than in the late colonial period and it is probable that numbers will further increase, changing the environmental infrastructure significantly.

With the increase in wildlife, not only do options change, but so do challenges. It is very obvious that human–wildlife conflict is on the increase all over the Kunene Region, and farmers campaign for the restriction of predator numbers. The Desert Lion Project reported the poisoning of a pride of lions in the western parts of the Kaokoveld.[8] During the past few years elephants have also come under renewed attack. The number of elephants in the Hoanib and Hoarusib valleys decreased post-2012, after two decades of increases. While some animals died naturally, others were hunted (Ramey and Brown 2014). In March 2014 three Chinese men were found with fourteen rhino horns at Hosea Kutako airport.[9] Allegedly some of the horns

---

[8] www.desertlion.info/. The website reports that the entire pride, dubbed the Musketeers, were poisoned by enraged villagers near Tomakas in the south-western Kaokoveld. The site reports that villagers accused conservationists and government of conspiring to protect predators more than they develop the well-being of people.

[9] *The Namibian*, 26/3/2014, 'Chinese men charged with rhinohorn smuggling'.

originated from rhino poached in the Kunene Region.[10] Since then a number of rhino poaching cases have been reported, often with the alleged or proven involvement of Chinese nationals. The very active Chinese business community in Namibia tried to emphasise its pro-conservationist stand when contributing N$30,000 (about €2,100) to rhino conservation measures in December 2016.[11]

How do pastures feature in the 'Arid Eden' scenario? Do they feature at all? In Chapter 8 I outlined the change in pasture composition after the increase in herd numbers since the mid-1950s. Perennial grasses have long been on the retreat, and annual grasses dominate. In recent decades a significant impoverishment of the layer of annual grasses and nearly complete demise of perennial grasses in many pastures was noticed. There has been a significant shift towards the hardy but low-yielding *Aristida* species. The Holistic Range Management Programme, which was launched by IRDNC in 2006 and continued to be funded under the Millennium Challenge Account between 2011 and 2015, set out to implement a new grazing regime. The strict management of herds (amalgamation of individual herds into village herds, delineated grazing territories, short and intensive impact grazing, and long resting periods) was instituted in a few localities. It was the declared aim of these micro-projects to restore the grass cover. In an online report,[12] IRDNC, as the facilitating NGO,[13] claimed that after only a few years of engagement annual grasses had replaced bare soil in many localities and that also perennial grasses are recovering gradually.[14] Planned grazing is also compatible with tourism. In park areas livestock managed following the approach of Planned Grazing through Herding (PGH strategy) can even improve the habitat for highly valued wildlife 'by changing the morphology of perennial grasses to more palatable growth forms. Furthermore, large herds have the ability to flatten coarse grass onto the ground – making new

---

[10] *The Namibian*, 19/1/2015, 'Wildlife staff probed in Kunene rhino poaching'.
[11] *The Namibian*, 6/12/2016, 'Chinese pledge N$ 30,000 to save rhino'.
[12] http://dry-net.org/initiatives/development-of-sustainable-rangeland-management-practises-in-the-communal-lands-of-namibia/.
[13] In 2015 the holistic range management component split from IRDNC to form the NGO Conservation Agriculture Namibia (CAN).
[14] There is no indication whether we must read 'over time' as a multi-year or a multi-decade projection.

growth available for selective feeders.'[15] In this way, wildlife and livestock can potentially be grazed in harmony in the future.

11.2 Economic Scenarios

Namibia's Vision 2030, adopted and publicised in 2004, developed a set of socio-economic scenarios for the country. The document envisions food security, sustainability, and high standards of living for the entire Namibian population by 2030. It proposes that inequalities which are so prominent in present-day Namibia be reduced and human development significantly improved. Vision 2030 devotes a long chapter to addressing future challenges and possible approaches to natural resource management, and outlines a future that combines sustainable livestock husbandry, wildlife management, and mining. For northwestern Namibia four different economic scenarios are narrativised by different sets of actors.

The Conservation Scenario

Many protagonists of community-based conservation approaches see Namibia's Kunene Region as an ideal of community involvement in wildlife conservation and an exemplary case for future-oriented public–private partnerships. Increasing wildlife numbers obviously testify to a successful community-based approach to conservation, and the rapid spread of conservancies is evidence that the sympathies and aspirations of the local population accord with such an approach. Kunene Region's conservancies and the NGO facilitating their emergence and maintenance, IRDNC, have won a number of international prizes and gained substantial donor support over almost three decades. Whether public–private partnerships are in fact as successful as depicted is not yet clear, and remains disputed. Schnegg and Kiaka (2018) show that just 20 per cent of the gains remains with the communities, while the major share of the profit goes to the private sector. In trophy-hunting, figures remain uncertain, as only the fees given by professional hunting companies to conservancies are well documented; it is not clear what these businesses originally receive from their clients and it is assumed that a major percentage of the gain

---

[15] See note 12.

stays with the company. Naidoo et al. (2016) describe that lately trophy-hunting has increased its share, while conservancies' income from other forms of tourism has risen moderately. Conservancies compete for hunting operators and sometimes feel forced to enter into agreements in order to prevent the operator from going to a neighbouring conservancy. The foundation of a conservancy-owned trophy-hunting company, Conservancy Safaris Namibia (CSN), was a reaction to that: it started business with the idea that larger shares of the gains would stay with local conservancies if they ran the trophy-hunting company themselves.[16] A recent guest comment on CSN's website reveals and certainly elicits fictional expectations on the part of its readers:

This is the least commercial, most benevolent, best access to the real Namibia, with superb guiding, animal tracking and local know-how. Let Boas and the others guide you with good humor and exquisite patience through the bush to a waiting Rhino, or back up in perfect viewing of an elephant cow cooling off with her calf by spraying herself with her own saliva, or sit on the veranda in their elegant and tasteful stone lodge at Etaambura, from which you sojourn virtually alone with the Himba tribesmen, who greet your guides as that rarest of things in Africa, honest allies accepted and revered by the locals because they reciprocate the respect. Give CSN some time. You will never forget it.

This is, of course, very close to Eden! A number of tourist companies have built lodges and camps in the Kaokoveld in recent years. They pay rent to local communities, and employ locals. Community-based conservation as envisioned by planners in the 1990s, and as cherished by Namibia's Vision 2030, is not possible without the engagement of the private sector.

How do the main actors judge the future of community-based conservation in the region? How can present successes be consolidated

---

[16] The Conservancy Safaris Namibia website claims: 'Our owners are Puros, Orupembe, Sanitatas, Okonjombo and Marienfluss conservancies, covering more than 13,500 square kms. When CSN grows and accumulates wealth, it is the conservancies, not outsiders, who are the beneficiaries. Our business model builds on Namibia's community-based natural resource management successes, linking conservation to economic and social development. For wildlife and the environment to be protected meaningful benefits have to be generated for the people and local capacity has to be built.' www.kcs-namibia.com.na/our-vision.html.

and how can more income from conservation be channelled to the inhabitants of the Kaokoveld? How will markets for trophy-hunting be further developed, and how can other natural resources (perfumes, Devil's Claw) be introduced into value chains?[17] Are there ways to increase incomes from other forms of tourism (other than trophy-hunting)? Vision 2030 sees wildlife conservation as adding importantly to the 'social and economic well-being' of rural populations in communal areas, and fosters plans to facilitate 'opportunities for people to derive economic value from wildlife species that impact on farming and livelihoods' and to improve income generation in conservancies in order to 'lessen dependency on Government and other providers of support' (Republic of Namibia 2004b: 157).

Indeed, Vision 2030 devotes a whole section to the economic prospects of conservancies and CBNRM. The argument in favour of community-based tourism is habitually based on figures relating to incomes. Vision 2030 argues that since 1990 tourism has grown exponentially, from 254,978 international tourist arrivals in 1993 to 757,201 in 2002, representing a growth rate of almost 200 per cent. Tourist numbers have since swelled to 1.4 million (in 2014) and 1.5 million (in 2015).[18] Namibia's Vision 2030 predicts that tourism will become Namibia's leading economic sector in the near future. The paper lauds the potential of community-based tourism and adds some statistical data to its argument. Tourists visiting community-based tourism enterprises had increased from 30,000 in 1999 to more than 90,000 by 2004 (Republic of Namibia 2004b: 152). A NACSO report asserts that the overall returns from tourism to Namibian conservancies came to just under N$30 million in 2013.[19] This does not include incomes derived from tourism through employment in lodges and on camping grounds. Incomes result from direct employment in tourism enterprises, or from fees for trophy hunts. The figure documenting such potential increases in community income shows a scenario under which conservancy benefits would increase from c. N$200 million to c. N$1,000 million by 2030 (Republic of Namibia 2004b: 154).

---

[17] In early December 2017 *The Namibian* reported a 'bumper devil's claw harvest' valued more than N$1 million. 'Conservancies get bumper devil's claw harvest', *The Namibian*, 4/12/2017, online archive.

[18] www.namibian.com.na/155155/archive-read/Tourist-arrivals-minimal-in-2015, *The Namibian*, 9/2/2016, online archive.

[19] www.nacso.org.na/resources/state-of-community-conservation.

Documentation by NACSO shows that there are currently forty-two joint-venture lodges in Namibian conservancies. The document argues that while the main source of income is still farming, 'with the growing effects of climate change, access to alternative income streams will become increasingly important'.[20] Incomes to conservancies could be further improved if the Red Line were relocated northwards (to the Angolan border) or eastwards (to the Kunene/Omusati boundary): then it is projected that benefits of up to N$62 million could be gained by the sale of live wildlife by 2030 – these are fictional expectations of a thriving wildlife-based economy.

The contribution of conservancies to local incomes rests on their capacity to sell their wildlife quota to commercial hunters. Naidoo et al. (2016) show how important hunting is to the incomes of conservancies. Whether hunting is practised or not, however, does not so much depend on its economic effectiveness and its contribution to livelihoods, but is rather determined by global discussions of animal rights, conservation, and environmental justice.

What Vision 2030's section on the economic prospects of community-based conservation does not say, though, is that such exponential increase in economic volume depends on international investments to a large degree. Sullivan (2012) has argued that 'a spectacular investment frontier' is supplying funds to local conservation programmes in anticipation of sizeable returns and substantial moves towards climate adapted sustainable land management. Nature is progressively conceptualised as a 'service provider' offering a multitude of ecosystem services which seek a market. Sullivan (2012: 206) claims that 'Inhabitants of service-providing landscapes also are radically reframed as service maintainers for consumers elsewhere in the emerging global ledger of financialized environmental services.' New 'biodiversity derivatives' may be of significance in future conservation projects in north-western Namibia. This may bring the interests of conservationists, international capital agencies, governments and landowners to align as species are made more valuable and more tradable at the same time.

Future expectations for community-based conservation efforts are very much focused on the economic prospects of conservancies at the

---

[20] www.nacso.org.na/conservancies#statistics; www.nacso.org.na/conservancies#statistic, Zugriff, 11/4/2017.

beginning of the twenty-first century. But what about the social and political side of the conservancy programme that was so salient in the 1990s? Will new programmes bring about poverty alleviation and true participation of rural communities in their destiny? As yet, future expectations in regard to conservation are awkwardly focused on the commoditisable parts of the social-ecological system: wildlife and landscapes.

The Mining Scenario and the Emergence of Industrial Infrastructure

Mining had some prominence in the Kunene Region throughout the twentieth century, but since about the early 2000s a virtual run on mineral resources has been taking place.[21] In the future, mining may indeed become of major importance for the region. A map published by the Namibian Ministry of Mines and Energy in early 2017 shows the extent of potential mining operations. Large stretches of the Kunene Region are being surveyed and scrutinised for their potential (see Map 11.3).

The Epembe Tantalum Mining Project[22] was launched by the Australian company African Mining Capital (AMC). AMC established a Namibian branch, Kunene Resources Namibia (Pty), in 2011 in order to survey and exploit mineral resources in the northern Kunene Region. Interestingly it did so in partnership with the Namibian Robben Island Veterans Trust Fund. The liaison of an international stock market-listed mining company, with its business centre in Australia, and a trust symbolising Namibia's fight for independence gives the company's engagement a specific sheen of political correctness. The Namibian Robben Island Veterans Trust Fund, however, holds only a 5 per cent share in the project.[23] In 2013, AMC merged Kunene

[21] I did not have the opportunity to conduct interviews with people in the mining sector. Locally very few people have an insight into either the extent or the potential and inherent risks of future mining operations. Hence, the information in the following paragraphs is derived from Internet sources and newspaper clippings. I will briefly sketch two mining projects which may shape the future of the Kaokoveld.
[22] All information taken from: www.africanminingcapital.com/kunene-resources/.
[23] In total 61 Namibians were incarcerated on Robben Island. Since then 21 have died, while 14 are currently serving Namibian society in different capacities – the remaining 26 are said to be in dire need of shelter, food and clothing (*The Namibian*, 12/7/2004). To my knowledge nobody from the Kaokoveld belongs to the Trust.

Into the Future: Environmental Infrastructures 331

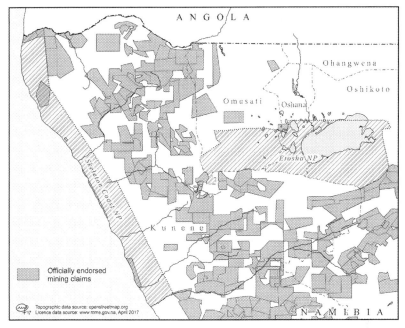

Map 11.3 Mining concessions in north-western Namibia.
Source: www.mme.gov.na (April 2017)

Resources with another company, Bannon Limited. Soon afterwards, Bannon Ltd changed its name to Kunene Resources Limited (KNE) to highlight the focus on the project in the Kaokoveld.[24] Ownership of the prospective mining project changed hands swiftly and the Kunene Region's mineral riches were negotiated on the Australian stock market: On 18 December 2015, KNE was acquired by Department 13, LLC. While this company's home base is West Perth, Australia[25]

---

[24] Financial structures underlying the mining project are confusing. AMC maintains its interest in the Epembe Project through Australian SPV Tandem JV Company Pty Ltd, of which AMC holds a 69 per cent share. The remaining 31 per cent is held by International Base Metals Limited (IBML), another Australia-based mining company which is currently developing the Omitiomire copper mine in Namibia. Tandem JV Company Pty Ltd in turn holds 95 per cent of Epembe Minerals (Pty) Ltd, with the remaining 5 per cent owned by The Namibian Former Robben Island Political Prisoners.
[25] www.bloomberg.com/research/stocks/private/snapshot.asp?privcapId=183287268. Interestingly, the website does not give any further information on the CEO or steering board.

the company's flagship project is the Kaokoveld scheme.[26] Kunene Resources holds seven prospecting licences north of Opuwo in the Kunene Region, totalling some 372,200 ha, and surveys the area according to its multi-commodity exploration licences. According to the company's website, around US$2.5 million was invested in exploration between 2012 and 2014. The Epembe site is apparently the most developed mining activity under the umbrella of KNE and a large deposit of tantalum has been located. The company's website claims there is potential for a multi-decade tantalum mine in a conflict-free zone 'with no barriers to development'.[27]

Another major mining project was reported in the Namibian press in 2012.[28] A giant iron ore deposit (an estimated 2.37 billion tonnes of ore) was found near Orumana, c. 30 km south of Opuwo. The prospecting company Namibia East China Non-Ferrous Investment, a Chinese company based in Namibia, forwarded plans not only for the establishment of a large iron ore mine but also for a major smelter in place. According to the company the mining activity and smelter could potentially create some 10,000 jobs. The company claimed that if mining went ahead at the ambitious rate of 20 million tonnes per year the mine could have a lifespan of some 100 years! Mining would begin, so the director informed the Namibian public, once an industrial town had been developed near Opuwo. The planning included major mining activities and also smelting and refinement of the ore. In February 2013 a delegation from Eastern China Non-Ferrous Metals Investment Holding (ECE) presented its proposal for iron ore mining and industrial park projects in the Kunene Region to Prime Minister Hage Geingob.[29] The Prime Minister welcomed the project but cautioned that the workforce had to come mainly from Namibia. A few months later another Chinese delegation visited the country, trying to negotiate special conditions for their mining project in the Kunene Region.[30] They demanded that the government of Namibia issue work

---

[26] According to its website Department 13 International Ltd acquires, explores, evaluates, and exploits mineral resources in Australia and Namibia.
[27] The latter apparently refers to other tantalum mines in war-torn Congo.
[28] www.observer.com.na/business/177-iron-ore-could-bring-10-000-jobs-to-kunene.
[29] www.trademarksa.org/news/chinese-invest-industrial-park-and-iron-mine.
[30] www.miningreview.com/news/chinese-want-own-labour-for-kunene-iron-ore-project/.

permits for the company's entire workforce for the planned iron ore mine and industrial park. The company also sought a wide range of tax reliefs. Apparently Namibia's Prime Minister Geingob reacted in a somewhat disgruntled way, and complained of a 'barrage of demands from the Chinese'.[31]

I have not found any more recent information regarding the project, and it seems somewhat mysterious how it surfaced sensationally in 2012 and then submerged in 2013.

None of the ambitious mining projects has yet become operational, but one is left with the impression that they could start at any time if world market prices were to make such a move profitable. The development of infrastructure (energy supply, harbours, roads) is highlighted in a number of planning documents: Only appropriate infrastructure will make an industrial future likely. Of major significance is the Oriokawe hydroelectric dam.

The Epupa Dam Debate of the 1990s and the Oriokawe Dam Debate of the 2010s

For more than two decades a dam in the lower reaches of the Kunene River has been negotiated,[32] and for all fictional expectations based upon the development of industries a hydroelectric dam is indispensable.[33] In 1993 plans were launched to have such a large dam built at Epupa. Amid substantial local opposition and staunch international protests the project was discarded in the late 1990s (Meissner 2016: 37–49). The campaigns of a coalition of local Namibian (e.g. Earthlife Namibia, Legal Assistance Centre, Epupa Action Campaign, National Socitiey for Human Rights), southern African (e.g. Environmental Monitoring Group), and international NGOs (Survival International,

---

[31] www.miningreview.com/news/chinese-want-own-labour-for-kunene-iron-ore-project/.
[32] www.nampower.com.na/Page.aspx?p=222.
[33] Meissner (2016: 11–27) shows that plans for a hydroelectric dam on the Kunene in the Epupa Region go far back into colonial times, when South African and Portuguese colonial authorities planned the hydroelectric and irrigation potential of the Kunene River basin. The Gove dam in the upper reaches of the Kunene, and the Ruacana dam at the border between Angola and Namibia, as well as the irrigation works starting off from Calueque dam and providing water to the Namibian Omusati Region (and the former homeland Ovamboland) originate from that planning-cum-construction period in the 1960s.

International Rivers Network, International Work Group for Indigenous Affairs, Society for Threatened Indigenous Communities) had a significant influence on international decision-makers (Meissner 2016: 40–1). Himba leaders oppositional to the dam were invited to tour Europe and to express their reasons for rejecting the dam in Germany, Great Britain, and Sweden. Other local leaders expressed their opposition to the dam at international workshops, for example in Cape Town (World Commission on Dams Hearing 1999), Arusha (Meeting of African Indigenous Communities), and Geneva (World Forum for Indigenous Communities). As a consequence of major protests and campaigns with a truly global reach, the World Bank formally expressed that it would not co-finance the project, and the African Development Bank expressed similar reluctance in the late 1990s.[34]

The Epupa debate had at once catapulted a local environmental issue into global debates. Whether the Namibian and Angolan government had any right to tap into local natural resources in a vast area sparsely populated by an indigenous community was hotly debated in many places of the world: salient reports on the topic were published by the International Rivers Network in San Francisco, by Survival International in London, and by the Society for Threatened Indigenous Communities in Göttingen (Germany), for example. Namibian newspapers reported widely on the trip of the two local chiefs travelling to Europe, an episode also captured in Craig Matthew's prizewinning film *Ochre and Water* (Matthews 2001).

The debate fell silent for five years after the Angolan government had decided that the dam was no longer a development priority in 2000 (Meissner 2016: 52), but was rejuvenated around 2005. By 2002 the Angolan civil war had finally come to an end and the future development of the Kunene basin again became a salient issue for both governments. Now a dam was proposed c. 50 km downstream from Epupa at Oriokawe. Such a dam, it was argued, would not affect the landscape beauty of the Kunene riverine oasis upstream from Epupa, and would not (or would hardly) affect Himba pastoralists making use of the Kunene Valley. Costs of the project were estimated to be US$1.2 billion. The feasibility study came up with very optimistic results and

---

[34] The Namibian government apparently was caught by surprise by the scale of the local resistance. In an awkward manner, local meetings of dam-opposers were hindered, traditional authorities were lured with promises, and the president and ministers accused 'foreigners' of stirring up mistrust within the local population.

proposed the bilateral Water Use Agreement on the Cunene River (dealing with issues such as the establishment of a Bi-National River Authority, the establishment of the Baynes Hydropower Company, and concessionary agreements between Angola and Namibia with the Baynes Hydropower Company for the development, operation, and maintenance of the power station). The dam is intended to produce some 600 MW of electricity, which would be shared by Namibia and Angola.

The proposed dam is a formidable construction: The maximum dam wall height will be 200 metres, and the reservoir will be 43 kilometres long and have a maximum width of 4 kilometres. The area inundated by the reservoir will be 57 km^2 and will possibly hold some 2,700 million m^3 of water, which is about half of the river's annual runoff of 5,000 million m^3. Although the capacity of the Baynes dam is smaller than that of Epupa's foreseen 7,500 million m^3, it has an annual average electricity generation of 1,610 GWh.[35] The construction phase is projected to take seven to ten years, and from its completion the dam would need another five to seven years to fill up: i.e. the dam could be operational by around 2030 at the earliest, and could then become the energy hub for future industrial development.

The dam issue heated up again after 2012 when both governments made a new effort to build a dam on the Kunene. In an effort to influence the local chief in favour of the dam, two Herero-speaking businessmen from central Namibia visited the chief frequently in his homestead. In early 2013 they visited the chief with representatives of a Chinese construction company, which was hoping to be selected for building the dam. They invited the chief and some of his councillors to come to China and to have a look at the manifold positive effects of dam construction there. In the end, the chief did not go to China, but a number of his councillors did. When they returned they found their chief was visiting the farm of one of the Herero-speaking businessmen close to Okahandja. The chief and some of his men stayed there for about three months. People in the Epupa area became severely irritated and rumours abounded. It was said that the chief had finally 'given away Epupa' (i.e. had given permission to build the dam on behalf of

---

[35] Kariba, one of the largest dams in the world, has an installed capacity of 1,200 MW and an annual generation of 6,400 GWh. Ruacana has a capacity of 330 MW.

his people) and was now afraid to return to his home area. When the chief finally returned to his homestead he was guarded by police officers, and people visiting him could only speak to him in the presence of a police officer. The chief claimed that his own people wanted to kill him and that there was an immediate need to protect him from assault. The atmosphere became heated, and a protest march involving several hundred Himba was staged in Epupa on 29 March 2014. A petition was handed over to the Regional Governor saying (amongst other things): 'we wish to make it categorically clear to the Government of the Republic of Namibia that we have at no point agreed and still do not agree to the construction of the Baynes Hydro Electric Dam. We will show our discontent with the planned construction of the dam by way of peaceful demonstration from Omuhandja up to Epupa Camp on Saturday 29th March.'[36] A few weeks later the chief admitted that he had not only agreed to the dam being built, but that he had also shifted his political allegiance from the oppositional DTA party (which is voted for by most Himba) to the ruling SWAPO party. Opposition to the chief now grew, and he was formally demoted and his younger brother enthroned. As the chief was not one of the three officially gazetted chiefs, the government did not intervene or comment, but some months later declared him the chief of Epupa, and hence negotiations could be continued with him.

The Namibian and the Angolan governments continued their efforts to start dam construction on the river, and in early 2016 the Namibian Minister for Mines and Energy 'finally set the wheels in motion for the construction of the power project which is expected to produce about 600 MW to commence as early as June 2017.'[37] Yet by mid-2019, construction had still not begun.

The mining scenario has not yet unleashed any economic activity but a flurry of fictional expectations are presented in the media, and fought over by international audiences as well as in localities in the Kaokoveld. Unlike for example in northern Kenya where the giant LAPSSET

---

[36] R. Sommer, 'Namibia: Semi-nomadic Himba march again in protest against dam construction and government attempt to bribe Himba chief's consent', 29 March 2014, https://intercontinentalcry.org/semi-nomadic-himba-march-protest-dam-attempted-bribery-chiefs/.

[37] P. Hashoongo, 'Baynes Hydropower project commences in 2017', www.primefocusmag.com/articles/969/baynes-hdropower-project-commences-in-2017, Zugriff, 15/9/2017.

corridor project has unleashed a run for land in the vicinity of nodal points of this large infrastructure project (Elliott 2016), or in western Uganda where oil finds ushered in a bonanza of speculation (Kathman and Shannon 2011), no major quest for land is evident. Nevertheless, the mining scenario is an important game changer: If only one of the projects comes about, other scenarios, notably the conservation scenario, are compromised.

The Social Transfer Scenario

While the 'Arid Eden' scenario and the mining scenario rest upon the assumption that value is produced within the region, social transfers are paid to inhabitants of the region without them necessarily contributing directly to the wealth of the nation. James Ferguson (2015) argues that such social transfers progressively contribute to local incomes in rural areas of southern Africa, and in fact in many marginalised regions of the globe.[38] He sees this trend towards social transfers as a significant shift from a production economy to an economy focused on the distribution of wealth. Ferguson (2015: 50–1) starts off from the assumption that people are the rightful owners of the whole country and therefore should receive a share of its wealth. The social transfer scenario has few characteristics of a true scenario: there are no outright plans to expand pension schemes or the like, no milestones established or targets given. Nevertheless, social transfers increasingly contribute to rural incomes, and feed into the creation of a scenario by default.

Significant numbers of households in the Kunene Region receive money from social transfers. Greiner (2008) ascertains that pensions stabilise rural households in agriculturally marginal areas of the southern Kunene Region. Little research on cash transfers has been done in Namibia. This is regrettable as gross figures indicate that incomes from cash transfers do impact rural household economies and are decisive for their vulnerability – perhaps it is not only planners and politicians that are fixed on a productionist paradigm but anthropologists too.

---

[38] Ferguson (2015: 13) speaks of a spread of cash transfers worldwide as a 'quiet revolution', and notes that such programmes are now estimated to reach between 0.75 and 1 billion people.

There are currently four types of non-contributory social cash transfers in Namibia. Old-age pensions, paid to everybody who is 60 and above, irrespective of prior employment status or income, for persons who are resident Namibian citizens or other permanent residents, are the most important kind of cash transfer. Pensions are not means tested and everybody has a right to them. A disability grant is transferred to people 16 years and older who have been diagnosed as being temporarily or permanently disabled. The third kind of social cash transfers are grants for orphans. Everybody below the age of 18 whose mother and father have died is entitled to a monthly grant, which is paid to the person in charge of that orphaned child. For some years also child grants of N$250 per child per month have been paid for all children officially registered.[39]

I would like to address the most pertinent type of cash transfer here in some detail: pensions. Pensions have been paid in Namibia since the 1980s. However, rates were adjusted according to racial and ethnic considerations before 1990. Pensions have substantially increased over the past two decades. While in 1994 some N$135 were paid, in 2008 this figure rose to N$450, in 2015 N$1,000, and in 2017 N$1,200 (about US$72) per month.[40] This is a few hundred Namibian dollars more than the official minimum wage for farm workers (N$888 in 2014).[41] In 2008 it was assumed that 9.7 per cent of the population in Kunene Region received an old-age pension: this would be roughly 5,900 people entitled to N$1,200 per month. A look at demographic figures for the year 2011 (Census of Namibia 2013) suggests that 1,255 people in Epupa (7.1 per cent of the population) and 1,761 in Opuwo constituencies (6.4 per cent) are over the age of 59, and are entitled to an old-age pension. This implies that currently c. N$3.6 million could potentially be paid to citizens of both constituencies per month. It is assumed that more than 90 per cent of those entitled actually receive pensions every month, i.e. it is likely that more than N$3 million are paid per month to c. 3,000 people. In a household

---

[39] In a survey in the Zambezi Region we found that apparently it takes considerable time to get children registered for this grant and often only one or two of a larger number of children were registered.

[40] www.namibian.com.na/159758/archive-read/June-pension-hike-despite-financial-woes.

[41] *The Namibian*, 17/6/2014, 'New minimum wage for farmworkers', www.namibian.com.na/index.php?id=124602&page=archive-read.

survey conducted in 2018 we found that out of 2,788 people enumerated in 235 households 405 people were eligible to some kind of grant. Out of these 144 got old-age pensions and 261 got child benefits. The community surveyed hence got some N$172,800 from old-age pensions and N$65,250 from child benefit payments; together N$238,050 were paid to 235 households resulting in an average payment of more than N$1,000 per household per month.

This is an enormous amount of cash, and certainly pays for major portions of staple foods needed, a fact that Diego Menestrey-Schwieger also observed ethnographically. These incomes are distributed, i.e. they are not centred upon a town but are spread across homesteads. While it is difficult to clearly ascertain exactly how much money pastoral households gain from livestock sales, the figures suggest rather low monetary profits. Social transfers are currently the major way to obtain cash.

There is a likelihood that the amount of money in such cash transfers will increase and that more people are made recipients of social transfer grants. Some years ago options for a basic income grant were discussed in Namibia (Ferguson 2015): basic income grants would endow every citizen (or every adult inhabitant) with a fixed sum of money paid on a monthly basis. The basic income grant scheme was test-run in eastern Namibia for three years, apparently with good results, but did not find political support after that. Nevertheless, the debate on the basic income grant is not dead, and given positive economic development, a further test-run and even a country-wide application is possible.

Ferguson (2015: 168) envisions a future in which poor rural populations in the Global South are given 'a rightful share' of national and possibly global wealth. Rural citizens in Namibia's north would certainly fall into this category. An economy based on (or accommodating) ideas of 'rightful' share would certainly lower local vulnerability; whether it would necessarily lessen the pressure on natural resources, however, is doubtful.

The Livestock Development Scenario

While in the 1950s and 1960s the Kaokoveld's future was seen in the expansion of livestock husbandry, in the early twenty-first century there seems to be little enthusiasm for this mode of production with planners. I treat this fourth economic scenario with caution: there is hardly any concise plan, let alone a vision for livestock husbandry in the twenty-first century in the Kunene Region. Limits for the expansion of pastoral land use are pointed out clearly, and a reduction of livestock numbers is promoted in some quarters. In 2000 a consultancy firm was gazetted to supply a report on the state and the possible future of livestock husbandry in the region. The report (IDC 2000: 27) specified that the stocking rate in the Kunene Region was possibly some 28 per cent above the proposed carrying capacity. As a consequence, the report claims, palatable grasses have been reduced or have disappeared altogether. The report advises that the agricultural potential lies in 'the upgrading and commercialization of the existing livestock population rather than the extension of livestock numbers' (IDC 2000: 40). How this could be done is not clearly specified. One catch-all argument (which has been consistently voiced since the 1960s) is that marketing facilities need to be improved.

Fifteen years later another report summarised and evaluated the effects of a well-funded livestock-focused programme which was run all over northern Namibia. In 2008 the Republic of Namibia and the US government signed a grant-funding agreement, the Millennium Challenge Account Namibia (MCA) Compact, to the value of US$304.5 million (N$3 billion). Projects were launched in the fields of education, agriculture, and tourism between 2009 and 2014.[42] It is remarkable that the major thrust of livestock-focused activities took place in the north-central and north-eastern regions, while in the Kunene Region activities were more oriented towards conservation and tourism.[43] In two fields of livestock husbandry, however, the project sought to have an impact also in the Kunene Region. In order to prepare cattle from the region to enter into commodity chains (inter alia to meet globally accepted meat product requirements) nearly 300,000 ear tags were distributed and c. 150,000 (c. 75 per cent) of the regional cattle herd were tagged[44] and thereby entered the Namibian digital traceability system. Now, each tagged animal was identifiable via barcode readers. The second big activity in the field of

[42] www.mcanamibia.org/files/files/KuneneFactsheetFinal.pdf.
[43] MCA 2014. Evaluation of MCA Namibia's Livestock Support Activity. July 2014.
[44] www.mcanamibia.org/files/files/KuneneFactsheetFinal.pdf; the evaluation report claims that c. N$6 million were paid for this.

livestock husbandry was the designation of grazing areas. In fourteen pilot areas holistic range management was supported through the implementation of new boreholes and the education of grazing guards. As said, all this does not come close to a scenario of fictional expectations, but it does show that livestock husbandry is meant to develop a greater market orientation (higher offtake, improved traceability) and improved sustainability (holistic range management). Steps in this direction, however, are piecemeal, and mainly depend upon external funding.

11.3 Social Scenarios: The Ethnicisation of Environmental Governance or Institutional Co-optation

How will the social organisation of resource governance change in the coming years? What are the fictional expectations for social change? While we have a number of projections and future-making narratives pertaining to the local economy or the ecology, there are few projections for the social system. There are two pertinent trends, though, which I would like to briefly address here. The first trend pertains to a progressive ethnicisation of resource governance. There are forceful demands made by the local population that natural resources should be governed (solely) by the local population and their traditional leaders in future. They envisage the semi-autonomy of ethnicised resource governance and demand exclusive rights of administration and management based on ethnic affiliation. The second scenario pertains to the development of institutions of co-management and public–private partnerships. In Chapter 10 I outlined the founding of a number of new institutions and organisational principles between the state and rural communities in the context of well-financed CBNRM programmes. Democratically constituted committees for wildlife, forests, and water, as well as a land board in which local stakeholders and also government officers are present govern natural resource management. In many ways both social change scenarios are contradictory: while the ethnicisation of resource governance accepts and deliberately seeks encapsulation, the co-management scenario counts on the positive effects of linking local institutions, actors, and practices with national and international frameworks. While the ethnicisation scenario counts on autonomy and identity, the co-management scenario emphasises citizenship, stewardship, and global responsibility.

Ethnicisation of Resource Governance

In 2012 a group of traditional leaders from the northern Kaokoveld complained to the UN that their rights as an indigenous minority were being disregarded by the Namibian government. Amongst a number of points (e.g. forms of school education unfit for pastoral populations) they raised issues directly alluding to resource governance and criticised the government for not consulting them regarding natural resource-related issues. I reproduce a larger portion of their statement verbatim as it elaborates their fictional expectations as semi-autonomous custodians of the land:

Indigenous Himba take fight to the UN, By Richard Lee February 28th, 2012. Osisa. Open Society Initiative for Southern Africa.

Our people and we [i.e. the traditional leaders of the Himba] strongly object to the state's ruthless interference by the Government of Namibia ... We are not consulted, included in any decision-making processes, nor are we heard when we object. We are therefore the marginalized and oppressed tribe in our country Namibia.

Because we are no longer allowed to govern, and are not recognized by the Government of Namibia as the legitimate leaders of our people and land, we see our traditional territory being invaded by the ruling Owambo ethnic group that controls the ruling SWAPO Party. We are currently facing a law that allows any citizen of Namibia to apply and receive 20 hectares of our land (Communal Land Reform Act 5 of 2002). We strongly object this law that is forced upon our throats against our will and consent. This is a land grab! We are losing our land. Our land is being fenced by outsiders.

We, the original people of this Kaokoland are semi nomadic people. We are roaming with our cattle, goat and sheep from place to place. We react to the change of climate in our semi desert environment, and follow the needs of our livestock and move them to grazing areas that are sufficient for them, especially during dry season. The fencing of our land is therefore not only a land right issue, and threatening our way of life, but more so a matter of our very survival. We won't be able to adapt and mitigate the negative effects of climate change when we are no longer able to access and roam freely our land.

We also face other forms of invasion into our territory by large-scale mining companies which will destroy huge areas of our environment without our free, prior and informed consent ... Today, we now also hear that the Government of Namibia wants to build again a dam in our territory, this time at Baynes Mountains, downstream of Epupa area. But as we have done so in the past, we strongly oppose and object to this. Again, the affected communities and traditional leaders have not been consulted, nor have we been included in any steps of the planning and decision-making levels. We will never give our consent to have our river being blocked ... and to have our environment being destroyed and our land being taken away from us.

We would use our graveyards and sacred places in those areas that would be flooded or destroyed through the construction of the dam. The population would become refugees, forced to move away with their animals to other areas that are already inhabited by others from our community. It would cause overpopulation and poverty due to overgrazing in the neighboring areas. Moreover, the beneficiaries of the hydroelectricity will be those who live in the cities and not us. ...

We demand that our Kaokoland to be legally recognized by the state as our territory, that we have traditionally occupied and owned for centuries.

We insist that the government stop the implementation of the Communal Land Reform Act that is resulting in the fencing off of our land and grabbing in Kaokoland.

We demand that Namibia halts its plans to build a dam downstream of Epupa in Baynes Mountains.

We further demand mining companies to be removed from our territory ... or otherwise we must be included in the entire process of giving out the mining permits and too the access on the benefits.

We insist that the government cease and desist from further interference, manipulations and disempowerment of our customary tribal ancestral institutions.

We demand that our traditional governance structure to be fully respected and our traditional authorities of Kaokoland by the government without delay.

What local leaders demand here from the Namibian government is nothing less than semi-autonomy founded upon ethnic institutions and local forms of authority. They first of all seek formal acknowledgement by the Namibian government as an indigenous and autochthonous community. In this text they do not directly link priority rights to such a status. Many interviews in the region, however, make clear that such a first-comer status would directly be connected to land rights and the rights to deny members of other ethnic communities the use of resources within a 'tribal' territory. Traditional authorities reject the Land Reform Act and the practice of land boards that are acting on the basis of this act. The Communal Land Reform Act of 2003 allows for leaseholds (which then may also be fenced) and it urges a formalisation of informal use-rights. While leaseholds have to be applied for with the land board and only need the consent of the chief, informal land rights are notified through the chief. In this way, the government becomes the repository of access rights, whether based on communal tenure or on leaseholds. The rights of administration as well as transfer rights and ownership rights are vested in the state. The cataloguing of informal rights has proceeded substantially in the Omusati, Ohangwena, Otjikoto, and Zambezi Regions. In Kunene Region the cataloguing of land rights has been slow due to local opposition, and only a few leaseholds have been registered. The UN appeal also rejects any form of large-scale infrastructure development in the region: mining companies are to be expelled and the government is asked to desist from implementing the ambitious plans for a large hydropower project.

Indirectly the document outlines a future that is based on pastoralism but which also (apparently) allows for additional incomes from tourism: there is no word in the document which is directed against the upcoming tourism industry. Traditional authorities also demand a school system that is 'culturally appropriate', i.e. which is attuned to the ethnic customs and local language use. If all this were to come about, the local population would be partially autonomous, follow its own regulations of resource governance, and receive a particular indigenised form of education.

A strong emphasis on ethnic identity and autonomy underlines this approach. Especially within the Himba community ethnic identity is progressively cherished. Friedman (2011) has depicted how neo-traditions are produced to equip contemporary leaders with legitimacy. The KovaHimba Association's planned cultural centre is meant to provide ground for such an approach. The association was founded by a French anthropologist, Solenn Bardet, and a number of local people. It strongly cherishes local ethnic identities. In a funding proposal for a cultural centre, the organisation advertises an economic future consisting of 'a combination of herding, tourism and the promotion of ... culture ... which would allow them to diversify their resources and give younger generations access to new types of jobs'. A 'new type of tourism where the Himbas and other minorities would play an active part, offering experiences tailored to the tourists' expectations while providing them with a decent income' is advertised, without offering much detail regarding how such an alternative form of tourism could look.

Ethnicity is progressively performed and regarded as a marketable resource. The future prospects for such anthropo-tourism are unclear.[45] Tourist numbers to the Kaokoveld during the past two decades have increased a lot, and indeed most tourists want to 'meet the Himba', to take a few photographs, or to shoot wildlife. Himba are presented as a quintessential traditional pastoral community, survivals of the 'old Africa'. Anthropologists (Bollig and Heinemann 2002) have outlined the fallacies of presenting the Himba as representatives of another epoch, as people out-of-time. Be that as it may, there is no denying that culture pays. If the Himba were paid a premium for all the photographs of them used in travel adverts, cosmetic adverts, book adverts etc. they would certainly gain substantially.

The vision of a semi-autonomous Kaokoveld which is partially administered by traditional leaders as custodians of indigenous land claims and in which resource ownership is held by the local people is not without precedent. In a court case the Canadian Cree gained far-reaching autonomy from the Canadian government and were granted semi-autonomous status, extensive rights of self-administration, and rights to manage natural resources (Johnson 2010).[46] Similar legal conditions pertain to the Scandinavian Sami, who have gained political

---

[45] Meiu (2017) depicts the commoditisation of ethnic identities in his study of ethno-erotic economies among the Kenyan Samburu. Like the Samburu, Himba actors perform ethnicity and at the same time explore new forms of protest.

[46] Ottawa, 18 July 2017, 'On Indigenous and Northern Affairs Canada': 'The Government of Canada and the Crees of Eeyou Istchee are taking a major step towards reconciliation today with the signing of an important governance agreement. ... The *Agreement on Cree Nation Governance* (Governance Agreement) was signed today by the Honourable Carolyn Bennett, Minister of Indigenous and Northern Affairs, for the Government of Canada, and by Grand Chief Dr. Matthew Coon Come for the Grand Council of the Crees (Eeyou Istchee)/Cree Nation Government. ... This Agreement and its companion, the Cree Constitution, set out a comprehensive regime of Cree self-governance on lands subject to federal jurisdiction under the *James Bay and Northern Québec Agreement* of 1975, the first modern Indigenous land claims agreement and treaty in Canada. ... The Governance Agreement sets out the power of the Cree First Nations to make laws (instead of by-laws) on a wide variety of local governance on Cree Category IA lands under federal jurisdiction, including environmental protection, public order and safety, land and resource use and planning. ... The Agreement maintains the existing land regime on these lands, including access and the grant of rights in lands and buildings. It also defines long-term financial arrangements with Canada.' www.canada.ca/en/indigenous-northern-affairs/news/2017/07/canada_and_the_creesofeeyouistcheesign agreementonc reenationgover.html.

recognition and far-reaching rights of self-governance (Henriksen 2009). Also for the Sami the argument is made that only self-governance and an autonomous handling of natural resources will ensure that the local population can meet the challenges of global climate change (Tyler et. al. 2007). Of course, semi-autonomy based on indigenous claims as granted to the Cree or Sami, and as considered for Australian Aborigines (Arthur 2001) or Brazilian Indians (Dove 2006), for example, has not been experimented with in Africa. Comparatively young national states have shied away from ceding part of their autonomy to indigenous communities within their territories, certainly fearing a domino effect, in that after granting such rights to one community other communities would stand up and request similar rights. The global shift towards recognition of indigenous rights and of semi-autonomous handling of natural resources by such communities, however, contributes to local aspirations in north-western Namibia. The confrontation with external mining companies and a government seeking to implement large-scale infrastructural projects may trigger court cases, which may proceed along exactly the same lines as the Cree and Sami cases. The future of social-ecological relations in north-western Namibia may also rest on the decisions in such court cases.

Co-Management of Resources through Institutions of the 'New Commons'

These processes of ethnicisation of political institutions and decision-making stand in contrast to Namibia's Vision 2030: here the future of resource tenure rests on the co-management of natural resources. Institutionalised co-management between administration and community-based organisations, as well as partnerships between local communities and private businesses, shape future social-ecological dynamics.

The legal reforms of the 1990s pertaining to a variety of natural resources established new institutional forms of commons management. Access rights and management rights over wildlife, water, pastures, and plants were newly defined, and for each of them different management bodies were inaugurated (Bollig 2016). All reforms adhered to blueprints of commons management designed by global organisations: (1) Natural resources have to be valorised in order to prevent overuse or to facilitate sustainable forms of use; those who use a resource must pay for it according to the value ascribed to the resource; (2) communities of resource users as well as resources themselves need to be clearly defined in order to guarantee institutional stability; (3) communities of resource users have to be steered by democratically (and not traditionally) legitimised committees which are capable of co-management with government institutions; (4) such committees need to have management plans and limited monitoring and sanctioning powers to be effective; and (5) the state has to devolve some management and transfer rights to the local level but must maintain its role as a supervisor.

Beyond this common ground in decentralisation efforts and common-pool management theory, each reform had its peculiarities. While wildlife had been the property of the state for nearly a century and had been anxiously guarded by state officials, now specific rights to wildlife and land were transferred to mandated communities, the so-called conservancies. In conjunction with NGOs the government established procedures stipulating how such conservancies had to be organised. While the conservancy was to manage all the wildlife in its territory, only specified wildlife quotas were to be used. With respect to land, the conservancy was permitted to transfer use-rights in the form of land rentals to private investors. Contracting between conservancies and private investors was guarded and monitored by state officials. Water-point associations were introduced compulsorily. Rural people were to take over the responsibility for their own water supply. While the government had managed boreholes and their machinery before and had even been responsible for the supply of diesel in the case of diesel-run engines, now the day-to-day management had to be handled by the communities themselves. User fees or some other financial mechanism had to be introduced to produce the funds to cover the day-to-day running costs of a borehole. Communities are split over the question of whether contributions should be proportionate to use or should be the same for all users. Schnegg et al. (2016) have demonstrated that the flat-rate system applied by many communities strongly favours the rich and contributes to more inequality.

Pasture management and community forest management are still incipient. The latter is closely aligned to the conservancies, and probably all that has been said with regard to the conservancies also pertains to the newly installed community forests. Indeed, their boundaries and management structures are the same. Pasture management along the lines of holistic range management is still at an experimental stage in a very few communities, but certainly has the potential to change grazing patterns in the long run. Foreseeably it will do so, however, only if the government decidedly pushes towards that end. While communities volunteered for conservancy status and were pressured into water-point associations, communities only rarely opted for communal range management if not greatly incentivised, and a number of communities which adopted it for some years dismissed it later when external funding ended.

Namibia's Vision 2030 (Republic of Namibia 2004b: 155–6) outlines an expansion of the conservancy approach. It depicts a scenario in which by 2030 conservancies also co-manage rangelands and forests within their territories in cooperation with administrative staff of various ministries. The governmental vision entails the management of environmental infrastructure by locals working along lines set by the government and organised along parameters of globalised resource governance: elected representatives, accountability of management, locally adapted plans for cost–benefit distribution and, perhaps most salient, a close nexus with the private sector. Financialisation of this vision is originating with national and international capital and where necessary globally operating NGOs and funding organisations.

PART 6

Theorising Time, Space, and Change in a Pastoral System

Within a period of roughly 150 years the environmental infrastructure of north-western Namibia has changed dramatically. Livelihoods and power relations within and between the local community and other political entities before the 1870s were grossly dissimilar from those after the 1910s. The repastoralisation of communities in north-western Namibia under the auspices of the emergent colonial state brought about fundamental changes pertaining to human–environment relations. This transformation was followed by four decades of pastoral specialisation: whereas by the beginning of the twentieth century only some households owned substantial numbers of cattle and foraging strategies were central, by the 1950s almost all households owned livestock; most owned at least some cattle and quite a number owned significant herds of cattle. The 1950s and 1960s saw a fundamental reorganisation of environmental infrastructure: the extensive borehole-drilling programme heralded the expansion of the ancillary infrastructures of the South African state and contributed to the rapid growth of the regional herd. Pastoral intensification and specialisation ruled for a couple of decades (roughly the 1960s to the 1990s). Other plans for a large-scale transformation of environmental infrastructure pertaining to an expansion of conservation areas, to large-scale irrigation, or to massive crossbreeding were not carried out. The recent phase of comprehensive reorganisation of natural resource management again brought about a social-ecological transformation, with conservancies and water-point associations emerging as entirely new social institutions of environmental governance, employment becoming an option, social transfers gaining in significance, and the commodification of wildlife and other natural resources bringing new non-pastoral incomes. The contemporary period of intensive experimentation with new social institutions under the guidance and with the financial backing of international conservation organisations may last for another two to three decades and may give way to large-scale mineral extraction run by international mining consortia, or enter decades in which the effects of global climatic change frame livelihoods more narrowly.

In this concluding chapter I would like to ask what such an in-depth ethnographic study of long-term social-ecological change can contribute to a more general understanding of the transformation and resilience of environmental infrastructure. What did we learn about coupling, environing, and environmental infrastructuring; about social institutions and about environmental governance? What understanding did we gain of the changing relations between local dynamics of pastoralism and the capitalist world system?

12 | *The Changing Environmental Infrastructure of the North-Western Namibian Savannah*

In this concluding chapter I will highlight some results of my case study that are generalisable on a regional scale and beyond. Change is punctuated and is characterised by distinct phases. Environmental infrastructure guarantees a degree of resilience for some time, but then due to internal contradictions or external forces becomes brittle and changeable, and is sometimes destroyed. Such infrastructure is territorialised – from the outside (e.g. by the colonial administration) but also from the inside (e.g. by chiefs, or conservancy committees). Power distribution determines who has the capacity to define the territorial scope of an environmental infrastructure and who can set its boundaries. Increasing complexity and progressive embeddedness in the capitalist world system are salient characteristics of temporal phases and processes of territorialisation. These dynamics result from a co-production by human and non-human agents.

12.1 Temporalising Social-Ecological Change

In stark contrast to images of north-western Namibia as remote and isolated, social-ecological dynamics have been entangled with global commodity markets through goods ranging from ostrich egg shells (nineteenth century), to ivory (since the mid-nineteenth century), to hippo skin (late nineteenth and early twentieth century), to game for trophy-hunting, wilderness landscapes, and ingredients for internationally distributed perfumes (at present). Only the 1920s to 1950s were exceptional in this respect: cattle were forcibly de-commoditised in an effort to encapsulate north-western Namibian livestock husbandry, and humans were almost violently decoupled from wildlife as African hunting became classed as poaching and was heavily punished.[1]

---

[1] Kreike (2010: 159) describes the encapsulation of livestock husbandry in the central Cuvelai plains. The colonial administration in the 1920s and 1930s

Colonisation in its early phase then rather decoupled the local pastoral system from capitalist dynamics and encapsulated the region as a frontier territory. Other changes were brought about by governmental programmes, for example the institution of fixed boundaries in the 1920s, the vaccination programmes of the 1930s, and the borehole-drilling programme of the 1960s and 1970s, or the community-based natural resource management programmes of the 1990s and early 2000s. Every thirty or forty years the social-ecological system has undergone major changes resulting in a grave transformation of environmental infrastructure. These changes have been material, social, political, and cultural. Not all such changes have originated in the activities of humans. In the late nineteenth century Rinderpest swept the region killing nearly all the cattle; contagious bovine pleuropneumonia has devastated cattle herds since the late nineteenth century and has remained a problem up to the present day due to frequent reinfections through unvaccinated Angolan cattle. Foot-and-mouth disease has been a recurrent problem since the 1950s. Of course, it was not only animals that were haunted by diseases: 'imported' venereal diseases like syphilis and gonorrhoea affected the human population by the early twentieth century at the latest, and significantly contributed to low demographic growth rates throughout that century. These epidemics challenged environmental infrastructures but did not lead to major social-ecological transformations.

Were all changes instigated by forces outside the system and beyond the confines of the Kaokoveld's communities? Anthropological accounts of change among East African pastoralists have shown that important drivers of change came from within. Sedentarisation, demographic growth, pasture degradation, privatisation, and the fragmentation of rangelands, as well as changing herding practices and altered herd structures, were linked to demographic growth, to the progressive engagement with markets, and to violent interactions between local communities (Fratkin and Ikeya 2005; Bollig 2006; Galaty 2016; Galvin 2009; Greiner 2012). This has not been the case in north-western

restricted the sale of livestock beyond the confines of the administrative boundaries of Ovamboland. Cattle were factually 'decommoditised', as Kreike puts it, and lost trade value. Also north-eastern Namibia, the former Caprivi and recent Zambezi Region experienced decades of decommodification in the 1920s and 1930s with a suppression of commercialised hunting and trans-boundary cattle trading (Bollig and Vehrs forthcoming).

Namibia: demographic growth was low, exchanges with markets were actively supressed by successive administrations, and violence was carried into the region (in the 1870s to 1890s and in the 1980s) rather than originating within it. What is remarkable though is the adaptive capacity with which the local population reacted to challenges. Only a decade or so after the introduction of boreholes the institutional regime managed a system of grossly altered options for accessing pastures. Only twenty years after the legislation for conservancies was launched most of the Kaokoveld's communities have adopted this institutional framework, and (try to) benefit from it. It is the adaptive response that makes social-ecological dynamics true transformations of environmental infrastructure.

In a contribution on social-ecological change in Eastern Africa (Bollig 2016) I postulated that the adaptive cycle of resilience theory provides new insights into long-term processes of pastoral social-ecological systems. Adaptive cycles are constituted by four distinct phases: exploitation (r), conservation (K), release (Ω), and reorganisation (α). Resilience develops during the r-phase and is fully established (e.g. as a knowledge system, as an institutional framework, or as a sustainable social-ecological formation) during the K-phase. I would like to expand this conceptual consideration here and argue that it is a particular environmental infrastructure that provides stability in this K-phase. During the release phase the system collapses and/or its constituents are reordered and finally reorganised.[2] By applying the adaptive cycle to Pokot pastoralism in northern Kenya, the emergence and decline of resilience within a pastoral setting, as well as pertinent changes relating to this, could be explained. Does the adaptive cycle model also have explanatory power for social-ecological dynamics in north-western Namibia? Was environmental infrastructure built up and lost again? The end of the phase of pastoralism-cum-foraging in the 1870s was extremely violent and abrupt, and certainly environmental infrastructure was lost at that time. However, there was no downturn and no apparent release phase as conceptualised in the adaptive cycle model: the actors of the previous phase were killed and expelled, their means of production stolen, and their institutions destroyed. There was,

---

[2] Adherents of the adaptive cycle concept allege that numerous adaptive cycles run at the same time within a single social-ecological system (Bollig 2014), but from an anthropological perspective it is certainly the cycle of the overall social-ecological system that is of key interest.

however, reorganisation which took place a couple of decades later. A pastoral environmental infrastructure was established under tight colonial control: the institution of boundaries and no-go areas as well as the prohibition against hunting and laying fires had substantial influence on the structure and dynamic interplay between diverse biota. Pastoralists were excluded from making use of large tracts of land in the southern Kaokoveld and along the Kunene River, and ancient migratory routes across the river were blocked, as were trade links with the polities of the north-central Namibian Cuvelai plains. Another significant change was the institution of powerful chiefs in the 1910s and 1920s who controlled access to territories and violently competed with each other. But colonialism also brought about non-controllable, erratic impacts: the two most vicious bovine diseases, Rinderpest and bovine pleuropneumonia, were brought into the region through circumstances framed by colonial regimes, in this case the international transportation of livestock, and later the encapsulation of indigenous livestock economies in the 1920s to 1940s. The strict administration also had stabilising effects: for more than three decades conditions for pastoralists were fairly well established, and power relations, intercommunity relations, and subsistence strategies remained stable by decree and certainly displayed the properties of a K-phase – stability by encapsulation well beyond the capitalist colonial economy.

The massive impact of the colonial administration's modernisation strategies regarding pastoralism since the mid-1950s resulted more from the government's wish to encourage livestock production in African reserves than from an actual crisis of the system. It did not stem from the idea that more livestock needed to be produced to be marketed, and that finally cattle needed to gain commodity status again, but rather from the absurd idea that African Bantustans should become self-sufficient in food production. There were a few inconclusive attempts to link local livestock production to larger markets, but by and large marketing cattle has remained a serious problem up to the present day. The intensification of livestock husbandry met local aspirations though. The possibility of herding larger herds of cattle and spreading over the landscape more widely was well received by local pastoralists, and governmental initiatives were appropriated quickly. There was no collapse or release phase, as predicted in the adaptive cycle: a previous phase simply came to its end due to government decree and due to massive technological and financial input. Local adaptation to the government programme was swift: grazing committees led by elders under the tutelage of a chief, administrative care for boreholes, chiefly wards with rather fixed territorial boundaries, and an incipient native bureaucracy (councillors, a tribal council, etc.) as much as an altered hydrological infrastructure, intensively used pastures and declining wildlife numbers were some characteristics of an environmental infrastructure in which local agents but also state actors progressively inscribed their agency. At the same time local strategies to provide resilience were developed masterfully, and ranged from extensive cattle-loaning networks and patronage, to ancestral rituals to ward off drought and other challenges. My 2006 book on risk management among the pastoral Himba relates to this c. 30- or 40-year-long phase of pastoral stability (Bollig 2006) and is an ethnography of this phase.

In the early 2000s a new phase was ushered in by the comprehensive reorganisation of natural resource management according to global blueprints (and with international funding) of sustainable and allegedly resilient common-pool resource management. Democratically elected committees were now teaming up with traditional authorities to manage the wildlife quotas allocated by the government, and to lease land to tourist businesses. Furthermore, this last move was not instigated by internal forces. It eventually emanated from quests for global environmental governance, sizeable funds generated at the international level to sustain and safeguard properties of north-western Namibia's social-ecological system, and governmental interests in decentralising natural resource management, to include rural populations in management decisions, and to democratise rural resource management.

What about the adaptive cycle, then? In the Namibian context we come across distinct phases of social-ecological development – but certainly not a cycle! Phases of stability and social-ecological resilience border upon phases of rapid change and reorganisation of environmental infrastructure. Such change is often brought about from the outside (e.g. due to violence, technological innovation, social engineering) but is rapidly indigenised. For each phase questions of sustainability, resilience, and risk management have to be answered anew, and local strategies have to be developed to meet these demands. In each phase social-ecological coupling and environing looks different, and environmental infrastructure is specific. Clearly there are also trajectories that connect these phases: for example the kinship system with its typical double descent structure remains astoundingly stable; ancestral beliefs are crucial at all stages; and settlements have a similar layout throughout the period under observation. As a first take-home message, then, I would suggest that environmental infrastructure and the social-ecological system of the Kaokoveld display distinct phases of a multi-decadal scale. Ruptures originate from violence, massive technological change, significant capital inflows, or comprehensive legal changes. Some of these changes may take place without any (initial) cooperation (e.g. the borehole-drilling programme initially met with great resistance), while others depend on cooperation right from the start (e.g. the conservancy programme). Environmental anthropologists have to be aware that their studies are habitually tied to one such phase, and that it is often difficult to see beyond the spatio-temporal borders of this phase. Environmental historians may acknowledge that phases of rapid change alternate with phases of stability. All too often we subscribe to an alleged ever-dynamic character of social-ecological systems and forget to ask what provides resilience. It is environmental infrastructure that provides resilience and entraps further action. It takes political power, capital, and technological advancement to unhinge such infrastructures and to transform them into something else.

12.2 Territorialising Environmental Infrastructures

Environmental infrastructures have a specific temporality but at the same time they are also territorial. They relate to a specific space and tend to have boundaries. From the local perspective the Kaokoveld today is a spatial entity, a pastoral landscape clearly discernible from neighbouring entities – the southern Angolan highlands to the north, the floodplains of north-central Namibia to the east, the inhospitable Namib Desert to the west, and the commercial farmlands to the south. Generally local people, and also planners from Windhoek, are fairly sure what to count as Kaokoveld and what not. They do so on ecological grounds, but also, and mainly, on socio-cultural ones: the Kaokoveld's places are well embedded in a network of place names and place-specific histories, thereby reaching back deeply in history. Successive colonial administrations have entrenched boundaries. These were not the same as the boundaries conventionally presented locally: to the north the Kunene River was defined and guarded as an international boundary since the early 1920s. This artificial boundary cut across the grazing lands of the Himba, for whom the Kunene was never a boundary but rather a pertinent perennial water source running through the midst of their grazing lands. To the east the early South African administration instituted a strictly guarded boundary to separate the Oshiwambo-speaking polities and agro-pastoral economies from Herero-speaking pastoralists, despite the fact that around 1900 the kings of Uukwaludhi and Ongandjera had extended their patronage system far into the Kaokoveld. The newly instituted colonial boundary here cut across older political affiliations and exchange systems.[3] It also divided cattle populations in an effort to control the expansion of viruses and microbes. Boundaries were violently guarded and reified when necessary. Trespassing cattle stood a high chance of being culled. The southern boundary was already instituted during German colonial times. In the 1920s the South African colonial government enforced a no-go zone of considerable breadth to institute the boundary, and in the late 1950s this boundary was marked by a double fence preventing any movement of livestock, wildlife, and people. The newly created boundary became a frontier zone of the South African empire *par excellence* – an area at the 'edge of space and time', as Anna Tsing has termed such areas peripheral to the capitalist world system (Tsing 2003: 5100). Of course, the enforced and violent encapsulation of the frontier did have an effect on social-ecological regulation: seasonal migrations of cattle herds from the Kaokoveld into the north-central Cuvelai floodplains came to an end in the 1920s, and migrations from and to southern Angola became exceedingly rare for fear of severe punishment. Migrations of livestock and wildlife across the infamous Red Line fence were impossible for many decades, and are still very difficult nowadays. Not only was the mobility of humans and their herds restricted, but so was the mobility of wildlife. Over the course of (almost) a century of colonial domination these boundaries became entrenched and they became material facts conditioning social-ecological processes within the delimitations of these boundaries. Transgressions of boundaries were severely punished and all forms of human and non-human mobility across boundaries were inhibited or at least strictly controlled. The boundaries that were

---

[3] The cattle e.g. Vedder found in Kaoko Otavi in 1914 were loaned animals that the king of Uukwaludhi had donated to some Tjimba clients (see Chapter 2).

artificial and merely politically set did not remain artificial but became naturalised over the coming decades, part and parcel of environmental infrastructures and true entrapments, in Ian Hodder's words (see Chapter 1; Hodder 2014). They conserved the frontier status. It was also due to the strictness of boundary regulations that the local, highly adapted Sanga cattle were protected from crossbreeding. High numbers of goats may have kept the bush encroachment problem at bay, an issue that is prevalent on the adjoining commercial farms to the south (Kreike 2013: 150–6).

While there is much greater contact across the Kaokoveld's outer boundaries, pertinent aspects of these boundaries are still maintained: Mobility with livestock, and transactions of livestock across these boundaries, are still barely possible. There are new internal boundaries emerging. The management maps of conservancies with their concisely drawn boundaries and their resource inventories are well represented on the Internet and accessible to anybody owning a smartphone. In virtual space and also increasingly in reality they establish new sub-units and are a first step towards village territories. Progressively environmental infrastructure is 'bound up with the technical, social, and organizational practices of large-scale computer-enabled information infrastructures' (Blok et al. 2016: 7). Livestock mobility across conservancy boundaries is still considerable, but in public discourse conservancy boundaries are increasingly being taken as a yardstick. In contrast to the outer boundaries these internal boundaries are negotiated and stipulated by internal actors who appropriate and indigenise a globally financed and nationally endorsed programme of conservation. This programme they use as a vehicle through which to constitute new boundaries. The new thrust towards conservation and tourism bargained on the earlier frontier narrative. Images of an untrammelled, wild nature are evoked, and landscape elements from previous livelihoods and ecologies are turned into a commodified wilderness (Brooks et al. 2011; Tsing 2003: 5100).

12.3 Coupling, Decoupling, and Recoupling as Processes of Environing and Environmental Infrastructuring

While the concept of adaptation is conventionally used to characterise the strategies of one species to cope with challenges posed by the environment, coupling focuses our attention on the interrelationship

The Changing Environmental Infrastructure

between species – in this case, humans and non-human entities, both living and non-living – on co-constitution, and on mutuality. Kreike's concept of environing stresses the creative aspects of coupling: for him social-ecological change is driven less by constraints than by human creativity, cultural values, and political aspirations. Non-human actors participate in this creative act of environing. Environmental infrastructuring focuses on the praxeological and performative aspects of coupling (Blok et al. 2016).

Environing and environmental infrastructuring are based on knowledge and the exchange of information, and hence are linked to local and supralocal power relations impacting the formation of knowledge. How and at what times pastures can be grazed sustainably (i.e. domesticated herbivores and pastures can be coupled) is a matter of experience and accumulated knowledge gained in situ; the borehole programme of the 1960s and the wildlife quotas of the 2000s were based on knowledge in a context where ideas about hydrology and assumptions about the relation between hydrological infrastructure and development mattered, and also where knowledge about the demographics of wildlife species and assumptions about the growing potential of wildlife for international tourism markets were significant. But is it only humans that accumulate knowledge and experience? Local pastoralists would ascertain that cattle also accumulate knowledge and put it to good use; they know grazing areas well, or else do not know them (in which case they then require more attendance by the shepherd); i.e. the environing of cattle is built upon experience, and they communicate such experience to humans via their behaviour. Elephants for that matter also learn. Vanderwalle and Alexander (2014) describe how elephants, driven by high elephant population densities in northern Botswana's Chobe National Park since the early 2010s, carefully (and systematically) explore areas in south-eastern Angola, gain experience in new territories, and are apparently able to communicate this.

Environmental infrastructures are important institutionalised means to channel coupling and to create powerful path dependencies. Whereas strategies are individual and can change, infrastructures are communal and hegemonic. Infrastructures keep coupling on specific tracks. The borehole-drilling programme is an excellent example in this direction: it is certainly interesting that in the 1950s and 1960s nobody in the administration doubted that boreholes were the solution to a perceived problem of underproduction, and after winning over the traditional authorities of the region the local population also shared in the belief that borehole-drilling and development were closely tied. Once it was established, it was nearly impossible to revise that infrastructure. Since the 1960s all coupling and environing between humans, livestock, and pastures has been entrapped by this very infrastructure. While its exact technologies changed (e.g. from wind-pumps to diesel pumps, and lately to pumps energised by solar power) and the governance of boreholes was overhauled, the environmental infrastructure, constituted to a significant degree by a network of boreholes tapping underground aquifers, remained intact.

In the context of this book, processes of enforced decoupling and recoupling are also significant, as some modes of environing were inhibited and supressed. In the first decades of the twentieth century the colonial administration instituted a strict ban on hunting and thereby enforced a partial decoupling of human population and wildlife (whereas, for example, the coupling between predators and livestock remained). Nowadays, trophy-hunting is allowed again in the context of conservancies. Increasing numbers of wildlife, along with this highly controlled and standardised access to wildlife, shape the recoupling of wildlife and human populations. Wildlife is being commoditised, and contributes (at least in some instances) to local economies. Elephants, who were the key commodity of the region before 1910, have regained that status: a single elephant given to trophy-hunting has a value much higher than the best of cattle. But recoupling comes at a price: human–wildlife cohabitation causes major problems as predators prey on local herds and elephants destroy valuable infrastructure. The environing of diverse species does not always result in harmonious cohabitation, but may also result in competition and degradation. These processes of decoupling and recoupling show coupling as an intensely political process with immediate material consequences. An administration can forcibly insist that a certain manner of environing should not be permitted. There are a good number of examples where not only the colonial administration but also the independent Namibian state instituted decoupling. Hefty fines, imprisonment, and enforced relocation were the means to drive decoupling during colonial days. In the early twenty-first century it is rather contractual ties between government and local community which organise decoupling. The core conservation areas of conservancies are a case in point: guided by blueprints

The Changing Environmental Infrastructure

delivered by development organisations and/or ministries communities decided by themselves which areas they wanted to exclude from day-to-day herding practices. Recoupling is based on a political agenda and a will to allow for and to encourage the coupling of human actors and other parts of the social-ecological system. While the results of these processes are very material, the decision to allow for them (or to discourage and even inhibit them) is first of all political and conditioned by standards of global environmental governance and national law. While political ecologists need to take into account these material processes which are caused by coupling, and also by de- and recoupling, social ecologists must acknowledge that the primary process is a political and not an ecological one.

12.4 Increasing Complexity and Ambivalent Inclusions in Capitalist Markets

During the course of the 150-year period I am considering, the social-ecological system of the Kaokoveld certainly became more complex. Increasing scale dependencies added to the complexity of the social-ecological system: The pastoralists of the early nineteenth century were not influenced in their decisions by external powers, kings in bordering areas, or administrations with a claim to the area. However, these early pastoralists were nevertheless connected to the dynamics of larger capitalist markets, even if indirectly. I pointed out that the migrations of Herero and Himba ancestors may have been the result of slave raiding in the seventeenth and eighteenth centuries in south-western Angola. People were forced to flee from the Kaokoveld by raiders originating from central Namibia preying on local cattle herds in the second half of the nineteenth century – cattle the raiders hoped to sell to livestock traders operating along the trading frontier expanding far inland from the Cape by the 1850s. Livelihoods were affected by the predatory elephant hunts of the Dorsland Trekkers operating from southern Angola around the turn of the nineteenth to the twentieth century. The ivory produced in the Kaokoveld was shipped across the Atlantic from southern Angolan ports. Slave raiders, livestock thieves, and elephant hunters came to the region to appropriate people, animals, and trophies for exchanges with the capitalist system. Decades before the Kaokoveld became part of the German Empire, global value chains embedded in the capitalist world system affected local social-ecological relations. But the first wave of globalisation also brought a loss of complexity: people reverted to hunting and dissolved into smaller mountain-dwelling bands, and many even left the area.

After 1900, inclusion in state administration became more systematic and also oppressive: The German colonial government prohibited the elephant hunts by the Dorsland Trekkers, and the South African administration attempted to inhibit all hunting and trading with livestock. While cutting off the Kaokoveld from many of its external exchange ties and effectively encapsulating and deglobalising the pastoral economy, colonialisation brought about a rupture of capitalist expansion, but added to the complexity of the political and technological situation in the region: Nominated chiefs controlling access to resources, the vaccination system brought in in the 1930s; a humble road network in the 1950s; boreholes, scientists planning future government activities in the 1960s; and, since the 1970s, environmentalists with global connections all added to the complexity of the system. The vaccines were transported from the South African Onderstepoort laboratories close to Pretoria and also from Nairobi veterinary laboratories (van Wolputte 2013); the fittings and machinery for the boreholes were imported from South Africa as well; and since the 1980s, and significantly so since the 1990s, donor money for projects of conservation came from Europe and North America. Environmental infrastructure was becoming more complex and was progressively established by external actors, occasionally working in conjunction with locals but frequently also without them. Colonial interventions were not based on capitalist considerations, let alone neo-liberal ones, but rather on the conviction that a strong state had to invest capital and establish new technologies to further development. The encapsulation paradigm ruled well into the 1970s, and only then very modest changes towards increased marketing of livestock and labour export came about. Only in the 1990s, and then more so in the first decade of the twenty-first century, did international actors, international capital, and international ideas have a significant impact on social-ecological relations in the Kaokoveld. These ideas were firmly based on the belief in capitalist exchanges: Wildlife would not only pay for itself but would also be a commodity of significance to develop the regional economy. A wildlife-based economy may become progressively interlinked with a pastoral economy; but whereas the pastoral economy is still encapsulated due to a number of regulations (particularly the Red Line), the booming wildlife economy is progressively fostered by new models of global financialisation and attracts global capital investing in species diversity and commercial options to explore it (Sullivan 2012). It would be short-sighted, though, to subsume all these developments under the label of neo-liberalism. There are also ideas of local participation and self-governance that underlie the Namibian conservancy programme. Traditional authorities vociferously voice ideas of local autonomy which, as yet, they see as potentially in harmony with conservation. However, if other development trajectories promise higher degrees of autonomy these traditional authorities will not cling to the conservation paradigm but will opt for solutions that best further their ends.

Increasing complexity is one characteristic of social-ecological dynamics in Namibia's north-west, while capitalist penetration is only so at certain times. This brings about a number of implications for research. During the twenty-five years I have been working in north-western Namibia I have experienced a push in complexity and capitalist penetration: in the mid-1990s mobile livestock husbandry was very much self-contained and subsistence-oriented. This was the result of decades of enforced encapsulation. If I were to redo my 1994/96 study today, twenty-five years later, I would still have to deal with mobile, subsistence-oriented livestock husbandry, yes, but additionally I would have to take into account trophy-hunting, incomes from tourism, natural resource harvesting of resins, the increasing relevance of social transfers, the implementation of elected committees according to global blueprints as a new form of resource governance, rapidly increasing connectedness of local actors via cell phones, etc. I would also have to deal with the financialisation of conservation and its impact on local social-ecological conditions.

12.5 Environmental Infrastructures and Multispecies Assemblages in North-Western Namibia in the Anthropocene

Contemporary literature has urged us to think beyond the nature/culture divide which has been so typical of Western European thinking since the Enlightenment (Kreike 2013; LeCain 2016). The sheer frequency of this call to embark on epistemological shifts tells us that this is not an easy task to accomplish. I hope that I have made some humble steps towards these ends and perhaps clarified some of the underlying salient questions, but I am sure that there is still a long way to go.

Anthropologists will stay close to an anthropocentric view of environmental infrastructures. This holds especially true if informants share some of their ideas on the nature/culture divide. North-west Namibia's pastoralists also partially subscribe to this divide; to divide the world in such a way is certainly not solely the prerogative of Westerners. The land of settlements is juxtaposed with bush country or with mountainous landscapes that are rarely used by livestock herds, where no permanent homesteads are located, and at a substantial distance from ancestral graveyards. These lands have been explored in the past by foragers, and in the twenty-first century they have become the core conservation and hunting zones of contemporary conservation efforts. In contrast to the Western fundamental nature/culture divide, however, local pastoralists would allow for mediating actors. Livestock may dwell in the wilderness, sometimes even unattended by shepherds. Mobile livestock camps may explore pastures in these stretches of land and make use of good grazing conditions for a couple of months during the dry season. Anthropologists are rather qualified to map the shifting boundaries of nature/culture divides and to produce ethnographies of interaction between species along these borders. If we include the histories and perhaps also the agency of non-human beings into our ethnographic approach, we do so with the methodological means and options of the social sciences and humanities. If information from the natural sciences is included it is analysed in a way that befits the anthropological narrative. I have attempted to give some insight into the environmental infrastructuring of elephants, with recourse to natural science data. I have also reported on some livestock diseases which followed their own courses. Even if both humans and non-humans are engaged in environing, we can only comprehend them through the anthropological lens.

Just as non-human actors are included in the anthropological narrative, the ethnography of technology has become a significant ingredient of ethnographies of environmental infrastructure. Like domestic livestock, technologically founded material infrastructure bridges the gap between culture and nature. Infrastructures, for example in the form of a vast network of boreholes drilled to a depth of about 60 to 100 metres at enormous costs, were considered at length in this book. They have become part of the landscape of north-western Namibia and have contributed to significant vegetation changes in their vicinity. Current legal reforms establishing specific social institutions to govern aspects of nature objectified as natural resources are a socio-technical way to bring about change. Here, too, anthropologists must widen their lens and include technology in their ethnographies. They have to consider to what extent uniform technological solutions contribute to a homogenisation of the landscape. All boreholes are drilled and built along similar lines, and they condition their surroundings to develop into certain directions (e.g. promoting heavy grazing in their immediate vicinities). These homogenising effects of a uniform hydrological regime are nowadays counteracted by the institution of conservation areas and an increase in wildlife, both contributing to a heterogenisation of the environment.

Climate forecasts tell us that north-western Namibia will be significantly changed by global climatic change in the coming decades, and that by the end of the twenty-first century the Kaokoveld will look very different from today. What is summarised as the Anthropocene seems to be right on the doorstep of the region. In only two or three decades the vicious impact of a drying climate will be felt, and perhaps the major drought which haunted north-western Namibia in 2019 is an apt forecast. This book has shown, however, that the landscape experienced as natural has actually been shaped by humans for a long time, and that environmental infrastructuring by the colonial regime transformed the environment profoundly, at least since the 1950s. A concept of the Anthropocene solely driven by climate considerations does not capture transformations of environmental infrastructure in a fine-grained manner, and it does not do justice to the inhabitants of the area who become victims in a global spectacle. Will there be space for local autonomy and for local environmental infrastructuring? Diverse attempts at future-making in and for the area point in very different directions. The mining scenario leaves little space for environing by locals; but against this scenario stand aspirations of more autonomous environing by culturally distinct people (self-) labelled as indigenous living with herds of livestock and cohabiting with abundant herds of wildlife. The drawn-out fight by the local population against the Epupa hydroelectric project has shown that local herders do not easily succumb to future-making agendas of the state, engineers, and investors, but cling to their own visions of a pastoral future within the Anthropocene.

Bibliography

Abel, H. (1954). Beiträge zur Landeskunde des Kaokoveldes (Südwestafrika). *Deutsche Geographische Blätter* 47, 7–120.
Acheson, J. M. (2006). Institutional failure in resource management. *Annual Review of Anthropology* 35, 117–34.
African Wildlife (1971). Vol. 25.
  (1976). Vol. 30.
Agrawal, A. (2001). Common property institutions and sustainable governance of institutions. *World Development* 29, 1649–72.
Alexander, C. (2001). Legal and binding: time, change and long-term transactions. *Journal of the Royal Anthropological Institute* 7, 467–85.
Alexander, J. (2006). *The Unsettled Land: State-Making and the Politics of Land in Zimbabwe 1893–2003*. Oxford: James Currey.
Allgemeine Zeitung (1981, 11 June).
Almeida, J. de (1936). *Sul de Angola. Relatório de um Govêrno de Distrito (1908–1910)*, 2nd ed. Lisboa: Divisao de Publicacoes e Biblioteca Agência Geral das Colónias.
Alpers, E. (1992). The ivory trade in Africa: a historical overview. In: D. Ross (ed.), *Elephant: The Animal and Its Ivory in African Culture*. Los Angeles: University of California Press, pp. 349–60.
Anderson, D. (2016). The beginning of time? Evidence for catastrophic drought in Baringo in the early nineteenth century. *Journal of East African Studies* 10, 45–66.
Anderson, K. J. (1863). Neuere Reisen nach dem Kunene- und Okavango-Flusse. In: H. Wagner (ed.), *Die neuesten Entdeckungsreisen an der Westküste Afrikas*. Leipzig: Otto Spamer, pp. 269–86.
Anderies, J. M., M. A. Janssen, and E. Ostrom (2004). A framework to analyze the robustness of social-ecological systems from an institutional perspective. *Ecology and Society* 9(1). www.ecologyandsociety.org/vol9/iss1/art18/.
Anonymous (1871). Herero-Land, Land und Leute. *Petermanns Mittheilungen* 24, 306–11.
Appadurai, A. (2013). *The Future as Cultural Fact: Essays on the Global Condition*. London: Verso.

Archer, S. (2003). Technology and ecology in the Karoo: a century of windmills, wire and changing farming practices. In: S. Dovers, R. Edgecombe, and B. Guest (eds.), *South Africa's Environmental History: Cases and Comparisons*. Athens: Ohio University Press, pp. 76–89.

Arends, N. and I. Stopforth (1967). *Trapping Safaris*. Cape Town: Nasionale Opvoedkundige Uitgewery Bpk.

Arthur, W. S. (2001). *Indigenous autonomy in Australia: some concepts, issues and examples*. Centre for Aboriginal Economic Policy. Discussion Paper 220.

Bassett, T. and D. Crummey (2003). *African Savannas: Global Narratives and Local Knowledge of Environmental Change in Africa*. Portsmouth, NH: Heinemann.

Baumann, H. (1975). Die Südwest-Bantu Provinz. In: H. Baumann (ed.), *Die Völker Afrikas und ihre traditionellen Kulturen*. Vol. 1. Wiesbaden: Steiner, pp. 473–512.

Beckert, J. (2013). Capitalism as a system of expectations: toward a sociological microfoundation of political economy. *Politics & Society* 41, 323–50.

Beer, Y. de, W. Kilian, W. Versfeld, and R. J. van Aarde (2006). Elephants and low rainfall alter woody vegetation in Etosha National Park, Namibia. *Journal of Arid Environments* 64, 412–21.

Behnke, R. (1998). *Grazing systems in the northern communal areas of Namibia: a summary of NOLIDEP socio-economic research on range management*. Manuscript. Windhoek.

Beinart, W. (2000). African history and environmental history. *African Affairs* 99, 269–302.

(2002). Environmental origins of the Pondoland Revolt. In: S. Dovers, R. Edgecombe, and B. Guest (eds.), *South Africa's Environmental History*. Athens: Ohio University Press, pp. 76–89.

(2007). Transhumance, animal diseases and environment in the Cape, South Africa. *South African Historical Journal*, 58, 17–41.

Beinart, W. and P. Coates (1995). *Environment and History: The Taming of Nature in the USA and South Africa*. London: Routledge.

Ben-Shahar, R. (1996). Do elephants over-utilize mopane woodlands in northern Botswana? *Journal of Tropical Ecology* 12, 505–15.

Berkes, F. (2006). From community-based resource management to complex systems. *Ecology and Society* 11(1). www.ecologyandsociety.org/vol11/iss1/art45/.

Blaikie, P. (1985). *The Political Economy of Soil Erosion in Developing Countries*. London: Longman.

Bleckmann, L. (2012). *Colonial trajectories and moving memories: performing past and identity in Southern Kaoko (Namibia)*. Dissertation, University of Leuven.

Blok, A., M. Nakazora, and B. Winthereik (2016). Infrastructuring environments. *Science as Culture* 25, 1–22.

Blümel, W. D., K. Hüser, and B. Eitel (2000). Landschaftsveränderungen in der Namib. Klimawandel oder Variabilität? *Geographische Rundschau* 52, 17–23.

Bollig, M. (1997). 'When War Came the Cattle Slept …': *Himba Oral Traditions*. With assistance of Tjakazapi Janson Mbunguha. Köln: Köppe.

— (1998a). Framing Kaokoland. In: W. Hartmann, J. Silvester, and P. Hayes (eds.), *The Colonising Camera: Photographs in the Making of Namibian History*. Cape Town: University of Cape Town Press, pp. 167–70.

— (1998b). Power & trade in precolonial and early colonial northern Kaokoland 1860s–1940s. In: P. Hayes, J. Silvester, M. Wallace, and W. Hartmann (eds.), *Namibia under South African Rule: Mobility & Containment, 1915–46*. Oxford: James Currey, pp. 175–93.

— (1998c). Zur Konstruktion ethnischer Grenzen im Nordwesten Namibias (ca. 1880–1940). Ethnohistorische Dekonstruktion im Spannungsfeld zwischen indigenen Ethnographien und kolonialen Texten. In: H. Behrend and T. Geider (eds.), *Afrikaner schreiben zurück. Texte und Bilder afrikanischer Ethnographen*. Köln: Köppe, pp. 245–74.

— (2004). Hunters, foragers, and singing smiths: the metamorphoses of peripatetic peoples in Africa. In: J. Berland and A. Rao (eds.), *Customary Strangers: New Perspectives on the Peripatetic Peoples in the Middle East, Africa and Asia*. Wesport, CT: Praeger, pp. 195–232.

— (2006). *Risk Management in a Hazardous Environment: A Comparative Study of Two Pastoral Societies*. New York: Springer.

— (2012). Social-ecological change and the changing structure of risk and risk management in a pastoral community in north-western Namibia. In: L. Bloemertz, M. Doevenspeck, E. Macamo, and D. Müller-Mahn (eds.), *Risk and Africa: Multi-disciplinary Empirical Approaches*. Zürich: LIT Verlag, pp. 107–34.

— (2013). Social-ecological change and institutional development in a pastoral community in north-western Namibia. In: M. Bollig, M. Schnegg, and H.-P. Wotzka (eds.), *Pastoralism in Africa: Past, Present and Future*. London: Berghahn Books, pp. 316–40.

— (2014). Resilience: analytical tool, bridging concept or development goal? Anthropological perspectives on the use of a border object. *Zeitschrift für Ethnologie* 139, 253–79.

(2016). Adaptive cycles in the savannah: pastoral specialization and diversification in northern Kenya. *Journal of East African Studies* 10, 21–44.

(2018). Naturschutz und Naturschutzgebiete weltweit: Chancen und Herausforderungen. *Geographische Rundschau* 70(12), 4–9.

Bollig, M., E. Brunotte, and T. Becker (eds.) (2002). *Interdisziplinäre Perspektiven zu Kultur- und Landschaftswandel im ariden und semiariden Nordwest Namibia*. Special Issue of *Kölner Geographische Arbeiten* 77.

Bollig, M. and J. Gewald (2000). People, cattle and land: transformations of a pastoral society – an introduction. In: M. Bollig and J. Gewald (eds.), *People, Cattle and Land: Transformations of a Pastoral Society*. Köln: Köppe, pp. 3–52.

Bollig, M. and H. Heinemann (2002). Nomadic savages, ochre people and heroic herders: visual presentations of the Himba of Namibia's Kaokoland. *Visual Anthropology* 15, 267–312.

(2004). Visual presentations of the people and land of north-western Namibia in German colonial times. In: W. Hartmann (ed.), *Hues between Black and White: Historical Photography from Colonial Namibia 1860s to 1915*. Windhoek: Out of Africa Publishers, pp. 259–78.

Bollig, M. and H. Lang (1999). Demographic growth and resource exploitation in two pastoral communities. *Nomadic Peoples* 3, 16–34.

Bollig, M. and C. Lesorogol (2016). The 'new pastoral commons' of Eastern and Southern Africa. *International Journal of the Commons* 10, 665–87.

Bollig, M. and D. A. Menestrey-Schwieger (2014). Fragmentation, cooperation and power: institutional dynamics in natural resource governance in north-western Namibia. *Human Ecology* 42, 167–81.

Bollig, M. and E. Olwage (2016). The political ecology of hunting in Namibia's Kaokoveld: from Dorsland Trekkers' elephant hunts to trophy-hunting in contemporary conservancies. *Journal of Contemporary African Studies* 34, 61–79.

Bollig, M. and A. Schulte (1999). Environmental change and pastoral perceptions: degradation and indigenous knowledge in two African pastoral communities. *Human Ecology* 27, 493–514.

Bollig, M., M. Schnegg, and H.-P. Wotzka (eds.) (2013). *Pastoralism in Africa: Past, Present and Future*. New York: Berghahn Books.

Bollig, M. and H. Vehrs (forthcoming). The making of a conservation landscape: the emergence of a conservationist environmental infrastructure in the Namibian Kwando Valley.

Bollig, M. and R. Vogelsang (2002). Naturraum und Besiedlungsgeschichte im Nordwesten Namibias. In: M. Bollig, E. Brunotte and T. Becker (eds.), *Interdisziplinäre Perspektiven zu Kultur- und Landschaftswandel im ariden und semiariden Nordwest Namibia. Kölner Geographische Arbeiten* 77, 145–58.

Botha, C. (2005). People and the environment in colonial Namibia. *South African Historical Journal* 52, 170–90.

(2013). The emergence of commercial ranching under state control and the encapsulation of pastoralism in African reserves. In: M. Bollig, M. Schnegg, and H.-P. Wotzka (eds.), *Pastoralism in Africa: Past, Present and Future*. New York: Berghahn Books, pp. 230–56.

Bousman, C. B. (1998). The chronological evidence for the introduction of domestic stock into southern Africa. *African Archaeological Review* 15, 133–50.

Brooks, S., M. Spierenburg, L. van Brakel, A. Kolk, and K. Lukhozi (2011). Creating a commodified wilderness: tourism, private game farming, and 'third nature' landscapes in Kwazulu-Natal. *Tijdschrift voor Economische en Sociale Geografie* 102, 260–74.

Brown, C. (2011). Analysis of human–wildlife conflict in the MCA-supported conservancies for the five-year period of 2006–2010. Namibia Nature Foundation, CDSS, September.

Bryant, R. L. (1998). Power, knowledge and political ecology in the third world: a review. *Progress in Physical Geography* 22, 79–94.

Büscher, B. and W. Dressler (2012). Commodity conservation: the restructuring of community conservation in South Africa and the Philippines. *Geoforum* 43, 367–76.

Butler, J., R. I. Rotberg, and J. Adams (1978). *The Black Homelands of South Africa: The Political and Economic Development of Bophuthatswana and KwaZulu*. Berkeley: University of California Press.

Carruthers, J. (1995). *The Kruger National Park: A Social and Political History*. Pietermaritzburg: University of Natal Press.

(2005). Changing perspectives on wildlife in Southern Africa, c.1840 to c.1914. *Society and Animals* 13(3), 183–200.

Chaiklin, M. (2010). Ivory in world history: early modern trade in context. *History Compass* 8(6), 530–42.

Chakrabarty, D. (2009). The climate of history: four theses. *Critical Inquiry*, 35, 197–222.

Chase, M. and C. Griffin (2008). Seasonal abundance and distribution of elephants in Sioma Ngwezi National Park, southwest Zambia. *Pachyderm*, 45, 88–97.

Ciskei, the Republic of (n.d.). *The Republic of Ciskei*. Johannesburg: C. van Rensburg Publications.

Clarence-Smith, W. G. (1978). Capitalist penetration among the Nyaneka of southern Angola, 1760s to 1920s. *African Studies* 37, 163–76.

(1979). *Slaves, Peasants and Capitalists in Southern Angola 1840–1926*. Cambridge: Cambridge University Press.
Cooke, C. K. 1965. Evidence of human migration from the rockart of Southern Rhodesia. *Africa* 35, 263–85.
Cox, M., G. Arnold, and S. Villamayor-Tomás (2010). A review of design principles for community-based natural resource management. *Ecology and Society* 15. www.ecologyandsociety.org/vol15/iss4/art38/.
Crandall, D. (1992). *The Ovahimba of Namibia: a study of dual descent and values*. PhD Dissertation, University of Oxford.
Crumley, C. L. (ed.) (1994). *Historical Ecology: Cultural Knowledge and Changing Landscapes*. Santa Fe, NM: School of American Research Press.
Dannert, E. (1905). *Zum Rechte der Herero, insbesondere über ihr Familien- und Erbrecht*. Berlin: Reimer.
De Vette, M., R.-M. Kashululu, and P. Hebinck (2012). Conservancies in Namibia: a discourse in action. In: B . Arts, S. van Bommel, M. Ros-Tonen, and G. Verschoor (eds.), *Forest–People Interfaces: Understanding Community Forestry and Biocultural Diversity*. Wageningen: Wageningen Academic Publishers, pp. 121–38.
De Wit, S. (2017). *Love in times of climate change: how an idea of adaptation to climate change travels to Northern Tanzania*. Dissertation, University of Cologne, Institute for Social and Cultural Anthropology.
Dedering, Tilman (1997). *Hate the Old and Follow the New: Khoekhoe and Missionaries in the Early Nineteenth Century*. Stuttgart. Steiner.
Dieckmann, U. (2007). *Hai//om in the Etosha Region: A History of Colonial Settlement, Ethnicity and Nature Conservation*. Basel: Basler Afrika Bibliographien.
(2011). Land, boreholes and fences: the development of commercial livestock farming in the Outjo District, Namibia. In: M. Bollig, M. Schnegg, and H. P. Wotzka (eds.), *Pastoralism in Africa: Past, Present and Futures*. London: Berghahn, pp. 257–88.
Dobler, G. (2008). From Scotch whisky to Chinese sneakers: international commodity flows and trade networks in Oshikango, Namibia. *Africa* 78, 410–32.
(2014). *Traders and Trade in Colonial Ovamboland 1925–1990: Elite Formation and the Politics of Consumption under Indirect Rule and Apartheid*. Basel: Basler Afrika Bibliographien.
Dove, M. (2006). Indigenous people and environmental politics. *Annual Reviews in Anthropology* 35, 191–208.
Du Pisani, André (ed.) (2010). *The Long Aftermath of War: Reconciliation and Transition in Namibia*. Freiburger Beiträge zu Entwicklung und Politik Nr. 37. Freiburg: Arnold-Bergstraesser-Institut.

Du Toit, A., S. R. Moe, and C. Skarpe (2014). Elephant-mediated ecosystem processes in Kalahari-sand woodlands. In: C. Skarpe, J. du Toit, and S. R. Moe (eds.), *Elephants and Savanna Woodland Ecosystems: A Study from Chobe National Park, Botswana*. London: Wiley, pp. 30–40.

Ehret, C. (1998). *An African Classical Age: Eastern and Southern Africa in World History, 1000 B.C. to A.D. 400*. Charlottesville: University Press of Virginia.

Eichhorn, B. and R. Vogelsang (2007). A pristine landscape? Archaeological and archaeobotanical research in the Skeleton Coast Park, northwestern Namibia. In: M. Bollig, O. Bubenzer, R. Vogelsang, and H.-P. Wotzka (eds.), *Aridity, Change and Conflict in Africa: Proceedings of an International ACACIA Conference held at Königswinter, Germany, October 1–3, 2003*. Köln: Heinrich-Barth-Institut (Colloquium africanum, 2), pp. 145–65.

Elliott, H. (2016). Planning, property and plots at the gateway to Kenya's 'new frontier'. *Journal of Eastern African Studies* 10(3), 511–29.

Ellis, S. (1994). Of elephants and men: politics and nature conservation in South Africa. *Journal of Southern African Studies* 20, 53–69.

Elphick, R. (1977). *Kraal and Castle: Khoikhoi and the Founding of White South Africa*. New Haven, CT: Yale University Press.

Emmett, R. and T. Lekan (eds.) (2016). *Whose Anthropocene? Revisiting Dipesh Chakrabarty's 'Four Theses'*. Special Issue of *Transformations in Environment and Society* 2.

Emmett, T. (1999). *Popular Resistance and the Roots of Nationalism in Namibia. 1890–1923*. Oxford: James Currey.

ENOK/FNDC [Eerste nasionale ontwikkelingskorporasie/First National Development Corporation] (1981). *ENOK Bulletin*. Windhoek.

Ensminger, J. (1992). *Making a Market: The Institutional Transformation of an African Society*. Cambridge: Cambridge University Press.

Estermann, C. (1981). *The Ethnography of Southwestern Angola III: The Herero People*. New York: Africana Publishing.

Fairhead, J. and M. Leach (1997). Deforestation in question: dialogue and dissonance in ecological, social and historical knowledge of West Africa; cases from Liberia and Sierra Leone. *Paideuma* 43, 193–225.

Fairhead, J., M. Leach, and I. Scoones (2012). Green grabbing: a new appropriation of nature? *Journal of Peasant Studies* 39, 237–61.

Ferguson, J. (2015). *Give a Man a Fish: Reflections on the New Politics of Distribution*. Durham, NC: Duke University Press.

Fleisch, A. and W. Möhlig (2002). *The Kavango Peoples in the Past: Local Historiographies from Northern Namibia*. Köln: Köppe.

Folke, C. (2006). Resilience: the emergence of a perspective for social–ecological systems analyses. *Global Environmental Change* 16, 253–67.

Fratkin, E. and K. Ikeya (eds.) (2005). *Pastoralists and Their Neighbors in Asia and Africa*. Senri Ethnological Studies no. 69. Osaka: National Museum of Ethnology.

Friedman, J. T. (2011). *Imagining the Post-Apartheid State: An Ethnographic Account of Namibia*. New York: Berghahn Books.

Galaty, J. (2016). Reasserting the commons: pastoral contestations of private and state lands in East Africa. *International Journal of the Commons* 10, 709–27.

Galvin, K. A. (2009). Transitions: pastoralists living with change. *Annual Review of Anthropology* 38, 185–98.

Gewald, J. (1999). *Herero Heroes: A Socio-Political History of the Herero of Namibia, 1890–1923*. Oxford: James Currey.

  (2011). On becoming a chief in the Kaokoveld, colonial Namibia, 1916–25. *Journal of African History* 52, 23–42.

Gil-Romera, G., L. Scott, E. Marais, and G. Brook (2007). Late Holocene environmental change in the northwestern Namib Desert margin: new fossil pollen evidence from hyrax middens. *Palaeogeography, Palaeoclimatology, Palaeoecology* 249, 1–17.

Gordon, R. (2000). The stat(us) of Namibian anthropology. *Cimbebasia* 6, 1–23.

Government of Namibia (1996). Government Notice No. 151: Promulgation of Nature Conservation Amendment Act, 1996 (Act 5 of 1996), of the Parliament.

Government of South Africa (1963). *The Odendaal Commission: The Commission of Enquiry into South West Africa Affairs 1962–63*. Pretoria: Government Printers.

Green, L. G. (1952). *Lords of the Last Frontier: The Story of South West Africa and Its People of All Races*. Cape Town: Howard B. Timmins.

Green, W. and A. Rothstein (1998). Translocation, hybridization, and the endangered Black-Faced Impala. *Conservation Biology* 12, 475–80.

Greenberg, J. B. and T. K. Park (1994). Political ecology. *Journal of Political Ecology* 1, 1–12.

Greiner, C. (2008). *Zwischen Ziegenkraal und Township. Migrationsprozesse in Nordwestnamibia*. Berlin: Reimer Verlag.

  (2012). Unexpected consequences: wildlife conservation and territorial conflict in northern Kenya. *Human Ecology* 40, 415–25.

Hahn, C. H. L., H. Vedder, and L. Fourie (eds.) (1928). *The Native Tribes of South West Africa*. Cape Town: Cape Times.

Håkansson, N. (2004). The human ecology of world systems in East Africa: the impact of the ivory trade. *Human Ecology* 32, 561–91.
Hall-Martin, A., C. Walker, and J. du P. Bothma (1988). *Kaokoveld: The Last Wilderness*. Johannesburg: Southern Book Publishers.
Hartmann, G. (1897). Das Kaoko-Gebiet in Deutsch-Südwest Afrika auf Grund eigener Reisen und Beobachtungen. *Verhandlungen der Gesellschaft für Erdkunde zu Berlin* 24, 113–41.
— (1902/1903). Meine Expedition 1900 ins nördliche Kaokofeld und 1901 durch das Amboland. *Beiträge zur Kolonialpolitik und Kolonialwirtschaft, Berlin* 20, 399–430.
— (1941). Die Bevölkerung des Kaokofeldes. *Deutsche Kolonialzeitung* 53, 29–33.
Hayes, P. (1992). *A history of the Ovambo of Namibia, c.1880–1935*. Dissertation, University of Cambridge.
— (1998). Northern exposures: the photography of C. H. L. Hahn, Native Commissioner of Ovamboland 1915–1946. In: W. Hartmann, J. Silvester, and P. Hayes (eds.), *The Colonising Camera: Photographs in the Making of Namibian History*. Cape Town: University of Cape Town Press, pp. 171–87.
— (2000). Camera Africa: indirect rule and landscape photographs of Kaoko, 1943. In: G. Miescher and D. Henrichsen (eds.), *New Notes on Kaoko: The Northern Kunene Region (Namibia) in Texts and Photographs*. Basel: Basler Afrika Bibliographien, pp. 48–73.
Henrichsen, D. (2000). Ozongombe, Omavita and Ozondjembo: the process of repastoralization amongst Herero in pre-colonial 19th century central Namibia. In: M. Bollig and J.-B. Gewald (eds.), *People, Cattle and Land: Transformations of a Pastoral Society in Southwestern Africa*. Köln: Köppe, pp. 149–86.
— (2011). *Herrschaft und Alltag im vorkolonialen Zentralnamibia. Das Herero- und Damaraland im 19. Jahrhundert*. Basel: Basler Afrika Bibliographien.
Henrichsen, D., G. Miescher, C. Rassool, and L. Rizzo (2015). Rethinking empire in Southern Africa. *Journal of Southern African Studies* 41, 431–5.
Henriksen, J. B. (ed.) (2009). *Sami Self-Determination: Autonomy and Self-Government – Education, Research and Culture*. Kautokeino: Gáldu.
Henshilwood, C. (1996). A revised chronology for pastoralism in southernmost Africa: new evidence of sheep at c. 2000 b.p. from Blombos Cave, South Africa. *Antiquity* 70, 945–9.
Heydinger, J., C. Packer, and J. Tsaneb (2019). Desert-adapted lions on communal land: surveying the costs incurred by, and perspectives of,

communal-area livestock owners in northwest Namibia. *Biological Conservation* 23, 496–504.

Heywood, A., B. Lau, and R. Ohly (eds.) (1992). *Warriors, Leaders, Sages and Outcasts in the Namibian Past: Narratives Collected from Herero Sources for the Michael Scott Oral Records Project 1985–6*. Windhoek: John Meinert.

Hitzeroth, H. W. (1976). On the identity of the stone-working Tjimba, South West Africa: a comparative study based on fingerprint pattern frequencies. *Cimbebasia* 2, 188–201.

Hjort, A. (1979). *Savannah Town: Rural Ties and Urban Opportunities in Northern Kenya*. Stockholm: University of Stockholm.

Hodder, I. (2014). The entanglements of humans and things: a long-term view. *New Literary History* 45, 19–36.

Holmgren, K. and H. Öberg (2006). Climate change in southern and eastern Africa during the past millennium and its implications for societal development. *Environment, Development and Sustainability* 9, 185–95.

Huntley, B. J. (1976). Angola: a situation report. *African WildLife* 30, 10–14.

Huntley, B. J. (2017). *Wildlife at War in Angola: The Rise and Fall of an African Eden*. Pretoria: Protea Book House.

IDC [International Development Consultancy] for the Ministry of Lands, Resettlement and Rehabilitation (2000). *Assessment and Development of Northern Communal Areas in Namibia*. Windhoek. 196 pp.

Igoe, J. and B. Croucher (2007). Conservation, commerce, and communities: the story of community-based wildlife management areas in Tanzania's northern tourist circuit. *Conservation and Society* 5, 534–61.

Illius, A. W. and T. G. O'Connor (1999). On the relevance of nonequilibrium concepts to arid and semiarid grazing systems. *Ecological Applications* 9, 798–813.

Irle, J. (1906). *Die Herero. Ein Beitrag zur Landes-, Volks- & Missionskunde*. Gütersloh: Bertelsmann.

Jackson, P. (1977). *World Wildlife Yearbook 1976–77*. Gland: World Wildlife Fund.

Jacobs, N. J. (2003). *Environment, Power, and Injustice: A South African History*. Cambridge: Cambridge University Press.

Jacobsohn, M. (1990). *Himba. Die Nomaden Namibias*. Hanover: Landbuch-Verlag.

Johnson, S. (2010). Cree autonomy: a re-examination of domestic dependence. *Indigenous Polity Journal* 21, 1–6.

Jones, B. (1999). Policy lessons from the evolution of a community-based approach to wildlife management, Kunene Region, Namibia. *Journal of International Development* 11, 295–304.

Jones, B. and M. W. Murphree (2001). The evolution of policy on community conservation in Namibia and Zimbabwe. In: D. Hulme and M. W. Murphree (eds.), *African Wildlife and Livelihoods: The Promise and Performance of Community Conservation*. Cape Town: David Philip, pp. 38–58.

Jones, B. and L. C. Weaver (2009). CBNRM in Namibia: growth, trends, lessons and constraints. In: H. Suich, B. Child, and A. Spenceley (eds.) *Evolution and Innovation in Wildlife Conservation Areas*. London: Earthscan, pp. 223–43.

Kathman, J. and M. Shannon (2011). Oil extraction and the potential for domestic instability in Uganda. *African Studies Quarterly* 12, 23–45.

Kelbert, T. (2016). *Encounters at the water-point: an ethnography of the travelling model of community-based water management and its application to rural water supply in Namibia*. PhD dissertation, University of Cologne.

Kiaka, R. (2018). *Environmental (in)justice in Namibia: costs and benefits of community-based water and wildlife management*. PhD dissertation, University of Hamburg.

Kinahan, J. (2000). *Cattle for Beads: The Archaeology of Historical Contact and Trade on the Namib Coast*. Uppsala: Uppsala University Press.

Klintenberg, P. and A. Verlinden (2008). Water points and their influence on grazing resources in central northern Namibia. *Land Degradation & Development* 19, 1–20.

Kottak, C. P. (1999). The new ecological anthropology. *American Anthropologist* 101, 23–35.

Kraak, M., R. van Tuinen, and K. Poortman (2013). *Authenticized: Authenticity Comes at a Price* (Film). https://cineblend.nl/programma/view/6/authenticized.

Kreike, E. (2009). De-globalisation and deforestation in colonial Africa: closed markets, the cattle complex, and environmental change in north-central Namibia, 1890–1990. *Journal of Southern African Studies* 35, 81–98.

(2010). *Deforestation and Reforestation in Namibia: The Global Consequences of Local Contradictions*. Leiden: Brill.

(2013). *Environmental Infrastructure in African History: Examining the Myth of Natural Resource Management in Namibia*. Cambridge: Cambridge University Press.

Kuntz, J. (1912a). Die Owatschimba im nördlichen Kaokofeld (Deutsch-Südwestafrika). *Dr. A. Petermanns Mitteilungen aus Justus Perthes' Geographischer Anstalt* 58, 206.

(1912b). Owatschimba-Typen aus dem nördlichen Kaokofeld (Deutsch-Südwestafrika). Nach Aufnahmen von Bergingenieur Julius Kuntz.

Dr. A. Petermanns Mitteilungen aus Justus Perthes' Geographischer Anstalt 58, Tafel 34.

(1912c). Flußtäler an den Rändern des Kaokofeldes (Deutsch-Südwestafrika). Nach Aufnahmen von Bergingenieur Julius Kuntz. Dr. A. Petermanns Mitteilungen aus Justus Perthes' Geographischer Anstalt 58(2), Tafel 32.

(1913). Die geographischen Resultate der Kaokofeld Expedition 1910/12. *Zeitschrift der Gesellschaft für Erdkunde* 6, 439–40.

Lau, B. (1981). 'Thank God the Germans came': Vedder and Namibian historiography. In: K. Gottschalk and C. Saunders (eds.), *Collected Seminar Papers*. Cape Town: University of Cape Town, pp. 24–53.

(1987). *Southern and Central Namibia in Jonker Afrikaner's Time*. Windhoek: National Archives of Namibia (Windhoek archives publication series, 8).

Laws, R. M. (1970). Elephants as agents of habitat and landscape change in East Africa. *OIKOS* 21, 1–15.

Leakey, L. S. B. (1936). *Stone Age Africa: An Outline of Prehistory in Africa*. London: Oxford University Press.

LeCain, T. J. (2016). Heralding a new humanism: the radical implications of Chakrabarty's four theses. In: R. Emmett and T. Lekan (eds.), *Whose Anthropocene? Revisiting Dipesh Chakrabarty's Four Theses. Transformations in Environment and Society* 2, 15–20.

(2017). *The Matter of History: How Things Create the Past*. New York: Cambridge University Press.

Leggett, K. (2006). Home range and seasonal movement of elephants in the Kunene Region, northwestern Namibia. *African Zoology* 41, 17–36.

Leggett, K., J. Fennessey, and S. Schneider (2003). Seasonal distributions and social dynamics of elephants in the Hoanib catchment, north-western Namibia. *African Zoology* 38, 305–16.

Leggett, K., L. Macalister Brown, and R. R. Ramey (2011). Matriarchal associations and reproduction in a remnant subpopulation of desert-dwelling elephants in Namibia, *Pachyderm* 49, 20–32.

Lenggenhager, L. (2018). *Ruling nature, controlling people: nature conservation, development and war in north-eastern Namibia since the 1920s*. PhD Dissertation, University of Zürich.

Leuthold, W. (1996). Recovery of woody vegetation in Tsavo National Park, Kenya, 1970–1994. *African Journal of Ecology* 34, 101–12.

LIFE (2008). *Integrated Community Based Natural Resource Management (CBNRM) for Economic Impact, Local Governance and Environmental Sustainability*. End of Project Report, Windhoek.

LINGS [Local Institutions in Globalized Societies] (2015). www.lings-net.de/.

Linke, T. (2017). *Kooperation unter Unsicherheit: Institutionelle Reformen und kommunale Wassernutzung im Nordwesten Namibias*. Bielefeld: Transcript Verlag.

MacCalman, H. R. and B. J. Grobbelaar (1965). Preliminary report of two stone-working Ovatjimba groups in the northern Kaokoveld of South West Africa. *Cimbebasia* 13, 1–39.

Malan, J. S. (1972). *Dubbele afkomsberekenings van die Himba, 'n hererosprekende volk in die Suidwest Afrika*. PhD Dissertation, University of Johannesburg.

Malan, J. S. and G. L. Owen-Smith (1974). The ethnobotany of Kaokoland. *Cimbebasia Series B* 2, 131–78.

Mathew, C. (2001). *Ochre and Water* (Film). www.unesco.org/archives/multimedia/?pg=33&s=films_details&id=3889.

McCabe, T. (2004). *Cattle Bring Us to Our Enemies: Turkana Ecology, Politics, and Raiding in a Disequilibrium System*. Ann Arbor, MI: University of Michigan Press.

McKittrick, M. (2002). *To Dwell Secure: Generation, Christianity, and Colonialism in Ovamboland, Northern Namibia*. New York. Heinemann.

Meissner, R. (2016). *Hydropolitics, Interest Groups and Governance: The Case of the Proposed Epupa Dam*. New York: Springer.

Meiu, G. P. (2017). *Ethno-Erotic Economies: Sexuality, Money, and Belonging in Kenya*. Chicago: University of Chicago Press.

Menestrey-Schwieger, D. A. (2017). *The Pump Keeps on Running: On the Emergence of Water Management Institutions between State Decentralization and Local Practices in Northern Kunene*. Berlin: Lit Verlag.

Meyer, J. (2007). *Die 'Wilden' und der 'Westen': Die Repräsentation des Fremden in der Dokusoap 'Wie die Wilden – Deutsche im Busch'*. MA thesis, Department of Social and Cultural Anthropology, University of Cologne.

Miescher, G. (2012). *Namibia's Red Line: The History of a Veterinary and Settlement Border*. New York: Palgrave Macmillan.

Miescher, G. and L. Rizzo (2000). Popular pictorial constructions of Kaoko in the 20th Century. In: G. Miescher and D. Henrichsen (eds.), *New Notes on Kaoko: The Northern Kunene Region (Namibia) in Texts and Photographs*. Basel: Basler Afrika Bibliographien, pp. 10–47.

Miller, J. C. (1988). *Way of Death: Merchant Capitalism and the Angolan Slave Trade, 1730–1830*. Madison, WI: University of Wisconsin Press.

Möhlig, W. (2000). The language history of Herero as a source of ethnohistorical interpretations. In: M. Bollig and J. B. Gewald (eds.), *People, Cattle and Land. Transformations of a Pastoral Society in Southwestern Africa*. Köln: Köppe, pp. 119–48.

(2002). Ethnohistorische Erkenntnisse aus sprachhistorischen Quellen im Herero. In: M. Bollig, E. Brunotte, and T. Becker (eds.), *Interdisziplinäre Perspektiven zu Kultur- und Landschaftswandel im ariden und semiariden Nordwest Namibia. Kölner Geographische Arbeiten*, 77, 159–70.

Moilanen, L. (2015). *A sub-basin water resource quantification and aquifer productivity assessment for the Northwest Borehole Scheme near Opuwo, Namibia*. Master's thesis, Michigan Technological University.

Müller-Friedman, F. (2005). 'Just build it modern': post-apartheid spaces on Namibia's urban frontier. In: S. Salm and T. Falola (eds.), *African Urban Spaces in Historical Perspective*. Rochester, NY: University of Rochester Press, pp. 48–70.

NACSO [The Namibian Association of Community Based Natural Resource Management Support Organisations] (2008). *Namibia's Communal Conservancies: A Review of Progress and Challenges in 2007*. Windhoek: NACSO.

NACSO (2012). *Namibia's Communal Conservancies: A Review of Progress and Challenges in 2010*. Windhoek: NACSO.

(2014). *The State of Community Conservation in Namibia: A Review of Communal Conservancies, Community Forests and Other CBNRM initiatives (2013 Annual Report)*. Windhoek: NACSO. www.nacso.org.na/dwnlds/SOC 2013.pdf.

(2017). *The State of Community Conservation in Namibia: A Review of Communal Conservancies, Community Forests and Other CBNRM initiatives (2016 Annual Report)*. Windhoek: NACSO. www.nacso.org.na/sites/default/files/State of Community Conservation book web_0.pdf.

(2018). *The State of Community Conservation in Namibia: A Review of Communal Conservancies, Community Forests and Other CBNRM initiatives (2017 Annual Report)*. Windhoek: NACSO. www.nacso.org.na/sites/default/files/State of Community Conservation book web_0.pdf.

Naidoo, R., L. C. Weaver, R. W. Diggle, G. Matongo, G. Stuart-Hill, and C. Thouless (2016). Complementary benefits of tourism and hunting to communal conservancies in Namibia. *Conservation Biology* 30, 628–38.

Naumann, C. (2014). Stability and transformation in a South African landscape: rural livelihoods, governmental interventions and agro-economic change in Thaba Nchu. *Journal of Southern African Studies* 40, 41–57.

Ohta, I. (2000). Drought and Mureti's grave: the 'we/us' boundaries between Kaokolanders and people of Okakarara in the early 1980s. In: M. Bollig and J. Gewald (eds.), *People, Cattle and Land: Transformations of a Pastoral Society*. Köln: Köppe, pp. 299–317.

Olwage, Elsemi (forthcoming). Cartographies of the everyday: rethinking the role of (im)mobilities in the co-production of public institutions in pastoralist societies, rural north-western Namibia. PhD dissertation, University of Cologne.

Ostrom, E. (1990). *Governing the Commons: The Evolution of Institutions for Collective Action*. Cambridge: Cambridge University Press.

Owen-Smith, G. L. (1972). Proposals for a game reserve in the Western Kaokoveld. *South African Journal of Science* 68, 29–37.

——— (2010). *An Arid Eden: A Personal Account of Conservation in the Kaokoveld*. Johannesburg: Jonathan Ball.

Page, D. (1975). *Evaluasie van die hulpbronne van Kaokoland en ontwikkelingsvoorstelle*. Stellenbosch: Universiteit van Stellenbosch.

Paratus (1982). *Kaokoland*, December issue.

Pauli, J. (2019). *The Decline of Marriage in Namibia: Kinship and Social Class in a Rural Community*. Bielefeld: Transcript Verlag.

Petermann, A. (1857). Die Reisen von Ladislaus Magyar in Südafrika. *Mitteilungen aus Justus Perthes' Geographischer Anstalt* 4, 181–99.

Pomeroy, R. S., B. M. Katon, and I. Harkes (2001). Conditions affecting the success of fisheries co-management: lessons from Asia. *Marine Policy* 25, 197–208.

Pyne, S. (2001). *Fire: A Brief History*. Seattle: University of Washington Press.

Ramey, R. and L. Brown (2014). *Desert Dwelling Elephants in the Hoarusib, Hoanib and Uniab Rivers*. Report prepared for the Ministry of Environment and Tourism. http://desertelephantconservation.org/NewsAndReports.html.

Ramutsindela, M., M. Spierenburg, and H. Wels (2011). *Sponsoring Nature: Environmental Philanthropy for Conservation*. London: Earthscan/Routledge.

Rand Daily Mail (1981a). Politics and war change the way of life in SWA (1981). *Rand Daily Mail*, 4 February.

——— (1981b). AK-47s bring the ways of the West to the Himba (1981). *Rand Daily Mail*, 10 December.

Rawlinson, J. (1994). *The Meat Industry of Namibia, 1835 to 1994*. Windhoek: Gamsberg Macmillan.

Reardon, M. (1986). *The Besieged Desert: War, Drought, Poaching in the Namib Desert*. London: Collins.

Reid, H., L. Sahlén, J. Stage, and J. MacGregor (2007). *The economic impact of climate change in Namibia: how climate change will affect the*

contribution of Namibia's natural resources to its economy. International Institute for Environment and Economy. Discussion Paper 07-02.
Reitz, D. (1943). *No Outspan*. London: Faber & Faber.
Republic of Namibia (1996). *Nature Conservation Amendment Act No. 5, 1996* (Act of 1996). Windhoek.
   (2004a). *Water Resources Management Act No. 24*. Windhoek.
   (2004b). *Namibia Vision 2030. Policy Framework for Long-Term National Development*. Windhoek: Namprint.
   (2009). *Namibia Policy on Human–Wildlife Conflict Management*. Windhoek.
   (2014). *Kunene Region. 2011. Census Regional Profile*. Windhoek.
   (2015). *Namibia Poverty Mapping Report 2015*. Windhoek: UNDP.
Republic of Transkei (1976). *The Republic of Transkei*. Johannesburg: C. van Rensburg Publications.
Rizzo, L. (2007). The elephant shooting: colonial law and indirect rule in Kaoko, Northwestern Namibia, in the 1920s and 1930s. *Journal of African History* 48, 245–66.
   (2012). *Gender and Colonialism: A History of Kaoko in North-Western Namibia, 1870s–1950s*. Basel: Basler Afrika Bibliographien (Basel Namibia Studies Series, 14).
Rohrbacher, P. (2002). *Die Geschichte des Hamiten-Mythos*. Veröffentlichungen der Institute für Afrikanistik und Ägyptologie der Universität Wien; 96 Beiträge zur Afrikanistik; Bd. 71. Wien: Afro-Pub.
Rudner, I. and J. Rudner (1997). *The Journal of Gustaf De Vylder: Naturalist in South-Western Africa, 1873–1875*. Translated from the original Swedish and edited by Ione and Jalmar Rudner. Cape Town: Van Riebeeck Society (Van Riebeeck Society, 2nd ser., no. 28).
SACAU [Southern African Confederation of Agricultural Unions] (2014). *New Minimum Wage for Namibia*. www.sacau.org/new-minimum-wage-for-namibia.
Sander, H., M. Bollig, and A. Schulte (1998). Himba paradise lost: stability, degradation and pastoralist management of the Omuhonga Basin (Namibia). *Die Erde* 129, 301–16.
Sanders, E. (1996). The Hamitic hypothesis: its origin in time. In R. O. Collins (ed.), *Problems in African History: The Precolonial Centuries*. New York: Markus Wiener Publishing, pp. 9–19.
Schnegg, M. and M. Bollig (2013). Introduction: specialisation and diversification among African pastoral societies. In: M. Bollig, M. Schnegg, and H.-P. Wotzka (eds.), *Pastoralism in Africa: Past, Present and Future*. New York: Berghahn Books, pp. 1–28.

(2016). Institutions put to the test: community-based water management in Namibia during a drought. *Journal of Arid Environments* 124, 62–71.

Schnegg, M., M. Bollig, and T. Linke (2016). Moral equality and success of common-pool water governance in Namibia. *Ambio* 45, 581–90.

Schnegg, M. and A. Bolten (2007). Sharing space and food in Namibia. In: O. Bubenzer, A. Bolten, and F. Darius (eds.), *Atlas of Cultural and Environmental Change in Arid Africa*. Cologne. Heinrich Barth Institute, pp. 194–7.

Schnegg, M. and R. D. Kiaka (2018). Subsidized elephants: community-based resource governance and environmental (in)justice in Namibia. *Geoforum* 93, 105–15.

Schnegg, M. and J. Pauli (2008). *Living Together, Writing Together: An Ethnographic Project on Culture and History in Fransfontein*. Windhoek: Klaus Hess Publishers.

Schneider, H. (1994). *Animal Health and Veterinary Medicine in Namibia: A Work of Reference on the Occurrence and Epidemiology of the Most Important Animal Diseases in Namibia during the Past 150 Years*. Windhoek: AGRIVET.

Schoeman, S. J. (1989). Recent research into the production potential of indigenous cattle with special reference to the Sanga. *South African Journal of Animal Sciences* 19, 55–61.

Schroeder, R. (2015). *Moving targets: shifting ethical standards in the safari hunting industry*. Contribution to the Conference on Hunting in Contemporary Africa. Convened by M. Bollig and R. Gordon at the University of Cologne.

Sheuyange, A., G. Obe, and R. Weladji (2005). Effects of anthropogenic fire history on savanna vegetation in north-eastern Namibia. *Journal of Environmental Management* 75, 189–98.

Shi, N., L. M. Dupont; H.-J. Beug, and R. Schneider (1998). Vegetation and climate changes during the last 21 000 years in S.W. Africa based on a marine pollen record. *Vegetation History and Archaeobotany* 7, 127–40.

(2000). Correlation between vegetation in Southwestern Africa and oceanic upwelling in the past 21,000 years. *Quaternary Research* 54, 72–80.

Shortridge, G. C. (1934). *The Mammals of South West Africa: A Biological Account of the Forms Occurring in that Region*. London: William Heinemann.

Siiskonen, H. (1990). *Trade and Socioeconomic Change in Ovamboland, 1850–1906*. Suomen Historiallinen Seura Studia Historica 35. Helsinki: Suomen Historiallinen Seura.

Silva, J. A. and A. W. Mosimane (2012). Conservation-based rural development in Namibia: a mixed-methods assessment of economic benefits. *Journal of Environment and Development* 22, 25–50.

(2014). How could I live here and not be a member? Economic versus social drivers of participation in Namibian conservation programs. *Human Ecology* 42, 183–97.

Silvester, J. (1998). Survival and the creation of pastoral economies in southern Namibia 1915–1935. In: P. Hayes, J. Silvester, M. Wallace, and W. Hartmann (eds.), *Namibia under South African Rule: Mobility & Containment 1915–1946*. Oxford: James Currey, pp. 95–116.

Silvester, J., M. Wallace, and P. Hayes (1998). 'Trees never meet': mobility and containment – an overview 1915–1946. In: P. Hayes, J. Silvester, M. Wallace, and W. Hartmann (eds.), *Namibia under South African Rule: Mobility & Containment 1915–1946*. Oxford: James Currey, pp. 3–48.

Skarpe, C., J. T. du Toit, and S. R. Moe (eds.) (2014). *Elephants and Savanna Woodland Ecosystems: A Study from Chobe National Park, Botswana*. London: Wiley.

Smallie, J. and T. G. O'Connor (2000). Elephant utilization of Colophospermum mopane: possible benefits of hedging. *African Journal of Ecology* 38, 352–9.

Spinage, C. A. (2012). *African Ecology: Benchmarks and Historical Perspectives*. New York: Springer.

Stals, E. L. P. (1988). *Die van der Merwes van Ehomba*. Windhoek: Gamsberg.

Stals, E. L. P. and A. Otto-Reiner (1999). *Oorlog en Vrede aan die Kunene. Die verhaal van Kaptein Vita ('Oorlog') Tom, of Harunga 1863–1937*. Windoek: Capital Press.

Stassen, N. (2010). *William Chapman, Reminiscences. Including: An account of the entry of the Trek Boers into Angola and of their sojourn during the forty-eight years they struggled in that country under Portuguese rule*. Pretoria: Protea Book House.

Steinhardt, J. (1922). *Ehombo*. Neudamm: Neumann.

Steinhart, E. (2001). Elephant hunting in 19th century Kenya: Kamba society and ecology in transformation. *International Journal of African Historical Studies* 33, 335–49.

Stoler, A. (2009). *Along the Archival Grain: Epistemic Anxieties and Colonial Common Sense*. Princeton, NJ: Princeton University Press.

Stow, G. W. (1905). *The Native Races of South Africa*. London: Swan.

Suich, H. (2009). *Livelihood impacts of CBNRM and related activities in IRDNC target areas: a meta-synthesis*. Manuscript. Windhoek: IRDNC.

Sullivan, S. (2012). Banking nature? The spectacular financialization of environmental conservation. *Antipode* 45, 198–217.
Sullivan, S., M. Hannis, A. Impey, C. Low, and R. Rohde (2016). Future pasts? Sustainabilities in west Namibia: a conceptual framework for research. Future Pasts Working Papers No. 1, 1–53.
Sundermeier, T. (1977). *Die Mbanderu. Studien zu ihrer Geschichte und Kultur.* Supplement by Silas Kuvare: The Kaokoveld Herero. Unter Mitarbeit von Silas Kuvare. St. Augustin: Anthropos-Institut. Collectanea Instituti Anthropos, 14.
Szalay, M. (1983). *Ethnologie und Geschichte. Zur Grundlegung einer ethnologischen Geschichtsschreibung. Mit Beispielen aus der Geschichte der Khoi-San in Südafrika.* Berlin: Reimer.
Thuening, M. (2018). *Causes of Expansion of Urban and Peri-Urban Cultivation in Northwest Namibia.* Culture and Environment in Africa Series 13. Cologne: African Studies Centre.
Tinley, K. (1971). Etosha and the Kaokoveld. Supplement to *African Wildlife* 25, 1–16,
Tönsjost, S. (2013). *Umverteilung und Egalität – Kapital und Konsummuster bei Ovaherero-Pastoralisten in Namibia.* Kölner Ethnologische Studien Band 35. Berlin: Lit Verlag.
Trawick, P. (2001). The moral economy of water: equity and antiquity in the Andean commons. *American Anthropologist* 103, 361–79.
Tsing, A. (2003). Natural resources and capitalist frontiers. *Economic and Political Weekly* 38, 5100–6.
Tyler, N. J. C., J. M. Turi, M. A. Sundset, K. Strøm Bull, M. N. Sara, E. Reinert, N. Oskal, N. Nellemann, J. J. McCarthyS. D. Mathiessen, M. L. Martello, O.H. Maggga, G. K. Hovelsrud, I. Hansen-Bauer, N. I. Eira, I. M. G. Eira, and R. W. Corell (2007). Saami reindeer pastoralism under climate change: applying a generalized framework for vulnerability studies to a sub-Arctic social-ecological system. *Global Environmental Change* 17, 191–206.
Van Warmelo, N. J. (1951). *Notes on the Kaokoveld (South West Africa) and Its People.* Pretoria: The Government Printer, Department of Native Affairs (Ethnological Publications, No. 26).
Van Wolputte, S. (2004). Hang on to yourself: of bodies, embodiment and selves. *Annual Review of Anthropology* 33, 251–69.
  (2007). Cattle works: livestock policy, apartheid and development in northwest Namibia, c. 1920–1980. *African Studies* 66, 103–28.
  (2013). Vicious vets and lazy locals: experimentation, politics and CBPP in north-west Namibia, 1925–1980. *Journal of Namibian Studies* 13, 79–100.

Vanderwalle, M. and K. Alexander (2014). Guns, ivory and disease: past influences on the present status of Botswana's elephants and their habitats. In: C. Skarpe, C. J. du Toit, and S. R. Moe (eds.), *Elephants and Savanna Woodland Ecosystems: A Study from Chobe National Park, Botswana*. London: Wiley, pp. 91–103.

Vansina, J. (2004). *How Societies Are Born: Governance in West Central Africa before 1600*. Charlottesville: University of Virginia Press.

Vedder, H. (1914). *Reisebericht des Missionars Vedder an den Bezirksamtmann von Zastrow*. Geographische und Ethnographische Forschungen im Kaokoveld 1900–1914. Namibia National Archives, J XIIIb5.

——— (1928). The Herero. In: C. H. L. Hahn, H. Vedder, and L. Fourie (eds.), *The Native Tribes of South West Africa*. Cape Town: Cape Times Ltd., pp. 153–211.

——— (1934). *Das alte Südwestafrika. Südwestafrikas Geschichte bis zum Tode Mahareros 1890. Nach den besten schriftlichen und mündlichen Quellen erzählt*. Berlin: Warneck.

Verschuren, D., K. R. Briffa, P. Hoelzman, K. Barber, P. Barker, L. Scott, I. Snowball, N. Roberts, and R. W. Battarbee, (2004). Climate variability in Europe and Africa: A Pages–PEP III Time Stream I synthesis. In: R. W. Battarbee, F. Gasse, and C. E. Stickley (eds.), *Past Climate Variability through Europe and Africa*. Dordrecht: Springer, pp. 567–82.

Viehe, G. (1902). Die Omaanda und Otuzo der Ovaherero. *Mittheilungen des Seminars für Orientalische Sprachen zu Berlin. Dritte Abteilung* 1, 109–17.

Vigne, P. (2001). *Cattle Marketing in the Epupa, Ruacana and Onesi Constituencies of Kunene and Omusati Regions. Report on a Pre-Implementation Base-Line Socio-Economic Survey for the Ruacana Quarantine Feedlot Project*. Presented to the Quarantine Enterprise Development Project Steering Committee, Windhoek, June.

Viljoen, P. J. (1988). The ecology of the desert-dwelling elephants *Loxodonta Africana* (Blumenbach 1797) of western Damaraland and Kaokoland. PhD Dissertation, University of Pretoria.

Vogelsang, R. (2002). Migration oder Diffusion? Frühe Viehhaltung im Kaokoland. In: M. Bollig, E. Brunotte, and T. Becker (eds.), *Interdisziplinäre Perspektiven zu Kultur- und Landschaftswandel im ariden und semiariden Nordwest Namibia. Kölner Geographische Arbeiten*, 77, 137–44.

Vogelsang, R. and B. Eichhorn (2011). *Under the Mopane Tree: Holocene Settlement in Northern Namibia*. Cologne: Heinrich Barth Institute.

Vogelsang, R., B. Eichhorn, and J. Richter (2002). Holocene human occupation and vegetation history in northern Namibia. *Die Erde* 133, 113–32.

Von Francois, C. (1899). *Deutsch Südwest-Afrika. Geschichte der Kolonisation bis zum Ausbruch des Krieges mit Witbooi*. Berlin: Reimer (reprint 1993).
Von Koenen, E. and H. von Koenen (1964). *Himba Harvest: S.W.A. Jaarboek 1964*. Windhoek: Scientific Society.
Von Moltke, J. (1943). *Jagkonings. Die Jagavonture van die Dorslandtrekkers*. Pretoria: Protea Boekhuis, 2nd ed. 2003.
Walker, P. A. (2005). Political ecology: where is the ecology? *Progress in Human Geography* 29, 73–82.
Wallace, M. (2011). *A History of Namibia: From the Beginning to 1990*. London: Hurst & Co.
Warnloef, C. (2000). The 'discovery' of the Himba: the politics of ethnographic film-making. *Africa* 70, 175–91.
Watts, M. (1983). *Silent Violence: Food, Famine and Peasantry in Northern Nigeria*. Berkeley, CA: University of California Press.
Weaver, L. C. and T. Petersen (2008). Namibia communal area conservancies. In: R. D. Baldus, G. R. Damm, and K.-U. Wollscheid (eds.), *Best Practices in Sustainable Hunting: A Guide to Best Practices from around the World*. Budakeszi: CIC – International Council for Game and Wildlife Conservation (CIC Technical Series Publication, 1), pp. 48–52.
Weiser, M., A. Kerkhoff, and P. Moriarty (2014). The latitudinal species richness gradient in New World woody angiosperms is consistent with the tropical conservatism hypothesis. *Proceedings of the National Academy of Sciences of the United States of America* 111, 8125–30.
Welle, T. (2007). Adaption strategies on a local scale in the context of global change? In: O. Bubenzer, A. Bolten, and F. Darius (eds.), *Atlas of Cultural and Environmental Change in Arid Africa*. Africa Prehistorica 21. Köln: Heinrich Barth Institut, pp. 110–11.
— (2009). Niederschlagsbestimmung aus METEOSAT-Second Generation-Zeitreihendaten mit dem Methodenverbund ORFEUSS – Fallbeispiel Namibia. Dissertation, Mathematisch-Naturwissenschaftliche Fakultät, University of Bonn.
Werner, W. (1990). 'Playing soldiers': the Truppenspieler movement among the Herero of Namibia, 1915 to ca. 1945. *Journal of Southern African Studies* 16, 476–502.
Wilgen, B. W. van (2009). The evolution of fire management practices in savanna protected areas in South Africa. *South African Journal of Science* 1005, 343–9.
Williams, F.-N. (1991). *Precolonial Communities of Southwestern Africa: A History of Owambo Kingdoms 1600–1920*. Windhoek: National Archives of Namibia.

Wilmsen, E. N. (1989). *Land Filled with Flies: A Political Economy of the Kalahari*. Chicago: University of Chicago Press.

Witz, L. (2015). Hunting for museums. *Journal of Southern African Studies* 41, 671–85.

Ziess, B. (2004). *Weide, Wasser, Wild – Ressourcennutzung und Konfliktmanagement in einer Conservancy im Norden Namibias*. Köln: Institut für Ethnologie (Kölner Ethnologische Beiträge, 15).

Zimmermann, J. (2009). *Population ecology of a dominant perennial grass: recruitment, growth and mortality in semi-arid savanna*. PhD Dissertation, Leipzig UFZ.

Articles and Issues from the Namibian Daily *The Namibian*

The Namibian 21/6/2004 article '"Government moves to eliminate veterinary cordon fence" reports the minister saying that the fence would be removed by 2010'

The Namibian 12/7/2004

The Namibian 14/8/2007 article 'Namibia feels effects of climate change'

The Namibian 26/3/2014 article 'Chinese men charged with rhinohorn smuggling'

The Namibian 19/1/2015 article 'Wildlife staff probed in Kunene rhino poaching'

The Namibian 6/12/2016 article 'Chinese pledged N$ 30.000 to save rhino'

The Namibian 26/4/2019

The Namibian 6/5/2019

Internet Sources

http://archives/un.org/sites/archives.un.org: Summary of AG-038 United Nations Transition Assistance Group (UNTAG) (1989–1990).

http://dry-net.org/initiatives/development-of-sustainable-rangeland-management-practises-in-the-communal-lands-of-namibia/.

https://reliefweb.int/map/world/africa-change-potential-cereal-output-2080.

www.africanminingcapital.com/kunene-resources/.

www.bloomberg.com/research/stocks/private/snapshot.asp?privcapId=183287268.

www.canada.ca/en/indigenous-northernaffairs/news/2017/07/canada_and_the_creesofeeyouistcheesignagreementoncreenationgover.html.

www.desertlion.info/.

www.giz.de/projektdaten/projects.action;jsessionid=9EC46B946DA3031ED92281FCE2402D04?request_locale=en_GB&pn=201397678.

www.irdnc.org.na/history.html.

www.kcs-namibia.com.na/our-vision.html.
www.mcanamibia.org/files/files/KuneneFactsheetFinal.pdf.
www.miningreview.com/news/chinese-want-own-labour-for-kunene-iron-ore-project/.
www.nacso.org.na/conservancies#statistics, Zugriff 11.4.2017.
www.nacso.org.na/index.php.
www.nacso.org.na/resources/state-of-community-conservation.
www.namibian.com.na/155155/archive-read/Tourist-arrivals-minimal-in-2015, *The Namibian* 2/9/2016, online archive.
www.namibian.com.na/159758/archive-read/June-pension-hike-despite-financial-woes.
www.namibian.com.na/index.php?id=6381&page=archive-read. www.oie.int/eng/maladies/Technical%20disease%20cards/CONTAGIOUS%20BOVINE%20: PLEUROPNEUMONIA_FINAL.pdf.
www.namibian.com.na/index.php?id=124602&page=archive-read.
www.nampower.com.na/Page.aspx?p=222.
www.observer.com.na/business/177-iron-ore-could-bring-10-000-jobs-to-kunene.
www.primefocusmag.com/articles/969/baynes-hdropower-project-commences-in-2017, Zugriff 15/9/2017.
www.the-eis.com/data/literature/Production_systems_in_Kunene_North_subregion.pdf.
www.theguardian.com/sustainable-business/2016/jul/13/namibia-drought-coca-cola-meat-construction-industry-water-crisis-climate-change.
www.trademarksa.org/news/chinese-invest-industrial-park-and-iron-mine.

Index

Abel, H., 82–83, 85
ACACIA. *See* Adaptation and Cultural Innovation in Africa
Acheson's lobster fisheries (Maine, US), 314
actor-networks, 8–9
Adaptation and Cultural Innovation in Africa (ACACIA), 12
adaptive cycle, 353–56
affect, colonial administration and, 72–73, 127, 156–57
African Mining Capital (AMC), 330–32
Afrikaner Bulls, importation of, 161–62, 179–80
agency, animal, 7
agricultural policy, 155–56, 161–65, 354–55
agriculture, 182–83
  climate change impacting, 320–22
  contemporary expansion of, 238, 273–76
Almeida, João de, 47–48
AMC. *See* African Mining Capital
Anderies, J. M., 13, 313
Angola, 223–24, 235–36
  civil war in, 198–99, 226, 230
  dam projects and, 333–36
  Humpata, 57–59, 64–65, 96
  poaching in, 225–26
Angola, colonial, 62–63, 93, 158, 197–98. *See also* Portuguese
  CBPP and, 141–42
  elephant hunting and, 56, 62, 64–65, 143–44, 361–62
  Kunene boundary with, 67, 122–24, 126–30, 356–57
  labor migration and, 136–37
  to Namibia, immigration from, 15, 29–30, 46–47, 68, 95–96, 101–2, 163

South Africa and, 106, 122–24, 127–31
  trade with, 127–31, 180–82
Anthropocene, 7–8, 363–65
anthropo-tourism, 344–45
Apartheid
  conservation and, 205, 211–12, 216–18
  development under, 161, 171
  game parks and, 205–6
Arends, Nicholas, 85, 87–88
Arid Eden, 3–5, 318–20, 323–26
assemblages, multi-species, 363–65

Bantu speakers
  as foragers, 23–24
  pastoralism of early, 3–5, 19, 23–24, 26–28, 30–32
Bantustans, 205–6, 231–32
Baumann, H., 29–30
Beinart, William, 9
big-men, 97–98, 101–4, 106
black-faced impala, 223, 226, 296–97, 303
Boer settlement, ivory trade and, 56–57
Bophuthatswana, 203, 206, 216–17
boreholes, 9–10
  cattle, growth of, and, 185
  CBNRM and, 280
  chiefs and, 174–75, 186–87
  communal management of, 12–13, 16–17, 308–9, 312
  conservation and, 214–15
  ecological impact of expanding, 175, 213–15, 228
  expansion of, 161–65, 167–78, 185–87, 193–95, 202, 209, 215, 277–78, 349–52, 359–60
  expansion of, contemporary, 238, 248–49

389

boreholes (cont.)
  expansion of, opposition to, 165–67, 356
  grazing and, 185–88
  as landscape, 364–65
  Marienfluss Valley, 175–76
  pastoral mobility and, 177–85
  separating groups and expansion of, 162, 167–68
  on settlements, impact of, 185–86
Botha, C., 199–200
Botswana, 50–51, 53, 359
boundaries, 356–58
  Angolan, army controlling, 197–98
  cattle and, 122–27
  conservancy, 289–90, 358
  Kunene, 122–24, 126–30, 356–57
  Ovamboland border, 120–21, 126, 140
  trade across, 130–37
Brown, Chris, 297–98
Bruwer, J. P., 171
bush-roads, 178, 184–85

capitalism. *See also* economic expectations
  boundaries in, 357
  complexity, increasing, and, 361–63
  conservancies and, 292–95, 299–302, 314–15, 326–30, 346–48
  environmental infrastructure and, 351–52
  expectations in, 317–19
  neo-liberalism, 279–80, 300, 362–63
  pastoralism and, 339–41, 351–52, 361–62
Carp, Bernhard, 84
  expedition of, 22–23, 82, 84–85, 87–88
  on *strandlopers*, 22–23, 85
cartography, 71
cattle, 6–8, 242, 359. *See also* contagious bovine pleuropneumonia; grazing; livestock; pastures
  Afrikaner Bulls, importation of, 161–62, 179–80
  borders and, 122–27
  boreholes and growth of, 185

breeding, intensified, of, 178–82, 194
contemporary, 248–56, 267–68, 276–78
decapitalisation of, 127
diseases of, mobility restrictions and, 120–21, 127, 138–43
in drought, 1980-82, 160–61, 196, 228, 231–36, 249
in early 20th century Kaokoveld, 98–102, 149–50
foot-and-mouth disease in, 149–50, 168, 351–52
Kreike on, 127, 162, 177–85, 242, 249–50, 351–52
leaders, pastoral, and, 101–4
loose herding of, 267–68
in Ovamboland, 242
ownership of, 252–54
in pre-colonial Kaokoveld, 42–43, 45
relocation and, 116–20
Rinderpest in, 47, 56–57, 68, 98–99, 138, 351–54
Sanga, 249–51, 276–77, 357–58
trade in, 128–29, 180–82, 202
vaccination of, 139–43, 168, 351–52, 362–63
wealth in, distribution of, 252–54, 288
wealth in, increasing, 186–87, 194
cattle population
  contemporary, 254–56
  rising, 193–95, 202, 248–49
CBNRM. *See* community-based natural resource management
CBPP. *See* contagious bovine pleuropneumonia
CBWM. *See* Community-Based Water Management
cell phones, 246
Chapman, William, 63
chiefs
  boreholes and, 174–75, 186–87
  to development, opposition of, 165–73
  under tribal council system, 154–55
Chinese, in Namibia, 245–46, 324–25, 332–33, 335
civil war, Angolan. *See* Angola
civil war, Namibian, 160–61, 241–42
  conservation stalled by, 199, 217–18, 242–43

Index

drought and, 227
Himba and, 229–31
livestock herding during, 242
settlement patterns disrupted by, 241
climate
   drought, 1980-82, and, 228–29
   pastoralism and changes in, 30–31
   in prehistorical north-western Namibia, 21
climate change
   on agriculture, impact of, 320–22
   conservancies and, 329
   drought and, 319–20, 322
   ethnicization and, 342–43, 345–46
   on livestock, impact of, 321–23
   local impact of, 321–23
   maps of, 320–21
   projections of, 317–23, 365
Cogill, Constable, 125–27
colonial reports, 71–73
co-management, 341, 346–48, 355
commodification
   decommodification, 351–52
   of environmental infrastructure, 314–15
commoditization
   of plants, 305–6, 327–28
   of wildlife, 360–61
common pool resource (CPR) management system, 5, 102–4, 346–48, 355
commons, new, 279–80, 314
   co-management, future, and, 346–48
   conservancies as, 292–95, 314–16
   governance of, 285–89
   water as, 314–16, 347–48
Communal Land Reform Acts, 280, 342–44
communal management, of boreholes, 12–13, 16–17, 308–9, 312
community-based natural resource management (CBNRM), 242–43, 279–81
Community-Based Water Management (CBWM), 308
complexity, increasing, 361–63
conservancies, 349–50, 356, 362–63. *See also* wildlife
   boundary making by, 289–90, 358

capitalist market and, 292–95, 299–302, 314–15, 326–30, 346–48
climate change and, 329
in co-management scenario, 346–48
coupling and, 360–61
Ehirovipuka, 291–95, 297–98
environmental governance through, 289–95
Epupa, 291–92, 294
game quotas of, 300–3, 346–48, 359
governance of, 285–89, 309–11
hunting in, 287–88, 292–95, 299–304, 326–29
HWC, increasing, and, 297–98
incomes from, 280–83, 287–89, 298–306, 314–15, 326–29, 346–48
in Kunene Region, expansion of, 281–85, 326–27
livestock in, 289–95
as new commons, 292–95, 314–16
NGOs and, 217–18, 281–84, 287–88, 290–92, 297–98, 301, 303–6, 326–27, 347–48
Okangundumba, 282–84
Ozondundu, 282–84
pastoralism and, 289–95
resource management and, 284
rural elites and, 288–89
tourism and, 280–83, 287–88, 290–95, 299–300, 318, 326–29, 355
wildlife, increase in, and, 295–97
in Zambesi Region, 282–83
zonation of, 290–95
Conservancy Safaris Namibia (CSN), 326–27
conservation, 5
   Apartheid government and, 205, 211–12, 216–18
   boreholes and, 214–15
   CBNRM and, 279–80
   civil war, Namibian, stalling, 199, 217–18, 242–43
   commercial ranching and, 200–2
   de la Bat Commission on, 203–6, 216
   development paradigm and, 202, 205–6, 208–9
   in economic expectations, 326–30

conservation (cont.)
  elephant research and, 218–22
  Eloff report on, 211–16, 218
  environmentalism, global, and, 202–3, 212–14, 216–17, 226–27
  future of, 16–17, 323, 326–30, 337, 365
  homelands and, 201–3, 206, 216–17
  hunting and, 199–204, 213–14, 225–27, 296–97
  IRDNC, 242–43, 282, 284, 303–6, 325–27
  livestock intensification and, 196
  NGOs and, 202, 206, 208, 211–12, 216–19, 225–27, 235–36, 242–43, 279–80, 325–26, 333–34, 349–50
  in 1980s, expansion of, 242–44
  in 1980s, grassroots, 242–43
  opposition to, 199–200, 202
  Owen-Smith report on, 209–14
  planning for, 203, 211–15, 217–18, 349–50
  poaching and, 200, 203–4, 213–14, 225–27
  productionist agenda and, 318–19
  Promulgation of Nature Conservation Amendment Act, 280–81
  re-emergence of, 196–203
  South Africa and, 15–16, 155–56, 205, 211–12, 216–18
  Tinley report on, 206–11
  wildlife, increase in, and, 295–97
contagious bovine pleuropneumonia (CBPP), 9–10
  mobility restrictions and fighting, 120–21, 138–43
  spread, impact of, 137–38, 149–50, 351–54
  vaccination, inoculation campaign against, 139–43
coupling, 13, 358–61
CPR management system. See common pool resource management system
Cree, Canadian, 345–46
CSN. See Conservancy Safaris Namibia

dams, 176–78, 185–86, 335
  Epupa project, 1990s, 333–35
  Oriokawe, 334–35

  plans for, 183, 319, 333–37, 342–44, 365
Dannert, E., 38–41
de la Bat Commission, 203–6, 216
decommodification, 351–52
decoupling. See coupling
demographic parameters, changing, 256–59
development, 15–16, 155
  agricultural policy and, 155–56, 161–65, 354–55
  conservation and, 202, 205–6, 208–9
  dams, 176–78, 183, 185–86, 319, 333–37, 342–44, 365
  ecological impact of, 196, 209, 228
  financialisation of, 167–68
  gardening, intensification of, 178, 182–84, 273–76
  livestock, future of, in, 339–41
  livestock breeding, intensification of, 178–82, 193–96, 202, 209, 354–55
  local opposition to, 165–73
  Odendaal Commission on, 171–74
  roads, 147–49, 178, 184–85, 238, 246
  separating communities and, 162, 167–68
  state-led, 151, 156–57, 193–95, 354–55
  tribal council system in, 153–55
devil's claw, 183–84, 327–28
diary entries, 77–78
Directorate of Rural Water Supply (DRWS), 308–9, 311–13
Dorsland Trekkers, 53, 63, 93, 95
  elephant hunting by, 14–15, 52–55, 57–61, 68, 361–62
  elephant hunting by, discontinued, 68, 143–44, 362–63
  in Humpata, 57–59, 64–65, 96
drought, 104
  climate change and, 319–20, 322
  recent, 289–90, 319–20, 322
  since 2014, wildlife decline from, 295
drought, 1980-82, 203, 227
  aid in, 231–32
  cattle in, 160–61, 196, 228, 231–36, 249
  climatic conditions and, 228–29

Index

migration, mobility, in, 232–35
pastoral decline and, 227–28, 232–36
personal recollections of, 232–35
wildlife decline and, 226–27
DRWS. *See* Directorate of Rural Water Supply
DTA (political party), 244–45, 336
Dublin Accord, 307
The Dying (*Otjita*). *See* drought, 1980-82

East Africa, 30, 282–83, 336–37
  elephant in, 49–50, 63–64
  pastoralists of, 269, 352–53
Eastern China Non-Ferrous Metals Investment Holding, 332–33
Eaton (native commissioner), 166–69
ecological expectations, 317–26
ecological impact
  of boreholes, 175, 213–15, 228
  of development, 196, 209, 228
  of pastoralism, expanding, 213–15, 228
ecology, political, 6, 10–11
  emancipatory orientation of, 11
  structuralist and poststructuralist, 10–11
economic expectations, 317
  conservation in, 326–30
  livestock development, 339–41
  mining, 330–33
  social transfers in, 318–19, 337–39
  Vision 2030, 317–19, 323, 326–29, 346, 348
economic growth, 1950s onward, 153–54
Eedes (native commissioner), 84, 134
Ehirovipuka conservancy, 291–95, 297–98
Eichhorn, B., 22–24, 30–31
elephant, 54–55, 64–65
  agency of, 7
  conservationism and research on, 218–22
  culling proposed for, 144, 199–200
  desert, 82–83, 158, 218–19
  in East Africa, 49–50, 63–64
  environing and, 359–61

on environmental infrastructure, impact of, 49–55, 149–50
  human conflict with, 144, 199–200, 205–6, 297–98, 360–61
  Kaokoveld, uniqueness of, 213–14
  on landscape, impact of, 49–51, 149–50
  migration of, 210–11
  on mopane savannah, impact of, 50–51
  Viljoen on, 51–52, 63, 158, 218–23
elephant hunting, 53, 58, 62, 64–65
  by Africans, local, 59–62
  by Dorsland Trekkers, 14–15, 52–55, 57–61, 68, 143–44, 361–63
  intensive, 3–5, 14–15, 48–50, 52–57
  ivory trade and, 55–62, 64–65, 106–7, 110–11, 143–44, 205–6, 223, 361–62
  Ovambo kingdoms and, 56, 60, 109–10
  poaching, 143–44, 158, 218–19, 221–25
  quotas for, 302–3
  social-ecological relations and, 63–64
  stratification and, 64–65
elephant population, 53
  contemporary, 295–96, 323–25
  decline in, 218–19, 221–23, 225, 260
  after hunting, 62–63
  before hunting, 52–54
  1960s and 1970s, 218, 221–22
  1980s, 222, 295–96
Eloff, Fritz, 212–14, 216, 218
Eloff report, 211–16, 218, 221
encapsulation
  of Kaokoveld, 106, 110–15, 132–33, 151, 351–54, 356–58
  of livestock, 351–54
Endangered Wildlife Trust, 199, 218–19, 225, 242–43
entanglement, 8–9
entrapment, 8–9
environing, 8–9, 150, 359, 363–64
  cattle and, 359
  coupling in, 13, 358–61
  elephant and, 359–61
environmental degradation, 163–64
environmental history, 6, 9–10

environmental infrastructure, 8–9, 349–56
  in Anthropocene, 363–65
  capitalism and, 351–52
  commodification of, 314–15
  contemporary, 276–78, 349–50
  coupling in, 358–61
  early 20th century, 104–5, 149–50, 349–50
  elephant impacting, 49–55, 149–50
  foragers, early pastoralists, and, 43–44
  future of, 317–19
  gardening, expansion of, changing, 276
  under German colonialism, 67–68
  pastoralism and, 6–7, 43–44, 104–5
  prehistory of north-western Namibian, 19–20
  social-ecological system and, 13
  territorialization of, 351, 356–58
  transformation of, 1950s to 1980s, 15–16, 178, 193–95, 349–50
environmentalism, global, 202–3, 212–14, 216–17, 226–27
Epembe Tantalum Mining Project, 330–32
Epupa, dam projects for, 333–36, 365
Epupa conservancy, 291–92, 294
Epupa constituency, Namibia, 256–58, 302–3
Estermann, C., 29
ethnicization, 17, 341–46
Etosha Park (Game Park No. 2), 200, 220–21, 235, 281–82, 297
  establishment of, 106–10
  game parks, proposed, linked to, 205–10, 214–15
  opposition to, 166–67, 169, 172
exchange networks, livestock-based, 189–91, 194–95

famine, 129–30, 132–33, 203, 231–32
Ferguson, James, 151, 319, 337, 339
fieldwork, north-western Namibia, 11–13
fires, anthropogenic, 144–47, 149–50, 189, 194
foot-and-mouth disease, 149–50, 168, 351–52

foragers, 22–24, 31–32, 45–46, 158–59
  coastal, 22–23
  environmental infrastructure and, 43–44
  pastoralism and, 14, 31–41, 353–54
  resource utilization of, 40–41
  on social-ecological system, impact of, 24
Franke, Victor, 72–75, 86–87, 93–95, 108
Friedman, J. T., 344
frontier zone, Kaokoveld as, 357–58

Game Park No. 2. *See* Etosha Park
game parks, 211–12, 217–18, 228
  Angolan, 225–26
  for Bantustans, 205–6
  in Eloff report, 213–15
  in Owen-Smith report, 209–10
  proposed, Etosha Park linked to, 205–10, 214–15
  under South Africa, 80–81, 144, 155–56, 161, 205–7, 217
  in Tinley report, 206–9
gardening, 178, 182–84, 273–76
Gärtner (trader), 130–31
gender
  in conservancy governance, 286, 316
  matrilineal and patrilineal kinship, 103–4, 189–93, 252, 266
  wealth and, 253–54
genocide, Herero, 79, 87, 94–95, 115–16
German colonialism, 3–5, 15, 67, 93
  boundaries under, 356–58
  environmental infrastructure under, 67–68
  genocide under, 79, 87, 94–95, 115–16
  hunting policed under, 56–57, 65, 67–68, 143, 362–63
  maps under, 73–76
  migration under, 95–96
  mobility under, 115, 356–58
  photographs under, 78–79
  population growth under, 68, 93–98
  raiding ending under, 45, 67–68
  repastoralization under, 65, 68, 149–50
  reports collected under, 71–73, 82, 86

Index

South African conflict with, 68
wildlife protection under, 106–10
Gewald, J., 96
goat, 149–50, 251, 357–58
  environmental infrastructure and, 276–78
  population of, 254–56, 276–77
grasses
  grazing pressure on, 104–5, 147, 149–50, 188–89, 194, 209, 249–50, 278
  restoring, 325–26
  veld fires and, 144–47, 149–50, 189, 194
graveyards, ancestral, 7–8
grazing, 34, 150
  boreholes and, 185–88
  on conservancies, 289–90
  on grasses, pressure of, 104–5, 147, 149–50, 188–89, 194, 209, 249–50, 278
  Herero, contemporary, and, 263–69
  Himba, contemporary, and, 262–63, 266–70
  PGH strategy for, 325–26
groeipunte (rural growth points), 183, 194
Groll map, 74–76

HACCSIS. *See* Human-Animal Conflict Conservancy Self-Insurance Scheme
Hahn, Carl, 82, 86, 127, 156–57
  CBPP under, 138–39, 141–42
  famine under, 129–30
  game parks and, 80–81, 144, 207
  local informants used by, 88–91
  mobility restricted under, 112, 121, 125–28
  photographs by, 76–77, 79–80, 157
  relocation under, 116–19
  trade under, 129–31
Hakansson, N., 49–50, 56, 63–64
Hall-Martin, A., 223
Hartley, Willem, 91, 166, 168, 172
Hartmann, Georg
  expeditions of, 40, 72–76, 78, 86–87
  on Kaokoveld population, early 20th century, 41, 93–94
Hayes, P., 76–78, 80–81

Henrichsen, D., 31, 45–46
Herero, 3–4, 31, 38–39, 167–68, 356–57
  big-men among, 97
  conservancies and, 288, 290
  development and separating, 162, 167–68
  drought, 1980-82, and, 203, 227, 231–32, 235–36, 249
  early colonialism and, 63–65
  foraging by, 45–46
  gardening among contemporary, 275–76
  genocide of, 79, 87, 94–95, 115–16
  grazing and contemporary, 263–69
  Kaokoland homeland administered by, 241, 244
  land rights among, 266–67, 270–71
  livestock and, 179–81, 235–36, 242, 249, 252–53, 263–65, 267–68, 288
  livestock inheritance among, 189–90
  migration of, 26–28, 95–97
  parties supported by, 244–45
  pastoralism, emerging, and, 26–32
  pastoralism of contemporary, 252–53
  pastures and contemporary, 266–73
  population growth of, contemporary, 258
  population of, 19th century, 41–42
  Portuguese and, 46–47, 95–96, 158
  raiding and, 44, 361–62
  relocation of, 119–20
  settlement patterns of contemporary, 263–65
  under South African rule, 112–13
  stratification, accumulation among, 63
  SWAPO and, 244–45
  trade and, 128, 132
  van der Merwes, Stals on, 158
  Vedder on, 26–28, 79–80
Herero Authority, 155–57
Himba, 167, 242
  Angolan, Kunene boundary and, 122–24
  army, police recruiting, 229–30
  cattle among contemporary, 249–52, 267
  civil war, Namibian, and, 229–31
  conservancies and, 288, 290

Himba (cont.)
  dams, plans for, and, 334, 336, 342–44
  development and separating, 162, 167–68
  drought, 1980-82, and, 203, 227–28, 235–36
  early colonialism and, 63–65
  Epupa dam opposed by, 333–34
  ethnicization and, 342–46
  gardening among contemporary, 252–76
  grazing and contemporary, 262–63, 266–70
  land rights among, 266–67
  livestock and, 242, 249–52, 267, 288
  livestock inheritance among, 189–91
  livestock loaning among, 191–93
  mercenaries of, 47–48
  on mining, 343–44, 346
  parties supported by, 244–45, 336
  pastoralism of, 11–13, 215, 249–53, 259–63, 266–67, 355
  pasture access among contemporary, 266–73
  plants, commoditizing, and, 305
  population growth of, 256–60
  Portuguese colonial economy and, 46–47, 62, 127
  raiding and, 45–46, 361–62
  resource management demands of, 342–46
  spatial organization of contemporary, 259–63, 265
  stratification, accumulation among, 63
  surveys of, 12–13
  SWAPO and, 244–45, 336, 342
  tourism and, 344–45
  trade of, 62
hippo, 58–59, 63, 351–52
Hitzeroth, H. W., 158–59
HIV/AIDS, 256–58
Holistic Range Management Programme, 325–26, 347–48
homeland, Kaokoland, 241, 244–45
homelands, South African, 201–3, 206, 216–17. *See also* Bantustans
homesteads, 97–98, 102
Human-Animal Conflict Conservancy Self-Insurance Scheme (HACCSIS), 297–98
human-wildlife conflicts (HWC), 297–98, 324–25
Humpata, Angola, 57–59, 64–65, 96
hunting, 143–44, 351–52, 360–61. *See also* poaching
  black-faced impala, 223, 226, 303
  in conservancies, 287–88, 292–95, 299–304, 326–29
  conservation and, 199–204, 213–14, 225–27, 296–97
  de la Bat Commission on, 205–6
  Eloff report on, 213–14
  under German colonialism, policing, 56–57, 65, 67–68, 143, 362–63
  hippo, 58–59, 63, 351–52
  jackal, 199–200, 303
  persistence of, 143–44
  rhino, 59, 63, 223, 225–26, 324–25
  under South Africa, policing of, 143–44, 362–63
  wildlife, conservation and, 200–2
  wildlife, legal, 224–25
hunting, elephant. *See* elephant
HWC. *See* human-wildlife conflicts
hydrological revolution, Kaokoveld, 5, 161–63, 178, 193–95, 359

independence, Namibian, 5, 16–17, 196–99, 235–36
  infrastructure after, 245–48
  in Kaokoveld, changes following, 245–48
  new government elected after, 244–45
  Opuwo growing after, 245–47, 259, 265–66
  population growth after, 237–38
  Red Line after, 16–17, 246
  resource management after, 12–13, 237–38, 279–80, 351–52, 355
  settlement patterns after, 241
  social-ecological changes of, 238
informants, local, 86–91
infrastructure, Namibian
  contemporary, 237–38, 245–48
  under German colonialism, 67–68
  in Opuwo, 238, 245–47
  roads, 147–49, 178, 184–85, 238, 246
infrastructuring environments, 9

inheritance, livestock, 189–92, 194–95
Integrated Rural Development and
    Nature Conservation (IRDNC),
    242–43
  conservancies and, 282, 284, 303–5,
    326–27
  Holistic Range Management
    Programme of, 325–26
  plants, commoditizing, and, 305–6
International Rivers Network,
    333–34
IRDNC. *See* Integrated Rural
    Development and Nature
    Conservation
Irle, J., 41–42, 45
irrigated farming, 183, 194
IUCN, 202, 218–19, 225
ivory. *See* elephant

jackal hunting, 199–200, 303
Jacobsohn, Margie, 229–30, 243
Jooste (native commissioner), 224–25

Kaiserreich, German, 3–5
Kakurukouye (Kasupi), 86–87, 94–96,
    110–11
Kambazembi, 41–42, 45
Kaokoland homeland. *See* homeland,
    Kaokoland
Kaokoveld. *See specific topics*
Kaputu, Alexander, 38–39
Karakul industry, 130–31
Kasupi. *See* Kakurukouye
Khoisan-speaking foragers, 22–23,
    31–32
Kiaka; R., 326–27
Klintenberg, P., 104–5
KNE. *See* Kunene Resources Limited
Kottak, Conrad P., 11
KovaHimba Association, 344
K-phase, 353–54
Kreike, E., 43–44
  on cattle, 127, 162, 177–85, 242,
    249–50, 351–52
  on environing, 8–9, 359
  on goat, 276–77
Kunene boundary, 67, 126, 356–57
  cattle and, 122–24
  trade across, 127–30
Kunene Region. *See specific topics*

Kunene Resources Limited (KNE),
    330–32
Kuntz, J., 54–55, 72–73, 75–76, 78–79,
    86–87, 93–95
Kwena. *See* Nama
Kwena Wars, 160–61

labor migration, 136–37
labor recruitment, 135–37, 163
land
  Communal Land Reform Acts, 280,
    342–44
  rights of, 266–68, 270–71
  use of, 98–105, 249–56, 339–40
landscape
  boreholes as, 364–65
  elephant impacting, 49–51,
    149–50
LAPC. *See* Long-term Agricultural
    Policy Commission
Latour, Bruno, 8–9
LeCain, T. J., 34
LINGS project, 261–62, 309–10,
    312–13
lion, 36, 303, 323–25
livestock, 6–7, 349–50
  agency of, 7
  breeding, intensified, of, 178–82,
    193–96, 202, 209, 354–55
  capitalism and, 339–41, 351–52
  in civil war, Namibian, 242
  climate change impacting, 321–23
  collapse of, 1980s, 248–49
  in conservancies, 289–95
  economy of, contemporary, 248–49,
    339–41
  encapsulation of, 351–54
  environmental consequences of, 196,
    209
  exchange networks of, expanded,
    189–91, 194–95
  gardening, expansion of, and, 276
  goat, 149–50, 251, 254–56, 276–78,
    357–58
  Herero and, 179–81, 189–90,
    235–36, 242, 249, 252–53,
    263–65, 267–68, 288
  Himba and, 189–93, 242, 249–52,
    267, 288
  inheritance of, 189–92, 194–95

livestock (cont.)
    loaning of, 189, 191–95, 252–53, 288, 357
    mortality of contemporary, 269–71
    population of, contemporary, 254–56
    recovery of, 248–49
    sale of, 180–82
    small-stock herds, contemporary, 253–56
    water management, communal, and, 313–14
local sources, 159–61
Longhorn cattle, 34
Long-term Agricultural Policy Commission (LAPC), 155–56

Malan, Johan, 158
Manning, C. N., 41
    disarmament by, 110–11, 115
    informants used by, 86, 88–91
    maps under, 76–77
    Ovamboland border under, 120–21
    on pastoralism, Kaokoveld, 97–98
    veld fires and, 145–47
maps, 71, 91–92
    climate change, 320–21
    under German administration, 73–76
    Groll map, 74–76
    under South African administration, 76–77
    Sprigade map, 75–76
Marienfluss Valley, 175–76
market. *See* capitalism
matrilineal kinship, 103–4, 189–93, 252, 266
Matthew, Craig, 239, 334
Mayuni conservancy, 283, 297
MCA. *See* Millennium Challenge Account Namibia Compact
Menestrey-Schwieger, Diego, 241, 339
mercenaries
    Himba, 47–48
    under Portuguese, 47, 59–60, 63–65, 101–2, 227
MET. *See* Ministry of Environment and Tourism, Namibian
migration
    in drought, 1980-82, 233–35
    Herero, 26–28, 95–97
    into Kunene Region, pastoralism and, 14, 26–28
    labor, 136–37
    Portuguese and, 15, 29–30, 95–96, 136–37
migration, wildlife, 209–10, 357–58
Millennium Challenge Account (MCA) Namibia Compact, 340
mining
    future of, 17, 317–19, 330–33, 336–37, 349–50, 365
    Himba on, 343–44, 346
Ministry of Environment and Tourism, Namibian (MET), 280–81, 284, 297–98, 301, 303–4
mobility. *See also* migration; relocation
    boreholes and, 177–85
    cattle diseases and, 120–21, 127, 138–43
    changes in, vegetation and, 188–89
    in drought, 1980-82, 232–33
    under German colonialism, 115, 356–58
    labor migration, 136–37
    in pastoralism, emergence of, 31–33
    under South Africa, restriction of, 68–69, 112–13, 115–28, 130–37, 150, 180–81, 356–58
modernization. *See* development
Möhlig, W., 28
mopane savannah, 19–21, 50–51
Mosimane, A. W., 282–83
Muhona Katiti, 77, 97–98, 125
    reserve of, 111–12
    road construction under, 147–48
    Vita Thom and, 96–97, 101–2, 110–11, 160–61
Muinimuhoro, 167, 170, 185–86
multi-species assemblages, 363–65
Muniombara, Katjira, 45–46
Mureti, 38–39, 41–42
Mutate, Thomas, 132
Muzuma, Kephas, 169, 172

Nama, 68. *See also* Kwena Wars
Namibia National Archives, 156–57, 238–39
Namibia Poverty Mapping Report, 248
Namibia Wildlife Trust, 199

Namibian Former Robben Island Political Prisoners Trust, 330–32
NamWater, 265–66
neo-liberalism, 279–80, 300, 362–63
new materialism, 6–9
Ngombe, Ndiri, 36–38
NGOs
  archival material of, 238–39
  commons, management of, and, 279
  conservancies and, 217–18, 281–84, 287–88, 290–92, 297–98, 301, 303–6, 326–27, 347–48
  conservation and, 202, 206, 208, 211–12, 216–19, 225–27, 235–36, 242–43, 279–80, 325–26, 349–50
  Epupa dam opposed by, 333–34
  local social-ecological dynamics and, 237–38
  mining and, 330–32
  1980s, 242–44
  Owen-Smith starting, 242–43
  plants, commoditizing, and, 305–6
  water management, community, and, 308–9
NPF (political party), 244–45

Ochre and Water (documentary), 239, 334
Odendaal Commission, 155, 161, 167–68, 171–74
  conservation and, 199–200, 204, 209, 228
  on population, 256
  Report of, 173–74
Okangundumba conservancy, 282–84
omumbiri, 305
omuni wehi (owner of the land), 266–67
Omusati Region, 288–89, 333
Ongandjera, 15, 356–57
ontwikkeling (development). *See* development
Oorlam, 44–45, 96
Oorlog. *See* Vita Thom
Opuwo, 4–9, 115
  cell phones in, 246
  gardening around, 275–76
  after independence, growth of, 245–47, 259, 265–66
  infrastructure in, 238, 245–47
  peri-urban area of, 238, 247
  water in, 265–66
Opuwo constituency
  demographics of, 256–58
  wildlife quotas in, 302–3
oral traditions, 102–3, 160–61
Oriokawe dam project, 334–35
Orma, Kenyan, 269
Oruuano Church, 153–54
ostrich egg shells, trade in, 61, 351–52
Ostrom, Elinor, 279–80, 307, 313
Otjita (The Dying). *See* drought, 1980-82
Otto-Reiner, A., 96, 102
Ovambo kingdoms, 60–62
  elephant hunting and, 56, 60, 109–10
  Ongandjera, 15, 356–57
  Uukwaludhi, 15, 60, 94, 120–21, 356–57
Ovamboland, 61, 198–99, 235
  Angola trade with, 180–81
  border of, 120–21, 126, 140
  cattle in, 242
overstocking, 163–64
Owen-Smith, Garth, 155, 158, 181, 188–89, 229–30
  conservation NGO of, 242–43
  on elephant, 218–19
  poaching and, 222–24
  report of, 209–14
owner of the land (*omuni wehi*), 266–67
Ozondundu conservancy, 282–84

Page, D., 183
pastoralism
  adaptive cycle and, 353–56
  big-men in early 20th century, 101–4, 106
  capitalism and, 339–41, 351–52, 361–62
  climatic changes and, 30–31
  conservancies and, 289–95
  contemporary, 16–17, 215, 238, 246–56, 259–63, 266–67, 276–78, 355
  contemporary, economy of, 248–49
  drought, 1980-82, and decline of, 227–28, 232–36

pastoralism (cont.)
  East African, 269, 352–53
  ecological impact of expanding, 213–15, 228
  elephant hunting and, 64–65
  environmental infrastructure and, 6–7, 43–44, 104–5
  foragers and, 31–41, 353–54
  Herero, 28–32, 252–53
  Himba, 11–13, 215, 249–53, 259–63, 266–67, 355
  homesteads in, 97–98, 102
  land use of, early 20th century, 98–105
  Opuwo and, 247
  pre-colonial, violence and, 44–48
  re-establishment of, early 20th century, 93–105
  relocation of, 116–20
  repastoralization, 64–65, 68, 73, 101–2, 149–50, 349–50
  under South African encapsulation, 113–14
  transhumant, 99–105, 267–68
  in 20th century, increasing, 3–5, 15–16
  wealth in, increasing, 186–87, 194
pastoralism, early, 361–62
  Bantu, 3–5, 19, 23–24, 26–28, 30–32
  environmental infrastructure and, 43–44
  settlements of, 31–39
  violence and, 44–48
pastoralism, emergence of, 3–5, 19–20, 23–26, 38–43
  foragers and, 14, 31–41
  Kunene Region, migration into, and, 14, 26–28
  mobility and socio-cultural dynamics in, 31–33
  as regional specialisation, 14, 28–31
pastures, 268, 347–48
  access to, 266–73
  Arid Eden, future of, and, 325–26
patrilineal kinship, 103–4, 266
pensions, 253, 256, 338–39
Peoples Liberation Army of Namibia (PLAN), 160–61, 198–99, 227, 229–31, 241–42

PGH. *See* Planned Grazing through Herding
photographs, 77–81, 157–58
  of Hahn, C., 76–77, 79–80, 157
  of Hartmann, 72–73, 78
  of Kuntz, 78–79
PLAN. *See* Peoples Liberation Army of Namibia
Planned Grazing through Herding (PGH), 325–26
plants, commoditizing of, 305–6, 327–28
poaching, 219, 223–26
  conservation and, 200, 203–4, 213–14, 225–27
  contemporary, 324–25
  elephant, 143–44, 158, 221–24
  elephant decline and, 218–19, 222–23, 225
  1970s and 1980s, 151, 203, 209, 211–14, 222–27, 242–43
population growth, 237–38, 245–46, 256–59, 277–78
Portuguese, 46–47, 93, 127, 158
  African mercenaries under, 47, 59–60, 63–65, 101–2, 227
  Angola granted independence by, 198–99
  Epupa dam planned under, 333
  migration and, 15, 29–30, 95–96, 136–37
  raiding and, 29–30, 62–63
  trade of, 62, 110–11, 127–31, 180–82
poverty, contemporary, 248, 254
pre-colonial Kaokoveld, 38–41
  cattle populations in, 42–43, 45
  human-environment relations in, 41–44
  pastoralists and foragers in, 14, 31–41, 43–44
  population of, 41–42
  raiding and, 41–48
  violence and breakdown of, 44–48
prehistory, north-western Namibia, 3–5
  archaeological evidence, sparse, on, 19, 21–24
  climate in, 21
  of environmental infrastructure, 19–20
  foragers in, 22–24
Promulgation of Nature Conservation Amendment Act (1996), 280–81

Index

quagga, 81–82

raiding
  under Germans, discontinued, 45, 67–68
  Herero and, 44, 361–62
  Himba and, 45–46, 361–62
  Oorlam, 44–45
  Portuguese and, 29–30, 62–63
  pre-colonial Kaokoveld and, 41–48
Ramutsindela, M., 216
ranching, conservation and, 200–2
reality shows, 239
Reardon, Mitch, 223–24, 235–36
recoupling. *See* coupling
Red Cross, International, 231
Red Line, Namibian, 3–5, 180–81, 202, 235, 302
  after independence, 16–17, 246
  moving, 329
re-immigration, pastoralist, 93–98
Reitz, Deneys, 54–55, 101–2
religious dissent, 153–54
relocation, 116–17
  cattle and, 116–20
  of Herero, 119–20
  of pastoralists, 116–20
  water and, 116–19
  white settlement and, 119–20
repastoralization, 64–65, 68, 73, 101–2, 149–50, 349–50
resource management, 5, 9–10
  autonomous, future of, 318–19
  boreholes impacting, 186–87
  CBNRM, 242–43, 279–81
  co-management, 341, 346–48, 355
  conservancies and, 284
  CPR, 102–4, 355
  early 20th century Kaokoveld, 99–105
  ethnicization of, 341–46
  Himba on, 342–46
  market approach to, 279–80
  after Namibian independence, 12–13, 237–38, 279–80, 351–52, 355
  new commons, 279–80, 285–89, 292–95, 314–16, 346–48
  Water Point Associations, 306–16, 347–50

rhino, 59, 63, 223, 225–26, 296–97, 324–25
Rinderpest, 68, 351–54
  1887 epidemic, 47
  1897, 1898 epidemics, 56–57, 98–99, 138
Rio 1992 Earth Summit, 279–80
Rizzo, Lorena, 96, 98, 101–2
roads, 147–49, 178, 184–85, 238, 246
Roosevelt, Theodore, 89–90
Rupert, Anton, 211–12, 216–18, 226–27
rural elites, conservancies and, 288–89
rural growth points (*groeipunte*), 183, 194

SADF. *See* South African Defense Force
Samburu, Kenyan, 345
Sami, Scandinavian, 345–46
sand dams, 176–78
SANF. *See* South African Nature Foundation
Sanga cattle, 249–51, 276–77, 357–58
Schnegg, M., 313–14, 326–27, 346–48
scientific knowledge, 15
  Carp Expedition, 22–23, 82, 84–85, 87–88
  Hartmann, expeditions of, 40, 72–76, 78, 86–87
  local informants and, 86–91
  methodologies in collecting, 89–90
  photographs, 76–81, 87
  racial gaze of, 72–73
  reports, 71–73, 157–59
  Shortridge, expedition of, 82–83, 85, 87
  under South Africa, 68–69, 71–73, 81–85, 88–92
  under South Africa, expeditions, 22–23, 81–90
  transmission of, 83, 86–92
  van Warmelo, expeditions of, 82–84
  visual, 71–73, 91–92
segregation-with-development agenda, 161
Sesfontein, 44, 207–8
settlement patterns
  boreholes impacting, 185–86
  civil war, Namibian, disrupting, 241
  contemporary, 241, 259–65, 277–78
  elephant and, 54–55, 64–65
sheep, 130–33, 254–56

Shortridge, Guy Chester, 54–55, 71, 82–83, 85, 87, 97–98
Siiskonen, Harri, 56–57
slave trade, 29–30, 56, 361–62
small-stock herds, contemporary, 253–56
social transfers, 248, 253, 256, 338–39
  basic income grants, 339
  Ferguson on, 319, 337, 339
  for orphans, 338
  scenario for, 318–19
social-ecological system, 13, 351–56
  adaptive cycle in, 353–54
  climate change impacting, 319–23, 365
  collapse of, 228–29
  complexity, increasing, of, 361–63
  elephant hunting and, 63–64
  environmental infrastructure and, 13
  foragers impacting, 24
  future of, 319–26
  after Namibian independence, 238
  NGOs and local, 237–38
  1950s to 1970s, 151
  1990s to present, 237–38
  under South Africa, 68–69
South Africa, 3–5, 15, 127, 349–50
  agricultural policy under, 155–56, 161–65
  Angola, colonial, and, 106, 122–24, 127–31
  Apartheid government of, 161, 171, 205–6, 211–12, 216–18
  Bantustans, 205–6, 231–32
  borders, internal, under, 124–27
  boundaries under, 122–30, 356–58
  in civil war, Angolan, 198–99, 230
  conservation and, 15–16, 155–56, 205, 211–12, 216–18
  conservation and military of, 216–17
  Dorsland Trekkers, elephant hunting by, and, 53–54
  Epupa dam planned under, 333
  famine, drought relief under, 129–30, 132–33, 231–32
  game parks under, 80–81, 144, 155–56, 161, 205–7, 217
  Herero under, 112–13
  homelands of, 201–3, 206, 216–17
  hunting policed under, 143, 362–63
  from Kaokoveld, withdrawal of, 244
  Kaokoveld encapsulated by, 15, 65, 106, 110–15, 132–33, 151, 351–54, 356–58
  Kunene boundary under, 122–24, 126–30, 356–57
  mobility restricted under, 68–69, 112–13, 115–28, 130–37, 150, 180–81, 356–58
  Namibian occupation of, opposition to, 167, 197–98
  Ovamboland border under, 120–21, 126, 140
  relocation under, 116–20
  road construction under, 147–49
  scientific expeditions under, 22–23, 81–90
  scientific knowledge collected under, 68–69, 71–73, 81–85, 88–92
  SWAPO and, 196, 223–24, 229–31
  tourism and, 200–3
  trade under, 68–69, 127–37
  Vita Thom and, 73, 86, 95–97, 110–12, 118, 125, 147–48
  wildlife, increasing, in contemporary, 296–97
South African Defense Force (SADF), 260
  in civil war, Namibian, 160–61, 217–18, 227, 229–31, 241–42
  famine relief by, 231
  locals joining, 229–30, 244
South African Nature Foundation (SANF), 202, 211–12, 217–19, 225–27. *See also* World Wildlife Fund
South West Africa Territorial Force (SWATF), 198–99, 244
South West African Native Labour Association (SWANLA), 133–37, 163
Sprigade map, 75–76
Stals, E. L. P., 96, 102, 158, 182–83
stamfonds (tribal trust fund), 154–55, 165–68
state-led modernization, 151, 156–57, 193–95, 354–55
STDs, 256–58
strandlopers, 22–23, 85, 158–59
stratification, 63–65, 101–2
surveillance, 219

Index

SWANLA. *See* South West African Native Labour Association
SWANU (political party), 244–45
SWAPO, 284
    Himba, Herero, and, 244–45, 336, 342
    under South African rule, 196, 223–24, 229–31
SWATF. *See* South West Africa Territorial Force

Tanzania, 282–83
technology, ethnography of, 364–65
tenure system, 99–105, 186–87, 259–63, 266–68, 290, 292–95
territorialization, 351, 356–58
Third Nature, 292, 323
Thwa, 23–24, 60, 62
Tinley report, 206–14
Tjihahuarua, Langman, 169
Tjimba, 23–24, 158–59, 357
    development and separating, 162, 167–68
    elephant hunting by, 60–62, 64–65
    under Germans, migration of, 95
    Herero migration and, 95, 97
    population, early 20th century, 94
    trade of, 61–62
Tjongoha, 86, 101–2
Toennissen (explorer), 72–73
Toensjost, Silke, 252–54
Tomlinson Commission, 161
tourism, 238–39, 247–48
    anthropo-tourism, future of, 344–45
    conservancies and, 280–83, 287–88, 290–95, 299–300, 318, 326–29, 355
    conservation and, 16–17, 200–3, 205–6, 209, 211–13, 248, 281–83, 287–88, 290–95, 299–300, 318, 325–26
    MET, 280–81, 284, 297–98, 301, 303–4
    planning for, 211–13
trade, 127
    in cattle, 128–29, 202
    Herero and, 128, 132
    Himba, 62
    across Kunene boundary, 127–30
    with natives, prohibited, 134
    Portuguese, 62, 110–11, 127–31, 180–82
    in sheep, 130–33
    under South Africa, 68–69, 127–37
    across southern border, 130–37
    of Tjimba, 61–62
transhumance, 99–105, 267–68
Transkei, 201, 203, 206, 216–17
tribal council system, 153–55
tribal trust fund (*stamfonds*), 154–55, 165–68
Truppenspieler movement, 112–13, 116
Tsing, Anna, 357
Turnhalle constitutional conference, 197–98

Uarije, Franz, 34–36
Uganda, 63
UN. *See* United Nations
UNEP, 320–21
United Nations (UN), 342–46
United States (US), 198–99, 314, 340
UNTAG (UN peacekeepers), 244
US. *See* United States
USAID, 226–27, 242–43
Uukwaludhi, 15, 60, 94, 120–21, 356–57

vaccination. *See* cattle
Vahikura Kapika, 232
van Warmelo, 22
    ethnography by, 146–47, 158, 182–83
    on pastoralism, emergence of, 28, 31–32
    scientific expeditions by, 82–84
van Wolputte, Steven, 113–14, 162
    on CBPP campaigns, 138, 140, 142
    on development, local opposition to, 165, 168
Vansina, Jan, 30–32
Vedder, H., 26, 61, 101–2, 357
    on elephant, 54–55, 60, 109–10
    on Herero, 26–28, 79–80
    local informants and, 86–87
    on ostrich egg trade, 61
    on pastoralism, emergence of, 26–28, 31–32
    photographs by, 79
    on population, Kaokoveld, 41
    reports of, 72–74
    van Warmelo and, 83–84

veld fires, 144–47, 149–50, 189, 194
Viljoen, Philippus Jacobus
  on elephant population, 63, 158, 218–23
  on elephant-vegetation interaction, 51–52
villages. *See* settlement patterns
Vision 2030, Namibia, 318
  co-management in, 346, 348
  conservation in, 317–19, 323, 326–29, 346, 348
Vita Thom (Oorlog), 47
  community of, Stals on, 158
  disarmament and, 110–11
  group of, 95–97, 101–4
  homestead of, 97–98, 102
  as informant, 86, 88–91
  Kakurukouye and, 110–11
  Muhona Katiti and, 96–97, 101–2, 110–11, 160–61
  reserve of, 88–91, 111–12
  road construction under, 147–48
  sheep trade and, 131–32
  South African administration and, 73, 86, 95–97, 110–12, 118, 125, 147–48
  water conflicts of, 101–2
Vogelsang, Ralf, 22–24, 30–31
von Koenen, Eberhard, 40, 85, 157–58
von Lindequist (governor), 106–7
von Moltke, J.
  on elephant hunting, 52–54, 57–62
  on Thwa, 62

Walker, Clive, 218, 225
Wallace, Marion, 153, 159
water, 101–2, 104–5, 149–50, 162–63, 302–7
  CBNRM and, 280
  climate change impacting, 320–23
  DRWS, 308–9, 311–13
  in Global South, reconsideration of, 306–7
  Himba spatial organization and, 260–63
  livestock and communal management of, 313–14
  as new commons, communal management of, 314–16, 347–48
  NGOs and, 308–9
  in Opuwo, 265–66
  relocation and, 116–19
  rights to, 102–4
  separating communities and, 162
Water Affairs, Department of, 174–76
Water Point Associations, 306–16, 347–50
wealth
  age and, 254
  in cattle, distribution of, 252–54, 288
  in cattle, increasing, 186–87, 194
  gender and, 253–54
WESSA. *See* Wildlife and Environment Society of South Africa
white settlement, relocation and, 119–20
wildlife, 329, 349–50
  CBNRM and, 280
  collapse of, 203, 226–28
  commoditization of, 360–61
  concentration of, 219–21
  conservation and hunting, 200–2
  in conservation scenarios, future, 329
  drought and, 226–28
  under German colonialism, protection of, 106–10
  human conflict with, increasing, 297–98, 324–25
  increase in, 237–38, 295–97, 323–25
  legal hunting of, 224–25
  migration of, 209–10, 357–58
  population of, 1960s and 1970s, 219–21
  quotas of, 300–3, 329, 346–48, 359
Wildlife and Environment Society of South Africa (WESSA), 219
Wildlife Society of South Africa, 206, 208, 219
World Wildlife Fund (WWF), 226–27
  CBNRM and, 242–43
  conservancies and, 217–18, 303–4
  South Africans and, 202, 211–12, 216–18

Zambesi Region, 282–83, 297, 300, 338, 351–52
zonation, conservancy, 290–95

African Studies Series

1 *City Politics: A Study of Leopoldville, 1962–63*, J. S. La Fontaine
2 *Studies in Rural Capitalism in West Africa*, Polly Hill
3 *Land Policy in Buganda*, Henry W. West
4 *The Nigerian Military: A Sociological Analysis of Authority and Revolt, 1960–67*, Robin Luckham
5 *The Ghanaian Factory Worker: Industrial Man in Africa*, Margaret Peil
6 *Labour in the South African Gold Mines*, Francis Wilson
7 *The Price of Liberty: Personality and Politics in Colonial Nigeria*, Kenneth W. J. Post and George D. Jenkins
8 *Subsistence to Commercial Farming in Present-Day Buganda: An Economic and Anthropological Survey*, Audrey I. Richards, Fort Sturrock and Jean M. Fortt (eds)
9 *Dependence and Opportunity: Political Change in Ahafo*, John Dunn and A. F. Robertson
10 *African Railwaymen: Solidarity and Opposition in an East African Labour Force*, R. D. Grillo
11 *Islam and Tribal Art in West Africa*, René A. Bravmann
12 *Modern and Traditional Elites in the Politics of Lagos*, P. D. Cole
13 *Asante in the Nineteenth Century: The Structure and Evaluation of a Political Order*, Ivor Wilks
14 *Culture, Tradition and Society in the West African Novel*, Emmanuel Obiechina
15 *Saints and Politicians*, Donal B. Cruise O'Brien
16 *The Lions of Dagbon: Political Change in Northern Ghana*, Martin Staniland
17 *Politics of Decolonization: Kenya Europeans and the Land Issue 1960–1965*, Gary B. Wasserman
18 *Muslim Brotherhoods in the Nineteenth-Century Africa*, B. G. Martin
19 *Warfare in the Sokoto Caliphate: Historical and Sociological Perspectives*, Joseph P. Smaldone
20 *Liberia and Sierra Leone: An Essay in Comparative Politics*, Christopher Clapham
21 *Adam Kok's Griquas: A Study in the Development of Stratification in South Africa*, Robert Ross
22 *Class, Power and Ideology in Ghana: The Railwaymen of Sekondi*, Richard Jeffries
23 *West African States: Failure and Promise*, John Dunn (ed.)
24 *Afrikaaners of the Kalahari: White Minority in a Black State*, Margo Russell and Martin Russell
25 *A Modern History of Tanganyika*, John Iliffe

26 *A History of African Christianity 1950–1975*, Adrian Hastings
27 *Slaves, Peasants and Capitalists in Southern Angola, 1840–1926*, W. G. Clarence-Smith
28 *The Hidden Hippopotamus: Reappraised in African History: The Early Colonial Experience in Western Zambia*, Gywn Prins
29 *Families Divided: The Impact of Migrant Labour in Lesotho*, Colin Murray
30 *Slavery, Colonialism and Economic Growth in Dahomey, 1640–1960*, Patrick Manning
31 *Kings, Commoners and Concessionaries: The Evolution of Dissolution of the Nineteenth-Century Swazi State*, Philip Bonner
32 *Oral Poetry and Somali Nationalism: The Case of Sayid Mahammad 'Abdille Hasan*, Said S. Samatar
33 *The Political Economy of Pondoland 1860–1930*, William Beinart
34 *Volkskapitalisme: Class, Capitals and Ideology in the Development of Afrikaner Nationalism, 1934–1948*, Dan O'Meara
35 *The Settler Economies: Studies in the Economic History of Kenya and Rhodesia 1900–1963*, Paul Mosely
36 *Transformations in Slavery: A History of Slavery in Africa, 1st edition*, Paul Lovejoy
37 *Amilcar Cabral: Revolutionary Leadership and People's War*, Patrick Chabal
38 *Essays on the Political Economy of Rural Africa*, Robert H. Bates
39 *Ijeshas and Nigerians: The Incorporation of a Yoruba Kingdom, 1890s–1970s*, J. D. Y. Peel
40 *Black People and the South African War, 1899–1902*, Peter Warwick
41 *A History of Niger 1850–1960*, Finn Fuglestad
42 *Industrialisation and Trade Union Organization in South Africa, 1924–1955*, Stephen Ellis
43 *The Rising of the Red Shawls: A Revolt in Madagascar 1895–1899*, Stephen Ellis
44 *Slavery in Dutch South Africa*, Nigel Worden
45 *Law, Custom and Social Order: The Colonial Experience in Malawi and Zambia*, Martin Chanock
46 *Salt of the Desert Sun: A History of Salt Production and Trade in the Central Sudan*, Paul E. Lovejoy
47 *Marrying Well: Marriage, Status and Social Change among the Educated Elite in Colonial Lagos*, Kristin Mann
48 *Language and Colonial Power: The Appropriation of Swahili in the Former Belgian Congo, 1880–1938*, Johannes Fabian
49 *The Shell Money of the Slave Trade*, Jan Hogendorn and Marion Johnson

50 *Political Domination in Africa*, Patrick Chabal
51 *The Southern Marches of Imperial Ethiopia: Essays in History and Social Anthropology*, Donald Donham and Wendy James
52 *Islam and Urban Labor in Northern Nigeria: The Making of a Muslim Working Class*, Paul M. Lubeck
53 *Horn and Crescent: Cultural Change and Traditional Islam on the East African Coast, 800–1900*, Randall L. Pouwels
54 *Capital and Labour on the Kimberley Diamond Fields, 1871–1890*, Robert Vicat Turrell
55 *National and Class Conflict in the Horn of Africa*, John Markakis
56 *Democracy and Prebendal Politics in Nigeria: The Rise and Fall of the Second Republic*, Richard A. Joseph
57 *Entrepreneurs and Parasites: The Struggle for Indigenous Capitalism in Zaire*, Janet MacGaffey
58 *The African Poor: A History*, John Iliffe
59 *Palm Oil and Protest: An Economic History of the Ngwa Region, South-Eastern Nigeria, 1800–1980*, Susan M. Martin
60 *France and Islam in West Africa, 1860–1960*, Christopher Harrison
61 *Transformation and Continuity in Revolutionary Ethiopia*, Christopher Clapham
62 *Prelude to the Mahdiyya: Peasants and Traders in the Shendi Region, 1821–1885*, Anders Bjorkelo
63 *Wa and the Wala: Islam and Polity in Northwestern Ghana*, Ivor Wilks
64 *H. C. Bankole-Bright and Politics in Colonial Sierra Leone, 1919–1958*, Akintola Wyse
65 Contemporary West African States, Donal Cruise O'Brien, John Dunn, and Richard Rathbone (eds)
66 *The Oromo of Ethiopia: A History, 1570–1860*, Mohammed Hassen
67 *Slavery and African Life: Occidental, Oriental, and African Slave Trades*, Patrick Manning
68 *Abraham Esau's War: A Black South African War in the Cape, 1899–1902*, Bill Nasson
69 *The Politics of Harmony: Land Dispute Strategies in Swaziland*, Laurel L. Rose
70 *Zimbabwe's Guerrilla War: Peasant Voices*, Norma J. Kriger
71 *Ethiopia: Power and Protest: Peasant Revolts in the Twentieth-Century*, Gebru Tareke
72 *White Supremacy and Black Resistance in Pre-Industrial South Africa: The Making of the Colonial Order in the Eastern Cape, 1770–1865*, Clifton C. Crais
73 *The Elusive Granary: Herder, Farmer, and State in Northern Kenya*, Peter D. Little

74 *The Kanyok of Zaire: An Institutional and Ideological History to 1895*, John C. Yoder
75 *Pragmatism in the Age of Jihad: The Precolonial State of Bundu*, Michael A. Gomez
76 *Slow Death for Slavery: The Course of Abolition in Northern Nigeria, 1897–1936*, Paul E. Lovejoy and Jan S. Hogendorn
77 *West African Slavery and Atlantic Commerce: The Senegal River Valley, 1700–1860*, James F. Searing
78 *A South African Kingdom: The Pursuit of Security in Nineteenth-Century Lesotho*, Elizabeth A. Elredge
79 *State and Society in Pre-Colonial Asante*, T. C. McCaskie
80 *Islamic Society and State Power in Senegal: Disciples and Citizens in Fatick*, Leonardo A. Villalon
81 *Ethnic Pride and Racial Prejudice in Victorian Cape Town: Group Identity and Social Practice*, Vivian Bickford-Smith
82 *The Eritrean Struggle for Independence: Domination, Resistance and Nationalism, 1941–1993*, Ruth Iyob
83 *Corruption and State Politics in Sierra Leone*, William Reno
84 *The Culture of Politics in Modern Kenya*, Angelique Haugerud
85 *Africans: The History of a Continent, 1st edition*, John Iliffe
86 *From Slave Trade to 'Legitimate' Commerce: The Commercial Transition in Nineteenth-Century West Africa*, Robin Law (ed.)
87 *Leisure and Society in Colonial Brazzaville*, Phyllis Martin
88 *Kingship and State: The Buganda Dynasty*, Christopher Wrigley
89 *Decolonialization and African Life: The Labour Question in French and British Africa*, Frederick Cooper
90 *Misreading the African Landscape: Society and Ecology in an African Forest-Savannah Mosaic*, James Fairhead and Melissa Leach
91 *Peasant Revolution in Ethiopia: The Tigray People's Liberation Front, 1975–1991*, John Young
92 *Senegambia and the Atlantic Slave Trade*, Boubacar Barry
93 *Commerce and Economic Change in West Africa: The Oil Trade in the Nineteenth Century*, Martin Lynn
94 *Slavery and French Colonial Rule in West Africa: Senegal, Guinea and Mali*, Martin A. Klein
95 *East African Doctors: A History of the Modern Profession*, John Iliffe
96 *Middlemen of the Cameroons Rivers: The Duala and Their Hinterland, c.1600–1960*, Ralph Derrick, Ralph A. Austen and Jonathan Derrick
97 *Masters and Servants on the Cape Eastern Frontier, 1760–1803*, Susan Newton-King
98 *Status and Respectability in the Cape Colony, 1750–1870: A Tragedy of Manners*, Robert Ross

99 *Slaves, Freedmen and Indentured Laborers in Colonial Mauritius*, Richard B. Allen
100 *Transformations in Slavery: A History of Slavery in Africa, 2nd edition*, Paul E. Lovejoy
101 *The Peasant Cotton Revolution in West Africa: Côte d'Ivoire, 1880–1995*, Thomas E. Bassett
102 *Re-imagining Rwanda: Conflict, Survival and Disinformation in the Late Twentieth Century*, Johan Pottier
103 *The Politics of Evil: Magic, State Power and the Political Imagination in South Africa*, Clifton Crais
104 *Transforming Mozambique: The Politics of Privatization, 1975–2000*, M. Anne Pitcher
105 *Guerrilla Veterans in Post-War Zimbabwe: Symbolic and Violent Politics, 1980–1987*, Norma J. Kriger
106 *An Economic History of Imperial Madagascar, 1750–1895: The Rise and Fall of an Island Empire*, Gwyn Campbell
107 *Honour in African History*, John Iliffe
108 *Africans: A History of a Continent, 2nd edition*, John Iliffe
109 *Guns, Race, and Power in Colonial South Africa*, William Kelleher Storey
110 *Islam and Social Change in French West Africa: History of an Emancipatory Community*, Sean Hanretta
111 *Defeating Mau Mau, Creating Kenya: Counterinsurgency, Civil War and Decolonization*, Daniel Branch
112 *Christianity and Genocide in Rwanda*, Timothy Longman
113 *From Africa to Brazil: Culture, Identity, and an African Slave Trade, 1600–1830*, Walter Hawthorne
114 *Africa in the Time of Cholera: A History of Pandemics from 1817 to the Present*, Myron Echenberg
115 *A History of Race in Muslim West Africa, 1600–1960*, Bruce S. Hall
116 *Witchcraft and Colonial Rule in Kenya, 1900–1955*, Katherine Luongo
117 *Transformations in Slavery: A History of Slavery in Africa, 3rd edition*, Paul E. Lovejoy
118 *The Rise of the Trans-Atlantic Slave Trade in Western Africa, 1300–1589*, Toby Green
119 *Party Politics and Economic Reform in Africa's Democracies*, M. Anne Pitcher
120 *Smugglers and Saints of the Sahara: Regional Connectivity in the Twentieth Century*, Judith Scheele
121 *Cross-Cultural Exchange in the Atlantic World: Angola and Brazil during the Era of the Slave Trade*, Roquinaldo Ferreira
122 *Ethnic Patriotism and the East African Revival*, Derek Peterson

123 *Black Morocco: A History of Slavery and Islam*, Chouki El Hamel
124 *An African Slaving Port and the Atlantic World: Benguela and Its Hinterland*, Mariana Candido
125 *Making Citizens in Africa: Ethnicity, Gender, and National Identity in Ethiopia*, Lahra Smith
126 *Slavery and Emancipation in Islamic East Africa: From Honor to Respectability*, Elisabeth McMahon
127 *A History of African Motherhood: The Case of Uganda, 700–1900*, Rhiannon Stephens
128 *The Borders of Race in Colonial South Africa: The Kat River Settlement, 1829–1856*, Robert Ross
129 *From Empires to NGOs in the West African Sahel: The Road to Nongovernmentality*, Gregory Mann
130 *Dictators and Democracy in African Development: The Political Economy of Good Governance in Nigeria*, A. Carl LeVan
131 *Water, Civilization and Power in Sudan: The Political Economy of Military-Islamist State Building*, Harry Verhoeven
132 *The Fruits of Freedom in British Togoland: Literacy, Politics and Nationalism, 1914–2014*, Kate Skinner
133 *Political Thought and the Public Sphere in Tanzania: Freedom, Democracy and Citizenship in the Era of Decolonization*, Emma Hunter
134 *Political Identity and Conflict in Central Angola, 1975–2002*, Justin Pearce
135 *From Slavery to Aid: Politics, Labour, and Ecology in the Nigerian Sahel, 1800–2000*, Benedetta Rossi
136 *National Liberation in Postcolonial Southern Africa: A Historical Ethnography of SWAPO's Exile Camps*, Christian A. Williams
137 *Africans: A History of a Continent, 3rd edition*, John Iliffe
138 *Colonial Buganda and the End of Empire: Political Thought and Historical Imagination in Africa*, Jonathon L. Earle
139 *The Struggle over State Power in Zimbabwe: Law and Politics since 1950*, George Karekwaivanane
140 *Transforming Sudan: Decolonisation, Economic Development and State Formation*, Alden Young
141 *Colonizing Consent: Rape and Governance in South Africa's Eastern Cape*, Elizabeth Thornberry
142 *The Value of Disorder: Autonomy, Prosperity and Plunder in the Chadian Sahara*, Julien Brachet and Judith Scheele
143 *The Politics of Poverty: Policy-Making and Development in Rural Tanzania*, Felicitas Becker
144 *Boundaries, Communities, and State-Making in West Africa: The Centrality of the Margins*, Paul Nugent

145 *Politics and Violence in Burundi: The Language of Truth in an Emerging State*, Aidan Russell
146 *Power and the Presidency in Kenya: The Jomo Kenyatta Years*, Anaïs Angelo
147 *East Africa after Liberation: Conflict, Security and the State since the 1980s*, Jonathan Fisher
148 *Shaping the African Savannah: From Capitalist Frontier to Arid Eden in Namibia*, Michael Bollig

Printed in the United States
By Bookmasters